P9-AOP-608

PER VERBA
Testi mediolatini con traduzione

12

Fondazione Ezio Franceschini

PER VERBA

Testi mediolatini con traduzione

collana diretta da Claudio Leonardi

Comitato scientifico

Ferruccio Bertini, Enzo Cecchini, François Dolbeau, Louk J. Engels,
Louis Holtz, Peter Christian Jacobsen, Michael Lapidge, Bengt Löfstedt,
Enrico Menestò, Paul Meyvaert, Giovanni Orlandi, Giovanni Polara

ALEXANDER NECKAM

Suppletio Defectuum
Book 1

ALEXANDER NECKAM ON PLANTS, BIRDS AND ANIMALS

A Supplement to the *Laus Sapientie Divine*

edited from
PARIS, B. N. LAT., MS 11867

by
Christopher J. McDonough

SISMEL
EDIZIONI DEL GALLUZZO

ISBN 88-87027-37-4
© 1999 SISMEL – Edizioni del Galluzzo
Via di Colleramole 11 – 50029 loc. Bottai
Tavarnuzze – Impruneta – FIRENZE

For Hanna

Acknowledgments

It is a particular pleasure to record here the help of several friends and colleagues who with characteristic generosity helped to improve this book. Adding to earlier kindnesses, Professor Nicole Bériou expedited delivery of photocopies of the manuscript from the Bibiothèque Nationale, Paris. My enquiries about lexical matters were answered promptly by Dr. David Howlett, Medieval Latin Dictionary, Oxford, and by Dr. David Vitali, *Mittellateinisches Wörterbuch*, Munich. Professor Barrie Hall and Professor Giovanni Orlandi read the Latin text and offered a number of valuable suggestions for improving it, while Professor Michael Reeve kindly gave me the considerable benefit of his critical skills. Professor George Rigg encouraged the project from the start and gave the original typescript a critical and scholarly reading. My colleagues, Michael Dewar and E. Weinrib, answered assorted questions and Dr. Jonathan Black put his computer expertise at my disposal. I owe a special debt to the invigorating and scholarly ambience of Clare Hall, Cambridge, where the research for this book was completed. I am grateful to the Director of the Bibliothèque Nationale, Paris, for permission to publish Paris, B. N. lat. 11867, and to Mª Luisa López-Vidriero Abello, for consent to reproduce readings from Biblioteca de Palacio Real ex Oriente, II-468. Finally, I would like to express my gratitude to Professor Gian Carlo Garfagnini and Dr. Piero Bugiani for the many courtesies they extended to me in the course of preparing the book for publication.

Toronto, July, 1998

INTRODUCTION

1. LIFE OF ALEXANDER NECKAM

When Alexander Neckam[1] returned to England in 1216 after attending the Fourth Lateran Council, he found time to attend to unfinished literary business. He could not have known that the two books of poetry he wrote during the course of that year would be his last. Unlike most of Neckam's other writings, they can be dated with some precision, because he specifies the period during which he composed the poem by referring to the installation of pope Honorius III as a fait accompli (18 July 1216) and to King John's death in October 1216.[2] The work that resulted is known today as the *Suppletio defectuum*, according to the colophon in Paris, Bibliothèque Nationale, MS lat. 11867, a title that E. Renan found bizarre. The title, which gives no indication of the poem's contents, consists of a combination of nouns extrapolated from two separate passages, in which Neckam editorializes about the poem's relationship to its master text.[3] It clearly signals, however, the supplementary character of the work, which, Alexander explains, he intended to be attached in an ancil-

---

1. For an analysis of the evidence regarding the variously attested forms of Alexander's name, see R. W. Hunt, *The Schools and the Cloister. The Life and Writings of Alexander Nequam (1157-1217)*. Edited and revised by M. Gibson (Oxford, 1984), 17-8.

2. See Hunt ed. Gibson, *The Schools and the Cloister*, 28 and note 54; J. N. D. Kelly, *The Oxford Dictionary of Popes* (Oxford, 1986), 188-9. Research for the *SD* occurred over a number of years, according to Neckam in *SD* 2, 565-6 (*multis uigilatus ab annis / ...labor*).

3. The title appears in Paris, Bibliothèque Nationale, lat. 11867, f. 218va and the poem occupies ff. 218va-231va; for the wording of the title, cf. *SD* 1, 563-4 Quosdam *defectus* illius carminis istud / *Suplebit*; 2, 7-8 Carminis illius *suplecio*, parue libelle, / Diceris, cuius assecla fidus eris. E. Renan, «Sur l'étymologie du nom d'Abélard», *Revue celtique* 1 (1870-72), 266, described the *SD* as «un ouvrage bizarrement intitulé». M. Esposito, «On Some Unpublished Poems Attributed to Alexander Neckam», *EHR* 30 (1915), 450 and note 1, records information about the manuscript; at 460 he printed *SD* 1, 1-10, where he misread *fingis* [6] for *fingas*. Individual verses appear in E. du Méril, *Poésies inédites du moyen âge* (Paris, 1854), 170 (*SD* 1, 843-8), in E. Renan, «Sur l'étymologie du nom d'Abélard», *Revue celtique* 1 (1870-72), 266 (*SD* 2, 1575), in E. Jeauneau, «Note sur l'école de Chartres», 3 ser. *SM* 5 (1964), 833, note 75 (*SD* 2, 1575-6), and, more recently, in Hunt ed. Gibson, *The Schools and the Cloister*, 1, note 4; 5, 16-7, 49, 75, 76-80, in L. Minio-Paluello, «The 'Ars disserendi' of Adam of Balsham 'Parvipontanus'», *MRS* 3 (1954), 117, note 4; 161, and in T. A.-P. Klein, *Alexander Neckam Nouus Auianus* (Genova 1998), 115, 119, 121, 127, 131, 133.

lary way to an poem, already monumental in scale, the *Laus sapientie diuine*,[1] which he had written some years before. As preserved in the Paris codex, the poetic supplement is incomplete, the result, probably, of the uncertainties of transmission, although it may be that Alexander did not live to finish it. It is unique in being the only known codicil that Neckam appended to an earlier literary testament. Subordinate in status though it is, Alexander brought to it no less industry, craftsmanship, and wit than he had devoted to the much longer encyclopedic poem.

Alexander's intellectual interests led him, first, to the schoolroom and later in life to monastic administration. Yet his choice of an Augustinian house, with a rule less rigid than those of competing orders, did not cloister him from the world, and, in fact, the historical record shows that the latitude granted by the order allowed him to exercise the considerable diplomatic and judicial skills that brought him into contact with royal and high ecclesiastical circles.

By 1216 Neckam could look back upon a body of work that had secured for him a reputation in the world of learning that later led his first editor, Thomas Wright, to call him «one of the most distinguished scholars of the latter end of the twelfth century».[2] The sheer range of his academic reach confers some credibility on the claim. There was scarcely a field he left uncultivated. At different times during his career, he combined, often with a deal of inventiveness,[3] diverse interests in grammar, poetry, science, preaching, exegesis and theology. To some disciplines, like the teaching of the Latin language, he remained attached all his life. In one of his earliest works, the *De nominibus utensilium*, a class-glossary written sometime before he taught at Oxford (1190-97), he attempted to teach young boys the Latin names for everyday things.[4] Its lively contents

---

1. The *LSD* versifies substantial parts of the *DNR*. Neckam refers to the *LSD* at *SD* 1, 560-3, and in *SD* 2, 1334 he makes a cross-reference to it (*editus ante liber*). For medieval and Renaissance supplements to the lacunose archetype of Curtius Rufus's *Historia Alexandri*, see E. Smits, «A Medieval Supplement to the Beginning of Curtius Rufus's *Historia Alexandri*: An Edition with Introduction», *Viator* 18 (1987), 90-1.

2. *A Volume of Vocabularies* (Liverpool, 1857), 96, note 1; Hunt ed. Gibson, *The Schools and the Cloister*, 15, notes that Alexander's reputation was wide-spread enough for an anecdote about him to be included in a sermon written by Caesarius of Heisterbach c. 1220.

3. P. Lendinara, «The 'Oratio de utensilibus ad domum regendam pertinentibus' by Adam of Balsham», *Anglo-Norman Studies* 15 (1992), 175, credits him with the novelty of presenting Latin vocabulary in a kind of continuous discourse.

4. Cf. *A Volume of Vocabularies*, *DNV*, 97, note 1, *Intencio autoris est colligere sub compendio nomina utensilium. Causa suscepti operis est puerilis instructio.* T. Hunt, *Teaching and Learning Latin in*

reflect the new trades and economic changes that were taking place in English society and include object-lessons based on culinary instruments, vegetables, wine, the parts of a weaving apparatus, a baronial hall, the components of a ship, the assorted paraphernalia used by writers or a *librarius*, and various items of ecclesiastical furniture and vestments. Alexander's habit of viewing the world around him as a pedagogical resource never deserted him.

Despite the volume of Neckam's extant works, surprisingly little is known about the precise chronology of his life and the sequence of his works.[1] An addition of unknown provenance to a 14th-c. chronicle of excerpts from Nicholas Trivet's *Annals* states that Alexander was born at St Albans in September 1157, on the same night as the future king, Richard I, and that his mother, Hodierna, raised them both.[2] Alexander himself specifies St Albans as his birthplace.[3] Records confirm a royal connection, because on his accession Richard paid Hodierna a pension of seven pounds sterling per annum, which passed in 1220 to a Willelemus Mercator.[4] Of Alexander's father nothing is known.

After receiving an early education at St Albans, Neckam became a

---

13ᵗʰ- c. in England (Cambridge 1989), 1991, 1: 178, cites an *accessus* to the work: *Intentio autoris est nomina utensilium in summam unam colligere ad promotionem et ad instructionem minus provectorum*; S. Reynolds, *Medieval Reading. Grammar, Rhetoric and the Classical Text* (Cambridge, 1996), 63, 72, 152, comments on Neckam's concern with educating *pueri*, beginning students of Latin. R. Ellis, «A Contribution to the History of the Transmission of Classical Literature in the Middle Age, from Oxford MSS», *AJP* 10 (1889), 159, documents the *DNV*'s indebtedness to Isidore's *Origines* and its occasional references to Horace, Lucan, Juvenal and ps.-Vergil. For an introduction and a text of *DNV*, see T. Hunt, *Teaching and Learning*, 1991, 1: 177-90; P. Lendinara, «The 'Oratio de utensilibus'», 175, discusses the differences between Adam of Balsham's *Oratio* and Neckam's *DNV*. Alexander's last work on grammar, the so-called *Sacerdos ad altare*, a commentary for more advanced students, must now be dated much closer to the end of his life.

1. For a summary of Alexander's life and most important works, see R. Düchting, *Lexikon des Mittellalters* (Munich, 1980), 1: 378-9; A. G. Rigg, *A History of Anglo-Latin Literature 1066-1422* (Cambridge, 1992), 117-22; G. Garbugino, *Alessandro Neckam Novus Aesopus* (Genova, 1987), 13-8; R. Sharpe, *A Handlist of the Latin Writers of Great Britain and Ireland before 1540*, 51-3, provides the most up-to-date information on editions and manuscripts of Alexander's writings; for detailed discussion of the historical record, see Hunt ed. Gibson, *The Schools and the Cloister*, 1-18.

2. See J. C. Russell, «Alexander Neckam in England», *EHR* 47 (1932), 260; Hunt ed. Gibson, *The Schools and the Cloister*, 1, note 1; the biographical sketch of Neckam presented here rests on Hunt's analysis; Hodierna's name occurs three times cf. *SD* 1, 835, 853, 868.

3. Cf. *LSD* 10, 319 (p. 503W) *Hic locus aetatis nostrae primordia nouit*; J. C. Russell, «Alexander Neckam in England», *EHR* 47 (1932), 260.

4. Cf. Hunt ed. Gibson, *The Schools and the Cloister*, 2.

teacher in Dunstable and, later, in St Albans, although whether this period
of employment preceded or followed a stay in Paris as a student and master
is unknown. According to Hunt's plausible reconstruction, based on indirect evidence in Matthew Paris's account of Guarinus's election as abbot
of St Albans in 1183, Neckam served for a year in Dunstable in 1183-84
before he applied for the school at St Albans. On this basis, a period of
study in Paris might reasonably have occurred c. 1175-82, before he took
up teaching. In Paris he attended lectures at the school near the Petit-Pont,
which a fellow-Englishman, Adam of Balsham, had established some time
after 1132.[1] While there, he may also have heard Gilles of Corbeil, who
around 1175 was lecturing on the texts of Hippocrates with the commentaries of Galen, which Gilles had brought back with him from Italy.[2]
While this period of Alexander's life remains obscure in its details, firm
evidence places him after 1190 in Oxford, where he lectured in theology.[3]

At an unspecified time during his scholastic career, Alexander decided
to enter a monastery, a decision that contemporaries, including Peter of
Blois, applauded.[4] The Augustinian abbey of Cirencester received him
some time between 1197 and 1202. These dates are based on inferences
drawn from a letter of Pope Celestine III, dated 23 January 1195, which
names Neckam as «master Alexander of St Albans» without using the title
of canon, a designation that does appear in a later composition, dated to
1205. Since the latter document includes a letter of Innocent III, dated 8
May 1203, styling Alexander a canon of Cirencester, he was probably already a canon by the end of 1202.[5]

---

1. P. Lendinara, «The 'Oratio de utensilibus'», *Anglo-Norman Studies* 15 (1992), 162,
note 9, emphasizes the similar career paths of Adam, Neckam and John of Salisbury, all of
whom travelled to Paris for further education; cf. *LSD* 10, 334 (p. 503W).

2. M. H. Saffron, «Maurus of Salerno, Twelfth-Century 'Optimus Physicus'», *Transactions of the American Philosophical Society* N. S. 62, 1 (1972), 10, further suggests that Gilles
may have been the conduit for communicating Salernitan medical teachings and the contents of the *Articella* to Neckam cf. 10, note 40; 97, note 88 for evidence linking the head
of the school at Salerno, Maurus, with Alexander.

3. See Hunt ed. Gibson, *The Schools and the Cloister*, 7-8, on Alexander's sermon which
appealed for funds to repair St Frideswide's and on two other sermons addressed to Oxford
scholars, as well as the statement in his *Commentary on the Song of Songs* that he lectured
publicly on theology; J. C. Russell, «Alexander Neckam in England», *EHR* 47 (1932), 261-
2, also prints texts that associate Neckam with Oxford.

4. See *Ep.* 137 (*MPL* 207: 405a) *Totis medullis animae conversioni et conversationi vestrae con-
gratulor*; Hunt ed. Gibson, *The Schools and the Cloister*, 10 and note 45; J. C. Russell, «Alexander Neckam in England», *EHR* 47 (1932), 263.

5. See Hunt ed. Gibson, *The Schools and the Cloister*, 11-2, on this and other evidence.

Neckam's academic reputation was acknowledged by many. Alfred of Sareshel's dedication of the *De motu cordis* to him may be taken as a token of the wide esteem he enjoyed.[1] But Alexander did not confine his considerable energies solely to the library. His administrative skills were valued and recognised in his appointment at different times as a papal and ecclesiastical judge. He acted as advocate on behalf of the priory of Lanthony in 1204-5 and the years 1212-13 found him engaged on the king's business, inquiring into the royal rights in the priory of Kenilworth.[2] This period of intense activity, in which he completed the *Laus sapientie diuine*,[3] must have consolidated his reputation for diplomacy and integrity, qualities that surely played a part in securing his election in 1213 to the abbacy of Cirencester. It was in this capacity that he departed for the Fourth Lateran Council on 21 July 1215. Records show that he stopped on the journey long enough to transact some business, since he appended his signature to a charter at Dover on 12 September. He did not long survive his return to England. At the end of March 1217 he died at Kempsey and was buried in Worcester cathedral.[4]

2. *SUPPLETIO DEFECTUUM*

The authenticity of the *Suppletio defectuum* and its rightful place in Neckam's canon have never been questioned. He inscribes the poem both with his own name and that of his mother,[5] and, in addition, while discussing the poem's pedigree, he carefully includes two cross-references that define its relationship to the *Laus sapientie diuine*. In the first, he refers by title to the controlling text he had completed three years earlier, which the reader can use, Neckam tells us, in conjunction with the supplement. Neckam disarmingly acknowledges the deficits in the earlier poem and suggests that

---

1. Hunt ed. Gibson, *The Schools and the Cloister*, 12; on Alfred, see J. K. Otte, «The Life and Writings of Alfredus Anglicus», *Viator* 3 (1972), 275-91; C. H. Talbot, *Medicine in Medieval England* (London, 1967), 48-50, provides a convenient summary of the contents of the *De motu cordis*. M. H. Saffron, «Maurus of Salerno», *Transaction of the American Philosophical Society* N. S. 62, 1 (1972), 10, notes, however, that Alfred did not hold Salernitan *physici* in high esteem and made Aristotle, not Hippocrates, his main authority.

2. J. C. Russell, «Alexander Neckam in England», *EHR* 47 (1932), 263, provides details.

3. See Hunt ed. Gibson, *The Schools and the Cloister*, 27.

4. See J. C. Russell, «Alexander Neckam in England», *EHR* 47 (1932), 263-4; Hunt ed. Gibson, *The Schools and the Cloister*, 13-5.

5. At *SD* 1, 844 (Alexander), and 835, 853, 868 (Hodierna).

they symbolize his own imperfections, which he now undertakes to repair
(*SD* 1, 561-6). In the second authorial insertion, a summary list first recapitulates the broad range of topics covered in the *Laus sapientie diuine*;
Neckam then alludes to its name, predicts the title by which the companion volume will become known, and its ancillary nature (*SD* 2, 1-8):

> *Precinui stellas, mare, fontes, flumina, pisces*
> *et prolem capitis, seua Medusa, tui:*
> *Urbes descripsi cum gentis moribus, et quas*
> *prospiciens nobis terra recondit opes.*
> *Quod, diuina, tibi seruit, sapientia, carmen*
> *Explicat ista; tamen addere*[1] *plura libet.*
> *Carminis illius suplecio,*[2] *parue libelle,*
> *Diceris, cuius assecla fidus eris.*

In categorizing the poem as subsidiary to other disciplines (*seruit*),
Neckam reflects twelfth-century theoretical statements about one of poetry's functions.

Despite the work's supplementary status, Neckam was attentive to its
composition, although a firm assessment of its structural unity remains beyond reach because of its incomplete state. However, the poem's overall
movement suggest that Alexander planned the contents with some care.
Like Adelard of Bath's *Quaestiones Naturales*, which had appeared a centu-

---

1. In writing a prose counterpart to the *Carmen paschale*, Sedulius anticipated criticism
by explaining: *nostri prorsus ab sese libelli non discrepant, sed quae defuerant primis addita sunt
secundis... nec impares argumento uel ordine, sed stilo uidentur et oratione dissimiles* (*Ep. ad Macedonium*, ed. Huemer, *CSEL* 10: 171-3). M. Carruthers, *The Book of Memory. A Study of
Memory in Medieval Culture* (Cambridge, 1990), 211-4, emphasizes, while describing the
compositional stages of Anselm's *Proslogion*, how alien to medieval authorship was the
modern notion of a «finished» literary work.

2. The noun belonged to the technical vocabulary of grammar, and was used in theological exegesis in the sense of supplying a gloss to make clear, in cases where the Bible's
meaning was equivocal, which one was correct cf. G. R. Evans, «Suppletio», *ALMA* 42
(1982), 72-6. Largely synonymous with the word *completio*, in the general meaning of
«completion, supplement, complement», *suppletio* is found in the context of writing in
Burchardus, *Ursb. chron.* (*MGH, SRG* 16: 16, 8 *quem* (sc. *Liber Autenticorum*) *prefatus Iustin-
ianus ad suppletionem et correctionem legum imperialium superaddidit*, two other examples post-
date the *SD*: Chart. Bern. III, 58 (*Fontes rerum Bernensium*, 61, 11 [a. 1273)]) *quod illum
paragraphum, qui incipit «et hec sunt iura statuta» etc., ubi tangitur de sculteto dando, cum hac sup-
pletione volumus observari, videlicet quod...*; Constitutiones III, 216, 5 (ed. Schwalm, *MGH, Legum* sectio 4: 3, 200, 12-7 [a. 1278]) *serenitatem regiam rogamus..., quatinus eadem privile-
gia...suppleas et perfici facias et procures, quod principum...ad id accedat assensus, ita quod...nova
data suppletiones et perfectiones huiusmodi comprehendat.*

ry earlier,[1] and the more contemporary *Questiones phisicales*,[2] the subject matter moves from the biological-zoological to the cosmological.[3]

Neckam used a number of means to clarify for the reader the structure of the first book and to mark its major divisions. The process began in the introduction, which announced the theme and offered a structured table of contents for the reader to follow. In a series of short, declarative sentences Neckam describes the unity of creation and the parts played by God's power, wisdom, and bounty in directing the order of the universe. Issues of structure and arrangement are given prominence and within this scheme allusion is made to the concept of *ordo rectus*.[4] At the end of the prologue (35-6), Neckam thematizes the question of structure by setting out, in effect, a series of headings in precisely the order in which he will treat the matter of birds that comes immediately after (37-178):

> *Discernit uolucres locus, ars, sonus, esca, potestas,*
> *Calliditas, forme gloria, prolis amor.*

The beginning of the following section on trees (179-262) is marked with greater emphasis, with three words insisting on the break (179-80):

> *Arboreos etiam fetus herbasque salubres*
> *Distinguit, signat, separat alta Noys.*

A similar signpost (263-4) introduces the much longer treatment of plants (263-588):

> *En diuina Noys herbas discernit ab herbis;*
> *Vires atque color, forma locusque probant.*

The method of distinguishing between species and arranging them into hierarchies is explicitly made in the next transition (589-92):

---

1. Cf. M. Müller, «Die *Quaestiones naturales* des Adelardus von Bath», *BGPTM* 31, 2 (Münster i. W., 1934), 76-7, dates this seminal work between 1111-6; for Adelard's biography, see *Adelard of Bath* ed. C. Burnett, (Cambridge, 1998), XI-XIX.

2. Dated to the end of the 12th-c. and start of the 13th-c. by B. Lawn, *The Salernitan Questions* (Oxford, 1963), 40.

3. Hunt ed. Gibson, *The Schools and the Cloister*, 78-80; G. Garbugino, *Alessandro Neckam Novus Aesopus* (Genova, 1987), 2: 38-9, provides a summary of the contents of *SD* 1-2.

4. *SD* 1, 22 *ordo regit*; T. Haye, *Das lateinische Lehrgedicht im Mittelalter. Analyse einer Gattung* (Leiden, 1997), 170-96, contains an excellent analysis of the structural techniques Neckam used to arrange the massive *LSD*, including the functions carried out by the prologues, epilogues and excursuses.

Plantarum species paucas distinximus, et iam
Se subdit nostro res animata stilo.

Here the narrative structure is shaped by what Thomas Haye has happily termed the «Janus-Gesicht» of linguistic indicators that afforded a double perspective; the perfect tense provides a retrospective look at the preceding section, while the temporal adverb points forward.[1] In the next couplet (591-2), the *res animata* is further refined with the announcement of the category of birds (593-890), beginning with the eagle:

Precedant uolucres; ea que descendit ab alto
Pre foribus nostris regia clangit auis.

As a bridge to the final section of the poem (931-1458), Neckam uses a technique he had used in the *LSD*.[2] In a short excursus (891-906), he inserts a defence of his poetic approach to the material, which consists of mingling *ioca* with serious content. That the digression functions as part of a well-planned narrative becomes immediately clear, when he connects it to the didactic context by outlining the mixed nature of the bat (907-30), which is half-bird, half animal. By means of this legerdemain he effects an imaginative passage to the segment on beasts (931-1458).

Alexander uses a number of other techniques by which readers could orient themselves within the poem's structure, but the ones specified above identify the larger components. Viewed broadly, the contents of the *capitulum primum*, as the rubric describes it, comprise a herbal, which itemizes the medicinal powers of almost seventy plants and flowers, followed by a bestiary that consists of birds, animals and a smaller number of snakes and insects. These plants and fauna appear in a different order from the schema laid out in the *Laus sapientie diuine*.

The book falls into four main divisions: first, a brief section describes the habitat, calls and characteristics of birds (37-178), followed by the fruits of selected trees and their virtues (179-262); a more extensive segment details plants and the ailments they are good for (263-588), while the rest of the book is devoted to a miniature bestiary, a genre that the English found particularly congenial (589-1458).[3] Included in the final part is a

---

1. T. Haye, *Das lateinische Lehrgedicht*, 182-3; at 183, note 65; offers selected examples of this type of break in the *LSD*.

2. T. Haye, *Das lateinische Lehrgedicht*, 191-6, discusses the different functions that excursuses fill in the *LSD*.

3. M. R. James, *The Bestiary* (Oxford, 1928), 1-2, analyzes and classifies thirty four prose

specimen from a related literary mode, one in which birds and animals also played a central role, the beast fable. Like all such stories, the mythos of the mouse has an allegorical cast; in this case the moral tale deals with the sin of pride, as the rubric in P points out. Written in the elevated manner of mock-epic, the tale represented for Richard Hunt the only diversion in a book he judged to be unoriginal and, even with the new material, of little interest.[1]

Neckam begins the second book, termed a *distinctio* by the glossator, with a prologue that selectively recapitulates the contents of the *LSD*. He then turns to the subject of man, aspects of his psychology and his elemental nature, the union of soul and body in Adam, the question of original sin and an extended description of Paradise (431-532). The rest of the book is almost entirely given over to a series of astronomical problems. They include the phenomena of solar and lunar eclipses, questions concerning the computus, calculations regarding the Great Year, the arrangement and movements of the planets, problems concerning the moon and the Zodiac, observations about the equinox and the solstice, and the distances between the earth, moon, sun and stars.[2] The close attention to these *quaestiones* reflects the broader interest of English intellectuals in the practical implications of astrology. The concluding section attempts to justify the ways in which the liberal arts served the ends of theology (1379-95). Grammatica, Logica and Rhetorica enter as personified figures and each in turn proceeds to defend the utility of their disciplines in the service of theology.[3] How the book ended we can only

---

bestiaries of English provenance and notes that the bestiary assumed a standard form in England.

1. Hunt ed. Gibson, *The Schools and the Cloister*, 79; cf. his comments on p. 67 «His chief scientific works, the *De naturis rerum* and the *Laus sapientie diuine*, have long been in print, and the unpublished *Suppletio defectuum* does not add much that is really new.» Against this view should be set Neckam's own assertion of novelty (*nouitas*) for the style in which he presented his research cf. *SD* 2, 561-6.

2. R. K. French and C. Cunningham, *Before Science. The Invention of the Friars' Natural Philosophy* (Aldershot, 1996), 88-9, have recently drawn attention to the practical applications of astrological theory, including the role of the moon, which were used by physicians in matters like prognosis and the calculation of critical days.

3. In personifying the liberal arts, Neckam may have been influenced by Osbern Pinnock of Gloucester's *Derivationes*, who writes in the preface: *Martianum autem Capellam secutus, ipsam Grammaticam induxi loquentem, ut sicut ipsa de liberalibus disputans, singulas artes quasi uoce propria introduxit loquentes, sic et ego de Latinitate disserens ipsam Latinitatis matrem.. .feci disputare per plurima* (ed. Bertini, 1:3, 24). Neckam borrowed heavily from the *Derivationes* in compiling the *Sacerdos ad altare*.

guess, for it breaks off abruptly in the middle of defining the rhetorical figure *complexio*.[1]

3. BACKGROUND TO THE *SUPPLETIO DEFECTUUM*

As noted above, Neckam undertook the poem with a defined goal, namely to add supplementary material to a pre-existing work. This probably explains why he offers within the new work the merest sketch of the wider conceptual framework in which he operates. From Neckam's cursory explanation of causes in the *Suppletio*, he clearly assumed familiarity with the theory of the elements and humours that he had summarized in the parent text. There Neckam had offered a short versified account of the theory, precisely because he had treated the same matter at greater length in the prose encyclopedia *De naturis rerum*. It is to this work that readers must turn for the fullest articulation of Neckam's views.

Within the broad sweep of the *De naturis rerum* Neckam presents a symbolic understanding of nature, based on the belief that mankind could gain knowledge of the Creator by reading nature like a book. Within this interpretive approach, Neckam also demonstrates a keen interest in acquiring knowledge about the natural world through scientific methods.[2] He clearly kept himself informed about the developments that were occurring in contemporary science and medicine.

Alexander was one of many among the lively English clerical intelligentsia interested in the scientific developments that were emerging from

---

1. Based on the order of presentation in the *DNR* and *LSD*, it is reasonable to conjecture that the second book ended with presentations from the quadrivial arts; M. Fumagalli and M. Parodi, «Due enciclopedie dell'Occidente medievale: Alessandro Neckam e Bartolomeo Anglico», *Rivista di storia della filosofia* 40 (1985), 66, infer from the placement of the liberal arts at the end of the *DNR*, despite the amount of space allocated, a sign of their marginality in the hierarchy of studies; cf. *DNR* 2, 173 (p. 283W) *Artium liberalium studia, etsi in se maximam contineant utilitatem, curiosis tamen inquisitionibus multam ingerunt vanitatem*, Neckam seems to liken the liberal arts to a type of *vana curiositas* cf. 2, 173 (p. 307W) *Antequam igitur Ecclesiasten aggrediar, libet de nonnullis vanitatum speciebus mentionem facere*. M. B. Parkes, «The Influence of the Concepts of 'Ordinatio' and 'Compilatio' on the Development of the Book», in J. J. G. Alexander and M. T. Gibson edd. *Medieval Learning and Literature* (Oxford, 1976), 119, discusses the subordination of the sciences to theology in the 13th-c.

2. A. Speer, «The Discovery of Nature: The Contributions of the Chartrians to Twelfth-Century Attempts to Found a *scientia naturalis*», *Traditio* 52 (1997), 138, summarizes the distinctions between speculative and scientific explanations of nature in the 12th-c.

a number of quarters. But drawn as he was to the new intellectual vistas opened up by translations of Greek and Arabic texts, his writings on natural phenomena remained firmly located within the universalizing context of divine power. The *Suppletio* is no exception. In the introduction to the poem Neckam sketches a Christian model of the universe that is full of diversity, yet remains unitary and teleological, extending from the four elements to the stars. Within this universe he presents the many faces of nature, nature complex, bountiful, challenging, powerful, rich, playful, awesome and full of grace. Among these the most rhetorically effective in Neckam's enterprise was the miraculous.[1] Although Neckam states his subject to be the observation of the natural world,[2] he more than once points to wonder as a stimulus for delving into a knowledge of causes. Sometimes he isolates the extraordinary and the singular for amused comment or as the impulse to seek a naturalized explanation.[3] In another variation, a marvelling attitude at the universe is expressed by the reiteration of key words that emphasize diversity.[4] Yet underlying the complexity, as Neckam reads it, lies the unity of creation, expressed in the design and handiwork of a Christian deity. For Neckam, the material world not merely confirmed the existence of a divine creator, but was also a site for moral reading and instruction.

The twelfh century witnessed a renewed interest in the physical world that raised questions about nature's role within Creation and man's relation to the natural order. Wetherbee has set out with admirable clarity the

---

1. P. R. Hardie, *Virgil's Aeneid. Cosmos and Imperium* (Oxford, 1986), 169-72, discusses Lucretius's habit of looking at phenomena within a universalizing and generalizing context and the way in which many ancient natural philosophers progressed from viewing the visible cosmos as an object of scientific study to contemplating it as a source of wonder. On the various medieval discourses of wonder, see C. W. Bynum, «Wonder», *AHR* 102 (1997), 1-7.

2. E. g. *SD* 1, 45; 891 *Sollicitant animos leuium spectacula rerum*; 1257-8 *Que sunt arbitrio uisus obnoxia cano / Haut umquam mentem sollicitare solent.*

3. Among the sources of delight or amazement are the bat's anatomy (*SD* 1, 891-920) and the mysterious phenomenon of ebony's resistance to fire (209-22). Admiration at the appearance and texture of porcupine quills (*SD* 1, 1101-2 *mira potestas / Nature*) leads into an explanation based on the theory of humours; elsewhere, seemingly miraculous phenomena are explained by the laws of nature e. g. the vine's natural process in transforming water into wine (*SD* 1, 1257-66, esp. 1259 *Nature minus attendit miracula uulgus*); C. W. Bynum, «Wonder», *AHR* 102 (1997), 4-5, discusses medieval distinctions between *miracula* and *mirabilia*.

4. Cf. *SD* 1, 1-34; C. W. Bynum, «Wonder», *AHR* 102 (1997), 20-1, provides medieval examples of amazed reactions to diversity.

movements that lay behind this revival: the expansion of the study of medicine, the translation and dissemination of Greek and Arabic scientific texts, and the construction of a rational world-view, influenced by Plato's *Timaeus*, which emphasized the idea of a demiurge.[1] Bernard Silvestris's *Cosmographia*, which Neckam had read, presents Nature as a demiurgic figure, a secondary principle and providential force responsible for generating material things which had been formed on the template of the divine. In Bernard's cosmology, Noys, God's providence, orders matter out of the chaos, arranges the world and produces man. To Nature falls the task of generation in the celestial and earthly spheres; to this end she summons the assistance of Urania, who is at work among the stars, and Physis, an active force in the sublunary world. Any anomalies in the world of generation were the result of a mistake or a joke of nature (*natura ludens*).

Other figures, like William of Conches, attempted to read the book of nature literally. William developed a philosophy that sought to link the upper and lower realms, from the planets to the earthly elements, with the whole held together by God's power. In considering how God had ordered the material world out of the original chaos, his successors elaborated a system that allowed nature to function as an autonomous principle in the universe. By the end of twelfth century the division between nature, referring to God and the celestial world, and the works of nature in the sublunary world had become a commonplace.

Interest in nature was further stimulated in the second half of the twelfth century by the appearance of translations of medical and astronomical texts. Scientists were chiefly interested in Arabic astrology, because they believed that celestial phenomena influenced earthly events and could be analysed to predict them. This belief led in time to the view that the positions and motions of the planets directly caused changes in the lower world of nature. Hermann of Carinthia was among those who began to study Ptolemy's *Almagest* for its astrological techniques and mathematical astronomy. Gerard found Ptolemy's text in Cremona and began with the help of the Englishman, Daniel of Morley, to translate it. It is this intellectual climate that produced the extensive treatment of astronomical matters in the second book of the *Suppletio*.[2]

The study of the physical world included man's body, which was made

---

1. See W. Wetherbee, *The Cosmographia of Bernardus Silvestris* (New York, 1973), 2-3, 7-8; R. K. French, *Before Science*, 72-3, *Adelard of Bath* ed. C. Burnett, XXVII.

2. Neckam mentions a certain Heremannus in *SD* 2, 1251, though his identity remains uncertain cf. Hunt ed. Gibson, *The Schools and the Cloister*, 76.

up of the same elements as the macrocosmos. These concerns naturally led
to the study of Aristotelian texts on the natural world. By this route medical teaching with its knowledge of the natural world made its way to
those whose philosophical interests required it. Bartholomaeus of Salerno
encouraged the use of Joannitius's *Isagoge*[1] and Aristotle's *Metaphysics* and
by dividing the parts of philosophy into theory and practice he firmly an-
chored *medicina*, as part of *physica*, to the new *scientia naturalis*, the Arab-
Greek rational philosophy. Another important figure in this movement
was the Salernitan teacher Urso, who made use of Aristotelian nature
texts in his commentary on the *Aphorisms* of Hippocrates.

4. *DE NATURIS RERUM*

The intellectual currents sketched above run through Neckam's *De naturis rerum*, a work centrally concerned with the physical world and the
natures of things. It forms a long introduction to a commentary on the
book of *Ecclesiastes*.[2] For Neckam, the significance of scientific knowledge
and observation lay in nature's correspondence with divine reality and the
trinitarian nature of God. Intense though his interest was in natural questions, he insisted on finalizing all knowledge in the study of theology. Accordingly, in the prologue to the second book, the perfection of Creation
as a whole and every creature within it reveals the power of the Father,
the wisdom of the Son and the bounty of the Holy Spirit.[3] As he moves
between the natural and transcendental worlds, Alexander reads the physical and human world as a series of symbols, parts of a text inscribed by
God. In Neckam's speculative interpretation, while the wisdom of the

---

1. A convenient summary of the contents of this work is offered by L. J. Rather, «Systematic Medical Treatises from the Ninth to the Nineteenth Century: The Unchanging
Scope and Structure of Academic Medicine in the West», *Clio Medica* 11 (1976), 291-4.

2. Hunt ed. Gibson, *The Schools and the Cloister*, 81, explains that Alexander adopted
Origen's tripartite division of the sapiential books of Solomon, in which *Ecclesiastes* repre-
sented *physica*. For summaries of the contents of the *DNR*, see S. Viarre, *La survie d'Ovide
dans la littérature scientifique des XIIᵉ et XIIIᵉ siècles* (Poitiers, 1966), 35, note 4; G. Garbugino,
Alessandro Neckam Novus Aesopus (Genova, 1987), 2: 18-21; A. G. Rigg, *A History of Anglo-
Latin Literature* (Cambridge, 1992), 118-9; R. K. French, *Before Science*, 91-2.

3. See *DNR* 2, *prologus* (pp. 125-6W) cf. *SD* 1, 17-20 for the spheres of *potestas*, *bonitas*
and *sapientia*; M. Fumagalli and M. Parodi, «Due enciclopedie», *Rivista di storia della filosofia*
40 (1985), 52-3, underline the importance of Augustine's *De doctrina Christiana* on Neckam's scientific project and cultural program in the *DNR*.

Father produces and disposes, the divine word is viewed as the pen of a scribe through whom the Father expresses himself in all things.[1] In addition to the theological argument, the *De naturis rerum* also aimed to liberate man from the evil of ignorance.[2] Neckam's goal remains fixed on enabling mankind to read the world as the place where God has left his mark. Sounding a theme he will amplify in the later books of commentary on *Ecclesiastes*, Neckam periodically inserts warnings against arrogance, vanity and the desire for praise and idle curiosity.[3]

More importantly, he privileges the search for moral significance in the nature of things as a means of approaching a knowledge of God.[4] Fumagalli analyzes Neckam's use of Aristotle to show the rhetorical strategy at work.[5] For instance, on the subject of fire, Neckam cites Aristotle's *Posterior Analytics* and concludes: *Ignis...in multiplici analogia est*. From this he generates a complex of observations that embrace the dissemination of wisdom, the efficacy of love and charity, the action of the Holy Spirit, the flames of anger or arrogance which burn beneath the monastic habit.[6] Throughout, natural phenomena serve as examples to stimulate teachings about morality and to intimate deeper meaning.[7]

---

1. Cf. *DNR* 2, *prologus* (p. 125W) *Est etiam verbum istud calamus scribae velociter scribentis ita quod in rebus sapientia Dei elucet*; note Neckam's description of the *mundus* as *calamo Dei inscriptus* (p. 125W).

2. *DNR* 1, *prologus* (p. 2W) *Verus igitur sol justitiae, qui de tenebris facit lucem splendescere, tenebras ignorantiae erroneae in nobis cum vitiorum caligine expellat.*

3. Cf. *DNR* 2, 155 (p. 247W)...*infaustam procreat* (sc. scientia) *occasionaliter sobolem, scilicet arrogantiam*; 2, 174 (p. 311W); in the commentary on *Ecclesiastes*, he warns against the dangers of pride that attend the vain display or sale of knowledge. While disclaimimg any criticism of masters who supported their families by professing the liberal arts, he exhorts: *Ad maiora nati sumus; uacent spiritualibus spiritus infusi*

4. Cf. *DNR* 1, *prologus* (pp. 2-3W) *Nolo tamen ut opinetur lector me naturas rerum fugere volentes investigare velle philosophice aut physice, moralem enim libet instituere tractatum*; Comm. in Eccles. f. 145va *Animus humanus auidus scientie mundum cum contentis lustrat ut creatorem in creaturis reperiat, agnoscat, ueneretur.*

5. See M. Fumagalli, «Due enciclopedie», *Rivista di storia della filosofia* 40 (1985), 59, and *DNR* 1, 17 (pp. 57-61W) at p. 57W; S. Viarre, *La survie d'Ovide*, 74, remarks on Neckam's tendency to unite scientific explanation, mythology and moralization.

6. M. Fumagalli, «Due enciclopedie», *Rivista di storia della filosofia* 40 (1985), 61-3, discusses the rhetorical uses to which Neckam applied Aristotle's name; she draws attention to the great weight Neckam assigns to the Church Fathers, the bestiary tradition and the classical poets.

7. Cf. *DNR* 1, 14 (p. 53W) *Sed sciendum est, in signum et in instructionem nostri hoc factum esse*. In this spirit, Neckam finds analogies between the stars and *uiri spirituales*, the planets and the gifts of the Holy Spirit.

In examining themes of natural philosophy, the work affords an ob-lique glimpse into a society in intellectual ferment.In the treatise, a ten-sion exists between the claims of scientific works in the empirical-exper-imental sense[1] and the allegorical interpretation of the physical world.[2] On the one hand, Neckam's interest in scientific matters is evident in ma-terial he borrowed from natural philosophers. Birkenmajer was the first to discover embedded in the work material taken from the *Quaestiones natu-rales* of Adelard of Bath and from the Salernitan medical writer, Urso.[3] But Neckam's fascination with the new knowledge and the problems of contemporary science remains subordinate to the higher purpose of un-covering God's presence in Creation. In other words, he read the world not only *physice*, but *mistice* and *tropologice*.[4]

5. *LAUS SAPIENTIE DIUINE*

A decade after completing the *De naturis rerum*, Alexander versified its contents and published the poem under a thematic title that proclaimed its encomiastic function, *Laus sapientie diuine*.[5] What motivated him to do this is unclear. It may simply have been the age-old challenge of at-tempting a poetic treatment of a subject that was in many respects in-trinsically unpoetic. It has been suggested that Neckam took Bernard

---

1. For an example of Neckam's personal empirical observations see *DNR* 1, 4 (pp. 30-1W) or 1, 19 (pp. 63-4W) concerning proofs about the void: *Ad propositum etiam facit exper-imentum etiam vulgo notum* (p. 64W).

2. See E. Sada, «Genesi del lupo cattivo», 3 ser.*SM* 33 (1992), 793.

3. See Hunt ed. Gibson, *The Schools and the Cloister*, 70-3.

4. See R. K. French, *Before Science*, 91-2; M. Fumagalli, «Due enciclopedie», *Rivista di storia della filosofia* 40 (1985), 66, aptly remarks that Neckam's interest in the problem of lu-nar spots centres not so much on the various hypotheses to find a causal explanation for them, but rather on emphasizing how they remind man of his fallen state and the conse-quences that follow from that condition cf. *DNR* 1, 14 (p.54W).

5. G. Garbugino, *Alessandro Neckam Novus Aesopus* (Genova, 1987), 2: 37-8, synopsizes the contents of the *LSD*; cf. A. G. Rigg, *A History of Anglo-Latin Literature*, 119-21; Hunt ed. Gibson, *The Schools and the Cloister*, 13, dates the *LSD* to 1213, while Rigg *A History of Anglo-Latin Literature*, 119, assigns it to the years 1213-5. For comments on the literary genre of the *LSD*, a composite of epic paraphrase of Genesis and panegyric, see C. Moussy and C. Camus edd., Dracontius, *Oeuvres*, 1. *Louanges de Dieu* 1-2 (Paris, 1985), 46-9; N. Henkel, *Studien zum Physiologus im Mittelalter* (Tübingen, 1976), 155-6. Hunt ed. Gibson, *The Schools and the Cloister*, 138, corrects Wright's division of the poem. On Neckam's pressing of di-dactic poetry into theological service, see T. Haye, *Das lateinische Lehrgedicht*, 393-4.

Silvestris as the model and authority for his own poetic enterprise.[1] The practice of producing a work in two paired parts, one prose, the other verse, known as an *opus geminatum*, reached back to the activity of paraphrase (*conuersio*) in antiquity.[2] Over time the demands for fidelity to the original composition became more flexible and the conventions were loose enough to allow for additions.[3] Divided into seven distinctions, the *Laus sapientie diuine* roughly follows the order in which the subjects are covered in the *De naturis rerum*. The first sets out the orders of angels, the divisions in the heavens and an exhaustive enumeration of the stars and planets. In the second, Alexander treats the winds and birds, while the next *distinctio* begins by recapitulating the avian world, before it discusses various types of fountains, rivers and fish. The fourth distinction elaborates the theory of the four elements with copious illustrations. After a brief account of Paradise, the following book offers new material on the three parts of the world, Europe, Libya and Asia. Alexander uses this as a framework for a catalogue of cities and their famous men. The penultimate section is concerned with precious metals, gems, plants and trees. Next comes the animal world and the creation of man, before the poem oncludes with a synopsis of the liberal arts and a final meditation on man and God.[4]

---

1. T. Haye, *Das lateinische Lehrgedicht*, 73-4, argues that Neckam saw «eine texttypologische Nähe» between didactic poetry and the thematically related prosimetrum; he cites *LSD* 7, 355-60 (p. 481W), where Neckam lauds Bernardus's treatment of botany in the prosimetric *Cosmographia*.

2. For a survey of the *opus geminatum* from its origins to the Carolingian age, see P. Godman, *Alcuin. The Bishops, Kings, and Saints of York* (Oxford, 1982), lxxviii-lxxxviii; N. Henkel, *Studien zum Physiologus im Mittelalter* (Tübingen, 1976), 34-6, mentions the versification of the *De naturis rerum* in the course of discussing the metrical adaptation of the *Physiologus*.

3. P. Godman, *Alcuin. The Bishops, Kings, and Saints of York* (Oxford, 1982), lxxxiii, points out that Aldhelm, *CDV* 2446-2761 (*MGH, AA* 15: 452-65) lacks a counterpart in the prose version. T. Haye, *Das lateinische Lehrgedicht*, 368, note 34, refers to an unpublished dissertation by E. Walther, who takes the view that neither the *DNR* or the *LSD* qualify under the rubric of the *opus geminatum*, because each work was conceived as an independent literary work. I have not been able to consult the thesis.

4. T. Haye, *Das lateinische Lehrgedict*, 168, lists among the factors influencing the size of didactic poems the breadth of theme, the detail of treatment, and the poetic conception of the author.

6. SUPPLETIO DEFECTUUM

Neckam re-arranged the order of the subject matter to make the first book consist almost entirely of a herbal and a bestiary. In other words, it combines practical information for addressing medical disorders and descriptions of beasts' characteristics which are allegorized for moral profit. [1] This arrangement no doubt reflects the Christian concern that healing should include the physical and the spiritual. But the combination of the concrete and the moral further serves to illustrate the notion of utility that was implicit in the medieval attitude towards nature.

Changes in Christian attitudes towards the secular study of nature and medical knowledge evolved slowly and were the result of the interplay of complex forces. [2] Along with much else, authors like Isidore of Seville transmitted in condensed format numerous facts about science and medicine they had gleaned from ancient sources. The moral and social values implicit in Roman science were also passed on and were eventually transformed by Christian attitudes towards the world. Perhaps the most important in this development was the Roman view that placed mankind at the centre of nature and that adopted a teleological view of nature's bounty as existing to benefit human ends. This utilitarian view of the natural world was taken up and accomodated into Christian thinking about God's purposeful Creation, at the heart of which lay human salvation. The characteristic Roman emphasis on utility also left a deep mark on the subsequent study of nature and its diversity. In thinking about nature in this way, Christians united their concern with rectitude and with utility, which for them included both the practical and the moral. [3]

---

1. A. C. Henderson, «Medieval Beasts and Modern Cages: The Making of Meaning in Fables and Bestiaries», *PMLA* 97 (1982), 40-2, observes that both genres spell out their meanings and have explicit morals; however, the exegetical method of moralizing that invested the properties of animals with their own spiritual meanings is much more common in bestiaries and sermons than in fables.

2. For a discussion of some of the social, cultural and religious currents that promoted change, see J. Cadden, *The Meanings of Sex Difference in the Middle Ages* (Cambridge, 1993), 46-52.

3. J. Cadden, *The Meanings of Sex Difference*, 51-2, observes how an awareness of the practicality of a knowledge of nature and the body affected the forms that were redefined to organize it, e. g. lists of recipes, booklets, question literature and the commentary form.

7. THE HERBAL

Although there is little that is original in Alexander's medical knowledge,[1] it forms part of a monastic tradition that from the sixth century fostered study of secular medical books and the preservation and transmission of Greek and Roman herbal lore.[2] Derivative though that knowledge was, it expressed a continuing concern for the physical health of the body and for the possibility of healing members of religious communities as well as others.[3]

The use of herbs and other plants for their medicinal properties probably stretches back to pre-history and they remain in use as a source of alternative or complementary healing up to the present day.[4] In ancient Egypt, it has been calculated that drugs were prepared from well over a hundred plants, although only a small fraction can be identified with confidence. Using honey, milk, wine and beer as vehicles for administering the herbal preparations, Egyptian healers made extensive use of them as analgesics, purgatives, relief of coughs, and as remedies for urinary problems.[5] In turn, the Greeks expanded considerably the inventory of herbs and vegetables from which they extracted active ingredients to apply as medications. Among medical writers, Theophrastus described over five hundred plants and the work of Mithridates's physician, Kratevas,[6] on the usefulness of medicinal plants lived on in the *De materia medica* of

---

1. C. H. Talbot, *Medicine in Medieval England*, 48, characterizes it as «minimal», but medieval culture was less concerned about originality than about extracting, reproducing and transmitting useful information from ancient sources; on this tendency, see R. W. Southern, *The Making of the Middle Ages* (London, 1987), 182; M. L. Cameron, *Anglo-Saxon Medicine* (Cambridge, 1993), 74.

2. T. Hunt, *Popular Medicine in Thirteenth-Century England* (Cambridge, 1990), 6-16, summarizes the main stages in the development of Western medicine from Roman times up to the School of Salerno.

3. N. G. Siraisi, *Medieval and Early Renaissance Medicine* (Chicago, 1990), 7-12, discusses the impact of Christianization and the new context it offered for medical learning and practice.

4. See M. L. Cameron, *Anglo-Saxon Medicine*, 123, who provides an overview of the modern analysis regarding the therapeutic value of herbs; P. M. Jones, «Medicine», in F. A. C. Mantello and A. G. Rigg, *Medieval Latin. An Introduction and Bibliographical Guide* (Washington, D. C., 1996), 416-8, offers a succinct history.

5. W. R. Dawson, «Studies in Medical History: (a) The Origin of the Herbal», *Aegyptus* 10 (1929), 47-57.

6. On his life, see C. Singer, «The Herbal in Antiquity and its Transmission to Later Ages», *Journal of Hellenic Studies* 47 (1927), 5-18.

Dioscorides. The treatise, written in Greek, supplied the names, descriptions and healing properties of nearly 600 plants and its influence was to last into the 17th-c.[1] Dioscorides's herbal, translated into Latin by the sixth century, established the pattern for subsequent work.[2]

Strictly defined, a herbal comprised a series of descriptions of plants, considered medicinal, with data regarding their various names, uses and habitat. Originally intended to supply inexpensive, practical medical information to readers, they normally provided descriptions detailed enough to identify plants, a summary of the diseases for which they were thought useful, and instructions on preparation, dosage and application. The *Herbarium* of Pseudo-Apuleius, a remedy book influential throughout the medieval period, may serve to illustrate the approach. Written in Latin sometime in the fourth century, it contained about 130 illustrations of medicinal plants. Beneath each representation appears the Latin name of the plant, followed by prescriptions listing its medicinal qualities and efficacy in curing designated illnesses. For example, a sketch of plantain is accompanied by these words: AD MORSUM CANIS RABIOSI: *Herba plantago tunsa et imposita facillime sanat*; SI QUA DURITIA IN CORPORE EVENERIT: *Herba plantago pisata cum axungia sine sale: et quasi in malagma facta imponitur duritie statim emolliet.*[3]

The *Herbarium* was translated into English no later than the ninth or tenth century[4] and was undoubtedly consulted with an eye to practical use. Recently, Voigts and Cameron have made the case that the Anglo-Saxons organised the use of these plants on a rational basis. The evidence includes modifications made to the herbal's text during transmission, the addition of plant chapters, lists of synonyms supplied for plant names, extra information concerning habitat, and a colour-coded table of contents for

---

1. On Dioscorides, see C. Singer, «The Herbal in Antiquity», *JHS* 47 (1927), 19-29; A. Arber, *Herbals, Their Origin and Evolution* (Cambridge, 1987), 5-10, sketches the early history of medicinal botany; R. Jackson, *Doctors and Diseases in the Roman Empire* (London, 1988), 76.

2. On Dioscorides and the medieval translations of his work, see H. E. Sigerist, «Materia medica in the Middle Ages», *Bulletin of the History of Medicine* 7 (1939), 417-21; on the Latin Dioscorides, cf. C. Singer, «The Herbal in Antiquity», *JHS* 47 (1927), 34-7; Cassiodorus, *Inst.* 1, 31, 2 (ed. R. A. B. Mynors, 78, 25-79,1 [Oxford, 1937]); N. G. Siraisi, *Medieval and Early Renaissance Medicine*, 196, note 18, suggests «Dioscorides» may refer to a Latin herbal loosely based on Dioscorides.

3. See F. W. T. Hunger, *The Herbal of Pseudo-Apuleius* (Leyden, 1935), 10-1; C. Singer, «The Herbal in Antiquity», *JHS* 47 (1927), 37-47.

4. See M. L. Cameron, *Anglo-Saxon Medicine*, 25-9.

easy access to remedies. On the issue of the work's utility, the improvements made to the manuscripts by other users are equally revealing. They include *Nota* signs and the addition of a list, written in a 12th-c. hand, of the Latin names of more than seventy plants drawn from Macer's *De uiribus herbarum*, with Old English glosses written over twenty one of them. [1] Mediterranean and Eastern plants were available through barter or commercial transactions and xerothermic climatic conditions in Northern Europe from 1000-1200 also favoured the cultivation of southern European *flora* in herb gardens. [2] In short, the evidence cumulatively suggests that Anglo-Saxon practitioners had access to the medicinal plants recommended in the books that were produced in their own monastic scriptoria. [3]

The interest in reproducing medical texts continued into early 12th-c. England, as attested by a manuscript from the monastery of Bury Saint Edmunds during Baldwin's abbacy. The multifarious contents of this book, Oxford, Bodleian Library, MS 130, includes a copy of Pseudo-Apuleius's *Herbarium*, extracts from a herbal by Dioscorides, a series of medical recipes and an illustrated copy of a work attributed to Sextus Placitus which describes remedies from animals. Marginal notes of English equivalents for Latin plant names suggest that it was put to practical use. [4]

Despite a modern assessment of Macer's work as a «poorly arranged, sometimes medically dangerous, confused mass of material», [5] it served as Neckam's primary source for the section on herbs and flowers in both the *Laus sapientie diuine* and its supplement. [6] Whether Neckam's abbreviated

---

1. See L. E. Voigts, «Anglo-Saxon Plant Remedies and the Anglo-Saxons», *Isis* 70 (1979), 255-9, 265; the list occurs on f. 10v in London, B. M., Cotton Vitellius C. iii, facing the OE illustrated *Herbarium* of Pseudo-Apuleius cf. M. L. Cameron, *Anglo-Saxon Medicine*, 129.

2. Cf. L. E. Voigts, «Anglo-Saxon Plant Remedies», *Isis* 70 (1979), 259-64; C. H. Talbot, *Medicine in Medieval England*, 153, notes the 9th-c. plan for a herb garden at St. Gall.

3. On the Continent, Walahfrid Strabo celebrated the cultivation of plants for their therapeutic value in the *De cultura hortorum*, which listed twenty nine plants, most of which he grew in his own garden. On the influence of Macer's *De uiribus herbarum* on vernacular and Latin writings, see G. Keil, «The Textual Transmission of the *Codex* Berleburg», in M. R. Schleissner, *Manuscript Sources of Medieval Medicine* (New York, 1995), 20; P. M. Jones, «Harley MS. 2558», in M. R. Schleissner, *Manuscript Sources*, 45. Attributed to Odo of Meung in a 14th-c. manuscript or to Marbod of Rennes (so J. Riddle 1995, 152), the poem cannot be earlier than the 10th-c., because it cites Strabo's works; it depends heavily on Pliny's *Natural History* and, to a lesser extent, on Dioscorides and others cf. L. Choulant, *Macer Floridus*, (Leipzig, 1832), 14.

4. See E. J. Kealey, *Medieval Medicus*, 6, 9.

5. E. J. Kealey, *Medieval Medicus*, 192, note 32.

6. *LSD* 7, 5-6 (p. 472W) *Macer lege metri diffusius explicat ista, / Atque Dioscorides liberiore stilo*

herbal served the practical needs of the monks of Cirencester can only be guessed at.[1] The gynecological data on abortifacients, menstruation and the after-birth, though at first sight seemingly irrelevant in a monastic milieu, may have been collected precisely because monasteries operated as centres of medical healing for nearby communities.[2]

The herbal, though old and rooted in folklore, increasingly came to reflect contemporary developments in practical medicine. As Lawn has already observed,[3] Alexander's interest in the physical world and medicine[4] is reflected in the contents of the *De naturis rerum* and the *Laus sapientie diuine*. In the former he quotes the *Aphorisms* of the Salernitan scholar and medical writer Urso, together with the commentary on them.[5] The *De naturis rerum* also shows familiarity with the form and content of the question literature which transmitted the new medical learning from Italy.[6] Cast in the form of question and answer, it investigated anthropological and zoological matters with a sweep broad enough to embrace the superstitions, legends and accounts of the marvellous attributes of birds, animals, fishes and reptiles. While there is little evidence that other English authors in the second half of the twelfth century used Salernitan prose writings,[7] Neckam knew these or similar sets of questions that were circulating and that comprised the common intellectual property of the Salernitan *magistri*. How Neckam acquired this knowledge remains un-

---

[cf. Sedulius, *Ep. ad Macedonium*, ed. Huemer, *CSEL* 10: 171, 7]. For Henry of Huntington's use of Macer, see B. Ruppel, «Ein verschollenes Gedichte des 12. Jahrhunderts: Heinrichs von Huntington «De herbis», *Frühmittelalterliche Studien* 31 (1997), 197-213'.

1. The medical receipt consisted of four parts: a rubric, indication, composition, and preparation. The indication listed the disorders for which the recipe might be useful; the composition specified the ingredients, proportions, and amounts; the preparation gave details for producing and applying the medicine. However, many recipes often lacked details regarding dosage or the parts of the plant that were useful; see T. Hunt, *Popular Medicine*, 2, 8. The supplement's usefulness may have been limited by its lack of information about the dosage.

2. On this subject see N. G. Siraisi, *Medieval and Early Renaissance Medicine*, 10-1.

3. See B. Lawn, *Salernitan Questions*, xi; he discusses the dating on p. 40.

4. On the close connection between medicine and the physical world in the 12th. c. cf. R. K. French, *Before Science*, 88-9.

5. Urso was one of the channels for knowledge about Aristotle's books on the natural world; see Hunt ed. Gibson, *The Schools and the Cloister*, 70-2; D. Jacquart, «Aristotelian Thought in Salerno», in P. Dronke 1988, 408; R. K. French, *Before Science*, 89.

6. See J. Cadden, *The Meanings of Sex Difference*, 89-91 and note 110.

7. B. Lawn, *Salernitan Questions*, 63, notes that Alfred of Sareshel's *De motu cordis*, written c. 1210-15, shows a little knowledge of Constantinian translations, but nothing of Salernitan question literature. By contrast, the *DNR* is steeped with Salernitan learning, as mediated in the prose questions and in Urso's writings. For a brief history of the school of

known. Perhaps, after he returned to England as a master of the school at
St Albans c. 1185, he came into contact with Matthew, brother of Warin,
abbot of St Albans (1183-95), who studied medicine at Salerno. Both
brothers knew two Salernitans, Fabianus and Robert, and all entered monastic life.[1] If Hunt is correct that Neckam's period of study in Paris ended c. 1182, when he returned to teach at Dunstable, he would not have
heard Gilles of Corbeil's lectures on Salernitan medicine, which he began
c. 1194. Paris, Bibliothèque Nationale, MS lat. 18081, written in Paris c.
1230-40, places the arrival of the prose Salernitan questions in the first half
of the 13th.c.[2] By whatever route the questions reached Neckam, the
contents and format of the *De naturis rerum* mirror the fundamental interests of this, and other such, compilations.[3]

   Kristeller has drawn attention to the shift from practical to theoretical
instruction in medicine that occurred in Salerno during the twelfth century. The school came to depend increasingly on the works of Greek and
Arabic medicine which Constantine the African had translated.[4] A significant contribution to the philosophical literature of the school was made
by Urso of Calabria, known also as Urso Salernitanus, who was among the

---

Salerno cf. M. H. Saffron, «Maurus of Salerno», *Transactions of the American Philosophical So-
ciety* 62 (1972), 5-11, who offers the following periodization of its activities: 900-1110 Early,
Pre-Constantine; 1100-1225 The «Great» Period; 1225-1400 Late, Post-Neapolitan. The
Period of Decline (p. 7). For a discussion of Adelard of Bath's use of the natural-questions
genre and the channels by which the questions and answers reached him, see *Adelard of
Bath* ed. C. Burnett, XXII-XXVII.

   1. B. Lawn, *Salernitan Questions*, 64, further suggests that Neckam could have studied
physica later after joining the Austin canons c. 1197; Cirencester was close to Hereford, a
centre noted for the study of mathematical sciences, especially astronomy. As for the study
of medicine there, Lawn finds suggestive the fact that Alfred of Sareshel dedicated his work
De plantis to Roger, a canon of Hereford, the author of several astronomical works; see C.
H. Talbot, *Medicine in Medieval England*, 47-8.

   2. See Hunt ed. Gibson, *The Schools and the Cloister*, 4-7; B. Lawn, *Salernitan Questions*,
72.

   3. See B. Lawn, *Salernitan Questions*, 44; in 45, note 1, Lawn records correspondences between the *De naturis rerum* and the Salernitan prose collection. He concludes that Neckam
was probably not the author of the Salernitan *Questiones phisicales*, despite the few correspondences between the *Speculator* and the *Laus sapientie diuine*; from examining the *LSD* and the
SD and their treatment of ideas common to the *Questiones phisicales*, Lawn, 45-6, finds a con-
sistent «difference in vocabulary and methods of expression», which led him to favour Gilles
of Corbeil as a more likely candidate for authorship of the *Questiones phisicales*.

   4. See P. O. Kristeller, «*The School of Salerno*», *Bulletin of the History of Medicine* 17
(1945), 156-7; at 144-6 he notes that the early fame of the school rested on its practical skill
and ability to provide successful cures, rather than on any medical scholarship.

earliest to use the works of Aristotle on natural philosophy.[1] Urso's *Aph-orismi*, glossed with his own commentary, influenced Neckam's *De naturis rerum*, as mentioned above.[2] Although Neckam does not cite Urso's *Aph-orismi* in the *Laus sapientie diuine*, he honours him by name.[3] However, Al-exander's treatment of the theory of the elements may owe something to Urso's *De commixtionibus elementorum*.[4] In the supplement Neckam adapt-ed and expanded material from the *Aphorismi* to construct a bridge passage that commented on the silent but miraculous processes of nature.[5]

8. THE BESTIARY

Perhaps no medieval genre better integrated the study of nature with moral and spiritual concerns than the bestiary. Few books appealed to me-dieval readers more vividly than the collection of animals and birds they found assembled there. It described the often marvellous characteristics of real creatures and drew from them ethical and religious lessons that changed over time to reflect important preoccupations of medieval life.[6] As a genre, the bestiary was closely related to the *Physiologus*, a book of wonders drawn from the natural world, written in Greek sometime dur-ing the second century of our era. Indirect evidence suggests it was trans-lated into Latin by the end of the fourth century.[7] The order and contents

---

1. See P. O. Kristeller, «*The School of Salerno*», *Bulletin of the History of Medicine* 17 (1945) 161-2.

2. See B. Lawn, *Salernitan Questions*, 44; on Urso, see 31-4; Hunt ed. Gibson, *The Schools and the Cloister*, 71 and notes 28-30.

3. A. Birkenmajer, «Le rôle joué par les médicins et les naturalistes dans la réception d'Aristote au XIIe et XIIIe siécles», *Extrait da la Pologne au VIe Congrès International des Sci-ences Historiques*, Oslo, 1928 (Warsaw, 1930), 4, noted its presence in *LSD* 4, 235 (p. 425 W) *albet ut Urso docet*.

4. See Hunt ed. Gibson, *The Schools and the Cloister*, 71-2.

5. See *SD* 1, 1257-66.

6. On the bestiary as a response to changing concerns, see D. Hassig, *Medieval Bestiaries. Text, Image, Ideology* (Cambridge, 1995), 167.

7. F. McCulloch, *Mediaeval Latin and French Bestiaries*, (Chapel Hill, 1962), 19-34, divides the numerous manuscripts into families; from *Versio B* developed Latin versions in England and France, while *B-Is* incorporated additional material from Isidore's *Origines*. Parallel pas-sages in *Physiologus* and in Ambrose's *Hexaemeron* (6, 3, 13, ed. Schenkl, *CSEL* 32: 211, 5-18) point to the existence of a Latin version between 386 x 388 A.D. cf. M. J. Curley, *Physiologus* (Austin, 1979), xvii-xxi; for a discussion of the date of the Latin translation, see G. Orlandi, «La tradizione del 'Physiologus'», in *L'Uomo di fronte al mondo animale nell'alto medioevo* (Spo-leto, 1985), 2: 1066-70, 1089. On the *Physiologus*'s popularity as a medieval school text cf. G. Glauche, *Schullektüre*, 70; F. Diekstra, «The 'Physiologus', the Bestiaries and Medieval

of the successive Latin versions changed considerably over the centuries, with the number of chapters being doubled in the twelfth century. Non-scientific in its approach, the *Physiologus* catalogued animal behaviours, mingling elements drawn from philosophy, legend, myth, fable and personal observation. At its core lay a concern, not for natural history, but for the symbolic value of the beasts to teach morals and religion.[1] From this perspective the animal world was read for signs of God's presence in creation that could serve as the basis for moralizations. This approach owed much to Augustine's view, expressed in the *De doctrina Christiana*, that in the created world could be found the Creator's nature.

Through animals the multiple truths of morality and religion could be connected to human behaviours and attitudes. To take a popular example, so well-known to medieval readers that Neckam confidently omitted details of the story's central drama. The beaver was hunted because its glands were thought to contain a secretion with medicinal properties. When threatened with capture, the animal severed its testicles in the hope of escaping with its life. When targetted by other hunters, it lay on its back to show that it no longer possessed them.[2] Using allegorical interpretation, the medieval bestiarist could generate a number of meanings.[3] For example, by linking the beaver (*castor*) with chastity (*castus*) through etymology, verbal allegory could be used to promote a Christian virtue and to urge the faithful to rid themselves of vexatious impediments.[4]

Similarly, the elephant served in more than one capacity to reinforce Christian doctrine.[5] Its habit of giving birth while standing in water could

----

Animal Lore», *Neophilologus* 69 (1985), 143-4; J. Ziolkowski, *Talking Animals. Medieval Latin Beast Poetry 750-1150* (Philadelphia, 1993), 34-5.

1. F. Diekstra, «The 'Physiologus', the Bestiaries and Medieval Animal Lore», *Neophilologus* 69 (1985), 142, summarizes the influence of nature symbolism from *Physiologus*, noting how its imagery was assimilated into medieval literature and Christian iconography; M. J. Curley, *Physiologus* (Austin, 1979), xxiii-xxvi, emphasizes the extent to which the work's author altered numerous details of animal lore in order to align them with Christian doctrine and the Scriptures; cf. D. Hassig, *Medieval Bestiaries*, 169. M. Carruthers, *The Book of Memory*, 126-7, suggests that the real importance of the Bestiary descriptions lay in their capacity to function as «mental imaging» in the memory, available to be deployed to mark information within a mnemonic system.

2. See J. Cadden, *The Meanings of Sex Difference in the Middle Ages*, 49-50 and figure 2.

3. S. Reynolds, *Medieval Reading*, 134-40, discusses this mode of exegesis as a program for reading texts, theological and secular.

4. See *SD* 1, 1067-1070; on the transformation of the beaver's legend into Christian fable, see M. J. Curley, *Physiologus* (Austin, 1979), xxiii.

5. A. C. Henderson, «Medieval Beasts and Modern Cages», *PMLA* 97 (1982), 45, under-

signify the action of the Holy Spirit, which cleansed the soul of filth. If the sight of blood enraged and incited elephants to attack, the moralizer seized the chance to urge Christian love at the thought of Christ's blood offering.[1] Part of the genre's charm undoubtedly lay in the impossibility of predicting what spiritual or social applications would emerge from this analogical method, especially when deployed innovatively by «sportive bestiarists».[2]

The earliest bestiary, dating from the eleventh century, combined a version of the *Physiologus* text with excerpts from Isidore's *Origines*.[3] Its animal symbolism is predominantly theological, whereas many compilations from the 12th- and 13th-c. tend to emphasize moral and ethical lessons. In the schools, the bestiary became yet another means for teaching Christian ethics.[4] Imaginative descriptions, often accompanied with visual images, ensured its success as a text book. Some time after 1132, Hugh of Fouilloy made instrumental use of the *De auibus* to assist in the moral and spiritual instruction of monastic lay-brothers. An Augustinian house, the order to which Neckam himself belonged, was the destination of the Morgan bestiary that was specifically composed for the brothers' enlightenment.[5] An index of the text's popularity in twelfth-century En-

---

lines the fact that in bestiaries one animal can mean a number of things; he cites the example of the elephant, which could signify sometimes the presence of the old Adam, and at others, Christ.

1. Cf. *SD* 1, 1149-64. Sometimes Neckam's reliance upon his contemporaries' knowledge of animal lore led him to highly compressed formulations, which, when combined with lapidary expression, are obscure to modern readers e. g. *SD* 1, 973-4.

2. The phrase is that of A. C. Henderson, «Medieval Beasts and Modern Cages», *PMLA* 97 (1982), 46; he argues that originality in elaborating new meanings from animal lore was valued and that readers could not be sure what options fabulists or bestiarists would choose from the choices available to them, until the process of analogy was completed.

3. G. Orlandi, «La tradizione del 'Physiologus'», in *L'Uomo di fronte al mondo animale* (Spoleto, 1985), 2: 1094-6, discusses the dating of the B-Is redaction of the *Physiologus*.

4. See B. Rowland, «The Art of Memory and the Bestiary», in W. B. Clark and M. T. McMunn, *Beasts and Birds of the Middle Ages* (Philadelphia, 1989), 12-4. For the popularity of the bestiary as an instrument of instruction and edification in Augustinian milieux, see X. Muratova, «I manoscritti miniati del bestiario medievale», in *L'Uomo di fronte al mondo animale* (Spoleto, 1985), 2: 1341, 1346.

5. Cf. B. Rowland, «The Art of Memory», in W. B. Clark and M. T. McMunn, *Beasts and Birds*, 18; D. Hassig, *Medieval Bestiaries*, 171; X. Muratova, «I manoscritti miniati del bestiario medievale», in *L'Uomo di fronte al mondo animale* (Spoleto, 1985), 2: 1340, notes that New York, Pierpoint Morgan Library, MS 81, was donated by a canon of Lincoln Cathedral to the Augustinian priory of Radford (Worksop) in Nottinghamshire in 1187 «ad edificationem fratrum».

gland may be seen in the fact that the so-called Second Family version of the *Physiologus* was produced there.[1] From the nature of the moralizations in the *Suppletio*, we can surmise that Alexander's implied audience included not only himself in his capacity as abbot, but heads of other religious houses, teachers, masters and clerics with general responsibilities for the moral life of those committed to their charge.[2]

9. INVENTIO

According to classical rhetoric, successful writing depended upon an author's *ingenium*, *ars* and *exercitatio*. This programme, transmitted to the Middle Ages by Isidore,[3] Alexander appears to endorse at the poem's outset (*SD* 1, 45-6). Although the technical terms of invention, disposition and ornamentation do not appear in the work as definitions of the three steps in composition, from discursive comments on his own working methods it is clear that he was familiar with them.[4] When these remarks are set beside the treatises written by Matthew of Vendôme and Geoffrey of Vinsauf, they help to illuminate his poetic praxis. The works of Matthew and Geoffrey provide a convenient frame for assessing Alexander's *imitatio*.

The terms *suppletio* and *supplere* belong to the discourse of literary theory. The latter occurs in Matthew of Vendôme's chapter on *inventio*, the first step in composition, where he advises writers on procedures for treating the material at their disposal (*exsecutio materie*): *Debent enim minus dicta suppleri et inconcinna in melius permutari, superflua penitus aboleri.*[5] Dividing the

---

1. See F. McCulloch, *Medieval Latin and French Bestiaries*, 34-8.

2. Cf. *SD* 1, 594, 781, 879, 975, 1276 (*doctores*), 645-6, 717, 774, 802, 948, 1084; D. Hassig, *Medieval Bestiaries*, 171, mentions that monastic themes in the bestiaries included obedience to abbots, the virtues of the ascetic life and rejection of the world.

3. Cf. Isid., *Orig.* 2, 3, 2 *Ipsa autem peritia dicendi in tribus rebus consistit: natura, doctrina, usu. Natura ingenio, doctrina scientia, usus adsiduitate. Haec sunt enim quae non solum in oratore, sed in unoquoque homine artifice expectantur, ut aliquid efficiat.*

4. Neckam explicitly discusses composition in the word's narrower sense of arranging the words in a sentence and he also adverts to its sense of a poem's structural coherence. See below.

5. *Ars* 4, 2 (ed. Munari, 3: 194); cf. Sen., *Ep.* 79, 6 *Multum interest, utrum ad consumptam materiam an ad subactam accedas; crescit in dies, et inventuris inventa non obstant.* Cf. D. M. Hooley, *The Knotted Thong* (Ann Arbor, 1997), 242-67, discusses the tradition of *imitatio* from ancient to modern times.

subject into two parts, Matthew contrasts previously treated matter (*materia exsecuta* or *pertractata*) with material that had not been versified at all (*materia illibata*).[1] In the case of the former, he instructs poets to maintain the tenor of the source; changes were to be introduced only to remedy lexical and metrical faults or to improve the narrative's continuity or clarity. He encourages the poet to preserve the thought of the original, although he was free to vary its vocabulary and syntax and even to embellish it, if he wished. As for the latter, *materia illibata*, Matthew reiterated the importance of preserving the thought and ideas. Significant changes could be achieved by amplification and, where required, by abbreviation. Additions, whether already in verse or not, should be motivated by a need to fill in gaps.[2]

Geoffrey of Vinsauf specified a number of ways to appropriate subject matter that other poets had treated. The instructions fall under four main headings.[3] The two most important concern matters of emphasis and restructuring. First, the author should concentrate on material that had been lightly treated and vice-versa; then he should re-order the contents of the source text: ...*universitatem materiae speculantes ibi dicamus aliquid ubi dixerunt nihil, et ubi dixerunt aliquid, nos nihil; quod etiam prius, nos posterius, et e converso; et sic communia proprie dicemus.*[4] The third issue involved narrative consequence: no topic should be broached which made it impossible to return to the main body of the work. Fourth, the poem's beginning should avoid pretention. Both theorists concur that previously treated material posed the greater challenge to the aspiring writer: ...*difficile est materiam communem et usitatam convenienter et bene tractare; quanto difficilius, tanto laudabilius est bene tractare materiam talem, scilicet communem et usitatam, quam materiam aliam, scilicet novam et inusitatam.*[5] After warning against the inappropriate use of expansion and abbreviation, Geoffrey pointed out the pitfalls of digressions,[6] irrelevant descriptions and material so compressed as to be obscure.

---

1. Cf. *Ars* 4, 3 *exsecuta*, 4, 16 (ed. Munari, 3: 194, 202) *pertractata*; cf. *Ars* 4. 3 (ed. Munari, 3: 194) on *illibata*.

2. Cf. *Ars* 1, 38-40 (ed. Munari, 3: 59-60).

3. See D. Kelly, «The Scope of the Treatment of Composition in the Twelfth - and Thirteenth - Century Arts of Poetry», *Speculum* 41 (1966), 273; *id.* «Theory of Composition», *MS* 31 (1969), 128.

4. *Documentum*, 309-10, 134, cited by D. Kelly, «Theory of Composition», *MS* 31 (1969), 123

5. *Documentum*, 309, 132, cited by D. Kelly, «Theory of Composition in Medieval Narrative Poetry and Geoffrey of Vinsauf's *Poetria Nova*», *MS* 31 (1969), 120.

6. T. Haye, *Das lateinische Lehrgedicht*, 191-96, discusses Neckam's use of digressions in the *LSD*.

In light of these observations, what procedures did Neckam follow in assimilating matter from Macer's *De uiribus herbarum*? In a programmatic note to the *Laus sapientie diuine*, he outlines a scheme of abbreviation, selection and omission, and re-arrangement. He follows a principle of selectivity,[1] acknowledging that he has left much uncovered.[2] He admits to a limited knowledge of the medicinal powers of flowers (*florum vis mihi nota minus. / Quorum naturas tetigit veneranda vetustas, / sed sunt notitie subdita pauca meae*[3]), a fact that may be reflected in the position of the three floral entries at the end of the catalogue.[4]

The following examples show some of the ways Neckam re-arranged, varied, and telescoped Macer's text in the *Laus sapientie diuine*:

1. *LSD* 7, 71-3 (pp. 473-74 W) *Pulmonem, pectus... / ...juvat... /* Artheticis, tussi, *febri,* tiasique *medetur.*
   Macer 274-6 *Pulmones iuvat et pectus... / ... /* Arteticos sciasimque iuvat, *febrique medetur.*

2. *LSD* 7, 113 (p. 475 W) Vexatis tiasi confert *superaddita coxae.*
   Macer 600-1 Illi, qui sciasim patitur, *coxae superadde.*

3. *LSD* 7, 118 (p. 475 W) Singultum *tollit* associata mero
   Macer 624 *Tollere singultum* cum vino dicitur hausta.

4. *LSD* 7, 127 (p. 475 W) *vermes necat aure* latentes
   Macer 1943 *Auribus* infusus *vermes* succus *necat* eius.

5. *LSD* 7, 139-40 (p. 475 W) Quod dabis *acidulae,* concedit *Plinius* isti, / *Effectus* harum judicat *esse pares.*
   Macer 763-64 *Acidulae* similes huic pene per omnia vires / *Effectusque pares* testatur *Plinius esse.*

6. *LSD* 7, 141-42 (p. 475 W) *semen /* Haustum cum Baccho *somnia vana* fugat... /
   Macer 771 Lactucae *semen* compescit *somnia vana* / Cum vino...

7. *LSD* 7, 254 (p. 478 W) *Compescit tussim...*
   Macer 1751 *Tussim compescit...*

Alexander generally transfers the factual information straightforwardly, with the occasional mythological or biblical flourish to ornament Macer's plain style. Two illustrations make the point: to show purslane's protec-

---

1. Cf. *LSD* 7, 1-2 (p. 472 W) *Herbarum species paucis perstringere paucas / ...libet, 8 Lucida si fuerint, abbreviata juvant;* cf. 7, 351 (p. 480 W) *Herbarum vires nonnullas me tetigisse / Glorior,...*

2. Cf. *LSD* 7, 341 (p. 480 W) *Tot restant herbae, tot flores.*

3. *LSD* 7, 352-4 (p. 480 W), correcting Wright's misprint (*notitia*) in 354.

4. Cf. *rosa: LSD* 7, 295-314 (p. 479 W); *lilium:* 7, 315-34 (p. 480 W); *viola:* 7, 335-40 (p. 480 W).

tive powers against the sun's heat, Neckam introduces from the Old Testament the figure of Judith, with the remark that the plant would have
saved her from widowhood, an allusion to the death of her husband, Ma-
nasseh, by sunstroke. Macer merely records this property of purslane.[1]
Similarly, Alexander embellishes the entry on the plant centaury by refer-
ing to the centaur, Chiron, in his capacity as Achilles's tutor.[2]

Neckam's notice about the incomplete coverage of plants in the *Laus
sapientie diuine* left the door open for him to return to the subject. Although Neckam is silent about his source, one sign of Macer's continuing
influence is evident in the supplement's arrangement of the material,
which follows Macer's order of herbs and flowers in almost exactly the
same sequence.

Alexander often compresses the material from his model by using asyn-
deton to present multiple facts concisely.[3] Although there is some auto-
citation from the *Laus sapientie diuine*, Neckam usually recasts it by means
of minor dictional variation, a procedure that suggests he worked with a
copy of the monumental poem in front of him. However, he also deployed other rhetorical devices to enliven the supplementary material, including puns, onomastic games, academic periphrases, etymological play,
and witty allusions to historical and mythical figures.[4] As a rule, Neckam
avoids tranferring matter verbatim,[5] but it does occasionally happen.
Note, for instance, the identical phrase that concludes the section on the
mallow in the source text (*LSD* 7, 96 [p. 474W] *morsibus apta salus*) and

---

1. *LSD* 7, 137–8 (p. 475W) *Si portulacae vires experta fuisset / Judith, sol fervens non viduasset
eam* (cf. Jdt 8. 2–3); cf. Macer 760–1 *Fervorem solis aestate comesta nocere / Non sinit.*

2. *LSD* 7, 249–50 (p. 478W) *Centaurea tibi notissima, doctor Achillis, / Absque Machaonia
vulnera sanat ope*; cf. Macer 1709–27.

3. Note *SD* 1, 559 *Quasdam presenti perstrinxi carmine*; Alexander refers to techniques for
amplifying and abbreviating material and implies how demanding he found them at *SD* 1,
1056–7; 2, 1017–8 *Hinc placidi breuitate stili committere scripto / ...libet;* 1067–8 *Svccincte soleo perstringere nota relatu; / Digna tamen cupio nota carere nota.*

4. For an example of a pun cf. *SD* 1, 459 *colubri colubrina uenenum;* for extended play on
the name *maurella* cf. *SD* 1, 489–94; for periphrasis cf. *SD* 1, 501–2; *SD* 1, 446 on Romulus,
543–6 on the death of Socrates, 321 on Thersites, 410 on Thais.

5. E. g. with *LSD* 7, 107 (p. 474W) *Savinae virtus anthracis vim fugat atram* with *SD* 1, 295
...antraci sauina medetur, with *LSD* 7, 188 (p. 476W) *digeret ipsa* (sc. eruca) *cibos* cf. *SD* 1, 385–
6 *escas / Digerit* (sc. eruca); *LSD* 7, 257 (p. 478W) *Hujus* (sc. ellebori albi) *vi...vertigo recedit*
and *SD* 1, 469 *Eius ui cedit uertigo.* Greater verbal variation occurs between *LSD* 7, 193–4
(p. 476 W) *Sed quod flos candens ornat praestantius esse / Scitur* and *SD* 1, 393–4 *vtilitate / Prestat qui niueo gaudet honore nitor* (sc. papauer); cf. *LSD* 7, 221–2 (p. 477W) *Aristologiae speciem
medicina rotundam / Dicit* and *SD* 1, 421 *Aristologie que sperica fertur... .*

the distich on the same plant in the supplement (*SD* 1, 290). More extensive, and slightly modified, is the duplicated material on the plant catnip
(*LSD* 7, 115-6 [p. 475W]):

> ...*stomachoque dolenti,*
> *Leprae quae nomen ex elephante trahit.*

> ...*confert stomachoque lepreque*
> *Que notum nomen ex elephante trahit.*
> > *SD* 1, 303-4

Repetitions of this kind make it unlikely that Neckam intended the
new material to be inserted after the corresponding verses in the *Laus sapientie diuine*.[1] At the same time, other couplets composed of almost entirely new material, for example, the distichs on plantain (*SD* 1, 283-4),
garlic (*SD* 1, 281-2), mustard (*SD* 1, 405-6) and wild parsnip (*SD* 1, 409-
10),[2] form seamless codas to their counterparts.[3]

Neckam took care to take from Macer only items that he had not already included in the *Laus sapientie diuine*. Close analysis reveals that verses
on plants from the *Laus sapientie diuine* which reappear in the supplement[4]
contain at least one new fact.[5] As illustration, from the dozen verses devoted to the powers of parsley (*LSD* 7, 79-90 [p. 474W]) Neckam selected
one, which he rearranged to accomodate the new matter:

> Confert hydropicis, spleni, jecorique (sc. *apium*)...
> > *LSD* 7, 83

---

1. Cf. the phrase *somnia vana fugat* occurs in the same *sedes* at *LSD* 7, 142 (p. 475W) and *SD* 1, 314, an attribute of *lactuca*.

2. The same is true of the lines on the onion at *SD* 1, 397-400, which do not replicate data from *LSD* 7, 197-204 (p. 477W), *marrubium* (*LSD* 7, 225-6 [p. 477W] and *SD* 1, 417-20), hyssop (*LSD* 7, 229-30 [p. 477W) and *SD* 1, 425-34), mint (*LSD* 7, 233-6 [p. 478W] and *SD* 1, 439-42; groundsel (*LSD* 7, 245-6 [p. 478W] and *SD* 1, 451-4); centaury (*LSD* 7, 249-50 [p. 478W] and *SD* 1, 457-8); dragonwort (*LSD* 7, 251-4 [p. 478W] and *SD* 1, 459-60); *verbena* (*LSD* 7, 263-6 [p. 478W] and *SD* 1, 475-8); *millefolium* (*LSD* 7, 267-8 [p. 478W] and *SD* 1, 479-84); germander (*LSD* 7, 269-70 [p. 478W] and *SD* 1, 485-8); henbane (*LSD* 7, 275-6 [p. 479W] and *SD* 1, 505-18; mallow (*LSD* 7, 277-8 [p. 479W] and *SD* 1, 519-28; the couplet on wild-thyme (*SD* 1, 413-6) also mentions the effect of the herb on the liver.

3. See *LSD* 7, 61-7 (p. 473W) and 7, 53-60 (p. 473W).

4. Two examples are *LSD* 7, 11 (p. 472W) *Matricis vitium levat artemisia* cf. *SD* 1, 265 *Optima matricis est artemisia mater*, with *LSD* 7, 23-4 (p. 472W) *Auribus...confert* (betonica)... / ...*hydropicosque juvat* with *SD* 1, 293-4 *Bethonice uirtus auris...dolori,* / ...*ydropicis dat opem.*

5. Only the entries on *artemesia* (265-6: cf. *LSD* 7. 11-20 [p. 472W]), *anetum* (291-2: cf. *LSD* 7. 97-106 [p. 474W]) and *satureia* (347-8: cf. *LSD* 7. 149-54 [p. 475W]) add nothing new.

Ydropicis, spleni confert apium iecorique,
feniculi succus si societur ei.

SD 1, 287-8

Similarly, we now learn, cerefolium is beneficial for ailments involving intestinal worms, the stomach and nausea;[1] hyssop is good not only for hoarse voices, facial complexions and coughing, but it is also an effective laxative.[2] Moreover, new data on the curative powers of herbs also emerge from the items on garlic (281-2), onions (397-400), mustard (405-6), horehound (417-20), centaury (457-8) and germander (485-8).[3] Finally, five plants omitted from the *Laus sapientie diuine* now receive coverage.[4]

Neckam deploys many of the means Geoffrey of Vinsauf[5] had advocated for expanding material, including interpretation (331-40, 343-6, 351-64), circumlocution (304, 382, 489, 502), digression (315-22, 543-6, 559-70) and apostrophe (298, 387, 396, 446, 496, 498, 526). At times, he quietly inserts among the technical details texts from classical and contemporary poets (277-8, 587-8). The rhetorical figures and intertextual play are not limited to the section on plants.[6]

The shorter segment on trees displays several novelties. A place is found for the almond and cherry tree, earlier mentioned only in passing. The cypress, oak and box merit a single line each.[7] While the couplet on the ash-tree is recapitulative,[8] by contrast Neckam's section about the eb-

---

1. With *SD* 1, 373-5 cf. *LSD* 7, 171-2 (p. 476 W) *cerefolium.*

2. With *SD* 1, 425-34 cf. *LDS* 7, 229-30 (p. 477 W) *hysopum*; cf. also *SD* 1, 411-2 with *LSD* 7. 217-8 (p. 477 W) *origanum* and *SD* 1, 471-4 with *LSD* 7, 259-62 (p. 478 W) *helleborum nigrum.* Other examples include: *SD* 1, 296-7 adds savin's power to cure wounds and diseases induced by cold: cf. *LSD* 7, 107-8 (p. 474 W). The couplet on *nepta* (*SD* 1, 303-4) specifies its beneficial effects on fevers cf. *LSD* 7, 113-8 (p. 475 W).

3. Cf. the entries on *cepa LSD* 7, 197-204 (p. 477 W), *sinapis* 7, 209-10 (p. 477 W), *marrubium* 7, 225-6 (p. 477 W), *centaurea* 7, 249-50 (p. 478 W), *germandrea* 7, 269-70 (p. 478 W). For further details on the precise extent of borrowed material, consult the commentary.

4. These are *gaido* (461-2), *columbina* (547-70), *crocus* (571-6), *solsequium* (577-8) and *nardus* (435-8); items 2-4 do not appear in Macer either; Hunt ed. Gibson, *The Schools and the Cloister*, 75, note 52, observes that in the section on herbs in the *DNR* Neckam follows Macer's order «with scarcely a change».

5. For a complete list and discussion see D. Kelly, «Theory of Composition», *MS* 31 (1969), 130.

6. For Neckam's use of *prosopopeia* cf. *SD* 2, 1509-26 (*Grammatica*), 1530-49 (*Theologia*).

7. On the *cerasus* cf. *LSD* 8, 91 (p. 483 W) *Mespila cum cerasis et prunis...*); for the cypress *LSD* 8, 45 (p. 482 W), *quercus* 8, 49 (p. 482 W), the box 8, 55 (p. 482 W *Tecta virore caput, sed truncum pallida, buxus*).

8. Cf. Hunt ed. Gibson, *The Schools and the Cloister*, 79 and note 70, compares *LSD* 8, 53-4 (p. 482 W) with *SD* 1, 229-30 on *fraxinus.*

ony is both amusing and original. From a single couplet (*Laus sapientie diuine* 8, 65-6 [p. 483W]), the ebony-tree grows into more than twenty verses (*SD* 1, 209-228) before it is capped with a moralization.[1]

Novelty is also evident in Neckam's treatment of birds, especially in the catalogue of bird calls (*uoces animantium*) and in expanded descriptions.[2] In the *Laus sapientie diuine* moralizations of avian *characteristica* play little or no part. For the animals there is none at all. The sections on the mole (1421-36), the fox (1447-58) and the stag (1267-82) may serve as illustrations. The mole and fox do not figure in the longer poem at all. The moral for the former is drawn from the *De naturis rerum*,[3] the source also for the verses on the fox.[4] Of the remaining beasts in the supplement four appear for the first time.

In summary, Neckam took care to present the traditional material with a fresh face.[5] He is particularly adept at playing new variations on the old. Most prominent are the insertions that use selected animal characteristics as pretexts to integrate different aspects of his own biography. For example, the hoopoe's famous filial piety introduces a long eulogy and meditation on his dead mother, Hodierna.[6] In another case, the bat's exotic anatomy, part-bird, part-animal, is made to act as a structural device for a deft transition from the avian to the animal world. The bat's hybrid nature is further exploited as a metaphor as the poet defends playfulness as a legitimate element in serious writing.[7] Again, the word for saw-fish (*serra*) sets off a series of associations that end with a description and apologia of his own poetics.[8] In the same vein are Alexander's isolated comments on

---

1. The language of allegory includes the verbs *explanare*, *delucidare* (719), *signare* (735, 817, 889, 995, 1136, 1139), *designare* (879, 1097, 1189, 1250, 1440), *significare* (332), *figurare* (1137, 1189), *docere* (740) and *notare* (742); cf. *tipus* (679), *tipice* (889).

2. Cf. *uoces animantium* at *SD* 1, 49-61; *passer. SD* 1, 701-6 with *LSD* 2, 783-8 (p. 391W); *turtur. SD* 1, 653-66 with *LSD* 2, 855-64 (pp. 392-3W). Hunt ed. Gibson, *The Schools and the Cloister*, 79, claims that in the section on birds and animals «the 'facts' are the same, but a new moral is given or one supplied if it was lacking».

3. With *DNR* 2, 122 (p. 200W) *ambitio...circa terrena semper occupata* cf. *SD* 1, 1429-30.

4. Cf. *DNR* 2, 125 (p. 205W). Note also that the stag's moralization (*SD* 1, 1275-6) differs from the account in *DNR* 2, 135 (p. 216W) and that, whereas the episode on the *barrus* in *LSD* 9, 47-90 (pp. 487-88W) lacks a moral, Neckam develops matter from *DNR* 2, 145 (pp. 225-6W).

5. The quatrain on the wild-cat, which takes over material from *LSD* 9, 275-8 (p. 492W) is an exception; *LSD* 6, 245-6 (p. 469W) on the lynx does not moralize the stone; cf. *SD* 1, 1311-22.

6. Cf. *SD* 1, 829-870.

7. Cf. *SD* 1, 891-930.

8. Cf. *SD* 1, 1009-1066.

literary decorum, apostrophes to his detractors, apprehensions about the poem's reception, and claims on behalf of his own poetic merit.

As noted above, the *Physiologus* formed part of the school curriculum and was studied with the *auctores* as a work of religious instruction. The text's broad dissemination meant that educated readers were familiar with its contents, a fact that allowed Neckam some latitude in presenting the incidental properties of individual animals. Thus, the distich on the ape (1227-8), a quotation from Bernard Silvestris, contains no `facts' about the animal, but is inserted solely to point the moral.[1] Similarly, the *passer* (701-6) is introduced as an index of man's efforts to elude the devil's snares. When the ape reappears (1287-1302), readers' expectations that Neckam will retell the well-known story about the ape and its twins are disappointed. Instead, they are surprised by a miniature Gigantomachy, which serves as a preface for a novel explanation of the beast's origin.

Neckam also rejuvenated the material by adding fresh moralizations. Now the hare furnishes a lesson absent from the *Laus sapientie diuine*,[2] and one that offers a different moral from the one drawn in the *De naturis rerum*, namely, that effeminate men imitate the animal.[3] The wolf[4] too carries a new signification. In contrast to the solo appearance of the crocodile in the earlier poem, it now takes the stage alongside its deadly enemy, the water-snake.[5] The entries on the sawfish (1009-14), the hedgehog (1073-90), the porcupine (1099-1148), the snail and the beetle (1185-90), and the more ambitious tale about the mouse (1323-1420) are original productions composed for the supplement.

The larger scale of the inserted Aesopic fable[6] merits detailed comment. Superficially, it narrates the story of a mouse who searches for a

---

1. Cf. *LSD* 9, 107-8 (p. 488W), where the ape is not moralized.

2. Cf. with *LSD* 9, 151-2 (p. 489W) cf. *SD* 1, 1001-2.

3. Cf. *DNR* 2, 134 (p. 215W). Other differences in moralizations occur for the camel at *DNR* 2, 141 (p. 221W) *Per camelum oneriferum designatur sollicitudo super rebus terrenis habita* (cf. *SD* 1, 989-92); for the bat in *LSD* 2, 583-4 (p. 386W) [cf. *SD* 1, 921-2]; for the fox in *DNR* 2, 125 (p. 205W) *Quid igitur melius per vulpem quam dolositas accipitur?* (cf. *SD* 1, 995-6); for the crocodile in *DNR* 2, 101 (p. 186W) *Sic et sunt quidam qui devoti videntur esse in ecclesia, rapinis tamen et turpibus lucris et questibus inhiant* (cf. *SD* 1, 1143-6); for the stag in *DNR* 2, 135 (p. 216W) *In hoc monemur ut unusquisque nostrum alteri condescendat, secundum quod dicitur: «Alter alterius onera portate.»* (cf. *SD* 1. 1275-6 *ecce monetur / Doctorum cetus ordinis esse memor*).

4. Cf. *SD* 1, 1243-56.

5. Cf. *LSD* 9, 155-62 (p. 489W).

6. For a discussion of Aesopic tales in ancient and medieval sources cf. J. Ziolkowski, *Talking Animals*, 15-32; S. Reynolds, *Medieval Reading*, 143, noting that such stories formed

suitable marriage partner of whom the gods will approve. After a debate, the mouse visits in succession the courts of the sun, the clouds, the wind, the rain, and the earth. They all in turn rebuff his request to marry their daughters, until finally Cybele intervenes to pronounce that, according to Ovid's teaching, like should be joined to like. The goddess decrees he must marry a mouse. She supports her decision with an argument from nature, drawn from the world of birds and animals. At the end, the narrator draws a moral about the dangers of arrogance.

The beast fable follows the generic pattern, but the context and the use of the term *fabula* hint that the fiction covers deeper truths, which turn out to involve physical theories about the world.[1] In the opening praise of divine wisdom, Neckam mentions the role of the four elements in creation and how combinations of them underlay phenomena ranging from the world's structure to man's temperament.[2] Although he does not present a theory of the elements[3] in the systematic manner of Adelard of Bath, Neckam was conversant with it. According to Adelard, while the pure elements were not accessible to man's senses, things arose from their mingling. As with plants,[4] so with animals; there were those with warmer, colder, more humid and more fiery complexions. References to this theory, and to its corollary,[5] the theory of the four humours, surface when needed to explain natural phenomena.[6] Basic to the theory was the principle that like demanded like.[7] Viewed in this light, the fable's subtext is an imaginative representation of the theory, in which earth (*mus* was et-

---

part of 12th-c. elementary education, adduces Neckam's *Novus Aesopus* and *Novus Avianus* as examples of this morally instructive genre of writing.

1. Cf. P. Dronke, *Fabula*, (Leiden, 1974), 18, 69, on the concept of *integumentum*; S. Reynolds, *Medieval Reading*, 141-2, discusses William of Conches's division of *fabulae* into Aesopic fables of moral instruction and those that concealed a truth of philosophical value.

2. Cf. *SD* 1, 11-2; 2, 213-4 *Quatuor humano concurrere des elementa / Corpore, set primum purius esse dabis.*

3. Cf. *LSD* 4, 810-9 (p. 439W); Hunt ed. Gibson, *The Schools and the Cloister*, 72, note 31.

4. In T. Wright, *A Volume of Vocabularies* (Liverpool, 1857), a mid-13th-c. treatise preserved in London, BM, MS Harl. 978, written between 1264-5, probably for a physician, plants are divided into two categories: *Chaudes Herbes* and *Freides Herbes*.

5. Cf. *SD* 2, 225-6 *Quatuor humores, tot uirtutes, elementa / Corpore terreno tot superesse docent.*

6. Cf. *caloris uis* (121-2), *calor ignitus* (601), *conplexio* (997), *ignea uis* (1005), *mixtus humor* (1102), *humor piger* (998, 1105), *humor aquosus / aquaticus* (1108, 1265), *Frigiditate potens humor sicco sociata* (1109).

7. Cf. Baumgartner, Adelard 82 «Die Ursache des Zerfalls der Organismen liegt in den Gesetz, dass Gleiches nach Gleichem verlangt.» Accordingly, a plant, in which the warm elements predominated, needed an environment of that kind; otherwise it could not renew

ymologically linked to *humus = terra*) attempts to bond unsuccessfully with the other elements, the sun (*ignis*), clouds and wind (*aer*) and rain (*aqua*), until Cybele, goddess of the earth, reaffirms the cosmic principle that holds creation together. The same point emerges from the account of man's creation in *SD* 2, 217-20:

> Plasmatum tamen e terra corpus prothoplasti
>   Legimus, at sensum consule: planus erit.
> Regnat predominans terreno corpore terra;
>   Officium complent cetera turba suum.

Since medieval readers were trained in allegoresis, a method of double reading, they could easily have decoded the tale's secondary meaning.

Neckam repeatedly raises issues of literary decorum, especially of the legitimacy of mingling *ludicra* with *seria*.[1] He defends this literary recipe on the grounds that it has a refreshing and salutary effect upon his audience (891-906). Arguing from nature, he playfully cites the bat's strange physiology as a precedent for combining the two kinds of discourse (909-10 *ridiculumue genus*).

Neckam's sense of humour is playful and learned. Consider how he treats the theme of the swan's song and its well-known associations with impending death. He animates the hackneyed topic by calling up the rites of a funeral mass, in which birds sing in the choir and a parrot, as celebrant, delivers the benediction (815-6).[2] Again, orthography is cited as the principle that guides cranes to form the letter Y as they fly (871-2). Proserpina, abducted to live in the Underworld, appears as a woman metamorphosed into a mole (1423), an object lesson against mankind's mad search for riches (an allusion to Pluto as Dis) that exist outside nature's realm. In discussing his poetics, Neckam has high fun with metaphors of marriage, divorce and re-marriage as he describes the agonies of composition and revision (1045-50). Nor does he miss the chance to refer to the beaver's (*castor*) severed testicles with the names of the twins, Castor and

---

new its existence; cf. Adelard,*Quaestiones Naturales*, ed. Mueller 6, 2-33 ...*in exterioribus elementis suum simile irritantibus et extrahentibus suisque qualitatibus idem exigentibus causam huius processionis pono. Unde ista inferiora perpetua dissolutione ad sua similia recedunt.*

1. In a notice of an author later than Neckam, John of Garland cautioned against introducing a comic component into serious subject matter and vice-versa (*incongrua materie variacio*); see D. Kelly, «Theory of Composition», *MS* 31 (1969), 124.

2. M. Bayless, *Parody in the Middle Ages. The Latin Tradition* (Ann Arbor, 1996), 177-212, explores the nature of religious humour in the Middle Ages.

Pollux (1067). In place of simple description, Neckam introduces two women from the Old Testament, one fertile, one barren (297-8), to illustrate the leek's power as an aphrodisiac. Finally, he often slips extracts from classical and medieval sources into new contexts. Thus Martial's couplet on gout turns up unannounced as a preface to noting this property of the nettle (277-8).

10. STYLE

Neckam's periodic characterizations of his compositional methods are orchestrated to serve a number of purposes. Taken as a whole, they validate his achievement and affirm his poetic merit. They are also functional, as mentioned above, in that the distribution of the narratorial comments throughout the book marks points of transition from one division to another. Moreover, as Alexander admits, they provide diversion for his readers. In one, Neckam pursues an encomiastic agenda. While he rejects claims to equal status with the ancients, he singles out his industry, diligence and painstaking craftmanship for praise: (*SD* 2, 561-6):

> Sim licet, ut uerum fatear, maioribus inpar,
>   Est tamen inuentis gratia danda meis.
> Subtili dicenda sibi nouitate[1] fauorem
>   Conciliant; veri lùx ratione micat.
> Prodeat in lucem multis uigilatus ab annis[2]
>   Detque fidem certam cum nouitate labor.[3]

In the section on the saw-fish (*SD* 1, 1009-66), he elaborates on the more formal aspects of composition. A description of the exotic fish is gradually shaped into a discussion of the choice and arrangement of words, of rhetorical ornamentation and of literary allusion.

The introductory frame repays close study. Neckam's compositional art did not escape the notice of the glossator, who perceptively remarked

---

1. The claim to poetic originality has a long history; cf. Alan of Lille, *Anticlaudianus*, pro- *logus*, 4-5 *Scribendi nouitate uetus iuuenescere carta / Gaudet; prologus* (ed. Bossuat, 55) *Quare...delectatione nouitatis illectus, lector accedat.* For comments on Neckam's *sphragis* at the end of the *LSD* and his awareness of his poetic achievement, see T. Haye, *Das lateinische Lehrgedicht*, 89.

2. Cf. *SD* 2, 1731-2 *Nobile Thebaidos carmen compleuit in annis / Bissex;* Stat., *Theb.* 12, 811-2 *o mihi bissenos multum uigilata per annos / Thebai.*

3. Cf. Baudri, *Carm.* 30, 1 *Frodo, labor magnus te uatibus equiperarat.*

on the poet's verbal and conceptual skills as he worked the semantic field
of the word *serra*. The play of ideas skips lightly from saw–fish to the saw
as material implement, until it comes to rest on another serrated tool, the
file. From here the leap to the file's metaphorical function and role in refining poetry is a short one. Next, the theme of literary decorum is raised
and linked to parts of his biography. Here an element of self–caricature
undercuts Neckam's disavowal of the playful element in his writing
(1017-20). In an adroit transition, admirably compressed, the poet addresses the reader about the direction of the argument:

> *Bestia displiceat: placeat tibi serra fabrilis*
> *Et poliat sceptum lima decenter opus.*
>   SD 1, 1023-4

In self-deprecating tones reminiscent of Horace, he poses questions
about literature's relationship to morality, the constant need for self-scru-
tiny, and the continual process of correction demanded by both life and
learning. The concerns eventually narrow to settle on related matters,
such as the choice of a poetic lexicon, the anxiety of writing after the classical achievement, and the subject of literary borrowing and allusion.

The connection between linguistic and ethical correction is reinforced
by the interwoven word order and the clever choice of words with meanings that overlap and resonate in both areas (*SD* 1, 1039-40):

> *Corripio mores, uersus emendo, reuoluo*
> *Sermonem, pingo uerba colore suo.*

The convergence is also apparent in the earlier critique of the *Laus sa-*
pientie diuine . After referring to unspecified deficits (*Quosdam defectus illius*
carminis [563]), he repeats the term and enlarges its meaning to include his
own life (565-6):

> *Defectus agnosco meos, quos carmine prudens*
> *Supleo presenti;*

Comments about revision, various types of locutions, and rhetoric's
ability to enhance words[1] culminate in observations about form, content
and style. Alexander rejects neologisms, meretricious ornamentation

---

1. In *SD* 2, 1676-8 Neckam alludes to these aspects of writing in his allegorical description of Rhetorica who is arrayed in multi-coloured clothing; cf. 1763-6 *Depingens* (sc. ars
rhetorica) *uariis depicta coloribus ista / Quod dignum laude est, quodlibet ornat opus. / Scemate*
multiplici disponit scemata queuis; / Ars est istius gracior artis ope, 1781-2 *Floribus est ornata suis re-*

(1042 *cum faleris uerba nouella*)[1] and turgid language (1043 *turgida*). Ignoring Matthew of Vendôme's caveat about the disadvantages of a mundane vocabulary (*verba cotidiana et nimium simplicia*),[2] he states a preference for *publica uerba* (1044). Next, he comments on disposition and the relationship of form to content (1046 *forma uenustet eam*). Using the rhetorical concept of *junctura uerborum* as a marriage,[3] he develops the conceit with the aid of technical grammatical terms. These in turn reinforce the idea with satisfying effect (1045):

> *Scinthasis ipsa docet ut nubat mobile fixo.*

In cases of incompatible lexical partnerships, the union is immediately dissolved and a second marriage follows on the divorce. Morals and language come together once more in the poet's wish (1051-2) for vice to be castigated with the same vigour as the Latin language rejects solecisms. He ends with an extended self-caricature of the moralist as poet. With playful self-deprecation, he portrays himself as a man in torment, reluctant to undertake the discipline of revision, until he finally abandons all thoughts of morality. Faced with imperfections in his own compositions, he begins to envy the literary merit of others. He is ready to admit their poetic achievement to himself, but he refuses to acknowledge it publicly. Yet even as he is openly critical of poetry he admires, he is marking lines for eventual inclusion in his own verse. In a humorous parting shot, expressed in polysemous language (1065-6 *improbus... censor, me iudice, .../... ingeniosus*), he gives an example of his own intertextual procedures, which are tailored to carry a denunciation of clever critics who denigrate the work of rivals. The point is reinforced by means of an Ovidian tag and a reformulated passage from Martial's prose preface to his book of epigrams.

---

sis uarioque, / Vt uulgo constat, picta colore nitent. While describing man's five senses, Neckam breaks off to comment on the licence of poets to deploy rhetorical figures in the service of faith: *SD 2, 123-6 Attendas resim uerbisque licentia detur; / Gaudet habere suos prosa soluta tropos. / Forcius ergo suis utantur metra figuris; / Scribenti metrice multa licere dabis.*

1. Cf. *SD 2, 1767-8 Cornipedem falere cultusque decencior ornat; NG M-N, 1440-3, s. v. novellus,* shows that the semantic range of the word includes newly-born animals, newly planted crops, newly founded monasteries and recently converted peoples, as well as newly fashioned words.

2. *Ars* 1, 31 (ed. Munari, 3: 56).

3. Cf. Matthew of Vendôme, *Ars* 1, 1 (ed. Munari, 3: 43-4) *Versus est metrica oratio succincte et clausulatim progrediens venusto verborum matrimonio et flosculis sententiarum picturata..facit versum ...elegans junctura dictionum.*

Despite the irony, the amalgam of theory and the wry observations regarding his practice may serve as a convenient starting point to review features of Neckam's style.

According to Geoffrey of Vinsauf, writers should consider content before form: *Cum constiterit de sententia, procedendum est ad verba, diligentiam adhibendo, ut series verborum sit ornata.*[1] Ornamentation (*elocutio*) should serve the poem's original conception (*inventio*) and order (*dispositio*), though it could vary according to the demands of the material. Subject matter determined the choice of one style over another. The selection and arrangement of words, tropes and figures were subject to the plan and purpose of the material (*materia*).

Like the writers of rhetorical manuals, Neckam acknowledged the primacy of content over form and the requirement that discourse be adapted to the subject matter.[2] Aside from Neckam's explicit comments, there is the evidence of the poetry itself. Even to an untutored eye, the unadorned style of the catalogue of herbs and flowers is markedly different from the elevated language adopted to narrate the fable of the mouse.

The section on plants, distilled from Macer's long poem, draws on the discourse of medicine, on the plain and technical language of herbal and medical literature. As the incorporating text, the *Suppletio* reproduces the formulaic language and uses repetitive and asyndetic phrasing to carry the entire section,[3] though it is interspersed with periodic flashes of wit, as

---

1. *Documentum*, 285, 2; cf. *Poetria Nova* 60-1 *Mentis in arcano cum rem digesserit ordo, / materiam verbis veniat vestire poesis*, cited by D. Kelly, «The Scope of the Treatment», *Speculum* 41 (1966), 273.

2. Cf. *SD* 1, 1041, 1046.

3. Recurring phrases from medical discourse include: *Subuenit ydropicis* (284) cf. Constantinus Africanus, 364 *ischiatis subuenit*; 356 *Aristolochia rotunda cum aqua bibita epilepticis, podagricis, et spasmum habentibus subuenit; Sanant...ictus* (281), *Vulnera...sanat* (461): cf. Constantinus, 364 *intestina uulnerata sanat; abscinthia cocta liquore* (269), *cocta mero* (541): cf. Constantinus, 344 *aqua rosata cocta cum uino iuuat caput* [cf. *SD* 1, 380 *Yctericos...iuuat*]; *Uirtus hebeni* (209), *bethonice uirtus* (293), *accidule uirtus* (309), *eruce uirtus* (385), *marrubii uirtus* (417), *Peonie uirtus* (445), *Verbene uirtus* (476), *uirtus herbe* (555): cf. Constantinus, 344 *Vnde quasi bellum facit* (sc. absinthium) [cf. *SD* 1, 379 *Vnguibus indicit bellum*], *quia uirtus laxatiua materiam mouet...et uirtus stiptica eam indurat; Origanum...tussique medetur* (411) cf. Dioscorides, *De medicinali materia*, 90v: *De origano: tussi medetur; Cuius uim laudant* (415), *celidonie uis* (455), *uis centauree* (457), *eius ui* (469), *sumpte uis malue* (519), *uiole uires* (557): cf. Dioscorides, 90r: *De hyssopo: Vim habet extenuandi; Prouocat urinam* (435): Constantinus, 363 [Anethum]...*urinam prouocat*, cf. 362, 346; *fugat serpentes* (201), *fugat omnem / Languorem* (447-78), *Oris fetorem fugat* (477); *sputa...fugat* (518), *signa..fugat* (520), *fugat uirtute uenena* (523): cf. Dioscorides, 90r *De abrotano: Serpentes ...fugat; Ad combusturas facit* (525): cf. Dioscorides, 94v

noted above. Among the most commonly used figures are anaphora[1] and paranomeon, the most sustained example of which is:

> **S**uccurrit **s**pleni, tussi **s**ciasique **s**inapis
> **S**crofis, serpentis....[2]

However, on occasion Neckam deploys the *stilus altisonus* associated with epic to make a satirical point. For example, to account for a monstrosity like the ape, he concocts an aetiology that involves the mythic story of the Giants' battle against the gods, which he tells in an elevated style (1287-96).[3] In the same grand manner stands the mouse fable (1323-1420), though it is larger in conception and execution.[4] What at first appears to be a stylistic solecism, an overlong and irrelevant digression,[5] turns out to fit the poem's overall design. For the alert reader Neckam encodes a sign about the fable's stylistic level:

> *Ha quociens effert humiles tumor assecla fastus!*[6]

The story of the grandiose mouse is matched by the style of the *genus grande*, which is here richly textured with Virgilian and Ovidian allusions.[7] The mouse, ironically cast as a monarch, is led through a maze of epic themes and conventions.[8] The stylistic unity is maintained to the end, where Neckam expresses the moral in a set of Virgilian similes and epic phrases.

Facit ad pectoris laterumque dolores; Matricem siccat (572): cf. Constantinus, 363-4 *ea omnino desiccat; morbis.. .prosunt* (245): cf. Dioscorides, 90r *De abrotano: Contra ictus eorum* (sc. serpentum) *cum uino potum prodest.*

1. SD 1, 1323 Cf. Matthew of Vendôme, *Ars* 3, 5 (ed. Munari, 3: 167); cf. SD 1, 77-8, 183-4, 331-4, 389-91, 476-7.

2. SD 1, 405-6; Matthew of Vendôme, *Ars*, 3, 10 (ed. Munari, 3: 170) gives the example: *Seva sedens super arma*; for other instances cf. SD 1, 271, 288, 305, 405, 577, 579, 588, 809, 850, 886. .

3. Cf. Claudian, *Carm min.* 53, 3 *omnia monstrifero conplebat Tartara fetu* (sc. Terra parens).

4. Note the polysemous terms in 1331-2: Set constare sibi uult de *uirtute* parentis, / Cuius *uim* laudent sydera, terra, mare.

5. See Geoffrey of Vinsauf, *Documentum* 313, 15 on *incompetens digressio*, cited by D. Kelly, «Theory of Composition», *MS* 31 (1969), 130.

6. SD 1, 1323; see Isid., *Orig.* 2, 17, 1 on the three styles: *humile, medium, grandiloquium*; Quint., *Inst.* 12, 10, 73 (ed. Winterbottom, 2: 738) *genus dicendi, quod... inmodico tumore turgescit*; for a further allusion to the grand style within the fable cf. SD 1, 1365 *Rex igitur tumido uoluens sub pectore curas.*

7. S. Viarre, *La survie d'Ovide*, 44, remarks on Neckam's concern to amuse his cultivated readers by inserting Ovidian excerpts in the *DNR*.

8. The themes include a royal council with a decision-making scene, a heavenly journey to the palace of the Sun, a catalogue of precious stones, standard epic formulas for

In yet another register, the moralizations attached to birds and animals use the discourse of exegetical literature. Normally placed as a separable unit, as a kind of appendix at the end of the entry, they are also often interwoven as part of a running commentary on the animal's traits. Here verbs and nouns dealing with signification (*signare*, *designare*, *typus*) predominate, and, less obviously, the hortatory aspect of the subjunctive mood. It is here too that Neckam tends to concentrate *exempla* based on Biblical events and persons.

II. RHETORICAL FIGURES

Neckam was a gifted rhetorician who painted his verse from a broad palette of colours. [1] The *figurae* and other grammatical tropes enhanced the poetry the better to serve Christian truth, as Grammatica points out to Theology (*SD* 2, 1537):

> *Iure tibi censes tropicas seruire figuras.*

The question of rhetoric's benefits for *scriptura sacra* is repeatedly canvassed in the second book (*SD* 2, 1737-8 *Quem sibi constituat finem facundia querunt / Et quid scripture conferat illa sacre*). The debate revolves around questions of form and content and the relative importance of rhetoric's utility and ornamental power (1741-2):

> *Aspectum recreat picture gratia; numquid*
> *Picture similis gloria resis erit?*

Rhetoric's case is presented by St Augustine, who is identified as both student and teacher of the art in Rome and Milan. Assuming rhetoric's practicality (1753 *Ars est celesti scripture commoda*), he first sketches its forensic utility (1753-60) before he turns to its decorative function. In a long

---

greeting strangers and inquiring why they have come, short formal speeches, and a divine pronouncement approved by a council of the gods. The social reality of medieval marriage dowry obtrudes at 1409-10.

1. Hunt ed. Gibson, *The Schools and the Cloister*, 64-6, sets out Alexander's favourite figures in his prose writings; cf. *LSD* 7, 357-8 (p. 481W) *Floribus ex variis contexit serta poesis, / Flores et Floram florida verba decent*; the «flower» was the conventional medieval name for a verbal trope; cf. Marbod, *De ornamentis verborum, prologus* (MPL 171: 1687) *Si potes his veluti gemmis et floribus uti, / Fiet opus clarum velut ortus deliciarum, / ... / Mens auditoris persuasa nitore coloris.*

development (1761-82), the saint valorizes rhetoric as a vital component in writings, both prose and verse (1763-4):

> Depingens uariis depicta coloribus ista
> Quod dignum laude est, quodlibet ornat opus.

1. Repetitio

In a list of rhetorical *flores* that is unfortunately incomplete, pride of place is given to the figure *repetitio*, which Neckam playfully illustrates in a tricolon that explains its advantages (*SD* 2, 1783-4):

> Quod repeticio sit gratus, quod sit color aptus
> Scripturis, quod sit primus in arte liquet. [1]

In the eulogy to his mother, Hodierna, Neckam deploys the same device effectively (839-42):

> Viuit amor, set uiuet amor; regnabit amoris
> Gratia; regnabit gloria, uiuit amor.
> Uiuit amor numquam moriturus, uiuet in euum.

2. Complexio.

The repetition *Viuit amor...uiuit amor*, which frames verses 839-40, also contains an example of the figure, *complexio*,[2] which is listed directly after *repetitio* in rhetoric's arsenal:

> color iste decenter
> Compositus finem principiumque tenet. [3]

3. Traductio

Repetitio includes alliteration. An extended example incorporates an instance of *traductio*, a figure that plays upon different grammatical forms of the same word. In the first, Neckam plays with the active and passive forms of the present tense, of the present participle and of the present infinitive of the verb *uincere* (933-8):

---

1. After reiterating *Roma, vale* ten times in *LSD* 5, 325-42 (p. 448W), Neckam wittily concludes (343-4): *Sed ne nugari videar tociens repetendo, / Roma, vale, cesso dicere, Roma, vale.*
2. In *SD* 2, 1792 *complexio* is glossed as *scilicet repeticionem et conuersionem.*
3. *SD* 2, 1794-5.

Vincitur ut *uincat; uincit uincatur* ut hostis;
  Uicto uincenti gloria maior adest;
Vincere me reputo maius quam *uincere* Parthum;
  Sic *uinci* quam sic *uincere* pluris erit.
Immo sic *uinci* des *uincere, uincere uinci*;
  Ergo cum *uinci* me sino, *uictor* ero.[1]

In a second case, Neckam rings the changes on the noun *cor* over four lines (849-52):

Quid miri, si *cor cordis* sic sit michi *cordi*
  Vt *cor* iam *cordis corde* carere querar?
Dimidio *cordis* me des aut *corde* carere,
  Nam falsi carie uerba carere decet.[2]

Shorter examples occur in the eulogy to his mother (843):

Tu michi mater *eras, es* mater, *ero* tibi natus,[3]

and in the definition of *repetitio* itself (SD 2, 1785):

Iste color primam *repetit repetenda* secundo.

Traductio could involve words of similar sounds, but different meanings, in the same sentence itself (SD 2, 1036):

Cor rapio multis quos bene *corripio.*

4. *Anaphora*

Anaphora, repetition at the start of lines, occurs at 1025-6:

Utilis est aliis, set se consumere nouit;
  Utilis est aliis, perniciosa sibi.[4]

---

1. Cf. *SD* 2, 1221-4 Orbis *honus* sustentat *honos* orbis, nec *honustum* / Tante molis *honus* censet *honoris honos*. / Non *honus* est *honeri* nec *honoris honus* set *honestas* / Atque *honor* est *honeris*; orbis egebat *honor*.

2. Less exuberant examples occur at *SD* 1, 869-70 Pro me flecte genu mentis, dulcissima *mater*, / *Matri* que *matrum* est gloria, gemma, decus; 1093 Fex est feda caro, fetens, *caries cariei*; 1096 Fedos *feda* iuuant, *turpia turpis* agit; 1089 Ne *concludatur* tibi, te *conclude* decenter. *Traductio* also covered the use of words with similar sounds but different meanings in the same sentence e. g. *SD* 1, 1030 *Officiosa* iuuant *officiendo* sibi; cf. Peter of Blois *Libellus*, ed. Camargo, 68, 907-8 *Studeant eandem sentenciam uerborum uarietate multipliciter mutare.*

3. Cf. *SD* 2, 1483 *Discretos discretus amat sapiens sapientes.*

4. Cf. *SD* 1, 165-8, 183-4, 331-4, 389-91, 601-3, 707-8, 907-9.

5. Anadiplosis

Anadiplosis is rarer, but two examples worth noting are: 854-5 *Iste dies / Iste dies* and 892-3 *seria mixta iocis / seria mixta iocis*.
Rhetorical questions and exclamations[1] regularly punctuate the verse.

12. SOURCES

In the last grammatical commentary he wrote, sometime after 1210, known today by its incipit as the *Sacerdos ad altare*, Neckam outlined a curriculum of reading that progressed from elementary books to more advanced texts. [2] Idealized though the list may be, Neckam's writings support the view that he was well-read in the *auctores*, even though he endorsed contemporary opinion about the ancillary role of the liberal arts. Following a long section on theology and some of its most eminent practitioners (*SD* 2, 1379-1498), a personified Grammatica demonstrates her discipline's support for theology by pointing to the Christian poets, Sedulius, Juvencus and Prudentius. [3] After Logica has argued for her utility, Rhetorica sweeps in with a retinue of classical poets, foremost among them Virgil:

> *En! uatum sequitur uenerabilis ordo; Maronem*
> *Mantua, Lucanum Corduba mittit; adest*
> *Stacius et Flaccus, cinicorum gloria, Naso*
> *Cui dulces elegos scribere ludus erat.*
> *Nobile Thebaidos carmen compleuit in annis*
> *Bissex; Eacide Stacius arma dedit.*[4]

As already mentioned, the case for Christian rhetoric emerges from St Augustine, who lists the advantages of an *ars... celesti scripture commoda* (*SD* 2, 1753):

> *Exanguis ne sit, ne sit uelud arrida queuis*
> *Pagina, prosa, metrum postulat eius opem.*
> *Depingens uariis depicta coloribus ista*
> *Quod dignum laude est, quodlibet ornat opus.*[5]

---

1. E. g. *SD* 1, 7, 117, 777, 781, 783-4, 952, 966, 1019, 1201-2, 1323.
2. See C. H. Haskins, *Studies in the History of Mediaeval Science* (Cambridge, MA., 1924), 365-76; S. Reynolds, *Medieval Reading*, 7-12, 108-9.
3. *SD* 2, 1517-20 *Iuuenco / Seruiui gaudens Sedulioque tuo. / Himpni quos dilecta canit uenerandaque mater / Se debent ueluti Sychomachia metris.*
4. *SD* 2, 1727-32.
5. *SD* 2, 1761-4.

In several grammatical works antedating the *Suppletio*, Neckam shows his familiarity with the works of the poets named in the *Suppletio*. By his own account, he read with an eye to his own compositions, ready with pen to mark verbal tags, phrases and entire verses for possible future use. The range of Neckam's reading, whether acquired from florilegia, grammatical works or from the classical texts themselves, has already been marked.[1] The following sketch aims to outline the nature and scope of literary allusion that Neckam practised in the *Suppletio*.

While Macer's *De uiribus herbarum* represents the largest and most obvious of Neckam's sources, fragments from other literary texts have been seamlessly sewn into the book's fabric. Most of these intertexts have been refashioned to express what he wanted to say. An instance in the section on trees (247-54) illustrates the method. In the opening couplet on quinces, chestnuts and pears, Neckam dovetails phrases from Martial and Virgil to fit the new syntax through minor modifications:

> Coctana Uulcani *lento decocta uapore*
> *Castaneeque nuces* atque uolema placent.

For the third distich he recalled the legend of Neptune's and Minerva's contest to name Athens. Drawing on material from Servius's commentary on the *Georgics*, Neckam had used it in an early work, the commentary on Martianus Capella's *De Nuptiis Philologiae et Mercurii*. It now resurfaces in verse form, together with another borrowing from Martial to describe the goddess's contribution:

> Armatum *Neptunus equum produxit Athenis*;
> Quam *tribuit Pallas,* pluris oliua fuit.

The lines encapsulate features that are characteristic of Alexander's *imitatio* as a whole: an ability to recast prose into verse, a talent for seeing the potential of classical poetry and the bible when relocated in new environments, and evidence of focussed reading in pursuit of his research.

Neckam set out to engage his critical readers (1173 *Lectori tetrico*). By informing them that he made a practice of quietly inserting source texts among his own words, he implicitly challenges them to identify the allusions, in much the same spirit as Ovid reportedly did when he mentioned his own borrowing from Virgil.[2] A near contemporary reader, the glossa-

---

1. Hunt ed. Gibson, *The Schools and the Cloister*, 43-53.
2. Cf. Sen., *Suas.* 3, 7 (ed. Winterbottom).

tor of **P**, began that process by recording in the margin of the manuscript the names of Bernard Silvestris, Ovid, Martial and Claudian against the as-similated texts.[1] From these classical and medieval poets Neckam appro-priated material about trees, animals, and birds.

Among secular Latin poets he mentions only Virgil (898) and Ovid (1405), using the proper names as allusion markers. Neckam's debt to Ovid runs deep and is most on display in the beast fable, where lines from the *Metamorphoses* introduce a brief ekphrasis of the Sun's palace.[2] In the same story, a verse from the *Heroides* is found to express Cybele's precept that like should marry like.[3] Elsewhere, Neckam signals his sources more gen-erally. Thus a reference to *uatum dicta* (82) alerts readers to a congeries of classical quotations which culminates with a modified line from the *Meta-morphoses*.[4] But as a rule Alexander does not advertise his thefts, trusting his audience's sensitivity to pick up the literary signals without overt signs.

Neckam adapts a variety of means to remodel the source texts. He may substitute metrical equivalents to bend a thematically useful Ovidian line to his own thought, as in:

et sub iudicium singula *verba vocem* mores

Ov., *Pont.* 1, 5, 20

Uix sub iudicium conuoco, *uerba uoco*

SD 1, 1054

Although he expresses the view that Ovid's *Fasti* were not essential reading,[5] it was not advice he followed himself. Observe how he partially reproduces Ovid's metrical structure in the first half of a pentameter:

erroremque suum quo tueatur *habet.*

Fast. 1, 32

Erroremque suum sompnus *habere* cupit

SD 1, 942

---

1. For Bernard Silvestris, see notes in the commentary to *SD* 1, 1223-4, 1227-34; for Ovid, see notes to 764, 1053-4, 1341-2; for Martial, see notes to 277-8, 636; for Claudian, see notes to 77-80, 149-52.

2. Ov., *Met.* 2, 1-2 = *SD* 1, 1341-2 (cf. *SA* f. 19b). S. Viarre, *La survie d'Ovide*, 155, dis-cusses the influence of the *Metamorphoses* on the *DNR* and the *LSD*.

3. Ov., *Ep.* 9, 32 = *SD* 1, 1406; cf. *SD* 1, 764 = Ov., *Pont.* 1, 5, 6.

4. Cf. *SD* 1, 77-82 and Ov., *Met.* 15, 394.

5. Cf. *SA* f. 48b *librum Fastorum non esse legendum nonnullis placet;* S. Viarre, *La survie d'Ovide*, 52, notes the presence of the *Fasti* in *LSD* 2, 531 (p. 385 W).

At other times, he abandons the Ovidian pattern entirely, while retain-
ing Ovid's words and meaning:

> et *docuit iungi* cum *pare* quemque sua
>> *Fast.* 4, 98

> Par igitur *iungenda pari* Nasone *docente*
>> *SD* 1, 1405

Ovidian diction colours Neckam's writing in less obtrusive ways, as the
following three examples make clear:

> *simplicitas digna favore* fuit
>> *Ep.* 2, 64

> Est et *simplicitas* quarundam *digna fauore*
>> *SD* 1, 125

> paulum *cervice reflexa* femina
>> *Ars* 3, 779

> Solsequium sequitur solem *ceruice reflexa*
>> *SD* 1, 579

> littera, sermonis *fida ministra* mei!
>> *Tr.* 3, 7, 2

> *Fida ministra* Noe fictaque Cilla colit
>> *SD* 1, 40

Neckam alludes to borrowed Virgilian material more subtly. Unsur-
prisingly, in light of the supplement's subject matter, he often retains or
adapts distinctive phrases from Virgil's *Georgics* and the *Eclogues*, while he
modifes the metrical patterning of the original:

> et sulco *attritus splendescere uomer*
>> *G.* 1, 46

> *Attritus uomer splendet*
>> *SD* 1, 763

> *leuium spectacula rerum*
>> *G.* 4, 3

> Sollicitant animos *leuium spectacula rerum*
>> *SD* 1, 891

> tamen haec quoque... / *exuerint siluestrem* animum
> > G. 2, 49-51

> *Siluestres* mores *exue*
> > *SD* 1, 720

> ipse ego cana legam tenera lanugine mala
> *Castaneasque nuces*
> > E. 2, 51-2

> *Castaneeque nuces*
> > *SD* 1, 248

When Virgil's name appears (898), it signals the presence of a series of pseudo-Virgilian texts. They begin with a quotation of two verses from the *Copa*,[1] followed by an inventory of *incipits* from several works contained in the *Appendix Vergiliana*. From the *De rosis nascentibus*, a remembered phrase is reworked to describe the rose; to make it fit, he inverts the order of the conceit and condenses the thought of the entire line into three words:

> quam modo nascentem rutilus conspexit Eoos,
> hanc rediens sero *uespere uidit anum*
> > *DRN* 45-6

> *Vespera cernit anum* quam uidit mane puellam
> > *SD* 1, 329

Lucan appears second only to Virgil in Rhetorica's train of venerable poets. Although Neckam used him often as a source of illustrative quotations in the *Sacerdos ad altare*, he found little use for the epic poet here. An exception is a slightly altered line that Neckam could have found in intermediate sources:

> Et *turbata perit* dispersis *littera* pinnis
> > Luc. 5, 716

> *Obscurata* prius *littera* tota *perit*
> > *SD* 1, 878

Although Juvenal's *moralia dicta* are commended in a grammatical treatise,[2] the satirist's name is absent from the *Suppletio*. But one memorable verse describing the Roman empress, Messalina, as she returns to the

---

1. *SD* 1, 899-900 = *Copa* 37-8.
2. *SA* f. 48a.

palace after a night of continuous sexual activity, is rejuvenated to refer to
the wolf's inexhaustible appetite for blood:

> et *lassata* viris *necdum satiata recessit*
>
> > Juv. 6, 130
>
> .... *lassus non saciatus abit*
> > > SD 1, 1246

From Horace's *Epistles* he took phrases, *rumpere claustra* and *ad sese...red-
it*, both of which he recycled into his account of the ostrich.[1] Greater skill
is shown in integrating a popular verse from the *Epistles*. This contextually
significant line had a particular resonance for Alexander, who was enter-
ing his sixtieth year:[2]

> nec *lusisse* pudet, *sed non incidere ludum.*
> > > Ep. 1, 14, 36
>
> *Lusimus* ha! nimium, *set non incidere ludum*
> Presertim senibus dedecus esse puta.
> > > SD 1, 1019-20

The only vestige of Statius's poetry is a clever allusion to a proverbial
line from the *Thebaid*.[3] By contrast, he found much to his purpose in the
minor poems of the late antique poet Claudian, whose *De raptu Proserpinae*
formed part of the elementary curriculum, along with the *Disticha Catonis*,
Maximianus's *Elegiae* and the *Ecloga* of Theodolus;[4] consider the following appropriations from Claudian:

> *igneus ambit*
> > > Carm. min. 22, 60
>
> *igneus ambit* honos
> > > SD 1, 152

> *Dulce malum* pelago *Sirenae*
> > > Carm. min. app. 1, 1
>
> Dulce melos reddit *dulce Syrena malum*
> > > SD 1, 704

---

1. See notes to *SD* 1, 108, 692.
2. Hor., *Ars* 131 *publica* materies *privati iuris* erit, left a mark on *SD* 2, 151-2 *iuris / Priuati*
faciat *publica*.
3. Cf. *SD* 1, 30 with Stat., *Theb.* 2, 446.
4. See Hunt ed. Gibson, *The Schools and the Cloister*, 47-8.

Claudian's description of the porcupine is treated more radically, but enough of the original survives to establish lines of continuity:

> Os longius illi
> Adsimulat *porcum*
>
> *Carm. min.* 9, 6-7

> stat corpore toto
> *Silva minax*
>
> *Carm. min.* 9, 10-11

> Densa tegit *porcum* iaculorum *silua minacem*
> SD 1, 1099

An entire line from the *Disticha Catonis*[1] turns up to moralize the swallow, while diction borrowed from the *Elegiae* of Maximianus[2] and Theodolus's *Ecloga*[3] emerge in new contexts.

The popular triad of Christian Latin poets, Sedulius,[4] Juvencus and Prudentius have left not a trace, except for a cadence from the *Psychomachia*,[5] which reappears in the same *sedes* to make a grammatical point about gender:

> *uirgo Pudicitia* speciosis fulget in armis
> Psych. 41

> *Uirgo pudicicia* se probet esse marem.
> SD 1, 76

Knowledge of Dracontius *De laudibus Dei* rests on a few phrases:[6]

> *carbunculus ardet* honore
> DLD 1, 322

---

1. *Disticha Catonis* 1, 27, 2 at *SD* 1, 703; in *SA* ff. 47b-48a Neckam describes it as *illud utile moralitatis compendium quod Catonis esse uulgus opinatur*, cf. Hunt ed. Gibson, *The Schools and the Cloister*, 47, note 27.

2. *Carm.* 1, 134 at *SD* 1, 428; *Carm.* 1, 101 at *SD* 1, 1018.

3. 252 at *SD* 1, 794

4. The phrase *infelix Arrius* at *SD* 1, 783 may derive from Sedulius, *Carm. pasch.* 1, 300, but it recurs in Arator, 1, 444-5; with *SD* 1, 1261 *In uinum mutauit aquam* cf Sedulius, *Carm. pasch.* 3, 4 *In vinum convertit aquas*; for the presence of these Christian authors in Neckam's earlier work, see T. A.-P. Klein ed. *Alexander Neckam Nouus Auianus*, 105.

5. Cf. *SD* 1, 227.

6. Cf. *SD* 1, 1003 *natura...reddit* with Dracontius, *De laudibus Dei* 1, 680 *redditque... / depositum natura* suum. The context and metrical placement of *DLD* 1, 723-4 *quem mox inuitat ad escam / praepetis aut aquilae senio renouare iuuentam*, suggest that Neckam may have written at *SD* 1, 599 Instar auis dicte studeas *renouare iuuentam*.

Irradians in ea *carbunculus ardet*;

SD 1, 1343

If Neckam had read the poetry of Paulinus of Nola, Venantius Fortu-
natus and Aldhelm, it appears to have left no mark on the poem. There is,
however, compelling evidence that Hildebert's *Biblical Epigrams* had come
into his hands:

Eterne uite *corrumpi nescia cedrus*
spem mihi designat. [1]

Epig. 48, 6-7

Dissimilem, cum sit *corrumpi nescia, cedrum*
Virginibus nostri temporis esse putes.

SD 1, 205-6

Virtutum pennis ut aues tolluntur ad astra.

Epig. 52,10

Virtutum pennis ocius alta pete.

SD 1, 730

Early in his writing career Alexander versified some prose fables that
were part of the collection known as the *Romulus*. These formed the basis
for the *Nouus Esopus*, poems that testify to his skill in moving from one
medium into another. Three passages in the supplement show how Alexander appropriated prose writings. Two derive from classical sources and
are embedded in comments about his own poetry. The first caps a long
discussion of compositional techniques: [2]

Set tamen *improbus* est censor, me iudice, *scripto*
Quisquis in alterius ingeniosus erit.

The diction and thought derive from Martial's prose preface to his poems, in which he deplored critics who were clever at the expense of other
writers:

improba facit *qui in alieno libro ingeniosus* est.

The second adaptation occurs in the same argument that Neckam addresses to his readers regarding an adverse reception to his poem. He

---

1. Cf. *SD* 2, 1794-5 color iste decenter / Compositus *finem principiumque tenet* with
Hildebert, *Biblical Epigrams* 67, 2 *principium finemque tenet.*

2. *SD* 1, 1065-6.

compresses the substance of an anecdote, reported by Seneca the Elder, that showed Ovid to have been conscious of his poetic faults:

> habet *neuos forma decora suos*
>
> SD 1, 1180
>
> Aiebat interim *decentiorem faciem* esse in qua aliquis *naevos* esset.
>
> Sen. *Contr.* 2, 2, 12

More creative is the appropriation of Urso of Salerno's gloss on the *Aphorismi* of Hippocrates.[1] A item of wolf lore cues a transition based on a reference to the faculty of sight.[2] As Neckam develops a point regarding visible and invisible events, he remembered a passage from the Salernitan's commentary. Urso contrasts the occurrence of miraculous phenomena in the natural world with Christ's instrumental use of miracles to reveal his divinity to man by deeds and words. He then adduces the vine's production of wine from water, a natural process at which mankind ceased to marvel after the Fall. To raise man from sin, Christ employed the extra-rational means of miracles to change water into wine, in order to induce humankind to believe in the power of the Creator. Urso's conceptual framework and supporting illustration about wine and water suited Neckam's purpose admirably. Leaving the theological point undeveloped, Neckam opposes the common man's ignorance of the wondrous processes that occur daily in nature, on the one hand, to his amazement at the rare occurrences of miracles, like the one Christ performed at the marriage in Cana.

13. METRE

Little or no work has been devoted to analysing the structure of Neckam's verse.[3]

---

1. See Hunt ed. Gibson, *The Schools and the Cloister*, 71-2, for Neckam's debt to Urso's *Aphorismi* in the *DNR* and the inclusion of the medical writer's name in *LSD* 4, 235 (p. 425 W).

2. Cf. *SD* 1, 1242 and 1257 *uisus*.

3. I have been unable to consult the article devoted to the metrical analysis of *LSD* 1 by J. L. Gamboa Jiménez. For a detailed study of the metre and prosody of Neckam's *Novus Aesopus*, see G. Garbugino in G. Catanzaro, *La favolistica latina in distici elegiaci* (Assisi, 1991), 111-8. See also T. A.-P. Klein ed. *Alexander Neckam Nouus Auianus*, 106.

1. *Hexameter*

The following table shows in order of frequency the distribution of spondees and dactyls in the first four feet:[1]

1.	DSSS 101 [13%]	
2.	DDSS 82	
3.	SSSS 78	
4.	SDSS 70	
5.	DSDS 54	
6.	DSSD 50	
7.	SSDS 47	
8.	DDDS 44	
9.	SDSD 39	
10.	DDSD 35	
11.	SDDS 33	
11.	SSSD 33	
13.	DSDD 24	
14.	DDDD 13	
15.	SSDD 13	
16.	SDDD 10	

Neckam's most popular pattern, DSSS, is the one preferred by the Augustan poets, Lucan, Persius, Silius, Juvenal, as well as by the Christian poets Juvencus, Prosper and Avitus.[2] Taken as a percentage of the whole, its occurrence also falls within the range of other poets who use the same combination most often. For example, in Virgil's *Aeneid*, Horace's *Epistles* and in Juvencus, the figures for the sequence DSSS as a percentage of the total are 14.39%, 11.85% and 15.28% respectively.[3] Moreover, the distribution of the first eight metrical verse-types diverges only slightly from that found in Horace and Virgil. With them Neckam shares seven

---

1. The first eight patterns in *SD* 2 are DSSS, SSSS, DDSS, SDSS, DSDSD, DSSD, SSDS, SDDS; G. Garbugino in G. Catanzaro, *La favolistica latina*, 116, note 69, lists the eight most frequent combinations in Neckam's *Novus Aesopus*, an early work of Neckam, as follows: DSSS (11%), DSDS, DDSS, SSDS, SDSS, DDDS, SSSS, SDDS; G. E. Duckworth, *Vergil and Classical Hexameter Poetry* (Ann Arbor, 1969), 128, lists the patterns in Juvencus, Prosper, Avitus and the other Christian poets. G. Orlandi, «Metrica 'medievale' e metrica 'antichizzante' nella commedia elegiaca», in R. Cardini, *Tradizione classica e letteratura umanistica* (Rome, 1985), 1: 14, tabulates the distribution of dactyls and spondees in the works of several medieval poets.

2. See G. E. Duckworth, *Vergil and Classical Hexameter Poetry*, 6.

3. Cf. G. E. Duckworth, *Vergil and Classical Hexameter Poetry*, 5, 55.

out of the first eight patterns, though they do not follow exactly the same order.[1]

Neckam's overall distribution conforms to a pattern that Duckworth first observed in Virgil and in many other poets, namely that the most and least frequent patterns form reverse combinations.[2] Thus, in *SD* 1 the most frequent pattern DSSS is reversed in the least frequent SDDD, the second DDSS in SSDD, the third SSSS in DDDD, the fourth SDSS in DS-DD. Although this tendency breaks down in two cases, DSDS and DDDS, it reappears in the distributions of DSSD / SDDS and SSDS / DDSD. The arrangement of the metrical verse-types points to conscious variation; for example, the schema DDDD (553) is immediately counter-balanced with SSSS (555) and DSSS (681) with DDDS (683). In only two places does the same metrical pattern occur in three successive hexameters.[3]

Usually, a strong penthimimeral caesura breaks the line, but there are twenty eight verses with a trochee in the third foot[4] and twenty verses[5] without a penthimimeral caesura. Elision occurs in eight lines,[6] two in verses with a monsyllabic ending.[7] Forty six quadri-[8] and fourteen pentasyllabic[9] words are found at the end of the line. Hiatus is avoided.

---

1. Neckam's order is closer to that favoured by Juvencus; A. Orchard, *The Poetic Art of Aldhelm* (Cambridge, 1994), 89, note 64, lists Virgil's most popular patterns as DSSS, DDSS, DSDS, SDSS, SSSS, DDDS, SSDS and SDDS; in Juvencus they are DSSS, DDSS, SDSS, SSSS, DSDS, SSDS, DSSD, and SDDS.

2. See G. E. Duckworth, *Vergil and Classical Hexameter Poetry*, 25-32.

3. SSSD at 921, 923, 925; SSSS at 1305, 1307, 1309.

4. Cf. Verses 67, 77, 137, 169, 171, 187, 215, 251, 301, 479, 499, 523, 565, 611, 697, 725, 789, 839, 1029, 1067, 1219, 1229, 1233, 1261, 1275, 1364, 1389, 1405.

5. Cf. *SD* 1, 117, 143, 217, 225, 233, 289, 295, 297, 371, 400, 443, 621, 765, 865, 871, 879, 1223 [= Bernard Silvestris], 1259, 1327, 1399.

6. Between first and second foot: 899 *merum est*; at the beginning of the third foot: 729 *uite est*, 737 *grata est*; at the start of the fourth foot: 111, 643 *tanta est*; in the middle of the fourth foot: 7 *cunctarum est*; in the middle of the sixth foot: 185 *apta est*, 953 *ymago est*.

7. Cf. Four of the six monosyllabic endings in *SD* 2 involve *est*: 361 *origo est*, 607 *summa est*, 683 *minuta est*, 1243 *causa est*; in middle of the fourth foot: 7 *cunctarum est*, cf. 877 *in quo*, 1693 *in qua*.

8. Cf. *SD* 1, 51, 53, 69, 123, 131, 139, 195, 211, 287, 323, 327, 355, 373, 387, 455, 557, 567, 577, 587, 641, 643, 655, 685, 731, 793, 819, 853, 909, 1001, 1021, 1051, 1059, 1093, 1103, 1109, 1127, 1147, 1153, 1203, 1215, 1261, 1327, 1407, 1435, 1437, 1457. Two of these verses end with the enclitic *-que*: 287 *iecorique*, 455 *maculeque*; in *SD* 2 Neckam resorts to this device at 1323 *geminosque*, 1571 *Stoicosque*, 1781 *uarioque*.

9. Cf. *SD* 1, 307, 393, 403, 601, 619, 623, 795, 925, 1015, 1037, 1057, 1095, 1219, 1445. Only 307 ends in *-que*: *luminibusque*. There are three examples in *SD* 2: 95 *officioque*, 259 *corporeeque*, 1515 *psalterioque*.

Neckam occasionally uses rhyme to ornament his verse.[1] Rarely do successive lines have rhyme at the caesura or diaeresis and at the end of the verse, as happens in 5-6:

> Qui uarias *artes* auctores fingere *plures*
> Vsurpas, *uarios* fingis in orbe *deos.*

Leonine hexameters with rhyme at the strong caesura and at the end of the verse are much more common, as in 15:

> Tot rerum *facies,* tot sunt discrimina, *dotes.*[2]

Versus caudati occur when the hexameter and pentameter have rhyme at the end of the verse only, as in 45-6:

> Excitat ingenium natura, set ars iuuat, *vsus*
> Perficit; ars languet, ni repetatur *opus.*

or at 135-6

> Grus casu lapidis predicit callida *fraudes*
> Et replet ipsius sepe saburra *pedes.*[3]

As in the hexameters, rhyme at the diaeresis and at the end of pentameters is common, as in 48:

> Emittit *uarios* turba sonora *sonos*

or 64:

> Clamitat *irritans* gabio *gesticulans.*[4]

Very occasionally, rhyme at the caesura of the hexameter matches that at the pentameter's close, as in 239-40:

---

1. G. Garbugino in G. Catanzaro, *La favolistica latina,* 116, calculates that in the *Novus Aesopus* internal rhyme occurs in 22% of the hexameters and in 31% of the pentameters.

2. Cf. *SD* 1, 19, 25, 27, 29, 51, 141, 211, 263, 267, 279, 285, 347, 373, 413, 489, 495, 507, 523, 587, 609, 639, 658, 709, 717, 813, 883, 937, 965, 977, 1003, 1015, 1019, 1037, 1051, 1073, 1187, 1213, 1215, 1219, 1257, 1271, 1299, 1301, 1321, [1327], 1363, 1379.

3. Cf. *SD* 1, 165-6, 243-4, 581-2, 603-4, 643-4, 647-8, 687-88, 719-20, 805-6, 823-4, 837-8, 843-4, 895-6, 1227-8, 1239-40, 1321-2, 1327-8, 1339-40, 1341-2, 1347-8, 1377-8.

4. Cf. *SD* 1, 66, 202, 262, 284, 354, 378, 422, 482, 510, 512, 590, 592, 600, 648, 650, 654, 658, 666, 720, 738, 768, 802, 848, 860, 862, 874, 894, 952, 958, 980, 986, 1044, 1050, 1064, 1154, 1180, 1188, 1224, 1282, 1288, 1300, 1306, 1308, 1324, 1352, 1380, 1384, 1394, 1396, 1416.

At pirus *exurgens* superas petit ignea partes
Fructus precipui nobilitate *potens*.[1]

For rhyme at caesura and diaeresis only, note 391-2:

Est quod se *roseum* mentitur habere colorem;
Florem *subroseum* dicere iure potes.

Neckam comes closest to writing *unisoni* at 647-8 with

Ecclesie pacem des auctor pacis *oliue*
Ramo *signate*, spiritus alme, *tue*

and at 1039-40.[2]

2. *Pentameter*

Adhering to classical precedent, Neckam allows only dactyls after the diaeresis. The distribution of spondees and dactyls in the first half of the pentameter is as follows:[3]

1.	SS	246
2.	DS	198
3.	SD	176
4.	DD	108

Words of two or three syllables are found at the end of all pentameters in *SD* 1. A monosyllabic or pentasyllabic word never occurs in that position, although six verses end in words of four syllables.[4] Of twelve elisions, four are located in the second hemiepes, two of which occur in verses quoted from classical sources.[5]

---

1. Cf. *SD* 1, 351-2, 361-2, 405-6, 711-2.

2. Hunt ed. Gibson, *The Schools and the Cloister*, 62, records the *unisonus* at *LSD* 3, 85-6 (p. 399W) Curia se *curis* agitat, ferit alta *securis*, / Rebus *securis* ha! peritura *furis*.

3. G. Orlandi, «Metrica 'medievale' e metrica 'antichizzante'», in R. Cardini, *Tradizione classica e letteratura umanistica* (Spoleto, 1985), 1: 14, Table 2, lists figures compiled from the pentameters of medieval comedies.

4. See *SD* 1, 64 *gesticulans*, 616 *irradiat*, 672 *mundicie*, 946 *iusticie*, 1036 *corripio*, 1396 *Alcinoo*. There are 15 occurrences in *SD* 2; in three verses Neckam places Aristotle's name at the end of the verse (980, 1346 *Aristotilis*, 1564 *Aristoteles*). Monosyllabic words occur before the diaeresis at *SD* 1, 70, 194, 256, 296, 338, 372, 382, 402, 552, 616, 620, 652, 664, 690, 708, 716, 754, 794, 818, 864, 870, 890, 936, 980, 998, 1060, 1118, 1120, 1134, 1138, 1144, 1278, 1410, 1442, 1446, 1456.

5. Namely *SD* 1, 278 [= Martial], 900 [= Ps.-Virgil], 1400 *dea est*, 1428 *tibi est* (two elisions occur after the diaeresis at the end of the line in *SD* 2, 106 *uia est*, 658 *data est*). For the remaining elisions cf. *SD* 1, 338, 684, 818, 862, 870, 890, 1342, 1422.

14. PROSODY

Neckam generally adheres to the rules of classical prosody, with the exception of the following words: *apostema* (472, 531), *artemisia* (265), *cameleon* (98), *cuculus* (39, 52), *epar* (270, 409), *pastinaca* (409), *pellicanus* (606), *philosophari* (1092), *Siren* (704).[1]

15. THE MANUSCRIPT

Paris, Bibliothèque Nationale, MS lat. 11867 [**P**], a late 13th-c. English manuscript which at some point belonged to the abbey of Saint-Germain-des-Prés,[2] contains a number of classical and medieval rhetorical and devotional texts. A late 19th-c. cataloguer described its makeup on p. 1 as follows: «Volume de 244 Feuillets plus le feuillet A préliminaire, plus le feuillet 77 bis. Manque la Cote 738. Les feuillets 1, 2, 244 sont mutilés. 8 Février 1898.» The contents of **P**, as described by a later hand on p. A and in the right hand margin of f. 2, include letters of Pope Innocent III and Pope Gregory I, Cicero, *De amicitia*, Thomas of Capua, *Summa dictaminis*, selected letters of Peter of Blois, Petrus Alphonsi, *Disciplina clericalis*, and the *Constitutum Constantini*.

On f. 2 appear three shelf numerals: 798, 376, 798.

Neckam's hymns and minor verses appear in a random arrangement on ff. 189vb-240va.[3] The pages recording Neckam's poetry measure 350 x 245,[4] with a writing area of 285 x 175; each one contains a regular 63 lines. The first letter of each verse is capitalized and highlighted with red ink.

---

1. S. Gaselee, «Notes on the Vocabulary of Alexander Neckam», *Speculum* 14 (1939), 106, compiles a full list of Neckam's deviations from classical practice.

2. See Hunt ed. Gibson, *The Schools and the Cloister*, 54-5, 140-1; on the verso of a preliminary page A is written: *Sancti Germani a Pratis*; T. A.-P. Klein ed. *Alexander Neckam Nouus Auianus*, 110-1, provides a summary description of the contents of **P**; he notes Sh. J. Heathcote's suggestion that the manuscript may have belonged to the Benedictine abbey of Marmoutier in the diocese of Tours before it arrived at Saint-Germain cf. 110 and note 37. Klein, 109-10, also announces the presence in Madrid, Biblioteca de Palacio Real ex Oriente, II-468, ff. 151v-179v, [**M**] of extracts from the *Suppletio defectuum*. The readings of **M** are presented in the Appendix.

3. See Hunt ed. Gibson, *The Schools and the Cloister*, 141, for a detailed description of this section.

4. Hunt ed. Gibson, *The Schools and the Cloister*, 141, note 2, gives the measurements of the section on Neckam as 353 x 245mm.

Major subdivisions in the poem are signalled by means of *litterae nota-biliores*, conspicuously marked in blue or red, followed by a second, small-er, capital letter, also marked by colour. Paraphs in red frequently guide the reader between major sections of the poem and also point to the mor-alizations. Running titles, all copied out in red ink (except at *SD* 1, 1233 where *et lepore* was added in black), indicate new divisions in the text. In-terlinear and marginal glosses in black ink are marked with *signes de ren-voie*. Several longer glosses are confined within inverted triangular bor-ders, as in the case of the glosses on ff. 218va *discrimen*, 222va *Tam de*, 222vb *Soloe*, 226ra *Theodolo*, 226rb *In vua*, *Grossus*, 226va *Simile*, 226vb *Vir-gilius*, 228rb *Nomina sunt*, 230va *Figura est*. The scribe makes corrections by means of expunction marks (e. g. *SD* 1, 138, 1153), although sometimes he draws a red line through mistakes as well, e. g. *SD* 2, 110.

The text of *SD* 1 attracted a number of purely Latin glosses.[1] One Greek word in the text, *chere* (123), is explained with a latinized Greek gloss; the three Greek words, in turn, are accompanied by Latin transla-tions.[2] Of the glosses as a whole the most numerous are lexical. This type provides an equivalent Latin term for the lemma, usually prefaced by *id est*, though several lack any introductory word, e. g. *stere*] *matricis* (447). The glossator deals with equivocal words in different ways. For example, he differentiates two meanings of the noun *ficus* (397 «figs» and «piles») by quoting Martial's well-known couplet to Caecilianus (1, 65, 3-4). In the case of the word *serra* (1009), he distinguishes the meaning of «saw-fish» from that of the implement «saw». There is only one note on the length of syllables (1389), whereas four grammatical glosses identify a noun as a vocative (561), the mood of *uolet* as subjunctive (1446), *circum* as a noun, not an adverb (939), and the voice of *licet* as passive (1204).

The glossator was far more interested in identifying the source texts ap-propriated by Neckam. He does so in two ways. Most often, he merely cites the name of the author of the borrowed verse[3] (e. g. Bernard [Sil-vestris] 169, 188, 587, 1224, 1227, 1231; Ovid 183, 764, 1341; Martial 396,

---

1. The sole vernacular lexical gloss occurs at *SD* 2, 490, where the lemma *aurea mala* is followed after the citation of Verg., *E.* 3, 71 by *In gallico pommes orenges*: cf. T. Hunt, *Plant Names of Medieval England* (Cambridge, 1989), 84 s. v. *citragulus*; 300 s. v. *Pomme d'Orange*.

2. In discussing the glosses, I adopt the categories and terms used by G. R. Wieland, *The Latin Glosses on Arator and Prudentius in Cambridge University Library MS GG. 5. 35* (Toronto, 1983).

3. Hunt ed. Gibson, *The Schools and the Cloister*, 46, notes that Alexander placed in the margins of the *CNP* the names of poets from whom he borrowed material.

636). He may cite the poet's name, followed by a direct quotation without specifying the book in which it is found (30, 277, 536, 896). The remaining glosses are either encyclopedic, defining a medical term (302), a rare mythological (536) and geographical name (1052), or etymological (651, 909, 1389).[1] The incidence of several technical terms, like *mistice* (225) or *yronia* (1365), indicate an interest in reading beyond the literal level.

16. EDITORIAL PRACTICE

This edition is based on first hand consultation of Paris, Bibliothèque Nationale, MS lat. 11867 [**P**] and on photographs of Madrid, Biblioteca de Palacio Real ex Oriente, II-468 [**M**]. All departures from **P**'s readings are recorded in the textual notes, together with suggestions for emendation. The interlinear and marginal glosses scattered throughout **P** appear at the bottom of the pages of the English translation. For the reader's convenience, I have drawn together at the beginning of the poem the numerous marginal rubrics that were added to mark the location of individual plants, birds and animals. Although the scribe of **P** did not divide the verse into sections, I have signalled the major divisions of the poem's contents by leaving a space between them.

The orthography of **P** has been retained, including the scribe's distinction between the letters *u* and *v* and *i* and *y*. Medieval spellings that may perplex are noted in the commentary; punctuation and capitalization are editorial. Punctuating Neckam's verse is not a simple matter. His verbal dexterity allows certain lines to be punctuated in more than one way. In such cases, I offer a syntactic punctuation and alert readers to alternatives in the notes. I have tried not to overburden the poetry with punctuation that impedes its flow. All contractions have been silently expanded; words occasionally, but not always, abbreviated appear according to the full form written out elsewhere. Scribal deletions are indicated by [[ ]] and editorial supplements by < >.

The commentary aims to meet a number of needs. It documents the supplement's relationship to its controlling texts, Macer's *De uiribus herbarum*, the *Laus sapientie diuine* and, when necessary, to the text from

---

1. On the various types of glossing that formed part of the grammarian's expository program, see S. Reynolds, *Medieval Reading*, 28-64.

which that poem derived, *De naturis rerum*. This material will enable students to assess the extent and manner of Neckam's auto-citation and his method of appropriating material from external sources. Although Thomas Wright provided an invaluable service to Neckam studies by editing both the *DNR* and the *LSD*, the notes he supplied for them are minimal. In the absence of modern editions and commentaries, I have occasionally had to comment on the text and contents of the *LSD*. I have also supplied comparative material from the second book of the *Suppletio* according to the text preserved in **P**, as well as from other writings of Neckam which remain available only in manuscript form. As a writer, Alexander read widely, always alert for matter that he might excerpt for his own writings. It is not always possible to establish what came to Neckam directly or through intermediate sources. Whatever the means of transmission may have been, I have attempted to identify the ultimate source and have included in square brackets citations of the same phrase or expression I have found in other medieval works. In the notes, «cf» is used to mark parallels that illuminate some aspect of the verse, but it does not follow that the parallels are direct sources.

    P's readings are discussed when they violate sense, metre or grammar and alternatives are suggested. In two cases I have recorded in the *apparatus criticus* conjectures which were made by J. B. Hall (p. 12) and M. Reeve (p. 20) before I discovered them to be the readings of M.[1] Rare or uncommon words are noted. Since Neckam assumed that his readers had an intimate knowledge of animal and avian lore, his accounts are allusive and sometimes obscure. In the interests of clarity, I have attached brief summaries at the beginning of each section which set out the main characteristics of individual birds, fish and animals.

---

1. In this I follow the example of W. Clausen ed., *Persius* (Oxford, 1956), p. XXVII.

Bibliography

Abbreviations and short Titles

Consult the Bibliography for complete references. The abbreviations used to refer to classical writers and their works are those set out in *The Oxford Classical Dictionary*, IX-XX. Individual books of the Bible are noted by the sigla adopted in the *Novae Concordantiae Bibliorum Sacrorum*, 1: XIII-XV.

AHR = *The American Historical Review*
AJ = *Archaeological Journal*
AJP = *American Journal of Philology*
ALMA = *Archivum Latinitatis Medii Aevi*
BGPTM = *Beiträge zur Geschichte der Philosophie und Theologie des Mittelalters*
C = Cambridge, University Library, Gg. 6. 42
CCCM = *Corpus Christianorum, Continuatio Mediaevalis*. Turnhout, 1968-
CCSL = *Corpus Christianorum, Series Latina*. Turnhout, 1953-
CMC = Commentary on Martianus Capella, *De Nuptiis* (Oxford, Bodleian Library, Digby 221, ff. 34vb-87vb; Cambridge, Trinity College R. 14. 9, ff. 38r-63r)
CP = *Corrogationes Promethei* (London, British Library, Harley 6)
CNP = *Corrogationes noui Promethei*. L. S. Cropp ed.
CPV = *Corrogationes Promethei versified* (London, British Library, Royal 9. A. XIV)
CSEL = *Corpus Scriptorum Ecclesiasticorum Latinorum*. Vienna, 1866-
DMLBS = *Dictionary of Medieval Latin from British Sources*. London, 1975-
DNR = *De naturis rerum*. T. Wright ed.
DNV = *De nominibus utensilium*. T. Wright ed.; T. Hunt ed.
EHR = *English Historical Review*.
GLK = *Grammatici Latini*. H. Keil ed.
GP = *Gloss on the Psalter*
in Eccles. (*DNR* 3-5) = Cambridge, Trinity College, O. 4. 1
JHS = *Journal of Hellenic Studies*
LH-L = *Lateinisches Hexameter-Lexikon*
LSD = *Laus sapientie diuine*. T. Wright ed.
M = Madrid, Biblioteca de Palacio Real ex Oriente, II-468.
Macer. = *Macer Floridus: De viribus herbarum*. L. Choulant ed. Leipzig, 1832.
MJ = *Mittellateinisches Jahrbuch*

MGH = *Monumenta Germaniae historica*. Hannover and Leipzig, 1826–

AA = *Auctores antiquissimi*

Ep. = *Epistolae*

P. L. = *Poetae latini*

Scr. = *Scriptores*

SRG = *Scriptores rerum Germanicarum*

MPL = J.-P. Migne, *Patrologiae cursus completus, Series latina*. 221 vols. Paris, 1844–64

MRS = *Mediaeval and Renaissance Studies*

MS = *Mediaeval Studies*

NA = *Nouus Auianus*. T. A.-P. Klein ed.

NE = *Novus Aesopus*. G. Garbugino ed.

NG = *Novum Glossarium mediae Latinitatis*. Copenhagen, 1957

NP = *Novus Phisiologus*. A. P. Orbán ed.

OE = Old English

OLD = *The Oxford Latin Dictionary*

P = Paris, Bibliothèque Nationale, lat. 11867

PMLA = *Publications of the Modern Language Association of America*

Poems = M. Esposito, «On Some Unpublished Poems Attributed to Alexander Neckam», *EHR* 30 (1915), 450–71; H. Walther, «Eine moral-asketische Dichtung
des XIII. Jahrhunderts: *Prorogationes Novi Promethei* des Alexander Neckam», *Medium Aevum* 31 (1962), 33–42; *id.*, «Zu den kleineren Gedichten des Alexander
Neckam», *MJ* 2 (1965), 111–29.

RE = *Paulys Realencyclopädie der classischen Altertumswissenschaft*. G. Wissowa ed.
Stuttgart, 1893–

RS = Rolls Series

SA = *Sacerdos ad altare*. Cambridge, Gaius and Gonville College, 385

SD = *Suppletio defectuum*

SM = *Studi Medievali*, ser. 3

ThLL = *Thesaurus linguae Latinae*. Leipzig, 1900–

Bibliography

Full titles appear on the first occurrence in the notes; short titles thereafter.

Texts

Abelard. *Abélard. Historia calamitatum*. J. Monfrin ed. Paris, 1967.

Accessus ad auctores. R. B. C. Huygens ed. Berchem-Bruxelles, 1954.

Adam of Balsam. Minio-Paluello, L. *Adam Balsamiensis Parvipontani: Ars disserendi*.
Rome, 1956.

–. «The "Ars disserendi" of Adam of Balsham "Parvipontanus"», *MRS* 3 (1954),
116–69.

Adelard of Bath. *Die Quaestiones naturales des Adelardus von Bath*. M. Müller ed. *BGPTM*, 31, 2. Münster i. W., 1934.

Adelard of Bath. *Conversations with his Nephew. On the Same and the Different, Questions on Natural Science and On Birds*. C. Burnett ed. Cambridge Medieval Classics, 9, Cambridge, 1998.

Ademar. *Il monaco Ademaro e la sua raccolta di favole fedriane*. F. Bertini ed. 1975.

Ademar of Chabannes. *Ademaro di Chabannes Favole*. F. Bertini and P. Gatti ed. Favolisti Latini medievali, 3. Genova, 1988.

«Aegrum fama fuit». *MGH, P. L.* 1: 62. Berlin, 1881.

Alain of Lille. *Anticlaudianus*. R. Bossuat ed. Paris, 1955.

–. *De planctu naturae*. N. M. Häring ed. «Alan of Lille, "De Planctu naturae"», *Studi Medievali* 3 ser. 19 (1978), 797-879.

Alcuin. *De gallo*. *MGH, P. L.* 1: 262. Berlin, 1881.

Aldhelm. *Aldhelmi Opera omnia*. R. Ehwald ed. *MGH, AA* 15. München, 1984.

Alexander Neckam. *Corrogationes Noui Promethei*. L. S. Cropp ed. *A Critical Edition of Alexander Neckam's Corrogationes Noui Promethei with Introduction, Textual Notes and Commentary*. Dissertation, University of Toronto, 1991.

–. *Novus Aesopus. Alessandro Neckam Novus Aesopus*. G. Garbugino ed. Favolisti Latini medievali, 2. Genova, 1987

–. *Alexander Neckam Nouus Auianus*. Thomas A.-P. Klein ed. Favolisti Latini medievali 7. Genova 1998

–. *Alexandri Neckam de naturis rerum libri with…De laudibus diuinae sapientiae*. T. Wright ed. London, 1863

–. *Poems*. M. Esposito, «On Some Unpublished Poems Attributed to Alexander Neckam», *EHR* 30 (1915), 450-71.

–. *Poems*. H. Walther, «Zu den kleineren Gedichten des Alexanders Neckam», *MJ* 2 (1965), 111-29.

Altercatio Ganimedis et Helene. R. Lentzen, «*Altercatio Ganimedis et Helene*». Kritische Edition mit Kommentar», *MJ* 7 (1972), 161-86.

Anth. Anthologia Latina. F. Buecheler, A. Riese and E. Lommatzsch eds. 1: 1 Leipzig, 1894; repr. Amsterdam, 1973; vol. 1: 2 Leipzig, 1906; repr. Amsterdam, 1972.

–. D. R. Shackleton Bailey ed. Stuttgart, 1982.

Arator. *De actibus apostolorum*. A. P. McKinlay ed. *CSEL* 72. Vienna, 1951.

Arundel. *The Oxford Poems of Hugh Primas and the Arundel Lyrics*. C. J. McDonough ed. Toronto, 1984.

Augustine. *Confessionum libri tredecim*. P. Knöll ed. *CSEL* 33. Vienna, 1896.

–. *Contra Faustum*. I. Zycha ed. *CSEL* 25: 251-797. Vienna, 1891.

–. *De genesi ad litteram libri duodecim*. I. Zycha ed. *CSEL* 28: 1-456. Vienna, 1894.

–. *In Iohannis Evangelium Tractatus CXXIV*. D. R. Willems, OSB ed. *CCSL* 36. Turnhout, 1954.

Ausonius. *Opuscula*. C. Schenkl ed. *MGH, AA* 5. Berlin, 1883.

Avianus. *Fables*. F. Gaide ed. Paris, 1980.

Baudri (of Bourgueil). Baldricus Burgulianus *Carmina*. K. Hilbert ed. Heidelberg, 1979.

Bernardus Silvestris. *Cosmographia*. Peter Dronke ed. Leiden, 1978.

Boethius. *Boethii consolatio philosophiae*. L. Bieler, ed. *CCSL* 94 Turnhout, 1957.

Bulst, W. «Liebesbriefgedichte Marbods». In *Liber Floridus. Mittellateinische Studien* (St. Ottilien, 1950), 287-301.

Camargo, M. «A Twelfth-Century Treatise on 'Dictamen' and Metaphor», *Traditio* 47 (1992), 161-213.

Carmina Burana. A. Hilka, O. Schumann and B. Bischoff eds. 3 vols. Heidelberg, 1930, 1941, 1970.

Carmina Cantabrigiensia. The Cambridge Songs. J. Ziolkowski ed. New York, 1994.

Claudian. *Claudianus Carmina*. J. B. Hall ed. Leipzig, 1985.

Carmody, Francis J.. ed. *Physiologus Latinus*. Paris, 1939.

Cohen, G. *La «comédie» latine en France au XIIe siècle*. 2 vols. Paris, 1931.

Concordantia verbalia missalis Romani. T. A. Schnitker and W. A. Slaby eds. Münster, 1983.

Constantinus. Constantinus Africanus, *De omnium morborum qui homini accidere possunt cognitione et curatione*. 1536 pp. 1-167.

De bestiis. De bestiis et aliis rebus. MPL 177: 13-164.

Disticha Catonis. M. Boas ed. Amsterdam, 1952.

Doctrinale. Das Doctrinale des Alexander de Villa-Dei. D. Reichling ed. Berlin, 1893.

Dracontius. *Oeuvres* 1: *Louanges de Dieu* 1-2. C. Moussy and C. Camus eds. Paris, 1985.

—. *Oeuvres* 4: *Poèmes profanes* VI-X. Fragments. E. Wolff ed. Paris, 1996.

—. *Carmina*. F. Vollmer ed. *MGH, AA*, 14. Berlin, 1961.

du Méril, Edélestand. *Poésies inédites du moyen âge*. Paris, 1854.

Ecbasis captivi. Ecbasis cuisdam captivi per tropologiam. K. Strecker ed. Hannover, 1935; reprint 1977.

Ecloga Theoduli. Theoduli Ecloga. Johannes Osternacher ed. Urfahr, 1902.

Eugenius. Eugenii Toletani *Carmina*. F. Vollmer ed. *MGH, AA* 14. Berlin, 1905.

Fulgentius. *Fulgentii Opera*. R. Helm ed. Leipzig, 1898.

Garbugino, G. ed. *Alessandro Neckam Novus Aesopus*. Favolisti Latini medievali, 2. Genova, 1987.

Geoffrey of Monmouth. *Life of Merlin: Vita Merlini*. B. Clarke ed. Cardiff, 1973.

Gerald of Wales. *Giraldi cambrensis Opera*. J. F. Dimock ed. *Topographia Hibernica*, 5. London, 1867.

Glosule super Lucanum. Arnulfi Aurelianensis Glosule super Lucanum. B. Marti ed. American Academy in Rome, 1958.

Godman, Peter ed.. *Alcuin. The Bishops, Kings, and Saints of York*. Oxford 1982.

Herrmann, L. «Gallus et Vulpes», *Scriptorium* 1 (1946-47), 260-66.

Hildebert. *Carmina minora*. A. B. Scott ed. Leipzig, 1969.

–. *Biblical Epigrams*. Scott, A. B., Baker, D. F. and Rigg, A. G. «The *Biblical Epigrams* of Hildebert of Le Mans: A Critical Edition», *MS* 47 (1985), 272-316.

Holtz, L. *Donat et la tradition de l'enseignement grammaticale: étude sur l'Ars Donati et sa diffusion (IVe-IXe siècle) et édition critique*. Paris, 1981.

Horace. *Opera*. D. R. Shackleton Bailey ed. Stuttgart, 1985.

Hrabanus. *Hrabani Mauri Carmina*. E. Duemmler ed. *MGH, P. L.* 2. Berlin, 1884.

Hugh Primas. See *Arundel*.

Ibis. P. Ovidii Nasonis Ibis. F. W. Lenz ed. Torino, 1956.

Kästner, Heinrich, «Pseudo-Dioscorides *De herbis femininis*», *Hermes* 31 (1896), 578-636.

Jerome. *Epistulae*. I. Hilberg ed. *CSEL* 54. Vienna, 1996.

John of Salisbury. *Entheticus maior and minor*. J. van Laarhoven ed. 3 vols. Leiden, 1987.

–. *Policraticus*. *Ioannis Saresberiensis Policraticus*. K. S. B. Keats-Rohan ed. *CCCM* 118. Turnhout, 1993.

Lactantius Placidus. *Lactantius Placidus in Statii Thebaida commentum*. R. D. Sweeney ed. Stuttgart, 1997.

Long, R. J. «Alfred of Sareshel's commentary on the Pseudo-Aristotelian *De plantis*: A critical edition», *MS* 47 (1985), 125-67.

Lucan. *Belli civilis libri decem*. A. E. Housman ed. Oxford, 1927.

Macer. *Macer Floridus: De viribus herbarum*. L. Choulant ed. Leipzig, 1832.

Marbod. *Liber decem capitulorum*. R. Leotta ed. Rome, 1984.

–. *De lapidibus*. Marbode of Rennes' (1035-1123) *De lapidibus*. John M. Riddle ed. Sudhoffs Archiv. *Zeitschrift für Wissenschaftsgeschichte*, Beiheft 20. Wiesbaden, 1977.

–. *Carmina uaria*. *MPL* 171: 1717-36.

–. W. Bulst, «Studien zu Marbods Carmina varia und Liber decem capitulorum», Nachrichten von der Gesellschaft der Wissenschaften zu Göttingen, phil.-hist. N. F. Fachgruppe 4, Band 2 (1937-9) [Göttingen, 1939], 173-241.

M. Valerius. *Bucoliche*. F. Munari ed. Florence, 1970.

Mathew of Vendôme. *Mathei Vindocinensis Opera: Ars versificatoria*. F. Munari ed. 3 vols. Rome, 1977-88.

Martianus Capella. *Martianus Capella*. J. Willis ed. Leipzig, 1983.

Maximianus. *Massimiano*. S. Niccoli ed. Napoli, 1969.

Milo. *De mundi philosophia*. R. A. Pack ed. *Proceedings of the American Philosophical Society* 126, 2 (1982), 155-82.

Novus Aesopus. Hervieux, L. *Les fabulistes latins depuis le siècle d'Auguste jusqu'à la fin du moyen âge*. 5 vols. Paris, 1884-1899.

Orbán, A. P. *Novus Phisiologus nach Hs. Darmstadt 2780*. Leiden, 1989.

Osbern of Gloucester. Osberno, *Derivazioni*. F. Bertini and V. Ussani ed. 2 vols. Spoleto, 1996,

Ovid, *Am.*, *Ars*, *Rem.* *Amores*. E. J. Kenney ed. Oxford, 1968.

Ep. *Epistulae Heroidum*. H. Dörrie ed. Berlin, 1971.

Fast. *Fasti*. E. H. Alton et al. ed. Leipzig, 1978.

Met. *Metamorphoses*. W. S. Anderson ed. Leipzig, 1977.

Persius. Aulus Persius Flaccus *Satiren*. W. Kissel ed. Heidelberg, 1990.

Peter of Blois. *Libellus: Libellus de arte dictandi rhetorice*. In *Medieval Rhetorics* (ed. M. Camargo), 37-87.

–. *Petri Blesensis Carmina*. C. Wollin ed. *CCCM* 128. Turnhout, 1998.

Pfister, F. *Kleine Texte zum Alexanderroman*. Heidelberg, 1910.

Physiologus. Translated by M. J. Curley. Austin, 1979.

Physiologus Latinus. F. J. Carmody ed. Paris, 1939.

Pliny. *Naturalis Historia*. L. Ian and C. Mayhoff edd. 6 vols. Stuttgart, 1906; repr. 1967.

Prudentius. *Carmina*. M. P. Cunningham ed. *CCSL* 126. Turnhout, 1966.

Pseudo–Apuleius. *The Herbal of Pseudo-Apuleius (Codex Casinensis 97)* described and annotated by F. W. T. Hunger. Leyden, 1935.

Pseudo–Bede. *De mundi celestis terrestrisque constitutione*. A Treatise on the Universe and the Soul. Charles Burnett ed. London, 1985.

Ps.-Verg. *Appendix Vergiliana*. W. V. Clausen ed. Oxford, 1966.

Scholia in Horatium. H. J. Botschuyver ed. 4 vols. Amsterdam, 1935-42.

Sedulius. *Opera omnia*. I. Huemer ed. *CSEL* 10. Vienna, 1885.

Seneca the Elder. *Declamations. Controversiae and Suasoriae*. M. Winterbotton ed. 2 vols. Cambridge, MA. 1974.

Serlo of Bayeux. A. Boutemy, «Deux poèmes inconnus de Serlon de Bayeux et une copie nouvelle de son poème contre les moines de Caen» 3 ser., *Le moyen âge* 9 (1938), 241-69.

Servius. *In Vergilii carmina commentarii*. G. Thilo and H. Hagen ed. 3 vols. Leipzig, 1881-7; repr. Hildesheim, 1961.

Solinus. *Collectanea rerum memorabilium*. Th. Mommsen ed. Berlin, 1958.

Statius, *Ach. Achilleis*. A. Marastoni ed. Leipzig, 1974.

Suetonius. *Praeter Caesarum libros reliquiae*. A. Reifferschied ed. Hildesheim, 1971.

Theobaldi Physiologus. P. T. Eden ed. Leiden, 1972.

Theodulph. *Theodulfi Carmina*. E. Duemmler ed. *MGH, P. L.* 1. Berlin, 1881.

Thiele, G. *Der illustrierte lateinische Äsop in der Handschrift des Ademar. Codex Vossianus Lat. oct.* 15 *Fol.* 195-205. Leiden, 1905.

Urso of Salerno. R. Creutz ed. «Die medizinisch-naturphilosophischen Aphorismen und Kommentar des Magisters Urso Salernitanus», *Quellen und Studien zur Geschichte der Naturwissenschaften und der Medizin* 5, 1 (1936), 1-192.

–. *De commixtionibus elementorum libellus*. W. Stürner ed. Stuttgart, 1976.

Valerius Maximus. *Valerii Maximi factorum et dictorum memorabilium libri novem.* C. Kempf ed. Stuttgart, 1966.

Vatican Mythographers. *Le premier mythographe du Vatican.* N. Zorzetti ed. Paris, 1995.

Venantius. *Venanti Fortunati Carmina.* F. Leo ed. *MGH, AA* 4. Berlin, 1881.

Vita Aedwardi regis. F. Barlow ed. London, 1962.

Vriend, H. J. de ed. *The Old English Herbarium and Medicina de Quadrupedibus.* Oxford, 1984.

Walahfrid. *Walahfridi Strabonis Carmina.* E. Duemmler ed. *MGH, P. L.* 2. Berlin, 1884.

Walter of Châtillon. *Galteri de Castellione Alexandreis.* M. L. Colker ed. Padua, 1978

Walter of England. *The Fables of 'Walter of England.'* A. E. Wright ed. Toronto, 1997.

William of Conches. *Glosae super Platonem.* E. Jeauneau ed. Paris, 1965.

William of Malmesbury. *De gestis pontificum Anglorum.* N. E. Hamilton ed. London, 1870.

Wright, Thomas. *A Volume of Vocabularies.* Liverpool, 1857.

Ysopet-Avionnet: The Latin and French Texts. K. McKenzie and W. A. Oldfather eds. Urbana, University of Illinois, 1919.

Ysengrimus. *Ysengrimus. Text with Translation, Commentary and Introduction.* J. Mann ed. Leiden, 1987.

Zander, C. *Phaedrus solutus vel Phaedri fabulae novae XXX.* Lund, 1921.

Books and articles

Adrados, F. R. «La fabula de la golondrina de Grecia a la India y la Edad Media», *Emerita* 48 (1980), 185-208.

André, J. *Les noms d'oiseaux en latin.* Paris, 1967.

Arber, A. *Herbals, Their Origin and Evolution – A Chapter in the History of Botany* 1470-1670. Cambridge, 1987.

Arnould, D. «A la pêche au crocodile: La postérité d'Hérodote 11, 68-70», *Revue de philologie* 70 (1996), 13-24.

Bambeck, M. «Zur Geschichte vom die Farbe wechselnde «chamäleon»», *Fabula* 25 (1984), 66-75.

Bayless, M. *Parody in the Middle Ages. The Latin Tradition.* Ann Arbor, 1996.

Berry, Gregory Leo. *A Partial Edition of Alexander Neckam's Laus Sapientie Divine.* Dissertation, Yale University, 1978.

Birkenmajer, A. «Le rôle joué par les médicins et les naturalistes dans la réception d'Aristote au XIIe et XIIIe siècles», *Extrait de la Pologne au VIe Congrès International des Sciences Historiques*, Oslo, 1928 (Warsaw, 1930).

Blaise, A. *Dictionnaire latin-français des auteurs chrétiens.* Paris, 1954.

Bloomfield, M. W. «Allegory as Interpretation», *New Literary History* 3 (1971), 301-17.

Bond, G. A. *The Loving Subject. Desire, Eloquence, and Power in Romanesque France.* Philadelphia, 1995.

Boutemy, A. «Fragments d'une oeuvre perdue de Sigebert de Gembloux (Le commentaire métrique de l' 'Ecclésiaste')», *Latomus* 2 (1938), 196-220.

Bremness, L. *The Complete Book of Herbs.* New York, 1988.

Brody, S. N. *The Disease of the Soul. Leprosy in Medieval Literature.* Ithaca, 1974.

Broek, R. van den. *The Myth of the Phoenix according to Classical and Early Christian Traditions.* Leiden, 1972.

Burnett, C. F. «Arabic into Latin in Twelfth Century Spain: The Works of Hermann of Carinthia», *MJ* 13 (1978), 100-34.

—. «Scientific Speculations» and «Hermann of Carinthia». In P. Dronke ed., *A History of Twelfth-Century Western Philosophy* (Cambridge, 1988), 151-76, 386-404.

Bynum, C. W. «Wonder», *The American Historical Review* 102 (1997), 1-26.

Cadden, J. *The Meanings of Sex Difference in the Middle Ages. Medicine, Science and Culture.* Cambridge, 1993.

Cairns, F. «Ancient 'Etymology' and Tibullus: On the Classification of 'Etymologies' and on 'Etymological Markers'», *Proceedings of the Cambridge Philological Society* 42 (1996), 24-59.

Camargo, M. *Medieval Rhetorics of Prose Composition. Five English Artes Dictandi and their Tradition.* Binghamton, 1995.

Cameron, M. L. *Anglo-Saxon Medicine.* Cambridge, 1993.

Cardini, R. et al., *Tradizione classica e letteratura umanistica, Per Alessandro Perosa.* 2 vols. Rome, 1985.

Carmody, F. J. «*De Bestiis et aliis rebus* and the Latin *Physiologus*», *Speculum* 13 (1938), 153-9.

Carruthers, M. *The Book of Memory. A Study of Memory in Medieval Culture.* Cambridge, 1990.

—. «The Poet as Master Builder: Composition and Locational Memory in the Middle Ages», *New Literary History* 24 (1993), 881-904.

Cary, G. *The Medieval Alexander* (D. J. A. Ross ed.). Cambridge, 1956; repr. 1967.

Catanzaro, G. and Santucci, F. *La favolistica latina in distici elegiaci.* Atti del convegno internazionale, Assisi, 26-28 ottobre 1990. Assisi, 1991.

Clark, W. B. and McMunn, M. T. *Beasts and Birds of the Middle Ages: The Bestiary and its Legacy.* Philadelphia, 1989.

Connors, C. *Petronius the Poet.* Cambridge, 1998.

Cronin, G. Jr.. «The Bestiary and the Mediaeval Mind: Some Complexities», *Modern Language Quarterly* 2 (1941), 191-8.

Curletto, S. «Il lupo e la gru da Esopo a La Fontaine». In F. Bertini ed., *Favolisti latini medievali* 1 (Genova, 1984), 11-24.

Curtius, E. R. *European Literature and the Latin Middle Ages*. trans. by W. R. Trask. London, 1953.

Dawson, W. R. «Studies in Medical history: (a) The Origin of the Herbal. (b) Castor-oil in Antiquity», *Aegyptus* 10 (1929), 47-72.

de Boor, H. «Über Fabel und Bîspel», *Sitz. der Bayerischen Ak. der Wiss.*, phil.-hist. Klasse (1966), 3-40.

Dronke, P. *Fabula. Explorations into the Uses of Myth in Medieval Platonism*. Leiden, 1974

Dronke, P. *Intellectuals and Poets in Medieval Europe*. Rome, 1992.

Diaz y Diaz, M. «Sobre las series de voces de animales». In J. J. O'Meara and Naumann B. eds., *Latin Script and Letters A. D. 400-900* (Leiden, 1976), 148-55.

Dicke, G. and Grubmüller, K. *Die Fabeln des Mittelalters und der frühen Neuzeit. Ein Katalog der deutschen Versionen und ihrer lateinischen Entsprechungen*. Munich, 1987.

Diekstra, F. N. M. «The 'Physiologus', the Bestiaries and Medieval Animal Lore», *Neophilologus* 69 (1985), 142-55.

Druce, G. C. «The Symbolism of the Crocodile in the Middle Ages», *Archaeological Journal* 66 (1909), 311-38.

—. «The Caladrius and its Legend, Sculptured upon the Twelfth-Century Doorway of Alne Church, Yorkshire», *Archaeological Journal* 69 (1912), 381-416.

—. «The Legend of the *Serra* or Saw-Fish», *Proceedings of the Society of Antiquaries of London*. Second series, 31 (1918-1919), 20-35.

—. «The Elephant in Medieval Legend and Art», *Archaeological Journal* 76 (1919), 1-73.

—. «The Medieval Bestiaries, and their Influence on Ecclesiastical Decorative Art», *Journal of the British Archaeological Association* N. S. 25 (1919), 41-82.

Duckworth, G. E. *Vergil and Classical Hexameter Poetry. A Study in Metrical Variety*. Ann Arbor, 1969.

Dyck, A. R. *A Commentary on Cicero, De Officiis*. Ann Arbor, 1996.

El-Gammal, S. Y. «Garlic in History», *Hamdard Medicus* 28, 1 (1985), 85-9.

Ellis, R. «Notes of a Fortnight's Research in the Bibliothèque Nationale of Paris», *Journal of Philology* 15 (1886), 246-8.

—. «A Contribution to the History of the Transmission of Classical Literature in the Middle Age, from Oxford MSS», *American Journal of Philology* 10 (1889), 159-64.

Esposito M. «On Some Unpublished Poems Attributed to Alexander Neckam», *English Historical Review* 30 (1915), 450-71.

Evans, G. R. «Suppletio», *ALMA* 42 (1982), 73-8.

Fechter, W. *Lateinische Dichtkunst und deutsches Mittelalter*. Berlin, 1964.

Fleissner, R. F. *A Rose by Another name: A Survey of Literary Flora from Shakespeare to Eco*. West Cornwall, Ct. 1989.

Flood, Jr., B. P. «The Medieval Herbal Tradition of Macer Floridus», *Pharmacy in History* 18 (1976), 62-6.

−. «Pliny and the Medieval 'Macer' Medical Text», *Journal of the History of Medicine* 32 (1977), 395-402.

Frassetto, M. «Reaction and Reform: Reception of Heresy in Arras and Aquitaine in the Early Eleventh Century», *The Catholic Historical Review* 83 (1997), 385-400.

French, R. K. and Cunningham, C. *Before Science. The Invention of the Friars' Natural Philosophy*. Aldershot, 1996

Fumagalli, M. and Parodi, M. «Due enciclopedie dell'Occidente medievale: Alessandro Neckam e Bartolomeo Anglico», *Rivista di storia della filosofia* 40 (1985), 51-90.

Garbugino, G. «Il 'Novus Aesopus' di Alessandro Neckam». In G. Catanzaro ed., *La favolistica latina in distici elegiaci* (Assisi, 1991), 107-32.

Gaselee, S. «Natural Science in England at the End of the Twelfth Century», *Proceedings of the Royal Institution of Great Britain* 29 (1937), 397-417.

−. «Notes on the Vocabulary of Alexander Neckam», *Speculum* 14 (1939), 106-7.

Gatti, P. «Le favole del monaco Ademaro e la tradizione manoscritta del *corpus* Fedriano», *Sandalion* 2 (1979), 247-59.

Glauche G., Schullektüre im Mittelalter. Entstehung and Wandlungen des Lektürekanons bis 1200 nach den Quellen dargestellt. Munich, 1970.

Gold, B. K. «*Mitte sectari, rosa quo locorum sera moretur*: Time and Nature in Horace's Odes», *Classical Philology* 88 (1993), 16-31.

Goosens, J and Sodmann, T. *Third International Beast Epic. Fable and Fabliau Colloquium*, Münster, 1979. Proceedings. Cologne, 1981.

Grubmüller, K. *Meister Esopus: Untersuchungen zur Geschichte und Funktion der Fabel im Mittelalter*. Munich, 1977.

Gualandri, I. and G. Orlandi. «Contributi sulla commedia elegiaca *Lidia*. Questioni letterarie e testuali», *Paideia* 45 (1990), 199-238.

Hamilton, G. L. «A New Redaction (J3ᵃ) of the *Historia de Preliis* and the Date of Redaction J3», *Speculum* 2 (1927), 113-46.

Hardie P. R. *Virgil's Aeneid. Cosmos and Imperium*. Oxford, 1986.

Haskins, C. H., *Studies in the History of Mediaeval Science*. Cambridge, MA., 1924.

−. «Adelard of Bath», *EHR* 26 (1911), 491-8.

Hassig, D. *Medieval Bestiaries. Text, Image, Ideology*. Cambridge, 1995.

Haye, T. «Das 'Novale' des William Pore: ein Beitrag zur mittellateinischen Reisedichtung», *SM* 37 (1996), 387-442.

−. *Das lateinische Lehrgedicht im Mittelalter. Analyse einer Gattung*. Leiden, 1997.

Heider, G. «Physiologus nach einer Handschrift des XI Jahrhunderts», *Archiv für österreichischer Geschichts-Quellen* 2 (1850), 541-82.

Henderson, A. C. «Medieval Beasts and Modern Cages: The Making of Meaning in Fables and Bestiaries», *PMLA* 97 (1982), 40-9.

Henkel, N. *Studien zum Physiologus im Mittelalter*. Tübingen, 1976.

Heyser, K., «Die Alliumarten als Arzneimittel im Gebrauch der abendlandischen Medizin», *Kyklos* 1 (1928), 64-102.

Hirschfeld, E., «Studien zur Geschichte der Heilpflanzen 1. Lillium convallium», *Kyklos* 2 (1929), 145-62.

Holmes, Urban T. *Daily Living in the Twelfth Century. Based on the Observations of Alexander Neckam in London and Paris.* Madison, 1962.

Hooley, D. M. *The Knotted Thong. Structures of Mimesis in Persius.* Ann Arbor, 1997.

Hortulus of Walahfrid Strabo. Ed. and trans. by R. Payne with commentary by W. Blunt. Pittsburg, PA. 1960.

Hunt, R. W. «The 'lost' preface to the *Liber derivationum* of Osbern of Gloucester», *Mediaeval and Renaissance Studies* 4 (1958), 267-82.

–. *The Schools and the Cloister. The Life and Writings of Alexander Nequam* (1157-1217). Edited and revised by Margaret Gibson. Oxford, 1984.

Hunt, Tony. *Plant Names of Medieval England. Introduction and Texts.* D. S. Brewer, Cambridge, 1989.

–. *Popular Medicine in Thirteenth-Century England.* D. S. Brewer, Cambridge, 1990.

–. *Teaching and Learning Latin in Thirteenth-Century England.* 3 vols. D. S. Brewer, Woodbridge, 1991.

Jackson, R. *Doctors and Diseases in the Roman Empire.* British Museum Publications. London, 1988.

Jacquart, D. «De *crasis* à *complexio*: note sur le vocabulaire du tempérament en latin médiévale». In *Mémoires* V. *Textes médicaux latins antiques* (1984), 71-5.

–. «Aristotelian Thought in Salerno». In P. Dronke ed., *A History of Twelfth-Century Western Philosophy* (Cambridge, 1988), 407-28.

James M. R. ed. *The Bestiary, Being a Reproduction in Full of the Manuscript Ii. 4. 26 in the University Library, Cambridge.* Oxford, 1928.

Janson, H. W. *Apes and Ape Lore in the Middle Ages and the Renaissance.* London, 1952.

Jauss, H. R. *Untersuchungen zur mittelalterlichen Tierdichtung.* Beiheft zur *ZRPh* 100 (1959).

Jeauneau, E. «Note sur l'école de Chartres», 3 ser. *SM* 5 (1964), 821-65.

Jiménez, J. L. Gamboa, «Estudio métrico de la 'distinctio prima' del 'De laudibus Divinae sapientiae' de Alexander Neckam», *Analecta malacitana* 9 (1986), 249-63.

Jones, J. W. *An Aeneid Commentary of Mixed Type. The Glosses in MSS Harley* 4946 *and Ambrosianus G* 111 *inf. A Critical Edition.* Toronto, 1996.

Jones, P. M. «Harley MS. 2558: A Fifteenth-Century Medical Commonplace Book». In M. R. Schleissner, *Manuscript Sources of Medieval Medicine*, 35-54.

Kealey, E. J. *Medieval Medicus. A Social History of Anglo-Norman Medicine.* Baltimore, 1981.

Keil, G. «The Textual Transmission of the *Codex* Berleburg». In M. R. Schleissner, *Manuscript Sources of Medieval Medicine*, 19-33.

Kelly, D. «The Scope of the Treatment of Composition in the Twelfth- and Thirteenth-Century Arts of Poetry», *Speculum* 41 (1966), 261-78.

–. «Theory of Composition in Medieval Narrative Poetry and Geoffrey of Vinsauf's
Poetria Nova», *MS* 31 (1969), 117-48.

Kelly, J. N. D. *The Oxford Dictionary of Popes*. Oxford, 1986.

Kristeller, P. O. «The School of Salerno: Its Development and its Contribution to
the History of Learning», *Bulletin of the History of Medicine* 17 (1945), 138-94.

–. «Bartholomaeus, Musandinus and Maurus of Salerno and Other Early Commen-
tators of the 'Articella', with a Tentative List of Texts and Manuscripts», *Italia
medioevale e umanistica* 19 (1976), 57-87.

Latham, R. E. *Revised Medieval Latin Word-List from British and Irish Sources*. London, 1965.

Lauzi, E. «Lepre, donnola e iena: contributi alla storia di una metafora», 3 ser. *SM*
29 (1988), 539-59.

Lawn, Brian. *The Salernitan Questions. An Introduction to the History of Medieval and
Renaissance Problem Literature*. Oxford, 1963.

–. *The Prose Salernitan Questions: Edited from a Bodleian Manuscript (Auct. F. 3. 10)*.
London, 1979.

Leeman, A. D. and Pinkster, H. *M. Tullius Cicero De Oratore Libri* III. Heidelberg,
1981.

Lendinara, P. «The 'Oratio de utensilibus ad domum regendam pertinentibus' by
Adam of Balsham», *Anglo-Norman Studies* 15 (1992), 161-76.

Lindberg, D. C. *The Beginnings of Western Science*. Chicago, 1992.

Loewe, R and Hunt, R. W. «Alexander Neckam's Knowledge of Hebrew», *MRS*
4 (1958), 17-34.

L'Uomo di fronte al mondo animale nell'alto medioevo, 7-13 aprile 1983. Settimane di
studio del Centro Italiano di studi sull'alto medioevo, 31. 2 vols. Spoleto, 1985.

Lyne, R. O. A. M. *Words and the Poet. Characteristic Techniques of Style in Vergil's Aeneid*. Oxford, 1989.

Manitius, Max. *Geschichte der lateinischen Literatur des Mittelalters*. 3 vols. Munich,
1911-31.

Mann, J. «La favolistica latina». In C. Leonardi and G. Orlandi ed., *Aspetti della letteratura latina nel secolo XIII: Atti del primo Convegno internazionale di studi dell'Associazione per il Medioevo e l'Umanesimo Latini (AMUL)*, Perugia, 3-5 ottobre
1983, (1986), 193-219.

Mantello, F. A. C. and Rigg, A. G.. *Medieval Latin. An Introduction and Bibliographical Guide*. Washington D. C., 1996.

Marcovich, M. «Voces animantium and Suetonius», *Ziva Antika. Antiquité vivante*
21 (1971), 399-416.

Mastandrea, P. *De fine versus. Repertorio di clausole ricorrenti nella poesia dattilica Latina
dalle origini a Sidonio Apollinare*. 2 vols. Hildesheim, 1993.

McCulloch, F. *Mediaeval Latin and French Bestiaries*. Revised edition. Chapel Hill, 1962.

Merle, H. «Aptum natum esse. Aptitudo naturalis», *ALMA* 43 (1981-82), 122-39.

Mermier, R. «The Phoenix: Its Nature and its Place in the Tradition of the *Physiologus*». In W. B. Clark and M. T. McMunn, *Beasts and Birds in the Middle Ages* (Philadelphia, 1989), 69-85.

Meyers, Jean. *L'art de l'emprunt dans la poèsie de Sedulius Scottus*. Paris, 1986.

Minnis A. J. and Scott A. B. ed. *Medieval Literary Theory and Criticism c. 1100-c. 1375. The Commentary Tradition*. Oxford, 1988.

Mollard, A. «La diffusion de l'Institution oratoire au XIIe siècle», *Le moyen âge* 3e serie, 5 (44 of Collection) (1934), 161-75.

Morson, J. «The English Cistercians and the Bestiary», *Bulletin of the John Rylands Library* 39 (1956-57), 146-70.

Muratova, X. «I manoscritti miniati del bestiario medievale: Origine, formazione e sviluppo dei cicli di illustrazioni. I bestiari miniati in Inghilterra nei secoli XII-XIV». In *L'Uomo di fronte al mondo animale nell'alto medioevo* (Spoleto, 1985), 2: 1319-62.

Neudeck, Otto, «Möglichkeiten der Dichter-Stilisierung in Mittelhochdeutscher Literatur: Neidhart, Wolfram, Vergil», *Euphorion* 88 (1994), 339-55.

Niermeyer, J. F. *Mediae Latinitatis Lexicon Minus*. Leiden, 1976.

Nisbet, R. G. M. *Collected Papers on Latin Literature* ed. by S. J. Harrison. Oxford, 1995.

Novae Concordantiae Bibliorum Sacrorum. B. Fischer O.S.B. ed. Tubingen, 1977.

Novati, F. «'Le Dis du Koc' di Jean de Condé ed il gallo del Campanile nella poesia medievale», *SM* 1 (1904-5), 465-512.

Nutton, Vivian et al. *The Western Medical Tradition, 800 B. C. to A. D. 1800*. Cambridge, 1996.

—. «Velia and the School of Salerno», *Medical History* 15 (1971), 1-11.

O'Donnell, J. J. Augustine. *Confessions*. Oxford, 1992.

Olson, G. *Literature as Recreation in the Later Middle Ages*. Ithaca, 1982.

O'Meara, J. J. and Naumann, B. *Latin Script and Letters A. D. 400-900*. Leiden, 1976.

Orchard, Andy. *The Poetic Art of Aldhelm*. Cambridge, 1994.

Orlandi, G. «Metrica 'medievale' e metrica 'antichizzante' nella commedia elegiaca: La technica versificatoria del *Miles Gloriosus* e della *Lidia*». In. R. Cardini ed., *Tradizione classica e letteratura umanistica* (Rome, 1985), 1: 1-16.

—. «La tradizione del 'Physiologus' e i prodromi del bestiario Latino». In *L'Uomo di fronte al mondo animale nell'alto medioevo* (Spoleto, 1985), 2: 1057-1106.

Orlowsky, Ursula and Orlowsky, Rebekka, *Narziss und Narzissmus im Spiegel von Literatur, Bildender Kunst und Psychoanalyse. Vom Mythos zum leeren Selbstinszenierung*. Munich, 1992.

Parkes, M. B. «The Influence of the Concepts of 'Ordinatio' and 'Compilatio' on the Development of the Book». In J. J. G. Alexander and M. T. Gibson eds., *Medieval Learning and Literature* (Oxford 1976), 115-41.

Paschalis, M. *Virgil's Aeneid. Semantic Relations and Proper Names.* Oxford, 1997.

Pepin, R. E. «Autobiography in Alexander Neckam's 'Laus sapientiae divinae'», *Florilegium* 6 (1984), 103-18.

Rather, L. J. «Systematic Medical Treatises from the Ninth to the Nineteenth Century: The Unchanging Scope and Structure of Academic Medicine in the West», *Clio Medica* 11 (1976), 289-305.

Renan, E. «Sur l'étymologie du nom d'Abélard», *Revue celtique* 1 (1870-72), 265-8.

Reynolds, L. D. *Texts and Transmission. A Survey of the Latin Classics.* Oxford, 1983.

Reynolds, Suzanne. *Medieval Reading. Grammar, Rhetoric and the Classical Text.* Cambridge, 1996.

Riddle, John M. «Theory and Practice in Medieval Medicine», *Viator* 5 (1974), 157-84.

—. *Contraception and Abortion from the Ancient World to the Renaissance.* Cambridge MA., 1992.

—. «Manuscript Sources for Birth Control». In M. R. Schleissner ed., *Manuscript Sources of Medieval Medicine* (New York, 1995), 145-58.

Rigg, A. G. *A History of Anglo-Latin Literature 1066-1422.* Cambridge, 1992.

Rowland, B. «The Relationship of St. Basil's *Hexaemeron* to the *Physiologus*». In G. Bianciotto and M. Salvat, *Epopée animale, fable, fabliau.* Actes du IVe colloque de la société internationale Reynardienne. Evreux 7-11 septembre 1981 (Paris, 1984), 489-98.

—. «The Art of Memory and the Bestiary». In W. B. Clark and M. T. McMunn eds., *Beasts and Birds of the Middle Ages* (Philadelphia, 1989), 12-25.

—. «The Wisdom of the Cock». In J. Goosens ed., *Third International Beast Epic. Fable and Fabliau Colloquium*, Münster, 1979. (Cologne, 1981), 340-55.

Ruppel, B. «Ein verschollenes Gedichte des 12. Jahrhunderts: Heinrichs von Huntingdon 'De herbis'», *Frümittelalterliche Studien* 31 (1997), 197-213.

Russell, J. C. «Alexander Neckam in England», *EHR* 47 (1932), 260-8.

Sada, E. «Genesi del lupo cattivo», 3 ser. *SM* 33 (1992), 779-97.

Saffron, M. H. «Maurus of Salerno, Twelfth-Century 'Optimus Physicus'», *Transactions of the American Philosophical Society* N. S. 62, 1 (1972), 5-104.

Schaller, D. *Studien zur lateinischen Dichtung des Frühmittelalters.* Stuttgart, 1995.

Scherer, M. R. *The Legends of Troy in Art and Literature.* New York, 1963.

Schleissner, M. R. ed. *Manuscript Sources of Medieval Medicine. A Book of Essays.* New York, 1995.

Sharpe, R. *A Handlist of the Latin Writers of Great Britain and Ireland before 1540.* Turnhout, 1997.

Sigerist, H. E. «Materia medica in the Middle Ages», *Bulletin of the History of Medicine* 7 (1939), 417-23.

Simpson, James. *Sciences and the Self in Medieval Poetry*. Alan of Lille's *Anticlaudianus* and John Gower's *Confessio amantis*. Cambridge, 1995.

Singer, C. «The Herbal in Antiquity and its Transmission to Later Ages», *Journal of Hellenic Studies* 47 (1927), 1-52.

Siraisi, N. G. *Medieval and Early Renaissance Medicine*. *An Introduction to Knowledge and Practice*. Chicago, 1990.

Smith, W. and Wace, H. *A Dictionary of Christian Biography, Literature, Sects and Doctrines*. 4 vols. London, 1877-87.

Smits, E. R. «A Medieval Supplement to the Beginning of Curtius Rufus's *Historia Alexandri*: An Edition with Introduction», *Viator* 18 (1987), 89-124.

Southern, R. W. *The Making of the Middle Ages*. London, 1987.

–. «From Schools to University». In T. H. Aston ed., *The History of the University of Oxford* 1. *The Early Oxford Schools* ed. J. I. Catto. Oxford, 1984.

Speer, A. *Die entdeckte Natur. Untersuchungen zu Begründungsversuchen einer «scientia naturalis» im 12. Jahrhundert*. Leiden, 1995.

–. «The Discovery of Nature: The Contributions of the Chartrians to Twelfth-Century Attempts to Found a *scientia naturalis*», *Traditio* 52 (1997), 135-51.

Stannard Jerry W.. «Medieval Herbals and their Development», *Clio Medica* 9 (1974), 23-33.

–. «The Herbal as a Medical Document», *Bulletin of the History of Medicine* 43 (1969), 212-20.

–. «The Graeco-Roman Background of the Renaissance Herbal», *Organon* 4 (1967), 141-5.

–. «The Theoretical Bases of Medieval Herbalism», *Medical Heritage* 1 (1985), 186-98.

–. «The Multiple Uses of Dill (Anethum graveolens) in Medieval Medicine». In *Festschrift Willem F. Daems*, Wurzburger Medizinhistorische Forschungen 24 (Pattensen, Han., 1982), 411-24.

Steadman, J. M. «Chauntecleer and Medieval Natural History», *Isis* 50 (1959), 236-44.

Talbot, C. H. *Medicine in Medieval England*. London, 1967.

The Cosmographia of Bernardus Silvestris. A Translation with Introduction and Notes by Winthrop Wetherbee. New York and London, 1973.

The Medieval Book of Birds. Hugh of Fouilloy's *Aviarium*. Edition, Translation and Commentary by Willene B. Clark. Binghamton, N. Y., 1992.

Sudhoff. K. «Salerno, Montpellier und Paris um 1200», *Archiv für Geschichte der Medizin* 20 (1928), 51-62.

The Oxford Latin Dictionary. P. G. W. Glare ed. Oxford, 1994.

Thorndike, L. *The Herbal of Rufinus*. Chicago, 1946.

–. *A History of Magic and Experimental Science*. vol. 2. New York, 1929.

P. W. Travis, «Chaucer's Heliotropes and the Poetics of Metaphor», *Speculum* 72 (1997), 399-427.

Viarre, S. *La survie d'Ovide dans la littérature scientifique des XIIe et XIIIe siècles.* Poitiers, 1966.

Voigts, L. E. «Anglo-Saxon Plant Remedies and the Anglo-Saxons», *Isis* 70 (1979), 250-68.

Walther, H. «Eine moral-asketische Dichtung des XIII. Jahrhunderts: *Prorogationes Novi Promethei* des Alexander Neckam», *Medium Aevum* 31 (1962), 33-42.

—. «Zu den kleineren Gedichten des Alexander Neckam», *MJ* 2 (1965), 111-29.

—. *Proverbia Sententiaeque Latinitatis Medii Aevi: Lateinische Sprichwörter und Sentenzen des Mittelalters in alphabetischer Anordnung.* 5 vols. Göttingen, 1963-1967.

Wetherbee, W. «Philosophy, Cosmology, and the Twelfth-Century Renaissance». In P. Dronke ed., *A History of Twelfth-Century Western Philosophy* (Cambridge, 1988), 21-53.

—. *Platonism and Poetry in the Twelfth Century. The Literary Influence of the School of Chartres.* Princeton, 1972.

Wieland, Gernot R. *The Latin Glosses on Arator and Prudentius in Cambridge University Library, MS GG. 5. 35.* Toronto, 1983.

Yarnall, J. *Transformations of Circe. The History of an Enchantress.* Urbana and Chicago, 1994.

Ziolkowski, Jan M., «The Spirit of Play in the Poetry of St. Gall». In J. C. King ed., *Sangallensia in Washington. The Arts and Letters in Medieval and Baroque St. Gall Viewed from the Late Twentieth Century* (New York, 1993), 143-69.

—. *Talking Animals. Medieval Latin Beast Poetry 750-1150.* Philadelphia, 1993.

Zurli, L. ed., Astensis Poetae *Novus Avianus.* Favolisti Latini Medievali e Umanistici, 5. Genova, 1994.

SUPPLETIO DEFECTUUM
BOOK I

Sigla

M = Madrid, Biblioteca de Palacio Real ex Oriente, II-468, 13th/14th c.
P = Paris, Bibliothèque Nationale, lat. 11867, 13th/14th c.

1. To facilitate access to the text, I have assembled the separate section headings scattered throughout the margins of **P** at the head of the poem. I have also marked the major
divisions of the poem by inserting breaks into the text, which are not present in **P**.

1191–1222	De auaricia incidenter.
1223–26	De cane.
1227–28	De simia.
1229–30	De oue et capra.
1231–32	De sisimo.
1233–34	De bobus.
1235–56	De lupo.
1257–66	Transitus.
1267–82	De ceruo.
1283–86	De tygride.
1287–1302	De symia.
1303–6	De urso.
1307–10	De uncia.
1311–22	De lince.
1323–1420	Moralis constructio super fastu muris [muiis **P**].
1421–36	De talpa.
1437–46	De laro.
1447–58	Iterum de uulpe.

<f. 218va> Incipit suplecio defectuum operis magistri Alexandri quod deseruit laudi sapientie diuine: capitulum primum.

Ornatu uario mundus depingitur artis;
    Docta manus uarium nobilitauit opus.
In rebus lucet artis preclara potestas;
    Tot rerum species condidit una manus.
5   Qui uarias artes auctores fingere plures
    Vsurpas, uarios fingis in orbe deos.
Fauste, tace! rerum cunctarum est vnicus auctor;
    Ars est una, manus unica, uera Noys.
Materiam, formas, usyas, sydera, celos
10   Rex regum iussu ducit in esse suo.
Hic elementa ligat concordi federe; cunctis
    Quas statuit leges rebus inesse iubet.
Causas, effectus, motus, loca, tempora, uires,
    Ciues angelicos regula iusta regit.
15   Tot rerum facies, tot sunt discrimina, dotes
    Nature, leges, federa, iura, modi.
Res de non esse producit ad esse potestas;
    Vsum dat bonitas, seruat in esse, fouet;
Discernit, uariat, numerat sapientia, mutat,
20   Ornat, disponit et moderatur eas.
Nectit amor fedus, seruat concordia, nutrit
    Pax; docet ars artem, lex ligat, ordo regit.
f. 218vb Scintillant stelle fixe, radiare planeta
    Cernitur; hec lucet amplius, illa minus.
25   Aureus est istis color, est argenteus illis;
    Hinc fulget roseus, igneus inde rubor.
Orion spacio rutilans diffunditur amplo,
    Coniunctas Pliades area parua tenet.

25. istis **M**, illis **P**   **28.** area *ed.*, arca **P**, aera **M**

Here begins a supplement to repair deficits in the work of Master Alexander, which is devoted to the praises of divine wisdom: first chapter.

The universe is painted with the varied adornments of art; an expert hand has ennobled a richly decorated creation. The magnificent power of artistry shines within physical phenomena; so many forms of created life has a single hand established. Faustus, you assume that multiple authors have produced the different arts; [5] you suppose that in the world there are gods of many different kinds. Faustus, be silent! The originator of all created things is one and only. The artistry is unique, the hand singular, Noys true. At his command the king of kings brings matter into existence, together with forms, the essences, the stars and the heavens. [10] In this world he binds the elements in a harmonious compact; he commands the laws he has established to be immanent in everything. A recognized principle guides causes, effects, movements, stations, seasons, powers and the angelic hosts. Matter displays so many configurations and countless differences; Nature's endowments, [15] principles, bonds, laws, and methods are without number. Power draws things out of non-existence into being. Goodness grants their use, it preserves and fosters (them) in their existence. Wisdom confers difference, diversity and number; it transforms, adorns, regulates and governs created life. [20] Love forms the bond for the union, harmony preserves it, and peace nourishes it. Art informs art, a law unites it in harmony, and order directs it.

The fixed stars flash like fire; planets are observed radiating light; this star shines with greater intensity, that one with less. These stars have a golden colour, those shine like silver. [25] A red colour shines brightly, rose-coloured from one part of the sky, fiery from the other. Orion, flashing red, is spread out over a vast distance; a small space contains the constellation of the Pleiads in conjunction. As the sun sets,

15. discrimina] Discrimen: glabella, periculum, differencia ut hic.
18. Vsum] vtilitatem.

Hesperus occasu solis set Lucifer ortu
30   regnat; quod regnum sit breue, stella docet.
Plaustra regens Zephiri non nouit regna Boetes;
    Arcton tam terio quam Cinosura colit.
Quinque paralellis speram distingue, coluro
    Bino; set zonas aeris esse dabis.
35 Discernit uolucres locus, ars, sonus, esca, potestas,
    Calliditas, forme gloria, prolis amor.

Mergus aquas, heremum turtur, siluamque palumbes,
    Noctua busta colit, set philomena rubos.
Passer tecta, cauum cuculus petreque foramen
40   Fida ministra Noe fictaque Cilla colit.
Turres coruus amat; in ramis prouida cornix
    Suspendit nidum; psitacus horret aquas.
Ingenuas uolucres regit ars, informat, adaptat,
    Instruit; instructis prompcior usus adest.
45 Excitat ingenium natura, set ars iuuat, vsus
    Perficit; ars languet, ni repetatur opus.
Pro specie uaria lex est diuersa sonorum;
    Emittit uarios turba sonora sonos.
Regia clangit auis, uariis minturnit hirundo
50   Questibus, at turtur atque columba gemunt.
Que uentrem purgat rostro crepitans crotalizat;
    Nugatur cuculus, laudat alauda diem.
Drensat olor, pulpat uultur; coruum crocitare,
    Te cupidum prede, milue, lupire ferunt.
55 Plipiat accipiter, Iunonis paupulat ales,
    Zinziat hinc merulus, hinc philomena canit.
Grus gruit, at sclingens anser strepit inter olores;
    Perdices cacabant, leta tetrissat anas.
Soccitat hinc turdus, hinc sturnus passitat; ales
60   Ticiat hinc nomen a paciendo trahens.

---

42. horret **M**, horre **P**   49. minturnit **M**, mumurat **P**   51. Que **M**, Quem **P**
53. Drensat **M**, Drensit **P**   58. tetrissat *ed.,* tretrissat **PM**

the evening star is dominant, but when it rises, it holds sway as the morning star. The morning star teaches (us) that dominion lasts but a short time. [30] Bootes that rules the plough knows nothing of Zephyr's domain; it is in the north that the Plough Ox dwells, just as does the Bear. Mark off the globe with five parallels, with two great circles passing through the poles; but you will grant the existence of celestial zones in heaven's vault.

Birds are differentiated by habitat, behaviour, sound, food, power, [35] cunning, glory of form and affection for their offspring.

The habitats birds cultivate

The diver inhabits water, the turtle-dove deserted places, and doves the forest; the little owl frequents tombs, but the nightingale lives in prickly bushes. The sparrow makes its home on rooftops, the cuckoo in a hollow, and Noah's faithful servant and the deceitful Scylla in a rocky opening. [40] The raven loves towers; the provident crow builds its nest amid branches, while parrots shudder at water.

Art governs gentle birds; it moulds, adapts and instructs them. The exercize (of art) is more practicable for the instructed. Nature stimulates the intellect, but the methods of art support it and experience [45] perfects it. Art grows feeble, if the labour is not undertaken anew.

The law governing sounds differs according to the various species; the tuneful throng (of birds) emits sounds that differ in each case. The royal bird screams; the swallow twitters with numerous complaints in varied tones, but the turtle-dove and dove moan. [50] Clattering with the bill that cleans its breast, (the stork) rattles, the cuckoo talks nonsense, while the lark hymns the day. The swan cries; the vulture utters his distinctive sound. They say that the raven croaks, that the kite emits a peculiar cry when eager for prey. The hawk shrieks, while Juno's bird has a sound all its own; [55] from one side the blackbird utters a characteristic sound, from the other the nightingale sings. The crane crun-kles, but the goose cackles and clamours among the swans. Partridges emit a particular sound; the duck quacks happily. From one side comes the sound of the thrush, from the other a starling utters its distinctive song; next, a cry from the bird that acquires a name from its

30. Stacius: *Non parcit populo regnum breue* [Stat., *Theb.* 2, 446; Walther, *Prov.* 18197].
59. ales] scilicet passer.

Fringuliunt graculi, cucubit que luce sepulcra
    Incolit et noctes sollicitare solet.
Psitace, dulcifluo demulces aera cantu;
    Clamitat irritans gabio gesticulans:
65   Nunc se conformat reliquis modulamine leto,
    Ludens nunc proprios gaudet habere sonos;
Hinnitu mentitur equum, se risibus aptat;
    Nunc gemit et gemitum turturis esse putes.
Turba minor uolucrum dulci modulos modulatu
70   Dat quociens lux est leta, serena dies.
Plebs minor in laudes exurgit sedula, quando
    Desuper irradians gratia lucis adest.
Inter aues etiam solus mas gaudia mentis
    Declarat cantu deliciisque soni.
75   Feminei mores non flectunt numina cantu.
    Uirgo pudicicia se probet esse marem.
Non epulis saturare famem Iunonius ales,
    Non ullo nouit uincere fonte sitim:
Solis eum feruor alit, aure pabula libat;
80   Sepe dat equoreus huic alimenta uapor.
Nunc lacrimis thuris et succo uiuit amomi,
    Si uatum dictis est adhibenda fides.
Ficedulam recreat ficus cum dulcibus uuis;
    Frugifere Cereris grana columba legit.
85   Exilem solo uenatur hyrundo uolatu
f. 219ra   Predam, se modico papilione cibans.
Musca, culex, bibio cibat hanc cinifumque popellus
    et cibus est illi deliciosus apes.
Uenatur lepores Iouis ales; predo sinister
90   Aufert fecunde pignora grata sui.
Sepe parens fido coram custode querelam
    Deponens fetu stat uiduata suo.
Balatu tantos exponit mesta dolores;
    Quid? genius resim nouit habere suam.

---

61. graculi *ed.,* grabuli **P**   **81.** Nunc **PM** [cf. Ov., *Met.* 15, 393]   **84.** Cereris *Hall*; **M** terens **P**   **88.** est **M**, et **P**

suffering. **[60]** The jackdaws twitter, and the owl hoots, as by day it inhabits tombs and regularly troubles the night. The parrot entrances the air with a melodious song. The parrot with its gestures annoys as it continually squawks. At one moment he patterns himself after the rest in a pleasing harmony, **[65]** at another he plays and enjoys having his own sounds. Whinnying, it mimics a horse; it adapts itself to laughing. The moment it groans, you would think that it was the moaning of a turtle-dove.

The lesser host of birds emits melodies in sweet harmony, whenever the light pleases them and the day is cloudless. **[70]** When the grace of light attends them, shedding its rays from above, a smaller crowd devotedly rises up to sing its praises. Also among birds, the male alone proclaims the joys in its mind through song and sounds of delight. Feminine ways do not appease divine will with song. **[75]** Through chastity a virgin may prove herself to be masculine.

Juno's bird does not know how to satisfy its hunger with dainties, nor how to overcome its thirst from any fountain. The sun's heat provides it with food; it sips on the sustenance of a breeeze; often vapour from the sea provides it with nourishment. **[80]** Now, if we are to believe the pronouncements of poets, it lives on the gum of frankincense and the juice of amomum. The fig tree refreshes the fig-pecker with its sweet grapes and the dove selects the seeds of fruit-bringing Ceres. Only when the swallow is in flight does it hunt its slender prey, **[85]** feeding itself on a small butterfly. The fly, gnat, insects and a host of stinging insects provide food for this (bird), while the bee is also a delightful delicacy for it.

Jupiter's bird hunts hares; a dreaded predator, it carries off the darling offspring of the fertile sow. **[90]** Often, in the presence of its loyal guardian, a mother lays aside her mournful cry and stands firm, now bereft of her own young. In her misery she expresses her great sorrows by bleating. What? Natural instinct knows how to harness its own ex-

---

61. sepulcra] scilicet Noctua.
71, 74, 75. Adaptacio.
81. Ouidius.
94. resim] Naturam uel rationem.

95   Aurifrisius est unde populator; in esum
         Pisces, ut ferrum strucio, sumit auens.
      Accipitri perdix, ut Niso Cilla, fit esus;
         Aere contentum cameleonta ferunt.
      Illicitur coruus cornixque cadauere uili;
100   Alcinoi fructus plurima turba rapit.
      Confertur uolucri Iouiali magna potestas,
         Que clangore suo sistere cogit aues.
      In dumis predam latitantem cernit ab alto;
         Virtutis ualide strenuitate uiget.
105   Rupta prius series Fatorum fila renodat,
         Dum fenix lucem set renouatus adit.
      Strucio fulgentis radii uirtute tenellam
         Inclusam prolem rumpere claustra iubet.
      Accipitris clamor quibus incubat oua columbe
110   Auditus subito degenerare facit.
      Vocis perdicum tanta est uis, tanta potestas:
         Ad proprium redeunt agmina parua patrem;
      Instinctu genii pulsantis ad hostia cordis,
         Nutricem spernit paruula turba suam.
115   Membra paterna fouet plumis nudata sub alis
         Ales quem sub aquis frigida claudit yemps.
      O pietas! o nature ueneranda potestas!
         Proles obsequiis incipit esse parens;
      Indiga subsidii plumali ueste reiecta
120   Mater quem genuit gaudet habere patrem.
      Cesareum munus quod digestiua caloris
         Vis cito consumpsit, exitiale fuit.
      Corue, tibi «chere» nocuit tociens repetitum;
         Aurum larga manus misit, auara necem.
125   Est et simplicitas quarundam digna fauore:
         en cultrix heremi simplicitate placet,
      Et quas Phasis alit, quas Grecia nutrit, auisque

---

120. Mater **M**, Matre **P**   **127.** nutrit **M**, mittit **P**

pression. The osprey hunts in the deep; ravening for food, [95] it consumes fish, as the ostrich (swallows) iron. The partridge becomes a
meal for the hawk, as the ciris for the sea-eagle. Tradition holds that
the chameleon lives contentedly on air. The raven and the crow are
enticed by vile corpses. Most of the flock are eager to peck at Alcinous's fruit. [100]

Great power is conferred on Jupiter's bird, which compels birds to
stop in their tracks when they hear its screech. From on high it observes its prey lurking in thorn bushes. It is powerful with the energy
supplied by mighty strength.

The succession of Fates reties the threads that were previously broken, [105] as the phoenix approaches the light, but renewed.

The ostrich through the power inherent in the gleaming ray (of its
eyes) commands its tender offspring to shatter the bars that enclose them.

The hawk's screech, once heard, causes the eggs upon which the
dove sits to degenerate in a moment. [110]

The partridge's voice possesses immense force and great power; columns of its young troop back to their own father. Through the instinct
of the power that beats against the door of the heart, the crowd of small
birds rejects its own wet-nurse.

The bird enclosed by icy winter beneath the waters warms under its
wings the limbs of a father, who has been stripped of his feathers. [115]
What devotion! How nature's power deserves veneration! Through its
allegiance the offspring begins to be a parent. Her covering of feathers
cast off, the mother, in need of assistance, rejoices to have as her pro-
tector the child whom it produced. [120]

Caesar's gift, which the digestive power of heat quickly consumed,
was fatal. Raven, the «hail!» you so often repeated brought you to
harm; a bountiful hand sent gold, a greedy one death.

The simplicity of certain birds also merits favour. [125] Observe: the
bird that cultivates lonely places is pleasing in its simplicity, as (are the
birds) which Phasis nourishes, which Greece rears, as is the bird which

---

108. claustra] id est scalam oui.
123. chere] Chere cesar anichos Basileos (cf. *Fulgentii super Thebaiden Commentariolum* 91 [ed.
Sweeney, 701]) with *salue Inuicte rex* written superscript over the first, third and fourth words.
126. cultrix] scilicet turtur.
127. phasis] phasiani; grecia] picturate galline.

Quam reddit celebrem ramus, oliua, tuus.
Insignes reddit alias astucia: passer

130   Aucupis euitat recia, furta, dolos.
Cornix munitas acies rostro crepitante
    Ducit et officium gaudet habere ducis.
Preuidet hostiles concursus, prelia, casus;
    Nunc instare docet, nunc simulare fugam.

135 Grus casu lapidis predicit callida fraudes
    Et replet ipsius sepe saburra pedes.
Quin mansuescat obesse nequit prescripcio longi
    Temporis; applaudit, gesticulatur ouans.
Ludit adulatrix pro nucibus aspicientis;

140   Vt manus hortatur, motibus apta salit.
Nunc sese tensis extollit leniter alis,
    Sepe mouet corpus articulosque pedum;
Remigio nunc alarum se subuehit, hinc se
    Submittens giros circinat ima petens.

145 It redit, hinc equor metitur, circuit, inde
    Discurrit motus multiplicando nouos;
Nunc capud attollit, nunc deprimit; inde supinat
    Corpus, ludentes ingerit ore minas.

f. 219rb Archanum radiant oculi iubar, igneus ora

150   Cingit honos, rutilo uertice fulget apex.
Aurea crista capud munit tenebrasque serena
    Luce secat; pennas igneus ambit honos.
Ceruleo uestem depingi flore decoram
    Tinctaque purpureo murice crura putes.

155 Iocundus terror faciei, sidera bina,
    Gratia membrorum, forma, figura, decor
Commendant aquilam; fenici gloria forme
    Maior, plus aquile strenuitatis inest.
Depingit ludens uario Natura colore

160   Pauonem; superis forma uenusta placet.
Delectat uisum formosus Phasidos ales;

138. applaudit **M,** aplaudit **P**; gesticulantur **P** *with expunction marks under* **n**   **141.**
tensis *ed.,* extensis **P,** excelsis **M**   **145.** It **M,** Id **P**   **157.** Commendant **M,** Commendat **P**

the branch of the olive tree made famous. Cunning renders other (birds) remarkable; the sparrow avoids the nets, deceptions and stratagems of the fowler. [130]

As its bill rattles, the crow leads the serried ranks and enjoys having a leader's duty. It foresees hostile encounters, battles, and mishaps. Now it instructs (the birds it leads) to take a stand, now to feign flight.

By dropping a stone the cunning crane announces traps in advance [135] and sand frequently fills its talons. Lengthy superannuation cannot hinder it from becoming gentle. It applauds and makes joyful gestures. It fawns and frolics before the nods of an onlooker; as a hand urges it on, it leaps in concert with the movements. [140] Now it gently lifts itself up on extended wings; it often moves its body and the joints of its feet; at another time it raises itself up, using its wings as oars; next, as it makes for the lower reaches, it lets itself downwards and wheels through circling movements. It goes and returns; after that, it traverses the sea, moves in a circle, [145] then it runs around multiplying its new movements. Now it lifts up its head, now it presses it down; next it bends its body backwards; with its beak it executes playful threats.

Its eyes radiate a mysterious gleam; a fiery glory surrounds its face; a crest flashes on its red head. [150] A golden crest protects its head and cuts the darkness with its clear light. A fiery grace encircles its wings. You would think that the plumage, beautiful with its blue flowers, was painted and that its legs were dyed with a crimson purple.

A pleasing ferocity of appearance, two star-like eyes, [155] the grace of its limbs, its form, shape and beauty commend the eagle; the phoenix possesses greater glory of beauty, (but) the eagle possesses more strength.

In playful mood Nature painted the peacock in various hues; its graceful shape brings pleasure to the gods. [160] The handsome bird of Phasis delights the faculty of sight; the hawk, I admit, pleases me more with its beauty. This bird's wings are suitably marked with variegated spots.

---

128. tuus] scilicet columba.
149. Claudianus.

Accipitrix, fateor, plus mihi forma placet.
Hic maculis plumas uariis distinguitur apte;
    Que uisum recreat, plurima restat auis.
165 Restat fidus amans demulcens aera rauco
    Murmure; restat adhuc altilis apta coco.
Restat piscator quedam pictura potentis
    Nature; restant et Palamedis aues
Et solus qui sentit olor discrimine quanto
170   Viuitur et spreto funere cantor obit.
Hic niueo candore nitet, set ueste uirenti
    Psitacus ornatur, plus tamen ore placet.
Sepe colit lumbos Ueneri gratissimus ales
    Qui prolem tenere diligit atque parem.
175 Indulges soboli renouande, callide passer;
    Regia multiplicat nobile parra genus.
Non numquam cignus octona prole superbit,
    Que mensas ditat ceu Palamedis auis.

Arboreos etiam fetus herbasque salubres
180   Distinguit, signat, separat alta Noys.
Humentique loco prefert loca saxea buxus,
    Que nux alta uelud Phillidis arbor amat.
Ut platanus riuo gaudet, sic populus unda;
    Ut uitis colles, sic iuga cedrus amat.
185 Sambuccus floris usu laudabilis apta est
    Parthorum bellis; inuida taxus api.
Ruscus inhorrescens et eisdem ramnus in armis
    Non nisi callosas extimuere manus.
Aspera castaneas toga uestit, pilleus ornat
190   Glandem, lanugo Persica, testa nucem.
Testa toga uiridi uestitur, set leuis instar
    Interule nucleum proxima uestis obit.
Baccis ditatur laurus uiridissima, Phebi
    Primus amor, cui uix seuior aura nocet.

---

169. solus **M**, salus **P**   **178.** auis *ed.*, aues **P**, ales **M**; ceu *ed.*, seu **P**   **181.** buxus
M, ruxus **P**

Many a bird remains to refresh the eyes. There remains the faithful lover soothing the air with its hoarse cooing; [165] in addition, there remains a fattened fowl suitable for the cook. There remains the fisher, a painting executed by powerful Nature; there also remain Palamedes's birds. And the swan, which alone perceives with what great danger life is lived, spurns death and dies singing. [170] This (bird) is resplendent in his snowy whiteness; but the parrot is decked out in green plumage; however, it gives more pleasure with its mouth.

Venus's most darling bird, who shows tender love for its offspring and partner, cultivates its loins frequently. Clever sparrow, you are kind to your progeny which deserve to be renewed. [175] The regal owl multiplies its noble line. Sometimes the swan glories in offspring eight at a time, like the bird of Palamedes, which enrichs tables.

On trees

Lofty Noys likewise classifies, marks, and distinguishes between burgeoning trees and health-giving plants. [180] And the box-tree prefers rocky locations to a moist terrain, places which the tall almond-tree loves, as if it were the tree of Phyllis. As the plane tree thrives near a brook, so the poplar enjoys water; as the vine loves hills, so the cedar flourishes on ridges.

The elder-tree, praised for the enjoyment its flowers give, is suitable for wars against Parthians; [185] the yew-tree is ill-disposed to bees. The bristling butcher's broom and the buckthorn, bearing the same arms, fear nothing except hardened hands. A rough garment drapes the chestnut, a hat adorns the acorn, down covers peaches, and a shell encases the nut. [190] The shell is clothed in a green dress, but a wrapping surrounds the centre closely like a light undergarment.

The laurel in its deepest green, Phoebus's first love, is enriched with berries; a rather violent breeze inflicts hardly any damage upon it.

165. amans] scilicet turtur.
169-70. Bernardus.
172. ore] scilicet cantu.
173. ales] scilicet columba.
178. aues] scilicet grues.
183-4. Ouidius.
187-88. Bernardus.
192. obit] idest circuit.

195 Anno, palma, tibi decies deno reuoluto
    Dactilici fructus gloria prima datur.
Stipitis inferior pars est angusta: decentem
    Elate poteris assimilare comam.
Effugat a bustis uermes redigique cadauer
200   In cinerem Cinare filia Mirra uetat.
Uitis odora fugat serpentes floris odore
    Verni, dum gemmas parturit ipsa nouas.
Cum stellis euo contendere uelle uidetur
    Cedrus; in hac modicum tempora iuris habent.
205 Dissimilem, cum sit corrumpi nescia, cedrum
    Virginibus nostri temporis esse putes;
Legibus hec etiam cum sit putredinis expers,
    Dispar humane condicionis erit.
Quod uirtus hebeni non cedit uiribus ignis
210   Vesta stupet, queritur Lemnius, Ethna gemit.
Duriciam ferri dolet a ligno superari
f. 219va   Ciclops, quod reddit purius ignis edax.
Philosophus nescit que subsit causa dolore
    Defectus; Driades gaudia uana fouent.
215 Ex hebeno constructa fuit municio tuta
    Quam Macedo cinxit obsidione diu.
Teda uolat cum fomentis ignita, set ignis
    Sese ui lambens ligna carere stupet.
Lignea materies se conseruauit in esse
220   Nec septis languens flamma nocere potest.
Seruatrix hebeni ridet Natura; stupescit
    Rex; dehinc ad reliquam confugit artis opem.
Quid quod non aliud adeo nigredo uenustat
    Lignum? uix aliquid nigrius esse potest.
225 Nigram se set formosam dilecta fatetur;
    Formosam uirtus, dat labor esse nigram,
Set non exurit ignisue libidinis ardens
    Aut ire feruor inpacientis eam.
Fraxinus artificis manibus parere parata
230   Quem sitit humano tincta cruore madet,

198. poteris *Reeve*; **M**, pontis **P**   203. contendere **M**, contende **P**   213. que **M**, quem **P**

When a hundred years have rolled around, to you, palm tree, [195] the first glory of the date's fruit is yielded. The lower part of the trunk is narrow; you will be able to describe the graceful foliage of the palm's new growth by means of a comparison.

Mirra, the daughter of Cinyras, causes worms to flee from tombs and prevents corpses from being reduced to dust. [200] With the fragrance of its vernal flower, the redolent vine causes serpents to flee, while it produces new buds itself.

The yew-tree appears to want to compete in time with the stars; in this, the ages have a modicum of right. Since it is innocent of corruption, you may think that the yew-tree [205] bears no similarity to young women. Further, since the yew is devoid of putrefaction, it will bear no likeness to the laws of the human condition.

Vesta remains entranced, the Lemnian complains, and Etna groans, [210] because ebony's force does not succumb to the power of fire. The Cyclops grieves that the hardness of iron, which consuming flames render more refined, is overpowered by wood. In anguish, the philosopher does not know the underlying cause of the deficiency. The wood-nymphs cherish illusory joys. The fortification [215] which the Macedonian surrounded during a lengthy siege was securely built out of ebony. A torch ablaze with incendiary materials flies through the air, but as it licks itself, it is amazed that the wood remains unaffected by the fire's force. The wooden material has preserved itself to live on and the languishing flame lacks the power to harm the people fenced in. [220] A laugh issues from nature, ebony's protective patron. The king's astonishment grows; then he resorts to the remaining resources of his craft. What are we to make of the fact that blackness graces no other wood to such a degree? There can scarcely be anything more black in existence. The beloved confesses that she is black, but beautiful. [225] Virtue permits her to remain beautiful, suffering to be black. But she is seared neither by lust's ardent fire nor by the heat of intolerable anger.

The ash, prepared to comply with a craftman's hands, is dyed and drenched in the human blood it thirsts for. [230] And the cypress, suit-

225. fatetur] mistice.

Aptaque funereis pompis seruire cupressus
     Fetores placido uincit odore graues.
Fertur idonea materies abiegna galeis
     Et didicit tumido carbasa ferre sinu.
235   At quernum robur solida conpage carinas
     Robustas nectit ne tabulata gemant.
Mora gerit celsus foliis ornata uenustis,
     Pirrame, flos iuuenum, sanguine tincta tuo.
At pirus exurgens superas petit ignea partes
240   Fructus precipui nobilitate potens.
Ni Bachus desit, pira sunt gratissima cene;
     Leticie potus subsidium dat eis.
Ornatu placidi uestiris, amigdale, floris
     Et reliquas tempus anticipando preis.
245   At uariis morbis que gignis amigdala prosunt:
     Lac confert; nucleus utilis esse solet.
Coctana Uulcani lento decocta uapore
     Castaneeque nuces atque uolema placent.
Intellectum dat uexacio, sicut oliue
250   Augmentum fructus tunsio crebra dabit.
Armatum Neptunus equum produxit Athenis;
     Quam tribuit Pallas, pluris oliua fuit.
Det Neptunus opes uarias, det furta, rapinas;
     Bella ciat; pacis gloria maior erit.
255   Deliciis breuibus cerasus ieiunia soluit
     Aut obsonia dat tempore grata suo.
Mespila brumali iam iam decocta pruina
     Quamuis constipent stipticitate iuuant.
Cerea sunt quedam melliti pruna saporis,
260   Quedam iam uicta ponticitate placent.
Pampineas uites sibi federe nectit amico
     Vlmus et est Bachi fida ministra sui.

En diuina Noys herbas discernit ab herbis;
     Vires atque color, forma locusque probant.

---

255. cerasus *ed.,* cerasis **P**, casus **M**   **256.** obsonia **M**, obsenia **P**

able for service in funeral processions, overcomes the heavy stench
with its pleasing fragrance.

Fir is said to be suitable material for ships and it has learned to support sails as they swell and billow. But it is the strength of oak that links
in firm construction [235] the solid keels so as to prevent the boarded
deck from groaning.

The mulberry, decked out with graceful leaves, produces blackber-
ries that are dyed with your blood, Pirramus, flower among young
men.

But the fiery pear tree rises upward and makes for the upper regions,
mighty and renowned for its extraordinary fruit. [240] If accompanied
by wine, pears are extremely agreeable for dinner. The drink of happiness offers them assistance.

Almond tree, you are covered and adorned with pleasing flowers
and you precede other trees by anticipating time. But the almonds you
produce are beneficial for various diseases; [245] it contributes milk;
the kernel is generally useful.

Figs, when cooked over the slow heat of a fire, are delicious, as are
chestnuts and pears. Tribulation brings understanding, just as frequently pounding an olive will increase the supply of the fruit. [250] Neptune brought forth a winged horse for Athens. The olive that Pallas
conferred was of more value. Let Neptune offer his various resources,
let him unlease robbery and rapine, let him stir up battles: the glory of
peace will be greater.

With its short-lived delights the cherry tree breaks periods of fasting
[255] and supplies an agreeable fruit in its own season.

Although medlars bind the bowels, they offer a pleasing astringency,
after their wintry frost has been reduced by boiling for a time.

Some wax-coloured plums have the taste of honey; certain ones are
delightful, once their briny taste has been overcome. [260] The elm
tree binds to itself in a loving union vines and their tendrils, and is a
loyal instrument of Bacchus, its lord.

On plants

Look! Divine Noys is separating plant from plant; their properties
and colour as well as their shape and location recommend them.

265 Optima matricis est artemesia mater;
 Vim dat ei, uires deliciosus honos.
 Abrotanum non uos, pectus, precordia, lumbi,
 Solatur; contra sumpta uenena iuuat.
 At stomachum recreant abscinthia cocta liquore
270 Aerio: nardus si societur, epar;
 Spleni succurrunt, set si socientur aceto,
 Vulneribusque nouis trita iuuamen erunt.
 Tussi succurret urtica resumpta frequenter;
 Ictericis confert associata mero.
f. 219vb 275 At semen colicis sumptum cum melle medetur;
 Stat cruor emanans hac ope fronte lita.
 Litigat et podagra Diodorus, Flacce, laborat.
 Set nil patrono porrigit: hec ciragra est.
 Pulmoni sterili, podagre uentrisque tumori
280 Atque uenenatis morsibus addit opem.
 Sanant quos serpens uel scorpius intulit ictus;
 Lumbricos molles allia sumpta necant.
 Asmaticis confert, sedat plantago tumores;
 Subuenit ydropicis morsibus apta canis.
285 Arteticos, sciazim, matricem, menstrua, tussim,
 Pulmonem, pectus, lumina ruta iuuat.
 Ydropicis, spleni confert apium iecorique,
 feniculi succus si societur ei.
 Malua iuuans emoptoicos lapidemque resoluens
290 Duricias sedat, morsibus apta salus.
 Luminibus confert et uirge curat anetum
 Vlcera; nutricis ubera lacte replet.
 Bethonice uirtus auris capitisque dolori,
 Fracture capitis, ydropicis dat opem.
295 Vulneribus set et antraci sauina medetur
 Et morbis quos uis frigiditatis alit.
 Inuideat, conuicia det Fenenna frequenter;
 Si porrum sumas, conferet, Anna, tibi.
 Ebrietatis honus, si crudum sumpseris illud,
300 Alleuiat; contra sumpta uenena facit.

---

267. lumbi *ed.,* lumbos **PM**   **278.** ciragra *ed.,* cirogra **P**   **292.** Vlcera *ed.,* Vulnera **P**

Mugwort is the womb's best mother; **[265]** rich honour confers force and power upon it. Southernwood brings no consolation to the chest, breast and loins; it is effective when taken against poisons. But wormwood, when cooked in a frothy liquid, refreshes the stomach; if nard is added, it restores the liver. **[270]** But if joined to wine, it assists the spleen and, when ground up, will assist in treating fresh wounds. Nettle, if taken up frequently, will relieve a cough; when joined with wine it confers benefits on the jaundiced. But the seed, when taken with honey, heals those suffering from colic. **[275]** Blood flowing from a forehead congeals when smeared with this resource. Diodorus is in the courts, Flaccus, and suffering from gout, but nothing reaches out to the patron; this is a disease of the hand. It brings relief to an unproductive lung, to gout, to swelling in the belly and to poisonous bites. **[280]**

Garlic cures any blows inflicted by a snake or a scorpion; when ingested, garlic destroys soft intestinal worms. Plantain benefits asthmatics and reduces tumours; it is suitable for dog bites and assists those with dropsy. Rue is beneficial for the arthritic, sciatica, the womb, menses, coughing, **[285]** the lung, chest and eyes. Parsley confers benefits on people with dropsy, the spleen and the liver, if the essence of fennel is added to it. Mallow helps people who spit up blood and it breaks up the stone; it reduces any hardness and is a suitable remedy for bites. **[290]** Anise is beneficial for the eyes and for sores on the penis; it fills nurses's breasts with milk.

The power of betony provides assistance for pains in the ear and head, for head fractures and for the dropsical. Savin cures wounds, but virulent ulcers as well, **[295]** and diseases which the force of coldness maintains. Let Fennenna be envious, and let her hurl frequent insults; if you take a leek, Anna, it will benefit you. If you eat the leek raw, it alleviates the heaviness of the drunken state; it is active, when applied, against poisons. **[300]** Chamomile, a plant with a short life, when

---

277. Litigat] Marcialis: *Litigat et podagra Diodorus, Flacce, laborat. / Set nil patrono porrigit: hec ciragra est* [Mart., 1, 98].
284. canis] Qui fetidum habent anhelitum.

Herba breuis camamilla mero sociata lapillum
  Dissipat; egilopas yctericosque iuuat.
Nepta febri, sciasi confert stomachoque lepreque
  Que notum nomen ex elephante trahit.
305 Pulegium purgat pectus pellitque secundas;
  Spasmum cum podagra, dira uenena fugat.
Renibus, ydropisis, pulmoni luminibusque
  Auribus et stomacho uis maratri dat opem.
Accidule uirtus fastidia tollit et herpes
310   Et fluxus uentris indiget eius ope.
Portulaca febrem que causon dicitur arcet
  Nec soles capiti sumpta nocere sinit.
Que stomacho confert minuit lactuca calorem
  Et nutrix sompni sompnia uana fugat.
315 Celestis color est aurora iudice uernans
  Qui dici roseus purpureusue potest.
Illa rose gaudet se concessisse colorem
  Vultus quo superis terrigenisque placet.
Ergo rosam specie flores excellere censes;
320   Si non, aurore protinus hostis eris.
Quid? si Tersites, si Birria, si Dauus extas,
  Indicet rutilans prelia mane tibi.
Set quid? Mira rose uirtus speciem superare
  Noscitur et laudes utilitatis habet.
325 Igni namque sacro, capiti stomachoque medetur;
  Cedit ei feruor noxius atque dolor.
Set qua<m> sit fragilis species, quam sit fugitiua,
  Vernantis monstrat forma uenusta rose.
Vespera cernit anum quam uidit mane puellam;
330   Non mensis set anum perficit una dies.
Lilia sunt casti designatiua pudoris;
  Vt rosa, martirium significare solet.
Lilia uirgo manu, confessor lilia gestat;
  Lilia mons celi, lilia uallis habet.
335 Que generat tellus celestia lilia fient;
  Sic qui sunt uallis lilia, montis erunt.

313. Que *ed.*, Quem **P**   321. Birria *ed.*, buria **P**; Dauus *ed.*, danus **P**

joined to wine, dissolves the stone; it assists people suffering from dis-
eased eyes and jaundice. Cat-mint is beneficial for fever, sciatica, the
stomach and leprosy; the last draws the name by which it is known
from the elephant. Penny-royal purges the chest and expels the after-
birth; [305] it drives away spasms, gout and terrible poisons.

Fennel's power provides relief to kidneys, people with dropsy, the
lungs, the eyes, the ears and the stomach. Sorrel has the power to remove lack of appetite; both shingles and efflux from the belly require
its assistance. [310] Purslane prevents the fever which is called causon;
when taken, it prevents the sun's heat from harming the head. Lettuce,
which is good for the stomach, reduces heat and as it promotes sleep,
it chases away empty dreams.

As it blossoms, the colour, which can be termed rosy or dark red, is
heavenly [315] in dawn's judgement. She is pleased to have conferred
upon the rose a colour, by which its appearance delights the gods
above and people born on earth. Therefore, you judge that in appearance the rose is superior to (all other) flowers; if you do not, you will
immediately draw dawn's enmity. [320] What? If you live the life of a
Thersites, a Birria, or a Davus, in the morning, when the dawn is red,
she will declare war on you. But what of it? The rose's marvellous
power is known to surpass its appearance and wins praise for its utility.
It cures the holy fire, the head and the stomach; [325] harmful heat and
pain yield before it. But how fragile beauty is, how fugitive, is revealed
by the graceful form of the rose in bloom. Evening looks upon an aged
woman, (the same) person whom she saw as a girl that morning. Not a
month, but a single day completes the process of making her an old
woman. [330]

Lilies are symbolic of chaste modesty; like the rose, it usually signifies martyrdom. The virgin bears lilies in her hand, as does the confessor. The mountain of heaven holds lilies, as does the valley. Lilies produced by the earth will become heavenly. [335] In this way, the lilies
of the valley will be lilies of the mountain. To the hosts of angels will

---

302. egilopas] Egilopa est uicium gingiuarum uel palati.

Ciuibus angelicis cetus, qui celibe uita
f. 220ra
  Vsus in hac ualle est, associandus erit:
E<t> reliquis, quos a lapsu miseracio summa
340   Erexit, paries integer alter erit.
Exustis prosunt membris sedantque tumorem
  Lilia; simplicitas uera tumore caret.
Grata pudicicie comes est niueique pudoris
  Simplicitas; fastus nescit adesse tumor.
345 Quos prius exussit feruore libidinis ignis,
  Mundat mundicie flos niueusque pudor.
Confert letargo satureia, si sit aceto
  Iuncta; senes ad opus hec iuuenile uocat.
Saluia succurret iecori laterisque dolori
350   Et condimentum fruminis esse solet.
Ecclesie uariis ornatur floribus ortus;
  Sunt in eo uiole, lilia mixta rosis.
Ascensus gradibus certis distinguitur apte
  Et ferrugineus flos, niueus, roseus.
355 Incipientes sunt uiole, sunt proficientes
  Lilia, consummat gloria magna rosas.
Felices uiole que tandem lilia fiunt;
  Lilia martirii purpurat inde rosa.
Et uiole gaudent proprie uirtutis honore
360   Quas gestant manibus lilia sepe suis:
Et uiole uiolas et lilia lilia gestant
  Vernantesque gerunt lilia blanda rosas.
Gestantes uiole gestatis pluris habentur,
  Magna licet uirtus concomitetur eas.
365 Nam podagram sedant; oculis capitisque dolori,
  Matrici, tussi lene iuuamen erunt.
Balnea quos recreant mundare ligustica norunt;
  Radix plus foliis utilitatis habet.
Ista iuuant colicos, stomachi sedare querelas
370   Nouerunt; capiti sumpta iuuamen erunt.
Ostrucium iuuat yctericos, depellit abortum;
  Cuius ope stat splen, tussis hanela fugit.

---

371. Ostrucium *ed.*, Astrucium **P**

have to be joined the company which has enjoyed the celibate life in this vale. And for the rest, whom perfect compassion raised up after a fall, there will be another wall, intact. **[340]**

Lilies are beneficial for burned limbs and they reduce swelling; true simplicity lacks arrogance. Simplicity is the agreeable companion of modesty and of snow-white chastity; the arrogance of pride cannot attend it. The flower of purity and modesty, white as snow, cleanses those whom the fires of lust have previously seared with its heat. **[345]**

Savory, if joined to vinegar, brings relief to a lethargic person; this plant summons old men to act as the young do. Wood sage will provide relief to the liver and pains in the side and it is usual to find it as a spice for gruel. **[350]**

The church's garden is adorned with flowers of different colours; it contains violets and lilies, mingled with roses. The flower, dark purple, snow-white and rosy, is suitably marked off by fixed degrees of ascent. Beginners are violets, those in progress **[355]** are lilies, while great glory marks the perfection of roses. Blessed are the violets who finally become lilies; after that, the rose of martyrdom darkens the lilies. Violets, which lilies frequently bear in their own hands, **[360]** also delight in the honour of their own virtue; and violets produce violets and lilies lilies, and enchanting lilies bear blooming roses. Violets that produce are considered of greater worth that those that are produced, although great virtue accompanies them. For they quell the gout and will provide gentle assistance to the eyes, to headaches, to the womb and to coughing. **[365]**

Lovage possesses the power to cleanse those restored by baths. The root has more utility than the leaves. Lovage helps those suffering from colic and knows how to quiet stomach complaints. When taken, it will provide relief for the head. **[370]** Betony helps people with jaundice, and expels a dead fetus. By means of its resources the spleen remains firm and it drives off coughing that causes breathlessness. For malignant

---

342. simplicitas] moraliter [superscript].

Ui cerefolii cancris melli sociati
    Adde merum; laterum causa doloris abit.
375 Lumbrici, tinee, uenter, uomitus, tumor omnis,
    Vertigo capitis ipsius optat opem.
Atriplicis uirtus aluum lenit; sacer ignis
    Cedit ei: podagram cogit inire fugam.
Vnguibus indicit bellum superaddita scabris;
380   Yctericos uino sic sociata iuuat.
Ventrem constipant coriandri semina; febrem
    Cui nomen dat lux tercia grana fugant.
Antraci, veneri, sciasi nasturcia prosunt;
    Horum cum splene glabrio poscit opem.
385 Eruce uirtus urinam prouocat; escas
    Digerit et maculas cogit abire cutis.
Te, lentigo, fugat; tussim pellit puerilem,
    Extrahit os fractum, Cipridis auget opus.
Est cui flos niueo fulget candore papauer,
390   Est cui purpurei gloria f<l>oris adest.
Est quod se roseum mentitur habere colorem;
    Florem subroseum dicere iure potes.
Namque rubet pallor, pallet rubor; vtilitate
    Prestat qui niueo gaudet honore nitor.
395 Id genus et fluxum uentris sedare probatur,
    Indicitque fugam, lenta podagra, tibi.
Cepe poscit opem dens, dissenteria, ficus
    Nudatusque capud glabrio crine suo.
Hec aluum mollit, inducit sumpta soporem;
400   Hec oculos, melli sit sociata, iuuat.
f. 220rb Cardiacis et pulmoni sciasique iuuamen
    Lingua bouis, si sic su<m>pta frequenter erit.
Si Bacho nubat, conuiuas exhilarabit;
    Succus ui coleram purgat utramque sua.
405 Succurrit spleni, tussi sciasique sinapis
    Scrofis, serpentis morsibus atque tisi.
Vulneribus, neruis, ciringis, testibus, uue
    Ardentique febri brassica prebet opem.

---

373. cancris *ed.,* cancer **P**

tumours, add wine combined with chervil's power, joined to honey; the cause of the pain in the side disappears. Intestinal worms, maggots, a swelling belly, vomiting, all tumours, [375] dizziness in the head desire the relief it offers.

Orache's power alleviates the paunch; holy fire yields to it; it forces gout to depart quickly. When added, it declares war on rough nails. When joined to wine, it helps people with jaundice. [380] Coriander seeds pack the belly tight; coriander grains drive off the fever, upon which the third day confers a name. Cress is good for anthrax, sex, and sciatica; a bald head and the spleen demand its assistance. Cole-wort has the power to stimulate urine; it digests food [385] and compels spots on the skin to disappear. It banishes freckles; it drives children's coughing away; it draws out broken fragments of bone and increases sexual activity. There is a poppy whose bloom gleams with a snowy whiteness; there is one which possesses the glory of a crimson flower. [390] There is a (third) flower with pretensions to a rosy colour; you can justly state that the flower is somewhat reddish. For the pallor has a reddish tinge, the red colour is pale. Superior in utility is the brilliant flower which delights in its snowy honour. A flower of that type is a proven remedy for quelling the womb's flux [395] and it proclaims that lingering gout must fly away.

Teeth, dissentery, piles and baldness, a head deprived of its hair, demand the onion's assistance. This vegetable soothes the belly, and when eaten, induces sleep. Add it to honey and it relieves the eyes. [400] Oxtongue, if taken frequently, will provide help to people suffering from cardiac fever, to the lungs and to sciatica. If it is married to wine, it will make guests happy. The power of its juice purges both cholers. Mustard brings immediate relief to the spleen, coughing, sciatica, [405] colic, snake bites and consumption.

Cabbage provides assistance to wounds, sinews, suppurating sores, the testes, the soft palate and burning fever. Parsnip grants relief to

---

372. ope] sepe stillantis ocelli.
395. probatur] ab effectu.
396. marcialis.
f. 220ra bottom: *Dicemus ficus, quas scimus in arbore nasci;/ Dicemus ficus, Ceciliane, tuos* [Mart., 1, 65, 3-4].

Testiculis, epati dat pastinaca leuamen;
410   Votis lasciue Taidis ista fauet.
Origanum nigre colere tussique medetur;
        Aures, ydropicos yctericosque iuuat.
Absolui uinclis stupet indignata frenesis
        Iussis serpilli; splen eget eius ope:
415 Cuius uim laudant epatis tumor et stera; morsus
        Pestifer et uentris torcio cedit ei.
Marrubii uirtus auris laterumque dolori
        Et tisicis letos spondet adesse dies.
Vulnera sanari carnem mordencia lesam
420   Yctericos, tisicos imperiosa iubet.
Aristologie que sperica fertur obedit
        Splen, dens, singultus, fistula, uentris honus.
Enula, purgatrix matricis, renibus aptam
        Prebet opem; clausus cedit abortus ei.
425 Si tibi furetur uocem uiolentia risus
        Raui, subductas reddet ysopus opes.
Exhilarat faciem, pectus dilatat, abibit
        Qui tristis fuerat funereusque color.
Hec si forte tibi crebro sumatur in esum,
430   Ridebit leto letus in ore color.
Que modo rauca fuit uocem iubet esse canoram;
        Lumbricos perimens interiora iuuat.
Singultus, tussim, gemitus, suspiria sedat
        Et reserat uentris hostia clausa prius.
435 Prouocat urinam, deducit menstrua nardus
        Agrestis; sciasim spernere fata iubet.
Instar et ellebori candentis pondere uentrem
        Destituit; iecori sumpta iuuamen erit.
Si Cererem socians mente ieiunia soluas,
440   Vix aer poterit noxius esse tibi.
Lumbricis, mammis, stomacho lingueque medetur
        Atque dolor fugiens auris obedit ei.
Vis ciperi iubet urinam laxare meatus;
        Duricies lapidis cedere gaudet ei.
445 Peonie uirtus fantasmata uana repellit,
        Te quociens uexat, Romule, falsa quies.

the testicles and to the liver. That plant favours the wishes of wanton Thais. [410] Marjoram heals melancholy and coughing; it helps the ears, and people suffering from dropsy and jaundice. Madness is outraged and amazed at being released from its chains, when commanded by wild-thyme. The spleen requires its aid. A swollen liver and the womb praise its efficacy. [415] A pernicious bite and griping in the belly yields to it. The power of horehound guarantees the presence of happy days for sufferers of ear-ache, pleurisy and consumption. It imperiously imposes healing upon wounds that tear damaged flesh, as well as upon people afflicted with jaundice and consumption. [420]

The spleen, teeth, the hiccups, suppurating ulcers and a burdened belly obey the birthwort that is said to be round. Elecampane, which purges the womb, offers suitable assistance to the kidneys; the enclosed fetus yields to its power. If violent and harsh laughter steals your voice away, [425] hyssop will give back the resources that have been withdrawn. It gladdens the face, dilates the lungs; and an appearance which had been gloomy and funereal will disappear. If you happen to take this herb frequently as a meal, a joyful complexion will smile out from a happy face. [430] It commands the voice that was just now hoarse to be tuneful. As it destroys intestinal worms, it assists the innards. It allays the hiccups, coughing, groaning, sighs and opens up the belly's doors that were previously closed.

Wild nard stimulates urine and it brings on the menses; [435] it commands sciatica to scorn the fates. Like white hellebore, it relieves the belly of its burden; when ingested, it will provide assistance to the liver.

If you break a fast by joining grain to mint, the weather will scarcely be able to harm you. [440] It is good for intestinal worms, the breasts, the stomach and the tongue; and ear-ache flees in obedience to it.

Galingale has the power to command urine to loosen the channels. The stone's hardness is happy to yield to it. The peony's strength chases away insubstantial apparitions, [445] whenever, Romulus, deceptive

407. ciringis] fistule scilicet.

Deliciis Bachi sociata stere fugat omnem
    Languorem, Lachesi ducere fila iubens.
Mellis Aristeo celestia dona ministrat
450   Borago uiridis asmaticisque placet.
Inferior regio, testes, uesica, foramen
    Yctericusque petunt senicionis opem.
Occurrit uicio cordis iecorisque potenter;
    Dentibus et strumis utilis esse solet.
455   Grata celidonie uis est oculis maculeque
    Et uicium lesi dentis abire iubet.
Vis centauree sciasi neruisque medetur;
    Lumina, si melli sit sociata, iuuat.
Demulcens pectus colubri colubrina uenenum
460   Sputaque concreto sanguine tincta fugat.
Vulnera gaido sanat sedatque tumores;
    Tantam formidans uim sacer ignis abit.
Ellebori geminas species distingue: superna
f. 220va   Quod candet purgat corporis, ima nigrum.
465   Album quartanas superat tussique silere
    Imperat et stare membra caduca iubet.
Cui Lucina negat lucem subducere partum
    Nouit et indignans mania cedit ei.
Eius ui cedit uertigo, tremor; dat acumen
470   Luminibus; mures puluis abire iubet.
Elleboro nigro paralisis, fistula, uenter,
    Apostema tumens, articulare malum,
Dens, auris, macule, colere cum flegmate parent
    Lepraque cum scabie, fistula, lesa cutis.
475   Conuiuas reddit hilares gratissima Bacho
    Verbene uirtus; oris amica comes
Oris fetorem fugat, oris uulnera curat;
    Ori dulce sapit associata mero.
Plus foliis, uirtute minus ditatur amorem
480   Herba reconcilians; plebs tamen ista canit.
Vulnera consolidat foliorum grata uenustas;
    Cedit deformis forma tumoris eis.

457. neruisque *ed.,* ueriusque **P**   461. *[rubric]* de gai[[l]]done **P**   461. gaido *ed.,*
gaildo **P**   475. hillares **P** *with an expunction mark under the first* **l**.

dreams harrass you. When joined with wine's delights, it dismisses all lethargy in the womb, as it commands Lachesis to spin out the threads. Green borage provides the heavenly gifts of honey to Aristaeus and brings relief to asthmatics. [450]

The lower region, the testes, the bladder, the anus and the jaundiced person seek groundsel's assistance. It powerfully combats heart and liver disease; it is generally useful for teeth and swelling of the lymphatic glands. Celandine has a power that is welcome to eyes and to blemishes [455] and it commands pain to depart from a damaged tooth. Centaury has the power to heal sciatica and warts; if it is joined with honey, it is helpful to eyes.

While soothing the chest, dragonwort drives off snake poison and saliva tinged with congealed blood. [460] Woad heals wounds and reduces tumours; fearing its great power holy fire departs.

Distinguish two kinds of hellebore; the white one purges the body's upper parts, the black kind the lower. White hellebore overcomes quartan agues, imposes silence upon coughs [465] and commands failing limbs to stand firm. It knows how to draw out a fetus, to whom Lucina denies the light of day, and outraged madness yields to its power. Before its force dizzness and trembling depart; it confers acuity upon eyesight. Its powder commands mice to depart this life. [470] Obedient to black hellebore are paralysis, suppurating ulcers, the belly, swelling abscesses, rheumatism, teeth, ears, spots, jaundice, phlegm, leprosy with scabies, suppurating sores and damaged skin.

Vervain, most agreeable to Bacchus, has the power to make guests joyful. [475] The mouth's friendly companion, it banishes bad breath and cures oral sores; when mixed with wine, it tastes sweet in the mouth. The riches of the plant which restores love reside more in the leaves and less in its virtue; yet people sing its praises. [480] The agreeable grace of its foliage solidifies wounds. The shape of an ugly swell-

---

447. stere] matricis.

Cum liquor urine solito cursu caret, illam
    Acri iunge mero; dens eget eius ope.
485   Germandrea iuuat splenem; caliginis umbram
    Subducens oculis, membra calore fouet.
Morsibus occurrit, sordencia uulnera purgat;
    Hanc poscit partus, menstrua, tussis opem.
Dat color a Mauro sumptum tibi nomen; ab auro
490   Conueniens, uires consule, nomen erit.
Apcius esse puto tibi nomen uiribus aptum;
    Si capud amittas, gloria maior adest.
Parte tui dempta si desses, aurea fias
    Aut aurella uelis utilis esse michi.
495   Luminibus fer opem capitis mulcendo dolorem
    Vt te, prurigo, glandula uicta fugit.
Set quid? ni facies rerum diuersa molestet
    Te, strigni species quatuor esse dabis.
Vnius est iocundus odor, placidus sapor; igni
500   Sacro succurrit egilopasque fugat.
Estus infrigdat stomachi, iuuat altera glaucos;
    Illorum morbus ex aue nomen habet.
Ydropicis species alie solacia prebent;
    Succum iunge mero: dentibus aptus erit.
505   Iusquiami species dignissima semine gaudet
    Albo; si queris comoda, pluris erit.
Altera subruffo ditatur, tercia nigro;
    Que medio fertur, usibus apta minus.
Set tibi si prime non suppetit ulla facultas,
510   Accedet uotis sponte secunda tuis.
Ergo recens folium tere quod sociare polente
    Ne pigrites; tumidis hanc superadde locis.
Indignans fugiet tumor omnis; si sit aceto
    Cocta diu, dentes ore retenta iuuat.
515   Quo male uexaris succurrit gallia morbo;
    Matrix cum mammis ipsius optat opem.

---

491. uiribus uiribus aptum **P** *with expunction marks under the second word.*   **493.** si desses *ed.,* didesses? **P**   **513.** tumor *ed.,* timor **P**

ing bows before its power. When urine's water lacks its usual stream, join milfoil to strong wine; teeth require the plant's assistance. Germander helps the spleen; withdrawing the shadow of darkness [485] from eyes, it nurtures limbs with its warmth. It is helpful for bites and cleans dirty wounds. The fetus, menses, and coughing demand this plant's assistance.

Colour confers on you a name taken from a Moor; if you consult its virtues, a suitable name will be derived from gold. [490] I think a name congruent with its powers is more appropriate for you. If you lose your head, a greater glory attends you. If you were deficient, a part of yourself taken away, you would become golden or you would claim to be useful to me as aurella. Bring relief to the eyes as you sooth a head-ache, [495] as a tumour is overcome and flees you, itch. But what of it? If the diverse appearance of reality does not trouble you, you will grant the existence of four kinds of nightshade. One possesses a pleasant fragrance and a pleasing taste; it is helpful for assuaging holy fire and it drives away ocular diseases. [500] The second cools down turbulence in the stomach and helps people suffering from glaucoma. Their disease takes its name from a bird. The other kinds provide relief for the dropsical. Mix the juice in wine; it will be suitable for treating teeth. The most worthwhile kind of henbane delights in a white seed; [505] if you ask about its advantages, it will be of more value. The second kind is enriched with a somewhat reddish seed, the third with a black one. The one which is said to be in the middle is less suitable for applications. But if a supply of the first kind is unavailable to you, the second will willingly accede to your wishes. [510] Therefore, grind a fresh leaf, and you should waste no time in bringing it together with crushed grain; add this on top of places that are swollen. Every abscess will flee in anger. If it is boiled in vinegar for a long time, it helps any teeth retained in the mouth. The aromatic herb relieves the disease with which you are being painfully tormented. [515] The womb and breasts desire its aid. The juice's power,

489. auro] ad maurellam.
498. strigni] Quod et maurella.
515. morbo] scilicet sacro igni.

Auribus infusi succi uirtute necantur
  Vermes; sputa quidem tincta cruore fugat.
Sumpte uis malue uesice tedia tollit
520   Et capitis lixe signa pudenda fugat.
Denti lenimen prebet, depellit abortum
  Egilopasque; sacer hac eget ignis ope.
Membra leuat quassata, fugat uirtute uenena
  Set nec apum lesis tela nocere sinit.
525 Ad combusturas facit, at paratella lapillum
  Comminuit; mundat te, scabiosa cutis.
f. 220vb Menstrua constringit cum uentre comesta; dolori
  Auris succurrit yctericisque placet.
Vulneris abstergit sordes contrita nigella;
530   Indicit lepris imperiosa fugam.
Apostema iubet mollescere, uota secundat
  Lucine; sciasis postulat eius opem.
Ignes extinguit ueneris cu<n>ctosque cicuta
  Feruores nocuos frigiditate potens.
535 Ignis ei cedit sacer atque podagra; papillis
  Herba Terranee gratior esse nequid.
Que laxe fuerant ueris iam flore soluto
  Pomula uirginei pectoris esse putes.
Si uiridi succo folii frons sit lita, rident
540   Lumina que lacrimis inmaduere prius.
Acri cocta mero spleni succurrit; amicam
  Arteticis dat opem yliacisque placet.
Laudibus extollo dampnandam iure cicutam
  Que iussit mundum sole carere suo.
545 Ausa fuit Socrati legem prescribere pene;
  Indignans liquit philosophia solum.
Hasta uirens foliis modicis ornata columbas
  Connexus blando federe quinque gerit.
Illas depingit dulcis ferrugo – uolantes
550   Credas – et uultum simplicitatis habent.
Dum uisu recreor, studium commendo potentis

---

522. Egilopasque *ed.,* Egilipasque **P**   **525.** paratella *ed.,* paralella **P**

when dripped into the ears, is instrumental in destroying worms. It banishes saliva that is tinged with blood. Mallow's force, when taken, relieves discomfort in the bladder and (the power) of its water (?) causes shameful marks on the head to disappear. [520] It affords relief to teeth, it expels the fetus and drives off eye disease. Holy fire needs this plant's assistance. It eases shattered limbs and has the power to rout poisons and it does not permit bee-stings to harm those who have been hurt. It acts against burns, but water-dock diminishes the stone. [525] It cleans rough skin. When ingested, it limits the menses as well as any swelling in the belly. It is helpful for ear-ache and delights those with jaundice.

Black cumin, when crushed, cleans filth from a wound. It imperiously imposes flight upon leprosy. [530] It commands an abscess to soften, it favours prayers to Lucina, and sciatica demands its assistance. Hemlock, powerful in its coldness, extinguishes sexual passion and all harmful fevers. Holy fire and gout yield to it; [535] a herb belonging to the woman from Therapnae could not be more pleasing to breasts. You would think that breasts, which had been flabby, were little apples on a maiden's chest, after their spring bloom had already been released. If the forehead is smeared with green juice from the leaf, eyes that had been drenched in tears now smile. [540] When boiled in strong wine, it relieves the spleen. It affords kindly assistance to the arthritic and finds favour with people suffering from illness in the groin. I extol with praise hemlock that should by right be condemned, for it ordered the world to exist without its own sun. It dared to prescribe a law to punish Socrates. [545] Philosophy abandoned the world in outrage.

The green shaft adorned with modest leaves bears five doves, joined in a charming union. A sweet dusky colour paints them – one would believe that the doves were in flight – and they possess an appearance of simplicity. [550]

While I am refreshed by its appearance, I recommend the study of

---

520. lixe] Lixa est portitor aque. Lucanus loquens de Catone ait: *Stat dum lixa bibat* [Luc., 9, 593].

536. terranee] helene [superscript].

536. f. 220vb bottom: Ouidius: *Probra Teramnee* [= *Therapnaeae*] *se qui dixerat ante marite/Mox cecinit laudes prosperiore lira* [Ov., Ars 3, 49-50].

        Nature, que tam nobile finxit opus.
    Ipse color poterit sibi conciliare fauorem;
        Forma michi quadam simplicitate placet.
555   Set uirtus herbe forme preiudicat eius;
        Dotes uix potero claudere lege metri.
    Set uiole uires non ignotas medicorum
        Vsibus ut proprias uendicat ipsa sibi.
    Quasdam presenti perstrinxi carmine, quasdam
560   Concinis, in laudem scripte libelle Noys.
    Laudes namque tuas alio, Sapiencia, scripsi
        Carmine, quod lector huic sociare potest.
    Quosdam defectus illius carminis istud
        Suplebit; summe seruit utrumque Noy.
565   Defectus agnosco meos, quos carmine prudens
        Supleo presenti; prodeat istud opus,
    Prodeat in lucem quasi lucis opus: tenebrosas
        Iam didicit liuor Ditis adire fores.
    Inclusus numquam superas euadat ad auras,
570   Ne cinice nostrum rodere possit opus.
    Reuma nocens oculis reuocat lenitque tumores,
        Matricem siccat, yliacis dat opem.
    Ano solamen, uentris fastidia tollit,
        Multa subueniens utilitate cocis,
575   Extinguens ignem sacrum sedansque dolorem
        Auricule, prestans commoditate crocus.
    Solis sponsa suas ostentat opes uenienti
        Phebo; claudit eas sole petente solum.
    Solsequium sequitur solem ceruice reflexa
580   Et motu capitis sepe salutat eum.
    Letificat sponsam solis presencia sponsi;
        Absit sol, languet solis amore sui.
    Cum sol humanos solatur luce labores,
        Offert se soli deliciasque suas.
585   Solis in occasu se mesta recondit et intra
        Orbiculos sese colligit ipsa suos.
    Queque die clauso sibi clauditur, et reserato
        Se reserat, solem sponsa secuta suum.

571. nocens *ed.*, nocent **P**   580. eum *ed.*, eam **P**

powerful nature, who has fashioned so noble a creation. Its very colour will be able to win favour for its cause. Shape that has a certain simplicity pleases me. But a plant's power prejudges its form. [555] I will scarcely be competent to encompass her riches within the rules of metre. But she personally claims the violet's powers, which are not unknown to physicians' practices, as special to herself.

I have sketched certain of these in the present poem; the book I have already written celebrates in song certain (others), as it sings the praises of Noys. [560] For, Wisdom, I have written in praise of you in another work, which the reader can append to this one. This poem will supplement certain deficiencies in that one. Both are the servants of Noys on high. I acknowledge my failings, which I supply from my learning in the present poem. [565] Let that book come forth, let it emerge into the light, as if a work of light. Now envy has learned to approach the dark doors of Dis. Imprisoned, never let it make its way into the upper air, so that it may not have any power to gnaw at my work like a dog. [570]

Saffron turns back flux that is harmful to the eyes, soothes tumours, dries the womb, and brings aid to people suffering from illnesses of the groin. It provides relief to the anus and removes discomforts in the belly; it assists cooks with the many uses it can be put to, extinguishes holy fire and soothes ear-ache. [575] The sun's bride displays her riches to Phoebus as he arrives. As the sun heads for the earth, she hides them. The heliotrope follows the sun by bending its neck and frequently greets it by moving her head. [580] The presence of the sun, her betrothed, gladdens the bride. If the sun is away, she languishes with love for the sun, her lord. When the sun consoles mankind at its daily labours, she offers herself and her delights to the sun. At the sun's setting, she hides itself in sadness [585] and gathers herself up within her own little circles. At the close of day, she encloses herself and when the day reappears, she opens herself out, a bride in pursuit of her own sun.

561. sapiencia] o [superscript].

Plantarum species paucas distinximus, et iam
     Se subdit nostro res animata stilo.
Precedant uolucres; ea que descendit ab alto
     Pre foribus nostris regia clangit auis.

Vt uolucres sistunt aquile clangore potenti,
     Sic doctoris erit mox reuocare suos.
Solares radios prolem que ferre recusat,
     Tanquam degenerem regia spernit auis:
Ne cernas uerum si claudis lumina mentis,
     Celestis quod agis gratia spernet opus.
Instar auis dicte studeas reuocare iuuentam;
     Fons uite letas dat nouitatis aquas.
Ne calor ignitus ea cogat degenerare,
     Temperat oua lapis frigiditate potens.
Ne calor ignauus actus deformet honestos,
     Gemma pudicicie celibis ornet eos.
Soliuagi tenui macie confecta canora
     pellicani pellis arida menbra tegit.
Fecunde matri natos Natura ministrat;
     Presumit matrem ledere turba minor.
Seua parens rostro pullos turbacior equo
     Enecat, ha! prolis inmemor, immo sui.
Iam natis orbata suis ad cor redit; iram
     Multiplicat, sese dilacerare studet.
Sanguine respergit prolem; uirtute caloris
     Fomentisque piis perdita uita redit.
Accio perpetue uite meritoria proles
     Est anime, qua<m> lux desuper irradiat.
Set quandoque labor animo fastidia prebet
     Et cor uexatum culpa nociua premit;
Tunc actus studii felicis mortificantur
     Et perimit, ni sors grata reformet eos.
Set confessio sanguineo signata rubore
     Cordis contriti uiuificabit opus.

f. 221ra   590
595
600
605
610
615
620

613. respergit *corrected from* resperget **P**

We have recorded the differences between a few kinds of plants and now the animal realm sets itself before my pen. [590] Let precedence be accorded to birds; the royal bird that descends from on high thunders before my doors.

As birds stand motionless before the eagle's powerful thundering, so it will next be the part of the teacher to summon back his own charges directly. The royal bird rejects as though degenerate an eaglet who refuses to endure the sun's rays. [595] If you close the eyes of your mind to avoid discerning the truth, heaven's grace will reject the work you are pursuing. Like the aforementioned bird, you should endeavour to recover your youth. The fountain of life offers joyful waters of renewal. [600] To prevent fiery heat from causing inevitable degeneration to the eggs, a stone powerful in its coldness tempers them. To avoid the heat of base passion from disfiguring honourable actions, they should be adorned by the gem of celibate chastity.

A tuneful skin covers the withered limbs of the solitary pelican, [605] limbs that are worn out, slender and lean. Nature supplies young to the fertile mother. The younger brood dares to harm its mother. The savage parent, more violent than is right, kills off her brood with her bill; alas! she forgets her own offspring, indeed (even) herself. [610] Now, deprived of her children, she returns to her mind; her rage increases and in a passion she tears herself apart. She sprays her young with blood; through the power of its warmth and nourishment devotedly given, the life she destroyed returns. An action that merits eternal life is the product of the soul, [615] on which light shines down from above. But occasionally toil brings weariness upon the soul and a harmful crime burdens a troubled heart. Then the actions of happy endeavour are annulled and it annihilates them, did not beloved destiny alter them. [620] But a confession, sealed with a blush the colour of blood, will enliven the work of a contrite heart. In the same manner,

587-88. Bernardus.
590. animata] anima uegetata.

Sic proles anime premortua uiuificatur
  Sicque reuiuiscit mortificata prius.
625 Psitacus Oreades demulcet uoce sonora;
  Ingenium, cantus, forma colorque placent.
Set quid? abhorret aquas; cantu sis Orpheus alter,
  Forma Narcisus, pectus Ulixis habes.
Esto: mundiciam detestaris, fugis, horres;
630 Vmbra, uapor, squalor, fumus es, alga, cinis.
Ecce columba gemens occulta foramine petre
  Delicias ueri nutrit amoris amans.
Vulneribus Christi roseo respersa cruore
  Mens lateat; gemitus cantus amantis erit;
635 Mens sine teste gemat, gemitus sit testis amoris;
  Ille dolet uere qui sine teste dolet.
Eligit hec granum dedignans uile cadauer
  Tangere; diuinus sermo sit esca tibi.
Et quod uirgineo creuit feliciter orto
640 Granum triticeum sit tibi certa salus.
Etsi lactea sit caro Thaydis, hanc fatearis
  Carnem fetentem uermibus esse datam.
Simplicitas etiam tanta est; fouet hec alienos
  Que pullos nutrit sedulitate suos.
645 Seruet honestatem propriam moresque suorum
  Qui cupit auctori rite placere suo.
Ecclesie pacem des auctor pacis oliue
  Ramo signate, spiritus alme, tue.
Granis Gessemani te conformato, columbe
650 Istius purus si cupis esse cibus.
Ad nos uera quies, uerus Noe mittat eandem,
  Accipitris ne nos terreat umbra uetus.
f. 221rb Spernit amena loci uiridis nemorosaque Tempe
  Turtur cui sociam fata tulere suam.
655 Coniugii fedus animum carni sociauit;
  Hec sponse nomen optinet, ille uiri.

---

624. reuiuiscit *ed.*, uiuiuiscit **P** remuscit **M**   **628.** Ulixis *ed.*, ulixus **P** ulixes
M   **640.** triticeum **M**, tuticeum **P**   **643.** est u fouet **P** *with expunction marks*
under **u**   **656.** sponse nomen **P** *with a division mark placed after sponse*

the soul's offspring, too early dead, is restored to life and, so too, what was previously dead comes back to life again.

The parrot's sonorous voice soothes the mountain-nymphs; **[625]** its native ability, song, shape and colour are delightful. But what of this? It abhors water; though you may be a second Orpheus when you sing, though another Narcissus in your beauty, you have the courage of Ulysses. So be it! You detest cleanliness, you avoid it and shudder before it; you are but a shadow, steam, filth, smoke, sea-weed and dust. **[630]**

Observe the dove moaning in the hidden opening of a rock; loving-ly it nourishes the delights of true love. Let the mind lie concealed, spattered with the rose-coloured blood of Christ's wounds; a groan will be the lover's song. Let the mind lament without witnesses; lam-entation will be love's witness. **[635]** True grief is felt by a man who grieves when no witness is present. Refusing to touch vile corpses, this bird chooses grain; let the word of God be your sustenance. And let the grain of wheat, which fruitfully grew in the Virgin's garden, be your certain salvation. **[640]** Although Thais's flesh is as white as milk, you must confess that this stinking flesh has been consigned to worms. Great also is its simplicity. This bird, which feeds its own young with continuous care, nurtures the brood of others. Any one who desires to please his Maker aright should preserve his own honour and the mo-rality of his own people. **[645]**

Bountiful Spirit, marked by a branch of your olive tree, may you guarantee and grant peace to the church. If you desire to be the pure food of that dove, **[650]** fashion yourself to the grains of Gethsemani. Let true peace, the true Noe send the same bird to us, so that the hawk's ancient shadow may not terrify us.

When the Fates have carried off the dove's partner, it disdains the pleasures of verdant fields and Tempe's charming glades. A marriage compact united soul to body; **[655]** this female obtains the name of bride, that male the title of husband. The latter rules, the former sub-

---

625. sonora] uel canora.
636. Marcialis.
651. noe] Noe interpretatur quies [cf. Jerome, *Lib. Interp. Hebr. Nom.* 9, 4 (ed. P. Antin, CCSL 72: 69)].

Hic regit, hec regitur; hic imperat, illa tenetur
    Inperio sponsi sponte subesse sui.
Ad frugem uite melioris sepe marita
660   Se suffert; habitu rem probat esse nouo.
Assensum dat uir; decet ut moriatur uterque
    Mundo; par uoti nexus utrumque liget.
Ludi condicio libramine lancis inique
    Pensatur, nisi uir commoriatur here.
665 Ergo uoluptati misere deseruiet Adam,
    Eua deliciis iam moriente suis.
Effert phenicem laus uatum, gloria forme;
    Nam genius uariis cultibus ornat eum.
Hec auis est semper coitus ignara cibique;
670   Purior et potus rarior usus adest.
Felix sobrietas que tot conseruat in annos
    Hanc uolucrem, felix gratia mundicie.
O si uirtutum renouet precordia cordis
    Ignis aromaticus pectus amore replens.
675 Igneus iste calor demulcet rore benigno
    Pectora; naturam seruat, adornat, alit.
Irrorans ignis, fons igneus irrigat ortum
    Mentis; celestis feruet in amne calor.
Strucio desidie tipus et certissimus index
680   Aerias partes nescit adire Iouis.
Aera languenti pennarum uerberat ictu
    Et se Iunonis sub dicione tenet.
Desidie comes est Bromius uentrisque lacunar
    Implere in uotis desidiosus habet.
685 Deglutit ferrum; quem seua iuuant recreari
    Seuis Herodis atque Neronis erit.
Desinit esse parens quociens commendat harene
    Oua, fit et prolis inmemor ipse sue.
Esse tibi prolem mores censebis honestos,
690   Set neglectus in hiis perniciosus erit.
Set ne desperes, ne te demergat abyssus;

---

657. illa **M**, ille **P**   **673.** renouet *ed.*, remouet **P**   **676.** seruat *ed.*, feruat **P**
678. calor *ed.*, color **P**

mits; when he commands, she is bound to be subject voluntarily to the bidding of her own bridegroom. Often, the wife proffers herself to the reward of a better life. Life in a new habit proves the point. [660] The husband gives his assent; it is proper that both should die to the world; let a binding vow tie both together as a pair. In the balance of an unequal scale, the condition is considered to be a mockery, if a husband does not die to his mistress. Therefore, Adam will be a slave to vile pleasure, [665] as Eve now dies amid her particular delights.

The praise of poets and glorious beauty extol the phoenix; for genius adorns it with various refinements. This bird is forever innocent of sexual union and food. It is interested in a somewhat pure and rarer enjoyment of drink. [670] Blessed is the restraint which has preserved this bird for so many years; the grace of chastity is a productive thing. If only the fragrant fire of virtues would fill the breast with love and renew the seat of the heart! That fiery warmth soothes the breast with the dew of kindness; [675] it preserves, adorns and nurtures nature. A bedewing fire and a fiery fountain water the garden of the mind; heaven's glow boils up in the water.

The ostrich, an exemplar and most unerring index of sloth, lacks the ability to approach the airy realms of the sky. [680] With languid blows from its wings, it beats the air and keeps itself under Juno's dominion. Wine keeps sloth company and the sluggard includes among his prayers a wish to fill the vault that is his belly. The ostrich gulps down iron; anyone who delights in savage things to be recreated by cruelties, [685] will be counted a follower of Herod and Nero. The ostrich ceases to be a parent whenever it entrusts its eggs to the sand and personally becomes forgetful about his own young. .

In your case, you will consider the offspring to be honourable behaviour, but negligence in these matters will be destructive. [690] But you should not lose hope, you should not sink into the abyss! The os-

683. Moralitas.

Ad cor et ad sese strucio sepe redit.
Mentem maternus affectus lenit amice;
 Ha! neglecta prius respicit oua parens.
695 Tunc ui nature, radii uirtute potentis
 Rumpuntur prime testea scepta domus.
Expergiscere! lentus eras; sis promptulus: usu
 Promtus amoris eris promcior igne nouo.
Illustrans actus radiis sol uerus aduret
700 Pectus et optata prole beatus eris.
Hostiles laqueos deuites passeris instar;
 Tot laqueos hostis, tot parat arte dolos.
Fistula dulce canit, uolucrem dum decipit auceps;
 Dulce melos reddit dulce Syrena malum;
705 Aures obturat comitum munitus Ulixes,
 Ne circumueniat filia Solis eos.
Sunt uolucres quas mansuetas lux unica reddit,
 Sunt quas uis aut ars nulla domare potest.
Quedam furtiuis indulgent sepe lucellis,
710 Sunt quas delectat simplicitatis amor.
Cantibus indulgent quedam noctuque dieque,
 Quedam luce colunt cantica, nocte silent.
Sunt que sub quouis depromunt tempore cantus,
 Sunt quibus estatis tempora sola placent.
715 Sunt que deciduo, sunt que languente uolatu
f. 221va Vtuntur; sunt que lecius alta petunt.
Aut hec aut similis distinctio conpetit illis
 Quos habitus humilis, nobile scema beat.
Se res explanat, se res delucidat apte:
720 Siluestres mores exue, furta fuge.
Sis philomena canens estatis tempore, brume,
 Autumpni, ueris nocte dieque deo.
Ad laudes nati sumus; hiis instemus amantes.
 Ad quem tendis, homo, laus tibi finis erit.
725 Piscis aqua genitrice satus spaciatur in undis;
 Pisces mundani, set mare mundus erit.

714. Sunt *ed.,* Sub **P**

trich often returns to its senses and to itself. A mother's love assuages the mind in a kindly way. Ah! The mother casts her gaze at the eggs she has previously neglected. Then by a force of nature, through the strength of its powerful eyes, **[695]** the earthy shells that form their first home are shattered. Wake up! You were slow; you should be quick. Ready in practising love, you will be more ready when a new love appears. Illuminating actions with its rays, the true sun will burn into your heart and you will be happy with the offspring you longed for. **[700]**

Like the sparrow, you should avoid the snares set by your enemies. The traps and deceptions artfully prepared by the enemy are without number. The pipe sings out a sweet tune, as the fowler deceives the bird; the Siren, a sweet evil, gives out a sweet melody. Ulysses, protected, blocks the ears of his companions **[705]** so that the Sun's daughter does not ensnare them.

There are birds transformed into tame creatures within a single day; there are birds which no force or technique can domesticate. Certain birds often yield to small rewards, furtively offered; there are some who are delighted by love's simplicity. **[710]** Certain birds give themselves over to singing night and day; some practise their songs by day; at night they fall silent. There are birds which draw out their melodies any time at all; there are birds for whom the summer season alone suits their fancy. There are birds which employ a falling, languid flight; **[715]** there are birds which soar to the heights with great joy.

This or a similar differentiation corresponds to those who have found happiness in a lowly habit and in a noble plan. The matter is self explanatory, the subject fittingly illuminates itself: divest yourself of habits that belong to the wild, avoid stealing! **[720]** Be a nightingale singing God's praises, night and day, during all seasons, summer, winter, autumn and spring. We were born to give praise. In a spirit of love let us press on with these. Man, for you praise will be the goal towards which you are striving. Fish spawned from the mothering deep roam amid the waves. **[725]** The fish will be worldly people, but the sea will

Ornatus pennis genitricem laudat eandem
 Ales; baptismus est aqua, fastus auis;
Profectus uite est, quo tendis ad alta, uolatus;
730 Virtutum pennis ocius alta pete.
Reice torporem qui uictricus est probitatis,
 Corporis ac mentis proditor, hostis honus.
Pauo nature decor, ostentacio, ludus,
 Delicium, Iuno, gloria magna tibi.
735 Magnatem signat uariis ornatibus ample
 Munitum censu deliciisque nouis.
Uoce minus grata est uolucris; sic plena minarum
 Vox est magnatis, imperiosa nimis.
Mollior incessus se furis gressibus aptans
740 Magnatum fastus insidiasque docet.
At pars inferior florenti sydere fulgens
 Pompe mundane gaudia uana notat.
Cui Parce parcunt caladrius aspicit egrum;
 Auertit uultum si rapiendus erit.
745 Si non respiceret nos summi gratia regis,
 Mortalis numquam pena remissa foret.
Nulla salus aderit, nisi nos informet honestas,
 Ni det opem summi dextera summa patris.
Uite uita deus uitam dat, seruat, adornat;
750 Numquam tuta fuit absque salute salus.
Hec auis absque nota niueo candore nitescit;
 Dii bene, si mentis candida uestis erit.
Est anime uestis caro, que candore refulget
 Mundicie, cum mens uernat honore rose.
755 Excitat a sompno se gallus, uerberat alis
 Corpus ut ad cantum prompcior esse queat.
Obsequium cultus diuini te uocat; aptis
 Excercens studiis te macerare stude.
Affectus tibi sit stimulus probitatis honeste;
760 Languor iners mores degenerare facit.
Vepribus et tribulis tellus inculta repletur;
 Delicias mense culta labrusca dabit.

754. mens **M**, mer^s? **P**

be the world. Decked out in its plumage, the bird praises the same mother. Water means baptism, the bird pride; the flight by which you direct your course to the heights symbolizes the progress of life. Make more quickly for the heavens on the wings of virtues. [730] Cast off sloth, which is a step-father to honesty; it betrays body and mind and is a burden of the enemy.

The peacock, nature's beauty, exhibition, sport and delight, is a glory to you, Juno. It represents the grandee in his splendid clothes of various colours, amply protected [735] by his wealth and novel delights. The bird's voice gives less pleasure; in the same way, the voice of the great is filled with threats and imperious in the extreme. The bird's rather effeminate gait, modelling itself on a thief's steps, reveals the arrogance and deceptions of magnates. [740] But its lower part gleams with glittering stars and signifies the empty joys of worldly pomp.

The caladrius directs a look upon a sick man spared by the Fates; it averts its gaze, if he is destined to be carried off. If the grace of the highest king did not look back upon us, [745] the penalty of death would never have been remitted. No salvation will attend us, unless honour shapes our actions, unless the supreme right hand of the great father assists us. God, life of life, grants, preserves and adorns life. Deliverance without salvation was never secure. [750] This bird shines forth with a singular brilliance, without a mark. The gods will be well pleased, if the veil of your mind is pure. The body is the soul's attire; it gleams with radiant chastity, when the mind blooms with the beauty of a rose.

The cock awakens himself from sleep and beats his body with his wings [755] in order that he may be more ready to crow. The service of divine worship summons you; as you train yourself with appropriate studies, do not hold back from exhausting yourself. For you, let love be a goad to honourable goodness. Listless inactivity causes morals to degenerate. [760] Land, if left uncultivated, teems with brambles and thorns. The wild vine, when cultivated, will provide delights for the

706. filia] circe.
754. rose] scilicet verecundie.

Attritus uomer splendet, rubigine sordet,
    Et uicium capiunt, ni moueantur, aque.
765   Dedita uox excercitio sistemata flectit
    Apcius et cantus gratior usus erit.
Cantu distinguit solempni preco diei
    Horas; sit queuis usibus apta tuis.
Tempora consilio sunt distribuenda salubri:
770   Ista sibi Rachel uendicet, illa Lya;
Illa reseruentur nature, vendicet illa
    Lectio; sic poteris certior esse tui.
Dat granum socie quod purius eligit; aptum
    Quod nosti uerbum fratribus esse dabis.
775   Elige quod placeat uel quod de iure placere
    Debeat et studeas utilis esse tuis.
Prothdolor! in senium iam uergens ponere fertur
    Ouum quod lento buffo calore fouet.
f. 221vb In lucem prodit proles infausta, maligne
780   Heres nutricis, prodigiosa lues.
Ue cum doctores deliri noxia fingunt
    Dogmata! nam mundo noxius error obest.
O quantum nocuit infelix Arrius orbi!
    O quot fedauit fex, Manichee, tua!
785   Si uero galeam, calcaria, prelia, pectus
    Audax et mores consulo, galle, tuos,
Militis egregii formam geris, inpiger, acer,
    Strenue, promte, ferox, tot fera bella ciens.
Vxores regis, immo domas, cum uix domet unam
790   Princeps, quem nanum zelotipasse ferunt.
Set te seducunt qui subducunt tibi testes
    Et criste priuant nobilitate capud.
Coniuge, milicia, fastu, cantu, probitate
    Destituunt te. Quid? degenerare nequis.
795   Altilis efficeris horum que prenumeraui
    Iacturam redimens simplicitate noua.
Iam ditas mensam quam chors nutriuerat ante;

---

770. Ista **M**, illa **P**   787. geris **M**; *omitted in* **P**   790. nanum **M**, uarium **P**

table. The hoe shines when worn, (but) it is filthy with rust; and waters, unless they are in motion, embody disease. A voice dedicated to practicing modulates the notes [765] more suitably and the occasion of singing will be more pleasing.

With his solemn singing the herald of the day marks off the hours. Let any hour at all be suitable for your exercizes. Seasons must be assigned according to a beneficial plan. Let Rachel claim for herself those times, Lia these. [770] Those should be reserved for nature; reading may claim these. In this way you will be able to be more sure of yourself.

The cock gives to his partner the purer seed he has selected. You will grant that the word you know is suitable for your brothers. Choose what may be pleasing or what rightly ought to please [775] and you should strive to be useful to your people. For shame! As he now inclines towards old age, he is said to lay an egg which a toad keeps warm with a heat that lingers. Into the light there emerges an unpropitious offspring, the heir of a malignant nurse, a monstrous plague. [780] How dreadful it is when teachers in their madness devise harmful teachings! For criminal error injures the world. How much harm the ill-starred Arrius inflicted upon the world! Alas for the number of people defiled by your filth, you Manichee!

But if I consider the cock's helmet, spurs, battles, brave heart [785] and morals, you carry the form of an outstanding soldier, vigorous and brave, as you energetically stir up so many savage conflicts with ready ferocity. You rule, indeed you subdue, your wives, whereas the prince, who, they say, being a dwarf, was a jealous man, could scarcely tame one. [790] But those who take away your testes lead you astray and they deprive your head of the grandeur of your crest. They defraud you of your wife, your courage, your pride, your song and your honour. What? You are not capable of degenerating. Of those birds I enumerated earlier, [795] you will become a fattened fowl, redeeming loss with a fresh simplicity. Previously you had been fed in a farm-yard,

764. Ouidius.
780. Heres] Basiliscus.
790. Princeps] Constantinus.

Delicias querens curia leta uidet.
Te, Progne, solo tenuis cibat esca uolatu;
800   Paucis se recreat mente superna petens.
Nocturnas poscit sibi pullus hirundinis escas;
         Sic studiis uite te recreare stude.
Presens uita quid est nisi nox, si mente reuoluis,
         Que confert superis gaudia uera quies?
805 Approbat utilitas lapidem quem nutrit hirundo;
         Virtutum niteat pectore gemma tuo.
Hec amor est qui sic radioso lumine fulget
         Vt solem mentis hunc reputare queas.
Cigno cantanti mors astans admouet aurem;
810   Indignans Parcam rumpere fila iubet.
Nouit quod celo tegitur qui non habet urnam;
         Quod sit pena diu uiuere nouit olor.
Naiades adductis quas mittit Flora Napeis
         In uiridi gaudent menbra locare solo.
815 Exequias celebrant uolucres cunctisque peractis
         Psitacus exclamat: «Ilicet ire licet.»
Illum signat olor qui gaudet linquere mundum,
         Cui mors in uoto est, uiuere pena grauis.
Sustinet ut uiuat, optans tamen ut moriatur;
820   Hoc suffert, illud eligit, optat, auet.
Vpupa busta colit, at tu succurre sepultis
         Orans; mendicis distribuenda dato.
Et tibi dilectos quondam uel mente recense
         Artus; in cinerem corpora uersa uide
825 Deliciis exquisitis nutrita potentum.
         Iam uermis quondam menbra decora rapit;
Mausolea colit coluber qui deuorat illam
         Carnem, quam superis ha! placuisse ferunt.
Exhibet obsequium predulce parentibus; alis
830   Iam spoliata togis frigida menbra fouet.
Filia iam mater matrem cibat, educat, arcet
         Frigus et innato menbra calore iuuat.

---

823. dilectos **M**, dilectas **P**

now you enrich a table. In its search for delights, the court looks upon you with joy.

Delicate food feeds you, Progne, only when you are in flight. A person who mentally makes for the celestial realm refeshes himself with few things. **[800]** The swallow's young demands food for itself at night; in the same way, eagerly strive to renew yourself in the pursuit of (eternal) life. If you reflect in your mind, what is our present life but darkness? What joys does true peace confer upon those living on earth? Utility approves the stone which the swallow nourishes; **[805]** let a jewel composed of virtues shine from your heart. This is the love which gleams with a light so radiant that you could reckon it to be the sun of the mind.

Death, standing nearby, lends a ear to the swan as it sings; in anger he commands the Fate to snap the threads. **[810]** He knows that the person without an urn is covered by the sky. The swan knows that long life is a punishment. After the woodland nymphs sent by Flora have been led in, the Naiades are glad to settle their limbs on the green turf. The birds celebrate the funeral rites and after everything has been completed, **[815]** the parrot proclaims: «It is over, you may go.» The swan signifies that person who feels joy at leaving the world, one who prays for death, for whom life is a heavy penalty. He bears up so that he may live, while at the same time he nevertheless wishes for death. He puts up with the former; the latter he chooses, desires and yearns for. **[820]**

The hoopoe frequents tombs, but you should run to assist the buried with your prayers; give to the needy alms that should be distributed to them. And, if you will, review in your mind's eye the limbs you once loved; observe that the bodies of the powerful, fed on exquisite delights, have been turned to dust. **[825]** Now a worm lays waste limbs that once were beautiful; tombs provide a sanctuary for the serpent who devours the famed flesh which once, they say, gave pleasure to the living. Ha! The hoopoe displays a very sweet compliance to its parents; with its wings it warms limbs grown cold now that they have been stripped of their covering. **[830]** The daughter, a mother now, feeds her mother, rears her, fends off the cold and assists her limbs with nat-

O quam degeneres nati sumus; hupupa nostros
    Mores condempnat ha! racione nocet?
835   Vix, Hodierna, tui dignantur adire locellum,
    Quo, mater, felix et miseranda iaces.
Illis mater eras, dum uixisti; michi uiuis,
    Nec michi defuncto mortua mater eris.
Viuit amor, set uiuet amor; regnabit amoris
840   Gratia; regnabit gloria, uiuit amor.
Uiuit amor numquam moriturus, uiuet in euum

f. 222ra   Felix qui mortis nescius extat amor.
Tu michi mater eras, es mater, ero tibi natus;
    Numquid Alexander desinet esse tuus?
845   Mens mea semper erit thalamus tibi siue sepulchrum
    Quo tua, fida parens, molliter ossa cubent.
In thalamo cordis tua set mea menbra quiescent;
    Cor mausoleum sit tibi, queso, meum.
Quid miri, si cor cordis sic sit michi cordi
850   Vt cor iam cordis corde carere querar?
Dimidio cordis me des aut corde carere,
    Nam falsi carie uerba carere decet.
Lux hodierna tibi semper lucens, Hodierna,
    Luceat; est presens iugiter iste dies.
855   Iste dies hodie lucet, quia iu<n>gitur illis
    Quos tenet in uero lumine uera dies.
Fertur habere diem mera gratia, gloria perpes;
    Ipse deus proprium gaudet habere diem.
Immo dies uerus deus est: «hodie genui te»
860   Alloquitur natum sic pater ipse suum.
Sol eterne, tui luces in luce diei;
    Eterni est talem solis habere diem.
Sol est eternus, lux est eterna diei;
    Tres persone sunt: sol, deus atque dies.
865   Hic in luce coeternum genitor sibi natum
    Equalem generat consimilemque sibi.
Lux hodie que cras nescit tibi lucida detur;

---

837. Illis **M**, Iillis **P**   855. iungitur *ed.*, iugiter **PM**   857. mera *ed.*, mora **PM**
864. atque **M**, at **P**

ural warmth. Oh! What a degenerate state we were born into! The hoopoe condemns the ways we behave. Ha! is reason harmful?

Hodierna, they scarcely think it worth while to approach your casket, [835] where, mother, you lie in a state of bliss, lamented by me. While you lived, you were a mother to them. For me you live on, nor, even when I have departed this life, will you be a mother who is dead in my eyes. Love is alive, but love will endure; the grace of love will prevail, its glory will reign supreme; love lives on. [840] Love, destined never to die, endures. Love which stands firm, innocent of death, will live on happily forever. To me you were a mother; you remain my mother; to you I will be a son. Will Alexander cease being your very own? My mind will forever be a chamber or burial place for you, [845] where, loyal parent, your bones will lie in a gentle sleep. But in the chamber of my heart your limbs, but also mine, will find rest; let my heart be your resting place, I pray. What is amazing, if my heart's heart is so loved by me that I mourn that now my heart is without the heart of my heart? [850] You must grant that I lack half of my heart or my heart, for it is proper that my words should be devoid of falsehood's corruption.

Hodierna, may the light that shines upon you today shine brightly upon you forever; that day is perpetually present. The light of that day shines today, because it is joined to those [855] who are held by true daylight in the light of truth. Pure grace and eternal glory are said to have their appointed time. God himself rejoices to have a day appointed as his own. Indeed, the light of day is the true God: «Today I have begotten you»: with these words the father addresses his own son in person. [860] Eternal sun, you are visible in the light of your own day. It is a mark of the eternal sun to have a day such as this. The sun is everlasting; everlasting is the light of day. There are three persons: God, the sun and the light of day. Here, in light the Father creates a co-eternal Son, [865] equal to himself and in his likeness. Today let brilliant light, which knows no tomorrow, be granted you. Upon you, Hodierna, let the light shine eternal. On my behalf bend the knee of your

Luceat eternum lux, Hodierna, tibi.
Pro me flecte genu mentis, dulcissima mater,
870   Matri que matrum est gloria, gemma, decus.
Ordo gruum sibi succedens formando figuram
       Ut bene seruetur ortographia monet.
Debita distinctis spaciis proporcio seruit
       Et ne deliret linea queque cauet.
875   Se que precedit testatur uoce magistram;
       Respondet placide cetera turba duci.
Si uenti rabies insurgens aera turbet,
       Obscurata prius littera tota perit.
Doctoris regimen designat preuia turba,
880   Illos quos patrum regula certa regit.
Insidiis hostis uenerabilis ordo fatescit
       Et que recta stetit regula curua iacet.
Excitat a sompno socias nocturna lapillo;
       Custos iusticie sit rigor iste tibi.
885   Secum directas acies in prelia ducit;
       Arma, quibus tutus te tueare, para.
Esca iam dignam sobolem dat Apollinis ales
       Dum nigra cernit corpora ueste tegi.
Sudorem tipice signat color iste uirilem;
890   Ecce relatiuo est dignus honore labor.

Sollicitant animos leuium spectacula rerum;
       Nunc ioca, nunc recreant seria mixta iocis.
Seria mixta iocis sunt seria. Quid? ioca rite
       Interserta iocis seria dico suis.
895   Seria sepe iocos admittunt, sepe repellunt;
       Eacidem cithara se recreasse ferunt;
Demulcet fidibus crinitus Apollo canoris
       Numina; Uirgilii Musa iocosa iubet:
«Pone merum et talos; pereat qui crastina curat:
900   Mors aurem uellens, 'Viuite' ait, 'venio'.»
Copa, liber Culicis, 'Est et non', 'Ver erat', atque

875. Se **M**, Et **P**   886. tutus **M**, tutis **P**   893. ioca **M**, loca **P**   900. aurem
M, autem **P**

mind, sweetest of mothers, before the mother who is the glory, jewel and splendor of mothers. [870]

As a procession of cranes follows one after the other to form the figure (of a letter), it reminds us that we do well to pay attention to correct writing. The due proportion is useful for the defined spaces and every crane guards against the line becoming crooked. And the crane which leads the way attests by its cry its role as instructor. [875] The rest of the flock responds calmly to its guide. If a turbulent wind arises and disturbs the atmosphere, the letter is first obscured and then vanishes entirely. The bird that leads the way for the flock symbolizes a teacher's guidance, those who are directed by the established rule of the Fathers. [880] The venerable order grows weary before the enemy's snares and the rule that once stood firm and upright lies fallen and stooped.

At night, the crane rouses its comrades from sleeping by means of a stone; let that firmness act as your guardian of what is just. He leads into battles the lines that have been aligned with him. [885] Prepare the arms by which you may protect yourself and remain secure.

Apollo's bird allows that his offspring are worth feeding in the moment when he sees their bodies are covered with black feathers. Allegorically, that colour represents the sweat of man. Observe! toil is worthy of the honour that relates one man to another. [890]

The spectacle of light matters stimulates our minds. Sometimes humour refreshes, sometimes a mixture of seriousness and humour does so. Serious discourse mingled with the playful constitutes serious business. What? I maintain that playfulness duly inserted in the right places is serious. Serious affairs frequently admit lightness, and often they reject it. [895] Tradition tells that Aeacus's grandson refreshed himself by playing the lyre. Long-haired Apollo soothes the gods with tunes from his strings. Vergil's muse facetiously commands: «Set up the wine and the dice; let any person concerned with tomorrow perish. Death plucks the ear and says, 'Enjoy your life, I am on my way.'» [900] The *Copa*, the book entitled *Culex*, the *Est et non*, «It was spring», and «Now night

---

897. Virgilius: *Priamiden Helene gratas regnasse per urbes* [cf. Verg., *A*. **3**, **295**]. In **M** f. 161r this verse is included in the text after v. 896 as follows: *Priamidem helenum graias regnasse per urbes*. **901.** Nomina librorum quos Virgilius conposuit [in red ink].

'Iam nox hibernas' digna fauore canunt.
Detinuit Sceuolam pila, circos cerne Catonem
    Intrantem, capitur ipsa Minerua iocis.

f. 222rb   905   Regia maiestas post ludos sceptra resumit;
    Seria qui cecini ludicra sponte cano.
Aut oblita sui Natura fuisse uidetur
    Aut uolucrum proprii nescia iuris erat
Aut lusit fidens cum uesperte dicioni
910   Concessit uolucrem ridiculumue genus.
Nonne uolat quociens girando circinat auras?
    Alarum numquid aera transit ope?
Adde quod ex ouo prorumpit in esse, set ecce
    In lucem tali reptile lege uenit.
915   Numquid item pennis aut plumis ala carebit?
    Quid quod bis geminos scitur habere pedes?
Soricis ergo sibi confert menbrana uolatum,
    Vt pisces ingens pinna uolare facit.
Dentibus armatur; magnas pro corpore gestat
920   Aures, munitum cornibus esse putes.
Sese munitam mentitur ypocrisis alis
    Virtutum, monstris connumeranda lues.
Alas mendaces huic gloria prebet inanis;
    Dum terrena sapit, non petit alta uolans.
925   Dum uisus tantum considerat exteriora,
    Tutum sub misera ueste latere putat.
Sese commendans aliorum carpere gaudet
    Mores nec cinico dente carere potest.
Arrectas placidis aperit rumoribus aures;
930   De se presumens cornua fastus habet.
Poscenti ueniam prebens arcensque rebellem
    Magnates uincit nobilitate leo.
Vincitur ut uincat; uincit uincatur ut hostis;
    Uicto uincenti gloria maior adest;
935   Vincere me reputo maius quam uincere Parthum;

---

904. ipsa **M**, illa **P**   916. quod sit bis **P** *with expunction marks under sit*   **931.**
arcensque **P** *with que added by a corrector in different ink.*

the wintry...» deserve acclamation for their poetic subjects. Exercising with a ball engaged Scaevola; observe Cato, as he enters the games; Minerva is herself enchanted by jests. After playing, royal majesty takes up the sceptre once more. [905] I, who have celebrated serious subjects in poetry, compose light verse willingly.

Nature appears either to have forgotten herself or she was ignorant of the law proper to birds or she amused herself, when she confidently yielded her flying and laughable offspring to evening's domain. [910] Does it not fly whenever it wheels around, as it flies in a circular course? Does it pass through the air assisted by wings? Add the fact that it breaks out from an egg into life; but look! into the light comes a reptile in such a condition. Likewise, will the wing lack feathers or plumage? [915] What of the fact that it is known to have four feet? Therefore, the membrane of a shrew-mouse allows it to fly, just as a huge wing causes fish to take flight. It is armed with teeth; in front of its body it sports large ears; you would think it was protected with horns. [920]

Hypocrisy, a plague to be counted among monsters, pretends that it is protected by squadrons of virtues. Vainglory supplies her with counterfeit wings. While it savours earthly matters, it does not soar and make for the heights. Since the faculty of sight looks attentively only at externals, [925] hypocrisy imagines that it is secure as it lurks beneath its contemptible surface. As it commends itself, it enjoys criticizing the morals of others and it cannot live without teeth to gnaw at them. It pricks up its ears and opens them to seductive rumours; presuming on itself, it possesses horns of pride. [930]

Because he shows mercy to those who beg for pardon and he keeps the rebellious at a distance, the lion surpasses potentates in nobility. He is overcome in order to gain victory; he prevails in order to defeat the enemy. Greater glory attends the conqueror than the defeated. I reckon self-mastery to be a greater feat than conquering the Parthians. [935]

---

909. uesperte] Vesperta est dea que preest hore uespertine.

Sic uinci quam sic uincere pluris erit.
Immo sic uinci des uincere, uincere uinci;
Ergo cum uinci me sino, uictor ero.
Describit cauda circum clausasque minaci
940   Rugitu sistit anticipatque feras.
Luminibus quasi sit uigilans obdormit apertis
Erroremque suum sompnus habere cupit.
Ne, quamuis simulent, credas dormire potentes;
Horrida maiestas regia semper erit.
945   Rugitu patris proles animatur; habeto
Rugitum, leo fis formaque iusticie.
Insta, declara quam tutum uiuere rite:
Sic tibi commissus grex animatus erit.
Ne tamen extollat elacio ceca leonem,
950   Vox strepitus rede stridula terret eum.
Pallida mors curru residens, uelociter instans
Pre foribus sese clamat adesse: time!
Adde quod albus ei gallus terroris ymago est;
Clamat «defuncti, surgite» preco uigil.
955   Uerbere se caude cedit ruiturus in hostem;
Otia sectaris: emulus hostis adest.
Hostis adest semper uigilans semperque dolosis
Insidiis cupiens uincere, bella ciens.
Duret in articulum mortis constancia firma;
960   Spem palme certam uerbera crebra dabunt.
Febricitatque leo quauis estate; potentes
Tempore successus impacienter agunt.
Assit hyemps, cessat febris; assi<n>t nubila sortis
Tempora mutate, mox furor ille uacat.
965   Nescius est elephas sua flectere menbra; potestas
Nulli conpaciens prothdolor! ecce subit.
Eligit hic robur cui se conmittit ibique

---

946. fis **P**, sis *Orlandi*   **947.** Insta *Orlandi*; Iusta **P**   **957.** adest adest semper **P**
with expunction marks under second word   **967.** ibi que? **P**   **969.** alni *ed.*, alte **P**

It will be worth more to lose in this manner than to win on these terms. Indeed, you must grant that defeat in this way constitutes victory, victory defeat. Therefore, whenever I allow myself to be beaten, I shall emerge the victor.

With his tail the lion describes a circle and, roaring menacingly, he freezes the wild beasts he has encircled and forestalls their every move. [940] He falls asleep with his eyes open, as if he were awake; and sleep desires to have its own path to wander along. You should not believe that powerful people remain inactive, however much they pretend. Royal majesty will forever inspire fear. When he hears his father roaring, the offspring leaps to life; possess a roar, [945] you will become a lion and the incarnation of justice. Be insistent and demonstrate what security there is in living a just life. On the same principle, the flock entrusted to your care will be spurred to life.

However, to prevent pride from exalting the lion and blinding him, the screeching noise of a rumbling wagon terrifies him. [950] Pale death, sitting back in a chariot, swiftly approaches and proclaims its presence before your doors: be fearful! Add the fact that a white cock represents for a lion the image of terror; the vigilant herald cries out: «You who are dead, arise.»

The lion strikes himself by lashing his tail as he is about to rush upon his enemy. [955] If you pursue leisure, the envious enemy waits at your side. The enemy is present, ever watchful and, as he stirs up conflicts, longs at every instant to defeat you using his treacherous snares. Unswerving constancy will last right up to the critical moment of death. Frequent lashes will award the certain hope of victory. [960]

And every summer the lion grows feverish; during periods of success the powerful act impatiently. Let winter arrive, the fever subsides; let there be overcast periods when fortune has changed; soon that rage becomes empty.

The elephant is unable to bend his limbs. [965] Observe! power that feels compassion for no person draws near. What sorrow! This animal selects a tree on which he sets himself and there, needing to rest, he

---

939. circum] hic circus [same gloss on same lemma in **P** f. 213vb].
f. 222rb bottom: O mundum mundans mundo mundo [mendo? **P**] caro mundans/Cara carens menda, nos munda sanguinis unda [cf. *Poems* 3, 155; 4b, 13-4. (ed. Walther 1965, 121, 122)].

f. 222va   Indulget sompnis stando quietis egens.

          Arbor cui barrus innititur est honor alni

970   Mollis cui requiem fingit adesse potens.

          Succidit robur lucri uenator auarus

            Arte tegens fraudem; fallitur inde ruens.

          Surgere ui propria captus nequid, arte leuatur;

            Inserta domino sedulitate subest.

975   Lucrum uenatur animarum doctor honestus,

            Lucri sectator atque salutis auens.

          Ferro doctrine robur succidit acute

            Dum terrena diu nescia stare probat.

          O casus felix, dum spes cadit illa potentis

980   Quam deceptus in hiis finxerat esse bonis,

          Gratia subsequitur; nos gratia preuenit, actus

            Informat, uires prebet, adauget eas.

          Que uis nature? que gloria? quanta potestas?

            Ipsius effectus quis numerare queat?

985   Augustum cernit directo sydere: Roma

            Neronis torue respicit ora sui.

          Gibbosam prebet sellam Natura camelo;

            Plus illum recreat quam pede turbat aqua;

          Plus turbata placet heresi doctrina magistre

990   Erroris; gibbum linea curua facit.

          Rectos corde iuuat rectissima regula ueri;

            Illa decens recti tramitis odit iter.

          Eligit amfractus uulpis astuta recuruos,

            Que taxo misera surripit arte domum.

995   Hec heresim signat, fraudem quoque mentis auare;

            Nam lucris inhians fraus aliena rapit.

          Forme menbrorum leporis conplexio cedit;

            Humor enim piger hunc exigit esse pigrum,

          Set casus nigre colere, pedibus timor alas

1000   Addidit et celerem cogit inire fugam.

          Vrgens articulus indicit opus probitatis

---

972. tegens *ed.*, regens **P**   974. Dehinc inserta domino **P**   978. nescia stare *ed.*, stare nescia **P**   981. Gratia *ed.*, Grana **P**   986. sui *ed.*, tui **P**   999. alas **M**, alis **P**

gives himself up to sleep while standing. The peaceful tree on which
the elephant leans is the beautiful alder, in which the powerful animal
imagines that repose resides. [970] The hunter, greedy for gain, cuts
through the tree, skilfully concealing his deception. The elephant is
tricked and comes crashing to the ground from there. Trapped, he is
unable to rise using his own strength; he is raised aloft by a technique.
(A smaller elephant) takes up a position underneath the sovereign
beast, with continual effort applied.

The honourable teacher hunts to gain souls, [975] as he pursues
profit and yearns for salvation. He cuts through the hard core with an
iron blade of sharp learning, while he proves that earthly matters are
unable to exist for long. How fortunate the fall, when that hope,
which the powerful man in his delusion had imagined to exist in these
goods, drops away. [980] Grace follows close after; grace precedes us,
shapes our actions, affords us strength and increases it. What is the
force of its nature? What the essence of its glory? How great the extent
of its power? Who would be able to reckon the operations of grace itself? From the star directly above it perceives Augustus; Rome [985]
looks back fiercely upon the face of her own Nero.

Nature provides the camel with a hump-backed saddle. The water
he stirs up with his foot refreshes him more. Confused doctrine affords
more pleasure to heresy, the high priestess of error. A bent line causes
a hump. [990] The straightest rule of truth assists the virtuous at heart.
Heresy loathes a proper journey along a straight path.

The cunning fox, who steals the badger's lair through contemptible
trickery, chooses pathways that curve and meander. This animal symbolizes heresy, as well as the dangers of a greedy mind. [995] For deceit
gazes eagerly at gain and carries off what belongs to others. The hare's
constitution yields to the shape of his limbs; for a sluggish humour requires him to be inactive, but the accident of black choler and fear
added wings to his feet and compelled him to undertake swift flight.
[1000] A pressing crisis proclaims the need of goodness for the weak;

---

976. auens] idest cupiens.
995. Adaptacio.

Inualidis, ualidos esse necesse facit.
Si natura pigrum te reddit, gratia promptum
    Reddet; naturam gratia summa regit.
1005 Ignea uis animo quem noxia corpora tardant
    Succurret: virtus ignea semper erit.
Infirme carni dominetur spiritus intus
    Regnans; prebet ei feruor amoris opem.
Perplicito nexu ludentis cornua serre
1010   Obuoluit fruticum densa corona comis.
Clamor prodit eam; capitur seducta. Superbe
    Motus elati cornua mentis erunt;
Mens capud est; fruticum tibi sit perplexa corona
    Vrgens curarum sollicitudo uigil.
1015 Ludus erit mentis lasciuia luxuriantis;
    Mors ridet quociens horrida ludit anus;
Ludum sustineo iuuenis; lasciua senectus
    Est monstrum; crebro ludere turpe seni.
Lusimus ha! nimium, set non incidere ludum
1020   Presertim senibus dedecus esse puta.
Clamor fraudis erit detectio se manifestans;
    Venator querens quem uoret hostis erit.
Bestia displiceat: placeat tibi serra fabrilis
    Et poliat sceptum lima decenter opus.
1025 Utilis est aliis, set se consumere nouit;
    Utilis est aliis, perniciosa sibi.
Materialis obest sibi lima: polit tamen apte
    Atque perornat opus se minuendo tamen.
Aptat opus cui prebet opem seruitque magistra;
1030   Officiosa iuuat officiendo sibi.
f. 222vb Sic doctrina comes uite turpis nocet ipsi
    Auctori, multos utilitate iuuans.
Sic cos exacuit ferrum, candela ministrat
    Lumen, sic liram uomer arando facit.
1035 Lima mordaci, set prudens, sepius utor,

1033. cos **M**, quos **P**

necessity causes them to be strong. If nature has made you indolent, grace will render you quick to respond to any situation. From on high grace governs nature. A fiery force will rush to help a mind slowed down by injurious bodies; [1005] virtue will always be ardent. Let the spirit which rules within have dominion over the weak flesh. Love's passion provides it with power.

A crown of bushes, thick with leaves, completely covers the horns of the frolicking saw-fish in an intricate complex. [1010] A shout brings it to the surface. It is trapped after it has been led astray. The projections will be the exalted passions of an arrogant mind. The head is the mind; for you let the intricate crown of shrubs stand for the pressing anxiety of cares that keeps you awake at night. Playfulness will be the licentiousness of a wanton mind. [1015] Death laughs whenever an ugly old woman flirts. I maintain the frivolous behaviour of my youth; an old age spent playing around is a monstrous thing; to spend time in repeated diversions brings disgrace upon an old man. To my regret, I have been unserious far too much; but you should consider it shameful, especially for old men, not to put an end to games. [1020] The shout will be the unmasking of deceit, making itself plain. The hunter seeking a victim to devour will stand for the enemy.

Should the beast not please you, let the craftsman's saw bring you delight and let the file beautify and smooth the work I have begun. The saw has utility for others, but it recognizes that it consumes itself. While it confers advantages on others, it is ruinous to itself. [1025] The material file damages itself; nevertherless, it is suitable for polishing and constantly adorns the work even while it diminishes itself. It puts in order the work it assists and provides a masterful service. In its readiness to serve, it helps by being detrimental to itself. [1030] In the same way, learning accompanied by a disgraceful way of life harms the agent himself, even though its utility assists many. Similarly, a whetstone sharpens iron tools, a candle provides light; so too a ploughshare creates a furrow while ploughing.

I use the rasping file rather often, but judiciously. [1035] I tear out

1002. necesse] scilicet necessitas.
1009. serre] Tam de serra animali quam de serra instrumento quam de lima iudiciali.
1030. Officiendo] idest nocendo.

Cor rapio multis quos bene corripio;
Set nec parco michi sub lima iudiciali
    Cum uerbis mores corripiendo meos.
Corripio mores, uersus emendo, reuoluo
1040   Sermonem, pingo uerba colore suo.
Perscrutor sensum, sermonem rebus adapto,
    Vix michi cum faleris uerba nouella placent.
Barbariem uito uerborum, turgida semper
    Sperno; sedent animo publica uerba meo.
1045 Scinthasis ipsa docet ut nubat mobile fixo,
    Substet materies, forma uenustet eam.
Si male conueniat uirgo sociata marito
    Et sociam querulus respuat ille suam,
Coniugium soluo, celebro diuorcia, legem
1050   Indicens socio nubat ut illa nouo.
O si barbariem uiciorum sic reprobarem,
    Vt uicium soloes lingua Latina fugit.
Vt sit limatus sermo desidero, mores
    Uix sub iudicium conuoco, uerba uoco.
1055 Si tempus studiis dandum feliciter arto,
    Si male dilato que breuianda forent,
Dissimulo, sileo, conniueo; corripienda
    Producens, gemitus edo, dolore tremo.
Carminibus parco propriis, carpens aliena;
1060   Inuideo si quis nobile condat opus.
Que mens commendat os dampnat; singula prudens
    Que sunt apposite dicta reseruo michi.
Singula dampno, licet multo sint digna fauore,
    Et furtim scriptis insero multa meis.
1065 Set tamen improbus est censor, me iudice, scripto
    Quisquis in alterius ingeniosus erit.
Castora cum Polluce suo succidere castor
    Fertur ut euadat tela sequentis eum.
Castor eris, si sis castus; quod te male uexat

1036. Corrapio **P**, *which a corrector divided.*   1044. publica **M**, pblica **P**   1045.
Scinthasis **P**, syntaxis *Hunt ed. Gibson, against the metre* 16   1052. **P** *corrects* lasciua *to*
latina *by means of an expunction mark under* **s**   1057. corripienda *ed.,* corripiendam
PM   1060. conda^t **P** *with* **t** *superscript in different ink*

the hearts of many people whom I reproach with the best of intentions. But neither do I spare myself, when I criticize my morals and my words before the tribunal of revision. I chastise my habits, I correct my verses, I reflect upon what I have said, I paint words with their distinctive colours. [1040] I scrutinize my thought, I fit the discourse to the subject-matter. Novel words with their trappings scarcely afford me any pleasure. I avoid barbarisms in my language, I always reject inflated vocabulary; words that are shared by everybody settle into my mind.

Apposition personally advises that the mobile should be married to the fixed. [1045] Once the subject has firmly settled, form may beautify it. If a maiden's union to her husband results in an unhappy marriage, and the latter, full of complaints, rejects his partner, I dissolve the marriage, I solemnize a divorce, proclaiming the principle that she should wed a new partner. [1050]

If only I condemned the barbarism of my vices in the same way as the Latin language avoids solecisms. I long for my language to be elegant. I summon my words, but reluctantly do I assemble my morals before a tribunal. If I curtail the time that ought to be happily given over to study, [1055] if I clumsily amplify what ought to be shortened, I dissemble, I keep silent and I close my eyes. Bringing forward what has to be corrected, I emit groans, and I tremble in my distress. I show mercy to my own poems, but I slander the writings of others. I am envious if anyone has composed an outstanding work. [1060]. My mouth condemns what my judgement commends. Individual phrases which have been suitably expressed I judiciously save up for my own use. I censure individual points, though they deserve much acclaim, and I secretly insert many of them into my own writings. But in my judgement, anyone who is clever at the expense of what another has written [1065] is a dishonest critic.

The beaver is said to cut off Castor with his twin Pollux in order to escape the weapons of his pursuer. You will be a beaver, if you are

---

1052. soloes] Soloe ciuitas in confinio Lacii et barbariei sita corrupte loquens, a qua soloecismus dicitur.
1069. Moralitas.

1070   Reice, ne currens impediaris, honus.
            Segniciem generat Uenus; hanc cum matre relinquas.
                Currenti languens torpor obesse solet.
            Hericius spinis se circumuoluit acutis;
                Cui desunt uires indiget artis ope.
1075   Et miseris obsunt hostes; ni fallor, auarum
                Hostem non numquam preda pusilla iuuat.
            Quem male transacte uite iam penitet, hostem
                Horrens dum curis angitur arcet eum.
            Spinis cincta suis sese contricio munit;
1080   Ista timor cautus arma ministrat ei.
            Nunc uitis fructu generoso pascit alumpnos,
                Nunc pomis proli subuenit ipse sue.
            Diuini uerbi precioso germine natos
                Ut recrees proprios, pastor honeste, decet.
1085   Cum timor angit eum, sese concludit in orbem;
                Intra se tuto quisque latere potest.
            Intra claustra sue mentis se quisque recludat;
                Conclusus poterit tucior esse sui.
            Ne concludatur tibi, te conclude decenter;
1090   Experto credas: exteriora nocent.
            Svs inmunda luti feda se fece uolutat,
                Nec nisi limosa philosophatur humo.
            Fex est feda caro, fetens, caries cariei;
f. 223ra   Que sunt feda magis deliciosa putat.
1095   Fece uoluptatum caro fetida deliciatur;
                Fedos feda iuuant, turpia turpis agit.
            Seuiciam poterit tibi designare potentum
                Frendens fulmineo dente timendus aper.
            Densa tegit porcum iaculorum silua minacem;
1100   Abruptas rupes et iuga celsa colit.
            Tela, quibus tergum muniuit mira potestas
                Nature, mixtus exhibet humor ei.
            Flegmatis atque nigre colere uires sociantur
                Telaque sic uario picta colore nitent.

1100. iuga **M**, luga **P**

chaste. Remove any burden that causes you great distress so that you may not be hindered as you run. **[1070]** Sex produces inactivity; you should abandon Venus and her mother. Listless torpor is usually injurious to a runner.

The hedgehog rolls himself into a ball of sharp prickles; any creature that lacks strength needs the assistance provided by a skill. Enemies injure even the poor. If I am not mistaken, **[1075]** a very weak prey sometimes benefits a greedy enemy.

Anyone who now feels regret at a life spent in wickedness keeps the enemy at bay, as long as he is fearful and tormented with anxieties. Contrition fortifies itself with a wall made of its own thorns; prudent apprehension supplies it with those defenses. **[1080]**At one moment the hedgehog feeds its young upon the vine's excellent fruit, at another it personally assists them with apples. Honourable shepherd, it is fitting that you refresh your own sons with the precious offshoot of the divine word. When fear causes it distress, the hedgehog rolls itself into a ball. **[1085]** Each and every person can live a life secure within himself. Everyone should enclose himself within the confines of his own mind. The cloistered person will be able to be more secure in himself. Restrain yourself in a proper manner so that people do not draw the wrong conclusions about you. Believe one with experience: externals cause injury. **[1090]**

The filthy pig wallows in the disgusting filth of mud and does not philosophize unless he is mired in slimy ooze. The disgusting filth is the stinking flesh, corruption to end all corruption. The pig thinks what is loathsome is more delicious. The stinking flesh takes delight in the dregs of pleasures. **[1095]** What is abominable gives pleasure to vile people; base people pursue base acts.

The wild boar, an animal to be feared as it gnashes its murderous teeth, will have the power to represent the ferocity of powerful people.

A thick forest of bristles covers the menacing porcupine; the creature haunts precipitous cliffs and lofty ridges **[1100]**. In his case, a mixture of humours produces the weapons with which nature's amazing power has fortified his back. The properties of phlegm and black choler unite and the quills, painted as they are in a variety of colours, have

1075. Et] idest eciam.

1105   Humor qui piger est uestit nigredine partem
        Teli quod dici cornea uirga potest.
    Nam colere nigre proles est ipsa nigredo;
        Humor candorem prebet aquosus ei.
    Frigiditate potens humor sicco sociata
1110   Duricie rigida consolidauit opus.
    Cornea uirga uolat directo tramite; missa
        Arcu lunato Parthica tela putes.
    E tanta silua uirgarum dirigit unam
        Ac si sit docta missa sagitta manu.
1115   Ore miser patulo dormit cocodrillus, at illi
        Insidians ydrus preparat arte dolum.
    Corpus humo circumducit uoluendo tenaci
        Hostis ut intret in os lubricitatis ope.
    Intrat et absumptis uitalibus exit; auara
1120   Ad questus mens os cordis hiare facit.
    Sompnus auaricie curas subducere nescit;
        Mens dormit, uigilat ceca cupido tamen.
    Fraudis amor misere miser intrat pectus auarum
        Corrumpens hominis interioris opes.
1125   Hee sunt Nature dotes seu dona potentis;
        Corrumpit mentis interiora dolus.
    Oua fouet nunc mas, nunc femina que cocodrillus
        Ponit; bis geminos fertur habere pedes.
    Corporis in longum distenti linea recta
1130   Quinque quater cubitos exsuperare datur.
    Vnguibus armatur seuis et dente minaci;
        Ferrea tela cutem uix penetrare queunt.
    Vnguis auaricie rapidus, dens improbus; ouum
        False mendax est simplicitatis opus.
1135   Vngue rapit, cinico reprehendit singula dente,
        Seuo signatur vngue cupido rapax.
    Corporis extensi dimensio longa figurat
        Spem questus qua mens est crucianda diu.
    Duriciam mentis signat cutis aspera, tela
1140   Verba quibus pauper cor penetrare solet.

1105. est **M**; *omitted by* **P**   1140. Verba *ed.*, Verbera **P**

a brilliant sheen. The humour which is inert covers in black [1105] the part of the quill which can also be described as a rod made of horn. For blackness itself is the product of black choler; an aqueous humour supplies its brilliance. A humour, potent in its coldness, when joined to the dry has solidified the defensive work into a stiff hardness. [1110] A projectile made of cornel wood flies in a straight line; you would think they were Parthian, let fly from from crescent-shaped bows. From the great forest of quills the porcupine directs one in a straight line, as if he had fired an arrow from an experienced hand.

With its mouth open wide, the unfortunate crocodile sleeps, [1115] but the water snake, lying in wait for him, artfully sets up the deception beforehand. It draws its body into a ball as it rolls in the sticky mud so that, assisted by its slipperiness, it may enter into the enemy's jaws. It eases in and emerges after consuming the vital organs. A covetous disposition causes the mouth of the heart to gape wide for gain. [1120] Sleep cannot take away anxieties caused by avarice. Although the mind sleeps, blind desire stays awake, nevertheless. A contemptible passion for deplorable deceit penetrates the greedy heart, corrupting the resources of the inner man. These are the endowments or the gifts of powerful nature. [1125] Guile ruins the inner places of the mind.

Now the male, now the female warms the eggs laid by the crocodile; it is said to have four feet. The straight line of its body, when it stretched lengthwise, is said to surpass twenty cubits. [1130] He is armed with ferocious claws and menacing teeth. Iron weapons can scarcely penetrate his hide. The claws of avarice are fierce, its teeth violent; the egg is the deceptive product of a feigned simplicity.

With his claws he tears at every single thing, he seizes it with his gnawing teeth; [1135] rapacious desire is expressed by the cruel claws. The long dimension of the extended body is a figure of the hope for profit, with which the mind is destined to be tormented for a long time. The rough skin represents the mind's hardness, the weapons indicate the words which the poor regularly use to pierce the heart.

Set cor auaricie numquid penetrabit Ulixes
    Uerbis aut Cicero? Quintiliane, tace.
Belua dicta uorans hominem sua fletibus ora
    Irrigat ac si sit compacientis opus.
1145 Cum turpes actus conmittit auara potestas,
    Seuiciam uultu dissimulare solet.
Coniugis Herodes nate munus salienti
    Illicitum, tristem se simulando, dedit.
Indulget proli generande rara uoluptas
1150   Barri; cum partus instat, in amne parit.
Notas declinat fraudes hac arte draconis;
    Obsequio promptas Naiades esse puta.
Felicis studii felix opus est elephantis
    Fetus; habet propriam spiritus almus aquam.
1155 Abluit hec sordes anime mundatque, decorem
    Affert; mundicies causa decoris erit.
f. 223rb Humani generis hostis uetus est draco qui nos
    Infestans fraudes nectere promptus adest.
Cum congressuras acies iam prelia poscunt,
1160   Ostenso barrus sanguine bella sitit.
Sumpto cor feruet, tumet, iram concipit, hostes
    Impetit, ignito pectore seua fremit.
Ferueat ergo tibi cor, mentem spes leuet ardens;
    Libato Christi sanguine crescat amor.
1165 Hostis bella ciat occurrens; pugnat inhermis,
    Ni quod fraus uigilans arma ministrat ei.
Det tibi spes galeam, clipeum pacientia; mucro
    Sit tibi uera fides, lancea longus amor.
Iusticie uirtus tibi sit lorica, iuuamen
1170   Christus precedens, quo duce uictor eris.
Ora cum Moyse; Iosue pugnabit et hostem
    Cedet; sic cedet Amalechita tibi.
Lectori tetrico seruit mea pagina nolens,
    Immo uolens; cunctis debitor esse uolo.
1175 Grates persoluam magnas tibi, candide lector,

1153. Felicis *corrected from* Felices **P**   1159. prelia *Reeve*, plurima **PM**

[1140] But will Ulysses or Cicero penetrate the heart of avarice with their eloquence? Quintilian, be silent. The afore-mentioned beast floods its face with tears as it devours a man, as if it were the act of a compassionate being. When greed leads power to commit evil actions, [1145] as a rule it disguises the savagery on its face. By feigning unhappiness, Herod granted to his dancing daughter the unlawful gift demanded by his wife.

Seldom does the elephant indulge in the pleasure of creating offspring; when the birth is imminent, she produces the child in the river. [1150] By this device she avoids the serpent's well-known trickery; imagine that the water-nymphs are quick to comply. The elephant's young signifies the fruitful labour of productive study; the restorative Spirit has its own water. This washes away and cleanses filth from the soul [1155] and brings grace to it. Purity will result in beauty. The serpent is the long-standing enemy of the human race, who attacks us and is ever present, ready to contrive his deceptions. When combat summons the battle-lines now on the point of engaging, at the sight of blood the elephant thirsts for battle. [1160] Once he has tasted it, his heart rages, he becomes violent, he takes hold of his anger, he attacks the enemy and roars ferociously with emotions that have been set ablaze. Therefore, let your heart glow, let ardent hope lift up your soul. Let your love increase now that you have tasted Christ's blood. Let the enemy go out and stir up conflicts; he fights unarmed, [1165] except for the weapons supplied to him by vigilant deceit. Let hope supply you a helmet, endurance a shield; let true faith be your sword and unending love your lance. Let the virtue of justice be your defence, the Christ who leads the way your help; under his guidance you will be victorious. [1170] Pray with Moses; Joshua will fight and cut the enemy down; so will the Amalechite depart from you.

Whether I like it or not, my writing is in the service of the stern reader. I want to be under obligation to everyone. To you, fair reader, [1175]

Qui uultu placido carmina nostra probas.
Censor qui cinico me rodit dente libellum
    Condat; erit legi subditus ipse sue.
Numquam lima carens macula solacia mundo
1180   Prebet; habet neuos forma decora suos.
Marmorei lapidis facies non semper ad unguem
    Equatur; nodos cirpus habere solet.
Cur me succensens quasi cornibus impetis hostem?
    Cum tibi displiceant, cur mea scripta legis?
1185 Cornua limaci, scarabeo cornua dantur;
    Deformes secum gestat uterque notas.
Per loca que transit uestigia feda relinquit
    Limax; pollutis insidet ille locis.
Hic inmundiciam designat, at ille figurat
1190   Desidiam; queuis est fugienda tibi.
Estus auaricie quid non presumat amore
    Questus? emptores prothdolor! aspis habet.
Institor exponit ueno letale uenenum,
    Buffonis miseras conparat emptor opes.
1195 Immo reseruatur longeuo tempore monstrum
    Quod placidis epulis pascit auara manus.
Uirgis cesa lues uirus quod pectore gestat
    Effundit pelli; suscipit illud herus;
Sic alimenta suo domino cum fenore soluit;
1200   Auro preferri toxica, Crasse, uides?
O dolor! o gemitus! o tanti causa pudoris!
    Quam misere, miser, es condicionis, homo!
Emptores miseri contendunt se licitando
    Vincere, nam magni merx miseranda licet.
1205 Pluris constabit uirus quam gemma reclusa
    Corpore que uires fertur habere suas.
Ethiopi corpus merx est preciosa draconis,
    Nam capitis thalamo fulgida gemma latet.
Uilius humano quod corpus corpore censes,
1210   Si censor uerax cuncta notare uelis?
Nullam Narcisi florenti corpore gemmam

1190. Que uis **P**   1191. quid **M**, qui **P**   1211. narcissi **P** *with an expunction mark under first* **s**.

you who judge my poems with a gentle expression, I will render great thanks. Any critic who disparages me with cynical envy is free to produce a book; he will be subject to his own rules. A file that is free from stain never provides comfort to the world; elegant beauty has its own imperfections. [1180] The surface of a marble slab is not always perfectly smooth. A bull-rush usually contains knots. Why do you rage and attack me with your horns, as if I am an enemy? Since they give you no pleasure, why do you read my writings?

Feelers are assigned to the snail and antennae to the beetle; [1185] both creatures carry with them unsightly marks. The snail leaves disgusting trails along the paths it crosses; the latter settles in spots which are polluted. The latter describes a lack of purity, but the former defines idleness. You must avoid them both. [1190]

What would the heat of avarice not dare in its lust for profit? What a shame it is that the asp finds buyers! The hawker sets out lethal poison for sale, a buyer procures the toad's contemptible riches. Indeed the monster, fed by the hand of avarice on pleasing delicacies, is saved up for a long time. [1195] The plague, beaten with branches, spews out onto a skin the poison it harbours in its chest. The owner takes it up. In this way he discharges for his owner recompense for its rearing, with interest. Do you see, Crassus, that poisons are preferred to gold? [1200] What pain! What grief! What a cause for intense shame! Worthless man, what an unfortunate state you find yourself in! Despicable buyers compete to outdo themselves in the bidding, for the contemptible merchandise is for sale at a high price. The poison will cost more than any unearthed jewel, which is said to contain in its substance particular virtues. [1205] The precious merchandise is the body of the Ethiopian serpent, for the glittering gem lies hidden in the head's inner chamber. What body do you judge to be more vile than the human body, if you are truly a censor and wish to brand everything? [1210] You will discover no jewel on the body of Narcissus in his bloom; beneath a snow-

1204. licet] passiue.

Inuenies; niuea sub cute feda latent.
Syderea facie precellens forma Lacene,
Quam prefers stellis numinibusque, Pari,
1215   Est splendor misere cutis in cinerem redigende;
Ha! uermes paries, tam miseranda parens.
Quid? Pari, dum corpus tenerum tua brachia cingunt
Et nectar sapiunt oscula blanda tibi,
Illa caro tam cara tibi, tam deliciosa,
1220   Infaustam sobolem parturit, edit, alit.
Admittit tecum consortes candida bissus
Et tibi dat socios quo requiescis ebur.
Morato canis ingenio uel amicior usu
Pertulit humanas extimuisse minas.
1225   Blandus adulator, custos tutissimus arcens
Insidias furum, fidus amator heri.
Prodit et in risus hominum deformis ymago,
Simia, nature degenerantis homo.
Velleribus mollescit ouis, capreque maritus
1230   Et capra uestitur asperiore toga.
Scisimus obrepsit et uestitura potentes
Matrix et spolio non leuiore beuer.
Nascuntur seruire boues, animalque timoris
Crescit in auriculas, res fugitiua, lepus.
1235   Vocem predatur ramis uetus incola silue;
Est predo radius, dens animusque rapax.
Ascribunt radio quod sic subducitur usus
Sermonis; gelidi causa timoris obest.
Hinc pauor infrigidat artus, stupor occupat inde
1240   Sensus qui propria destituuntur ope.
Adde quod inficitur aer liuore maligni
Visus; infectus inficit inde uirum.
Fur nocturnus oues rapit; hinc suffocat, at inde
Suggillat fauces sicque cruore madet.

f. 223va (margin at 1220)

1215 (margin)
1225 (margin)
1230 (margin)
1235 (margin)
1240 (margin)

1223. uel **M**, ut et **P**   **1231.** Scisimus **M**, SIcimus **P**; [[ob]]repsit **P**   **1232.** matrix
P [= martix]; Martrix **M**; *NG* L–M **227.** s. v. *martur is m. notes Neckam DNV ed. Wright*, **99**: Penula mantelli sit ex scisimis, vel experiolis,...cujus urla sit ex sabelino et *matrice*, vel bivere...   **1233.** animalque **M**, animasque **P**   **1243.** oues *ed.*, opes **P**

white skin lurks the disgusting. The Spartan woman's beauty, supreme in its divine appearance, which you, Paris, prefer to the stars and the gods, is the brilliance of a worthless surface that is doomed to be reduced to dust. [1215] Alas! As a parent, you deserve so much pity, for you will spawn worms. What? Paris, while your arms encircle her soft body and her seductive kisses taste of honey on your lips, that flesh so dear to you, so full of delights, gives birth to, produces and nourishes an unpropitious offspring. [1220] The white linen sheets admit partners along with you and the ivory couch on which you relax supplies you with allies.

Somewhat friendly from its conditioned nature or through practice, the dog has put up with experiencing fear by facing threats from people. It is a fawning sycophant, a most protective guardian who fends off [1225] thieves and their traps, and a loyal friend to his master. The ape, a being of degenerate nature, a misshapen image of mankind, emerges to provoke laughter. With its fleece the sheep grows soft and the nanny-goat's husband and the she-goat are clothed in somewhat rougher dress. [1230] The squirrel approaches stealthily, as does the marten, whose purpose is to clothe the powerful, and the beaver, no less trivial a spoil. Oxen are born to slave and the hare, a fearful animal, a fugitive creature, grows into its ears.

The ancient inhabitant amid the forest's branches plunders the voice; [1235] the eye is the predator, and the tooth is a rapacious intellect. That the use of speech is withdrawn in this manner people attribute to the eye. Chilling fear constitutes the reason and it is harmful. Because of this, dread causes limbs to run cold; then stupefaction seizes the senses which are robbed of their own resources. [1240] Add the fact that the atmosphere is infected by the malice of an evil eye. The tainted air then corrupts man. At night a thief carries off the sheep; after this, he chokes them, but then he crushes their throats and, as a result, he is

1222. ebur] Eburneus lectus.
1224-25. Bernardus.
1227-30. Bernardus.
1231-34. Bernardus.

1245   Nec sedare sitim ualet ille sititor auarus
        Sanguinis et lassus non saciatus abit.
   Predo rapax Pharao uetus apti subripit usum
        Sermonis, rapiens simplicitatis oues.
   Inproba seuicies dens est, intencio uisus;
1250   Designes animi nomine uelle malum.
   En lupus! ergo canis si desit, si tibi cornu
        Vel baculi desit copia, Meri, fuge.
   Sit caule custos prudencia, sit tibi cornu
        Iudicii terror; hec ciet, ille fugat.
1255   Fistula dulce canens sermo diuinus; honesti
        pastoris baculus crux sacra siue fides.
   Que sunt arbitrio uisus obnoxia cano
        Haut umquam mentem sollicitare solent.
   Nature minus attendit miracula uulgus
1260   Set que miratur rarior usus habet.
   In uinum mutauit aquam uitis generosa,
        Cum mundator aque nobilitauit eam.
   Hoc insigne stupet opus orbis, cum tamen usus
        Ignorans cernat cotidianus idem.
1265   In ligno uitis putrescit aquaticus humor
        Transit et in uinum ros ueniens ab humo.
   Cornibus emunit ceruum Natura quotannis
        Et noua munifice larga ministrat ei.
   Innouat arma tue menti depicta decenter
1270   Fabri que stellas est fabricata manus.
   Quando procell<os>as agmen se mittit in undas,
        Cui robur maius preuius intrat eas.
   Qui sequitur placide capud aptat clunibus eius;
        Hoc sibi succedens ordine turba natat.
1275   Oppositum sic litus adit grex; ecce monetur
        Doctorum cetus ordinis esse memor.
   Fonte sitim sedans senii fastidia delet;
        Indignans super hoc tercia Parca gemit.
   Quamquam delires, poteris renouare iuuentam,

1258. umquam *ed.,* numquam **P**   1267. Cornibus *ed.,* ceruus **P**; quot annis
P   1271. undas *ed.,* undis **P**

drenched in blood. Nor with his insatiable thirst for blood is he able to quench his parched throat [1245] and he departs, exhausted but unsatisfied. The rapacious plunderer, Pharoah of old, steals away the practice of suitable discourse, carrying away the sheep of innocence; teeth symbolize fierce cruelty, the eye represents intention. With the name for the will you may describe an evil wish. [1250]

Look! A wolf! Therefore, if you do not have a dog, if you do not have available a bow or a bundle of sticks, Moeris, run away! Let discretion stand guard over the fold; let the bow represent for you terror before the Judgement; the latter rouses, the former puts to flight. The sweet sounding pipe is God's word; [1255] the honest shepherd's crook is the holy cross or faith.

Facts that are submitted to the mature judgement of sight do not as a rule ever disturb man's intellect. The common folk pay little attention to nature's miracles, but a more uncommon occasion contains aspects at which it does marvel. [1260] The fruitful vine changed water into wine, when He cleansed the water and ennobled it. The world stays entranced at this remarkable deed, though the everyday world witnesses the same, although it does not recognize the event. Aqueous humour putrifies in the wood of the vine [1265] and moisture, rising from the ground, passes through into wine.

Every year nature fortifies the stag with antlers and in her abundance she bountifully supplies it with fresh growth. The hand of the craftman, who fashioned the stars, renews armour appropriately conceived for your mind. [1270] When the column launches itself into stormy waters, the stag possessing the greater strength enters the waters, leading the way. The following stag gently nestles its head into the haunches (of the one in front). Following each other in this order the troop swims across. In this formation the herd makes its way to the opposite shore. [1275] Note: the crowd of teachers is advised to be mindful of order. Slaking his thirst with water, the stag abolishes the disgust that attaches to old age; the three Fates groan indignantly over this. Although you may be deranged, you will be able to renew your youth,

---

1261. uitis] Christus dicit: *ego sum uitis uera* [Jo 15, 1].

1280   Cum te mundauit fons pietatis aqua.
                    Vexantes ceruum uermes sub cornibus herent;
                        Cura ne curis sollicitere nouis.
f. 223vb   Orbate uitrea delusus ymagine feruor
                        Tigridis indignans linquere cepta dolet.
1285   Lucida set fragilis cum sit mundana uoluptas,
                        Ne te seducat tam fugitiua, caue.
                    Numina cum celum peterent tellure relicta,
                        Ingemuit natis Ops spoliata suis.
                    Indignans igitur fouet alto corde dolorem;
1290   Nature properat tristis adire domum.
                    Aduertens tanti causam Natura doloris
                        Irate uotis spondet adesse dee.
                    Inperat ut tellus pariat fecunda Gigantes,
                        Qui mox in superos prelia seua parent.
1295   Obsequitur iussis producens monstra tumensque
                        Contractis miserum naribus edit opus.
                    Gesticulans igitur a simo symia nomen
                        Contraxit naso lusibus apta nouis.
                    Mentiri risus, humanos fingere gestus
1300   Gaudet; gallus eam cogit inire fugam.
                    Deliciosus ei cibus est murena; leoni
                        Ergo maturam symia prebet opem.
                    Vnguibus armatus ursus deseuit in hostem,
                        Natiua languens debilitate capud.
1305   Viscose carni partus informis apertam
                        Dat formam lingue sedulitate sue.
                    Qve uis urinam mures infundere cogit
                        Morsibus infaustis, vncia seua, tuis?
                    Non illos rupes, non interualla locorum,
1310   Non mare nec prudens ars reuocare potest.
                    Vertitur in lapidem lincis liquor; inuida nostris
                        Usibus ut lateat sponte recondit eam.
                    Liuor, auariciam stimulas set et inficis; illa
                        Te fedat crucians, tabida, ceca lues.
1315   Nature munus luteo sub puluere claudis;

1294. Qui...parent *ed.,* Cui...patent **P**

when the fountain of piety has cleansed you in its waters. [1280] Snakes cling under the antlers, causing the stag distress. Take care that you are not harrassed by fresh anxieties.

Tricked by her reflection in a glass, the passionate tiger, stripped of its young, feels rage and pain at abandoning what it has begun. Since worldly pleasures are brilliant but brittle, [1285] take care that such fugitive matters do not lead you astray.

When the gods abandoned the earth and made for heaven, Ops, robbed of her children, mourned her loss. And so, she raged and nursed a pain deep in her heart. In sadness she hurried to consult nature in her home. [1290] Nature, observing the reasons from her great distress, solemnly promises that she will support the wishes of the angry goddess. She commands the fertile earth to create giants, that they may then prepare for violent warfare against the gods above. The earth complies with the orders and produces monsters; and from her swollen state [1295] she brings forth an unfortunate creation with flattened nostrils. As a result, the gesticulating ape, suited for fresh sport, contracted a name from its flat nose. It loves to feign laughter, to devise human gestures. The cock forces it to run in headlong flight. [1300] A lamprey is delicious food for it. The ape, therefore, provides the lion with ripe riches.

Armed with claws the bear rages against the enemy; her head droops from innate weakness. Through the continual application of her tongue, she imposes a clear [1305] form upon the viscous flesh of her shapeless young.

Fierce wildcat, what force compels mice to squirt urine on the unfortunate bites you inflict? No cliffs, no distance between places, no sea, no practised art can call them off. [1310]

The lynx's urine turns to stone. Begrudging our enjoyment of it, she instinctively buries it so that it may remain hidden. Envy, you incite avarice but you also taint it; that notoriously blind and wasting plague torments and defiles you. You hide nature's gift under the muddy

1288. ops] terra.

Quidnam gemma latens utilitatis habet?
　　Prodeat in lucem: lucebit gracius; usus
　　　　Natiuum lumen letius esse facit.
　　Obducant solem sic ut non luceat orbi
1320　　　　Nubila: nonne minor gloria solis erit?
　　Ergo sub modio non sit conclusa, set alto
　　　　Emineat placide lux radiosa loco.
　　Ha quociens effert humiles tumor assecla fastus!
　　　　Quos prius erexit spes, dolor inde premit.
1325　Informare potest moralis fabula mores;
　　　　Prebet iam dictis nostra fabella fidem.
　　Mvs igitur sibi concilium iussit celebrari,
　　　　Sciturus quenam danda sit uxor ei.
　　Facture iurat se ducere uelle potentis
1330　　　　Natam que superis iure placere queat.
　　Set constare sibi uult de uirtute parentis,
　　　　Cuius uim laudent sydera, terra, mare.
　　Dum rex declarat effectum mentis, ab ore
　　　　Ipsius pendet curia tota silens.
1335　Rege tacente subit murmur uarioque tumultu
　　　　Aula strepit; uariis dissona turba fauet.
　　Vna tamen cunctis tandem sentencia sedit
　　　　Vt rex proponat solis adire domum.
　　Uix emensus iter Phebi conscendit in aulam;
1340　　　　Gemmarum fulgor igneus ornat eam.
　　Regia solis erat sublimi<b>us alta columpnis
　　　　Clara micante auro stelliferisque gazis.
　　Irradians in ea carbunculus ardet; achatem
　　　　Non pallere sinit flammiger ille rubor.
1345　Examitum, rutam, laurum seseque smaragdi
f. 224ra　　　　Contendit placidus uincere posse uiror.
　　Crisolito cedit fului preciosa metalli
　　　　Gloria, scintillans vnio fulget ibi.
　　Dum celi facies ridet letissima, confer
1350　　　　Celo saphirum: par utriusque decor.

1316. Quidnam gemma latens *ed.,* Gemma latens quidnam **P**

earth. [1315] What utility does a hidden jewel have? Let it emerge into the light; its glitter will be more agreeable; enjoyment causes its natural light to shine with greater pleasure. If clouds cover the sun so that its light does not fall upon the world, will not the sun's glory be diminished? [1320] Therefore, do not confine your light under a bushel, but let it be conspicuous, calmly emitting its rays from a place on high.

Alas! How often arrogance, a hand-maiden to pride, carries the lowly away! Later, sorrow overwhelms people who previously had been buoyed by hope. A morality tale has the power to shape our behaviours. [1325] Now our short story will lend credibility to these assertions.

A mouse, therefore, ordered a council to be convened for him, so that he might know which woman was fated to be granted him as wife. He swears that he wants to marry the daughter of a powerful creature, one who would justly be able to satisfy the gods. [1330] But he wants to establish to his own satisfaction questions about the parent's power, whose excellence the stars, earth and sea would praise. While the king openly declared his mind's purpose, the entire court hung on his words in silence. As the king finished speaking, a murmur arose and the hall rumbled with various disturbances. [1335] The crowd disagreed and favoured differing options. However, everyone settled eventually upon one decision; as a result, the king resolved to approach the mansion of the sun. Having covered the journey with difficulty, he climbed up into Phoebus's palace, which was adorned with the fiery brilliance of jewels. [1340] The sun's palace, supported on raised columns, shone with the glitter of gold and riches supplied by the stars. Upon the walls a blazing carbuncle beams out its rays. Its well-known fiery redness did not permit the agate to lose its natural colour. The serene green of an emerald vied to use its power to overwhem the samite, the laurel and itself. [1345] The extravagant glory of the tawny metal yielded before a topaz; there gleamed a sparkling pearl. While the face of heaven presents its happiest smile, compare the saphire with the sky. Both are equally beautiful. [1350] The amethyst, jasper, topaz and the mixture

1341. Ouidius.

Iacinctus, iaspis, topazius atque piropus
    Contendunt radios uincere, Phebe, tuos.
Nocte relegata plus se debere fatetur
    Gemmis quam soli perpetuata dies.

1355 Sole salutato causaque uie reserata
    Sol sacra de sacro pectore uerba refert:
«Non te sollicitet, non gloria uexet inanis;
    Spes circumuentrix fallere blanda solet.
Cum michi subducat nubes tenuissima lumen

1360   Vt nequeam radiis exhilarare solum,
Ha! nostris uires nubis preferre licebit;
    Consors digna tibi filia nubis erit.
Vsibus apta tuis adeas umbracula nubis;
    Hec loca non poteris lucida ferre diu.»

1365 Rex igitur tumido uoluens sub pectore curas
    Indignans nubis tecta subire parat.
Intrat et aerio uelatam cernit amictu
    Reginam; pandit ordine cuncta suo.
Illa breui sermone refert: «Sum uiribus inpar

1370   Uento qui nutu concutit alta suo;
Menia, templa, domos subuertit; me fugat Arthos
    Nunc, me uexatam suscipit inde Nothus.
Ergo tuis uotis feliciter accidet, eius
    Si tibi legitime nubere nata uolet.»

1375 Rex spe delusus consumit gaudia uotis
    Et mox Eolii carceris ima petit.
Explicat aduentus causam; cui uentus: «Amoris
    Tu michi perpetuo federe uinctus eris:
Quid miri? tu me tanto dignaris honore

1380   Vt cupias natam ducere rite meam.
Set desunt uires quas ascribit michi uulgus,
    Namque meus modico uincitur imbre furor.
Ergo si pluuie nubat tibi filia, felix
    Et uoti conpos efficiare tui.»

1385 Spes motum geminat, iam tecta madencia cernit;

1369. refert *ed.*, referti? **P**   1374. uolet *ed.*, uelit *corrected from* uelet **P**   1384.
uoti conpos *ed.*, conpos uoti **P**; efficiare *ed.*, efficiere **P**

of gold and bronze eagerly compete to surpass the rays of the sun. When night has been banished, the uninterrupted light of day confesses that its debt to the gems is greater than to the sun.

After the mouse greeted the sun and disclosed the reason for his journey, [1355] the sun delivered from his holy heart hallowed words: «You should not be disturbed or plagued by vainglory. Hope is deceptive and is usually seductive and treacherous. Because the most insignificant cloud takes away my light so that I lose my power to gladden the earth with my rays, [1360] you will be at liberty to prefer its powers to mine. The cloud's daughter will prove a partner worthy of you. You should approach the shady places offered by the cloud, because they are suitable for your purposes. You will not be able to stand these realms of light for long.»

Therefore, the king turns over his concerns [1365] in a mind swollen with ambition, and readies himself to approach the house of the cloud, despite his impatience. As he enters, he sees the queen veiled in a mantle of air; he relates the whole story from the beginning. The cloud replies with a brief speech: «In strength I am unequal to the wind, who shakes the heights whenever he pleases; [1370] he brings walls, temples and houses tumbling down; at one moment, the North wind puts me to flight, from there the South wind harries and takes me up. Therefore, your wishes will turn out happily, if his daughter consents to marry you lawfully.»

Disappointed in his hopes, the king reduces the joy in his prayers to nothing [1375] and next he makes for the depths of Aeolus's cave. He unfolds the reason for his arrival, to which the wind replies: «You will be bound to me in an everlasting compact of love. Why do you marvel? You judge me worthy of an honour so great that you desire to marry my daughter with all proper ceremony. [1380] But I lack the powers which common folk attribute to me, for my fury is subdued by a moderate rain-storm. Therefore, if the rain-shower's daughter married you, you would become a happy man and possess what you wish for.» Hope redoubled his movements; already he has the dripping roof-

1365. yronia.
1379. tu me] cum accentu humiliacionis [superscript].

Rex rem declarat, subicit illa gemens:
«Publica priuate persona potensque maritam
    Exposcis natam; vera referre libet.
Est Cibele regina potens, generosa deorum
1390   Mater, que cunctis nobilitate preest.
Eius inexhaustas uires, cataclisme, probasti;
    Indignans imbres ebibit ipsa meos.
Absorbet quicquit effundo; rebus habundat
    Gemmis et plumis, Sardanapalle, tuis.
1395 Delicias Bachi Cererisque ministrat habunde;
    Hec mel Aristeo, poma dat Alcinoo,
Ferrum concedit Marti, Ianoque metalla
    Cetera; que uulgo nota referre pudet.»
Rex Cibelen adit exponens que causa laboris;
1400   Cui mox subridens talibus orsa dea est:
«Iungit amor similes: gaudet pare tigride tigris,
    Ceruo cerua placet, grus comes apta grui,
Vrsus et ursa pares; nubit tibi, regule, parra.
    Nec fas est aquilam nubere, rana, tibi.
1405 Par igitur iungenda pari Nasone docente;
    Si qua uoles apte nubere, nube pari.
Prodeat in medium terre soboles; societur
    Mus muri.» Ridet Iupiter, acta placent.
f. 224rb Mox assignatur sponse donacio propter
1410   Connubium. Quid ni? Dos datur apta uiro.
Non se presumat cedris conferre mirica,
    Non ulule cignis, non saliunca rose.
Alta petat fumus, mox euanescit in auras.
    Sceptra gerat Dauus regia, Dauus erit.
1415 Pelle leonina uestitur asellus, at illum
    Prodet uox, auris segniciesque grauis.
Solares radios, quia sic a sole repulsam
    Passus es, odisti, mus, latebrasque colis.
Dampnari tenebris quiuis de iure meretur

1386. declarat *ed.,* declarans **P**   1391. in exhaustas **P**; uires *ed.,* iure **P**   **1411.**
Nonse **P** *with a dividing line after* Non

tops in sight. [1385] After the king had publicly declared his purpose, the rain adds these words with a sigh: «You, a public and powerful figure, request from me, a private person, my daughter as your wife. I would like to call to mind a true story. Cibele is a mighty queen, a highborn mother of the gods, who surpasses all in her nobility. [1390] The deluge tested her inexhaustible strength. Indignant, she absorbs my rain-storms by herself. Whatever I pour forth she devours. She overflows with wealth, with jewels and, Sardanapallus, with your down pillows. She supplies the delights of Bachus and Ceres in abundance. [1395] This goddess provides Aristaeus with honey and Alcinous with apples. To Mars she yields iron and to Janus the other metals. I am ashamed to record facts that are common knowledge.»

The king approaches Cibele, explaining the reason for his distress. Then, smiling at him the goddess began her remarks as follows [1400]: «Love unites creatures that are alike; the tiger enjoys having a tigress as his mate; the doe delights a stag; a crane is suitable company for a crane. The bear and his mate are a pair. A barn owl marries you, small bird. It is not lawful for an eagle to marry a frog. According to Naso's teaching, like must be joined to like. [1405] If in some way you want to enter an appropriate marriage, marry an equal. Let an offspring from the earth come forward into our midst. Let a mouse be joined to a mouse.»

Jupiter smiles; the transactions are approved. Then, because of the marriage a gift is conferred upon the betrothed. Why not? A suitable dowry is given to the husband. [1410] The tamarisk should not presume to compare itself with a cedar, nor an owl with a swan, nor wild nard with the rose. If smoke curls up to higher altitudes, it soon vanishes into the air. Though Davus may bear the royal sceptre, he will remain Davus. Cover an ass with a lion skin; [1415] but his braying sound, his ears and ponderous slowness will betray him. Mouse, you dislike the rays of the sun, because you suffered rejection by the sun in this way, and you inhabit hidden recesses. Anyone hoisted, indeed

---

1389. cibele] Cibele quasi cubile, quia terra centrum est et prestat stabilitatem et sic producitur media (cf. J. W. Jones, 1996, 112, 106; 198, 92). Cum autem corripitur, greca dictio est et dicitur cibele quasi charombale a rotacione capitis [cf. Serv., A. 3, 111. (ed. Thilo-Hagen, 1: 362, 12-3)]. Marcialis: Et Cibeles picto stat choribante tholus [Mart., 1, 70, 10].
1396. Species pro genere.

1420   Quem fastus supra se uehit, immo rapit.
Delicias quas nec diues Natura creauit
      Appetere insani pectoris esse scias.
Hoc experta probat in talpam uersa puella,
      Triticee Cereris munera uana ferens.
1425 Hinc est quod terra tantum recreatur in esum;
      Ecce grauem culpam pena secuta grauis.
Panis confirmans hominis cor, lectio sacra
      Deliciosa minus, perfide Fauste, tibi est.
Pagina celestis tibi displicet; vtere terra.
1430   Disciplina tibi terrea dulce sapit;
Luminibus capti fodere cubilia talpe
      Et latebris heresis ceca latere solet.
Adde quod et luxum crebro comitatur egestas;
      Prodiga uirgo potens indiga fiet anus.
1435 Precessiua famis est crapula; nam Nabuzardan
      Subuertit Solime menia, templa, domos.
Est larus uolucris instar pennis decoratus;
      Nunc aqua, nunc tellus hospicium dat ei.
Effugit insidias pernici sepe uolatu;
1440   Designantur aqua mollia, dura solo.
Prospera mollia sunt, aduersaque dura uocantur;
      Nos exercet sors aspera, blanda iuuat.
Prosperitas fluidos, stabiles sors aspera reddit;
      Nunc sto cum terra, nunc uelud unda fluo.
1445 Set quid? siue dies sit lucida prosperitatis
      Seu sors nubila sit, mens uolet alta petens.
Prima senectutis actus prenuntiat etas;
      Balatu mores predicat agnus ouis.
Hinnulus indiciis certis se conprobat esse
1450   Ceruum. Quod rampno sit sata, spina probat.
En uulpis soboles thalamis inclusa parentis
      Declarat cuius condicionis erit.
Perforat ungue cutem quod conformandus auitis
      Moribus est; unguis asperitate docet.

1424. Triticee **M**, Tuticee **P**

snatched up, by pride above his station, rightly deserves to be sentenced to darkness. [1420]

You should know that it is characteristic of a mad mind to seek out delights that not even nature in all her richness created. The experience of the girl transformed into a mole proves this, as she receives the fruitless gifts of Ceres's wheat. This is the reason that from the earth so much is reproduced for food. [1425] Observe the heavy punishment that followed a serious crime. The bread that strengthens the heart of mankind, reading the holy book, brings no pleasure to your palate, faithless Faustus. The heavenly book offers you no delight; enjoy the earth. In your mouth earthly knowledge has a sweet taste. [1430] Because of deficient eyesight moles have dug lairs, while blind heresy as a rule skulks in hidden recesses. Add the fact that extreme poverty frequently accompanies even extravagance. A prodigal young woman, though powerful, will become a needy woman when old. Dissipation is the prelude to hunger. For Nabuzardan [1435] overthrew the walls, the temples and the houses of Jerusalem.

Like a bird, the amphibious animal is adorned with wings. At one moment, water offers it lodgings, at another, land. It often escapes traps through swift flight. Water represents easy triumphs, earth the harsh aspects of life. [1440] Successes are soft, while adversities are termed hard. A harsh destiny plagues us, an agreeable lot brings delight. Good fortune makes us soft, desperate conditions cause us to stand firm. Sometimes I stand immovable with the earth, at others I fluctuate like water. But what of it? Whether there appears a brilliantly successful day or an overcast condition looms, [1445] the mind should soar as it makes for the heights.

The first stage of life predicts the actions of old age. With its bleating the lamb broadcasts the nature of a sheep. A young stag demonstrates by unmistakable signs that it is a stag. A thorn shows that it originated from the buckthorn. [1450] Look! A fox's young, when enclosed in its mother's womb, openly declares what its nature will be. Using its claws, it cuts through the skin, because it has to conform to atavistic behaviours. The claw teaches by its roughness. A mind wickedly devoted to pursuing deception is tormented by malignant offspring,

1446. uolet] subiunctiui modi.

1455   Mens studio fraudis male dedita prole maligna
            Uexatur, quam fraus inproba mente parit.
        In predam predo fallax sese resupinans
            Insidias ueteres aucupis arte preit

[1455] which monstrous delusion engenders in the mind. The predator, full of guile, lies on his back waiting for prey and with this trick
tops the bird-catcher's time-honoured wiles.

NOTES

1-36. *Introduction*

In a condensed and partial account, the poet sketches the unity underlying the diversity of creation, as he passes from the First Cause through the firmament to the earth and the zone of the air inhabited by birds.

1. **Ornatu uario**: cf. *LSD* 2, 337 (p. 381W); 8, 155 (p. 485W); the epithet suggests profusion and complexity; **mundus**: the universe is painted with the colours of both nature and art; **depingitur**: the verb, in its meaning of «to represent (in words)» [*OLD* 4], overlays the creation of the universe with the theme of the poet's creation cf. Dronke, Bernardus Silvestris, *Cosmographia*, 58; **artis**: cf. Peter of Blois, *Carm.* 5, 8, 3, 7-8 *Arti diuine linquitur, / quod flos de spina nascitur.*

2. **Docta manus…opus**: cf. Hildebert, *Carm. min.* 46, 9-10 *et opus mirabile cernens, / est mirata suas hoc potuisse manus*; Alan of Lille, *Anticlaudianus* 2, 474 *Nam pictor predoctus eam descripserat*; cf. *SD* 1, 1270 *Fabri…manus*; **nobilitauit opus**: *LSD* 2, 360 (p. 381W); *SD* 2, 36, 1385-6 *Candida simplicitas roseo sociata pudori / Clarum nature nobilitauit opus*; cf. 2, 145 *Nobile condit opus quod totus predicet orbis*, 351-2 *spiritus ille perhennis / Se soli domino nobile debet opus*; Bernardus Silvestris, *Cosmographia* 1, 1, 63 (ed. Dronke, 98); *LSD* 3, 278 (p. 401W), 952 (p. 417W), 1040 (p. 419W); 4, 265 (p. 426W); 5, 292 (p. 447W), 486 (p. 451W); *SD* 1, 552, 1060 *Inuideo si quis nobile condat opus*; *LSD* 2, 204 (p. 378W) on the phoenix.

3. **In rebus lucet**: cf. *DNR* 2, Prologue (p. 125W) *in rebus sapientia Dei elucet*; **artis**: cf. *LSD* 4, 257 (p. 425W) *singula disponens, ars, noys, ordo, decor*; **potestas**: cf. *SD* 1, 17.

4. **Tot…species**: *LSD* 4, 314 (p. 427W), 10, 9 (p. 496W); **rerum species**: Bernardus Silvestris, *Cosmographia* 1, 2, 8 *rerum species reformauit* (sc. Noys); 1, 4, 8 (ed. Dronke, 101, 118); *SD* 1, 15 *Tot rerum facies*, 497; *NA* 2, 21 *Cernere tot rerum species cupiet Iouis ales*; **rerum… condidit**: Arator, *Ep. ad Florianum* 11 (ed. McKinlay, *CSEL* 72: 2) *Naturaeque modo, quam rerum condidit Auctor*, **una manus**: cf. *SD* 1, 8.

5. **uarias artes**: cf. Mart. 7, 32, 13 *per varias artes*; for Faustus's accomplishment in the liberal arts cf. Aug., *Conf.* 5, 3, 6 (ed. Knöll, *CSEL* 33: 93, 10-18).

6. **Vsurpas**: followed by an accusative and infinitive; *OLD* 5 «to make (frequent) use of (word, expression etc.) in speech»: note the repetition of *uarias…uarios*; **uarios…deos**: cf. *LSD* 1, 115 (p. 359W) *Auctores rerum geminos fingis* (of Faustus); Gnosticism, which survived in Manichean doctrine, held that the creator God, the Demiurge, was different from the supreme and unknowable Divine being. Christianity insisted on the identity of the two cf. *SD* 1, 7; for Faustus's position on the question and Augustine's response cf. *Contra Faustum* 21 (ed. Zycha, *CSEL* 25: 568-90).

7. **Fauste, tace!**: on the technique of addressing a fictive opponent to mark a break in a text's structure, see Haye 1997, 189; Faustus, together with Zoilus in *SD* 2, plays the stan-

dard foil to Neckam on a number of issues; the phrase recurs in *SD* 2, 403, 410, 414, 416, 418 *perfide Fauste, tace!*; *Poems* 3, 152 (ed. Walther, 1962, 121); *LSD* 1, 110, 112, 114 (p. 359W), 236 (p. 362W), 557, 567, 569, 571, 587 (p. 370W), 639 (p. 372W); 3, 8 (p. 395W); 5, 898 (p. 461W); Eugenius, *praefatio*, 7 (*MGH, AA* 14: 231) *invide, iam cessa, iam cessa, perfide, cessa*; at *SD* 2, 1465-6 Neckam puns on the meaning of Faustus's name (»Lucky«): *Pelagius pelagus heresum Faustusque recedit / Infaustus* [cf. Ov., *Fast.* 5, 453 *Faustulus infelix*]. Neckam characterizes heretics in terms established by Augustine; for this practice in the 11th-c., cf. M. Frassetto, «Reaction and Reform», *The Catholic Historical Review* 83 (1997), 385-400; Faustus of Milevis, born sometime before 350, became a bishop in the Manichean sect (cf. Aug., *Contra Faustum* 1, 1 [ed. Zycha, *CSEL* 25: 251, 1] *secta Manichaeus*; *LSD* 5, 451 (p. 450W) *Cur Fausti sequeris errores, cur Manichaei?*); with him Augustine studied for almost a decade before abandoning him as a teacher. Faustus was eloquent (*suauiloquentia*), though not deeply learned in the liberal arts cf. Aug., *Conf.* 5, 3, 3; 5, 6, 11 (ed. Knöll, *CSEL* 33: 90, 16-91, 13; 97, 17) *expertus sum prius hominem expertem liberalium disciplinarum nisi grammaticae.* O'Donnell, *Augustine* 2:285-6, outlines his career cf. *RE* 6: 2, 2092-3 s. v. *Faustus* no. 17. *LSD* 5, 442 equates Faustian Manicheanism with the dualist heresy of the Albigensians in southern France; cf. Berry 87; **vnicus auctor**: cf. Matthew of Vendôme, *Tob.* 2185-6 (ed. Munari, 2: 253) *Est personarum distinctio trina, sed una / Est usya, Deus unicus, una noys.*

8. I follow **P**'s punctuation of the line, though it could be divided at the diaeresis only. In either case, Neckam emphasizes the idea of unicity in contrast to claims for multiplicity; **una manus**: Ov., *Rem.* 44; Maximianus 5, 28; **uera Noys**: cf. *CMC* Oxford, Digby 221, 81va *Noys summa pars anime est quam mentem vocamus*; *LSD* 4, 257 (p. 426W); Bernardus Silvestris, *Cosmographia* 1, 1, 6 (ed. Dronke, 97) *michi vera Minerva*; *Doctrinale* 542 *non est Verbigena nisi Christus, vera sophia.*

9. **Materiam, formas**: *LSD* 1, 27 (p. 357W); **usyas**: see Wetherbee 1972, 145, note 8, on the meaning of the term in John Scotus Eriugena; cf. the account of creation in Geoffrey of Monmouth, *Vita Merlini* 737-819; **sydera, celos**: for variations of this clausula cf. Mastandrea 791.

10. **Rex...suo**: cf. *LSD* 1, 58 (p. 358W).

11. **ligat concordi federe**: cf. *DNR* 1, 16 (p. 55W) *Satis probabiliter persuaserunt sibi philosophi mundum subsistere non posse sine quadam concordi elementorum quatuor discordia*; *SD* 2, 15-6 *simplex inmensus amoris / Innati dulci federe cuncta ligans*; 1. 261; *Doctrinale* 2636 *Si sint res aliquae concordi foedere iunctae*; Lawn, *Salern. Questions*, 160, 43-4 *Quis gumfus visum fugiens discordia rerum / Semina concilians concordi pace ligavit?*; Urso, *De commixtionibus elem.* 2 (ed. Stürner, 46) *Unde Martianus «Complexuque sacro dissona nexa foves»*, idest elementa discordantia nectis amico complexu.

12. **leges**: cf. *LSD* 4, 321 (p. 427W) *gaudent singula lege sua.*

13. **Causas, effectus**: cf. *LSD* 4, 737-47 (p. 437W) on causes and effects; Burnett in P. Dronke 1988, 166-75, discusses the prominence of causes in 12th-c. physics and its impact on other disciplines; with the translation of Arabic texts in the second half of the 12th-c. a *scientia naturalis* developed, in which the upper world was thought to cause the lower world and its motions cf. French 81-8. Aristotle postulated four causes by which the natures of things become manifest: the efficient, formal, material and final cf. *SD* 2, 400-1 *uel que proxima causa mali? / Efficiens que causa mali?*; cf. *Poems* 1, 99 (ed. Walther, 1965, 114) *Tunc rerum causas, effectus, symbola, nexus / Inquiro*; **Causas...tempora**: In the *De essentiis* 58v b-d, Her-

mann of Carinthia named five ultimate principles, called essences, that underlie all change: cause, movement, place, time and «habitude»; cf. Burnett in P. Dronke 1988, 393-4.

14. **Ciues angelicos**: cf. *LSD* 1, 69-100 (pp. 358-9W); *SD* 1, 337; 2, 17; **regula...regit**: for the etymology cf. Isid., *Orig.* 6, 16, 2 *Alii dixerunt regulam dictam vel quod regat,...*; *SD* 1, 880; 2, 205 *Recta fides regit hunc*; *LSD* 4, 287 (p. 427W) *regula...regens*, 300-1.

15. **Tot...facies**: *LSD* 4, 308 (p. 427W); **rerum facies:** cf. Dracontius, *De laudibus Dei* 1, 121 (*MGH, AA* 14: 28) *lux facies rerum*; Arundel 4, 1a, 1-3; *SD* 1, 497; **dotes / Nature**: cf. *SD* 1, 1125 *nature dotes*.

15-16. **facies... / Nature**: cf. Urso, *De commixtionibus elem.* 4, 1 (ed. Stürner, 76-7) *Sunt autem nature motus sex, scilicet generatio, corruptio, augmentum, diminutio, alteratio et secundum locum mutatio.*

17-19. **potestas**; / **...bonitas...** / **...sapientia**: cf. *LSD* 1, 39 (p. 358W) *Esse Dei, bonitas, sapientia, vita, potestas*; for celebration of God's power and bounty as evidenced in Creation cf. Dracontius, *De laudibus Dei* 1, 115-555 (*MGH, AA* 14: 28-54); on the manifestation of the attributes of divine power, goodness and wisdom in the creation cf. William of Conches, *Glosae super Platonem* (ed. Jeauneau, 60).

17. **Res...ad esse**: Geoffrey of Vitry, *Commentary on Claudian De raptu Proserpinae* ed. A. K. Clarke (Leiden, 1973), p. 31; cf. Bernardus Silvestris, *Cosmographia* 1, 2, 1 (ed. Dronke, 99) *Inconsulto enim deo priusquam de composito sententia proferatur, rebus ad essentiam frustra maturius festinatur*, *DNR* 2, prologus, (pp. 125-6W) *Potentiam enim Patris loquuntur ea per quae res potens est. Substantiales autem proprietates potentem esse rem faciunt. Sapientiam autem Dei enarrant color rei, et pulchritudo, et forma, cum figura et dispositione partium et numero. Benignitatem autem artificis summi loquuntur conservatio rei in esse et utilitas ejusdem*, *LSD* 1, 57 (p. 358W) *De non esse potens produxit in esse potenter*, 9, 271-2 (p. 492W), 311 (p. 493W); *in Eccles.* f. 121ra *Perfectionis opera perfecta sunt et qui potenter res de non esse in esse produxit creando regit ipsas sapientissime, conseruat benignissime*, f. 160ra *De non esse produxit nos in esse diuina sapientia*; for *bonitas* presiding over seven *primordiales cause* (which include *sapientia* and *uirtus*) in a 12th-c. manuscript illustration, see Dronke 1992, 53.

18. **seruat in esse**: cf. *SD* 1, 219 *conseruauit in esse*; *LSD* 1, 31 (p. 357W) *Omnia disponit, regit et conservat in esse*; *Poems* 5, 3 (ed. Esposito, 455).

19. **discernit...sapientia**: cf. *SD* 1, 180 *Distinguit...Noys*, 263 *Noys...discernit*; **mutat**: cf. *SD* 2, 1197-8 *Set loca mutantur, mutantur tempora* [*Doctrinale* 2603], *scripta / Mutari coget pristina longa dies.*

19-20. **sapientia... / ...disponit**: Sap 8, 1 *et disponit omnia* (sc. sapientia); cf. *LSD* 4, 256-7 (p. 426W) *Lusit ab aeterno summi sapientia pectoris, / Singula disponens, ars, noys, ordo, decor*; Bernardus Silvestris, *Cosmographia* 1, 2, 1 (ed. Dronke, 99) *Noys ego, scientia et arbitraria divine voluntatis ad dispositionem rerum...*; **moderatur**: cf. Maximianus 5, 129 *ipsa etiam totum moderans sapientia mundum...*; Bernardus Silvestris, *Cosmographia* 1, 1, 62 (ed. Dronke, 98).

21. **Nectit amor**: cf. Boethius, *DCP* 2, M. 8, 13-5 (ed. Bieler, *CCSL* 94: 36) *hanc rerum seriem ligat / ... / ...amor*; *LSD* 4, 826 (p. 439W) *Haec connexa sibi firmo sociantur amore.*

23. **radiare planeta**: cf. *SD* 2, 31 *Septenam radiare iubet lux quarta planetam.*

25. **Aureus...color**: cf. Claudian, *De raptu* 1, 254 *nec color unus inest: stellas accendit in auro*, *CMC*, Oxford, Digby 221, f. 63rb *Unusquisque planetarum, teste Plinio, suum proprium possidet colorem.*

27-32. According to Southern 1987, 179, Orion and Bootes are mentioned in a set of simple astronomical instructions issued to a monk in a house near Orleans in the eleventh century, who kept watch through the night in order to mark the times for daily services according to the rising and setting of the stars.

28. **area parua**: cf. *CNP* 1352 *nam seiungit eos area parua loci.*

29. **Hesperus**: the same star as Lucifer cf. Isid., *Orig.* 3, 71, 19 *Fertur autem quod haec stella oriens luciferum, occidens vesperum facit. De qua Statius (Theb.* 6, 241): *Et alterno dependitur unus in ortu*; **Lucifer ortu**: cf. Mastandrea 461.

30. **regnum...breue**: cf. Stat., *Theb.* 2, 446 *non parcit populis regnum breue* [Matthew of Vendôme, *Ars* 3, 49 (ed. Munari, 3: 189); *in Eccles.* f. 155va]; cf. Walther, *Prov.* 18197; **stella**: i. e. Lucifer, the day star, with an allusion to the fallen angel, Lucifer, who was equated with Satan cf. Is. 14, 12 *quomodo cecidisti de caelo lucifer qui mane oriebaris*; *DMLBS* 5: 1651 s. v. *lucifer* 4.

31. **Plaustra...Boetes**: cf. Ov., *Met.* 10, 446-7; Boethius, *DCP* 4, M. 5, 3 (ed. Bieler, *CCSL* 94: 78) *cur legat tardus plaustra Bootes*; Isid., *Orig.* 3, 71, 8 *Eundem et Booten dixerunt, eo quod plaustro haerent*; for the constellation Bootes used as an equivalent for *Arctos* cf. *ThLL*, 2: 2128, 80; for the form *Boetes*, see *ThLL*, 2:2128, 31-2; *DMLBS* 1: 207 s. v. *Bootes.*

32. **terio quam Cinosura**: the constellations Septentriones and Ursa minor respectively, which belong to the far north cf. Nisbet 148; cf. *LSD* 1, 355 (p. 365W) *Bos, terio, plaustrum ducunt septem teriones, / Lento subsequitur hos cynosura gradu*; 2, 95-6 (p. 375W) *Respicit oppositum septentrio frigidus austrum, / Septenus terio nomine ditat eum*; Isid., *Orig.* 3, 71, 6 *Signorum primus Arcton...Nomen est Graecum, quod Latine dicitur ursa; quae quia in modum plaustri vertitur, nostri eam Septentrionem dixerunt. Triones enim proprie sunt boves aratorii, dicti eo quod terram terant, quasi teriones* (cf. Var., L. 7, 73-4; Gel. 2, 21); see McCulloch 148 on *bos*; **Cinosura**: the constellation Ursa Minor cf. Ov., *Fast.* 3, 107-8; **colit**: note the learned play on the sense «to cultivate, to till» after Bootes, the Ploughman, and *terio* (sc. bos), the Plough Ox cf. Gel., 2, 21, 8 *...qui «triones» ...boues appellatos scribunt quasi quosdam «terriones»*, hoc est arandae *colendaeque* terrae idoneos.

33. **distingue**: cf. Ov., *Met.* 1, 47 *onus inclusum* (sc. terram) *numero distinxit eodem* (sc.quinque zonis) *cura dei*; **coluro / Bino**: cf. *SD* 2, 1095 *Obliquando means geminos secat ipse coluros*; the colures were two circles that passed through the equinoctial and solstitial points; at the poles they intersected at right angles.

33-4 **Quinque... / ...dabis**: cf. Isid., *Orig.* 3, 44; Theodulf, *Carm.* 46, 76-8 (*MGH, P. L.* 1: 546) *Aetherias zonas at rota quinque tenet. / E quibus extremae geminae sunt frigore pressae, / Torrida per medium temperat una duas*; John of Salisbury, *Enthet. maior* 743 (ed. van Laarhoven, 1: 155) *Quinque polum zonae distinguunt, aera quinque.*

34. **zonas esse dabis**: cf. Verg., *G.* 1, 233 *quinque tenent caelum zonae*; *SD* 1, 498; *LSD* 6, 22 (p. 464W). The chapter on birds in *DNR* 1, 23 (p. 70W) also follows the discussion of the element air and related topics; on the scheme that organizes the treatise in descending order from the Trinity to man and his world, see Fumagalli 62.

35-6. **Discernit... / ...amor**: cf. Theodulf, *Carm.* 72, 145-6 (*MGH. P. L.* 1: 567) *Quis* (sc. uolucribus) *cibus est varius, cantus, color atque volatus, / Penna, ungues, rostrum, mos, locus, officium*; cf. Schaller 74-5; Bernardus Silvestris, *Cosmographia* 1, 3, 482 (ed. Dronke, 116) *Distarunt volucres, corpore, mente, loco*; *DNR* 1, 23 (p. 70-5W); avian attributes and behaviours are described in the following order: *locus* (37-42), *ars* (43-6), *sonus* (47-78), *esca* (79-100), *potestas* (101-24), *calliditas* (125-48), *forme gloria* (149-72), *prolis amor* (173-8). For a list of the differentiating characteristics of plants cf. *SD* 1, 264.

36. **forme gloria**: cf. *SD* 1, 667, Maximianus 1. 17 *gloria formae*; Aldhelm, *Enig.* 96, 9 (*MGH, AA* 15: 143).

37-42. *The habitats of birds*

37. **Mergus aquas**: Ov., *Pont.* 1, 6, 52; Matthew of Vendôme, *Ep. prologus*, 36 (ed. Munari, 2: 77); **heremum turtur**: cf. Isid., *Orig.* 12, 7, 60; on different avian habitats cf. Theodulf, *Carm.* 72, 143-4 (*MGH, P. L.* 1: 567).

38. **busta colit**: *LSD* 2, 580 (p. 386W); cf. Verg., *A.* 12, 863-5 (of the owl) *quae quondam in bustis... / nocte sedens serum canit*; *SD* 1, 821 *Vpupa busta colit*; McCulloch 126; **philomena rubos**: cf. *Novale* 251 (ed. Haye, 427) *Non canit in rubeis dulcis phylomena rubetis*.

39. **petreque foramen**: cf. Ct 2, 14 *in foraminibus petrae*; Jr 13, 4; *SD* 1, 631.

40. **fida ministra**: an Ovidian phrase for Noah's dove: Ov., *Tr.* 3, 7, 2 *littera, sermonis fida ministra mei*; Gn 8, 8-11; cf. *LSD* 2, 704 (p. 389W); *SD* 1, 262;

40. **fictaque Cilla**: Nisus, king of Megara, was betrayed by his daughter Scylla, who was subsequently changed into the bird *ciris*; cf. Ov., *Met.* 8, 151; *LSD* 2, 307-14 (p. 380W).

41. **Turres coruus amat**: cf. *DNR* 1, 61 (p. 110W) *Turres item inhabitat* (sc. coruus); **prouida**: cf. *SD* 1, 133 *Preuidet* (sc. cornix) *hostiles concursus*.

42. **Suspendit nidum**: cf. Verg., *G.* 4, 307 *nidum suspendat*; **horret aquas**: Ov., *Pont.* 2, 7, 8 *naufragus horret aquas*; *SD* 1, 627 *abhorret aquas* (sc. psittacus).

43-46. *About art*

43. **Ingenuas uolucres**: cf. *CNP* 1301 *si sors ingenue uolucris conatibus obstat*; for *ingenuus* meaning *natiuitate liber* (cf. *ThLL*, 7: 1544, 1) applied to an animal cf. Hor., *S.* 2, 3, 186 '*astuta ingenuum vulpes imitata leonem*'; it is used of the sounds of birds by Dracontius, *Romul.* 7, 103 (*MGH, AA* 14: 154) *ingenuos dat capta sonos quasi libera .../... avis*; **ars**: the artistry of Noys (cf. *SD* 1, 3) and the skill exercised by birds; the word also wittily plays on a secondary meaning of *ingenuus*: «liberally educated» cf. *ThLL*, 7: 1547, 27; Cic., *de orat.* 1, 73 *omnibus ingenuis artibus instructus*, an idea carried on in *SD* 1, 44 with *Instruit*; *instructis* (cf. *DNR* 2, 173 (p. 300W) *ut patet instructo in geometria*); *SD* 2, 1379 *Iam libet ingenuas artes perstringere*; [cf. Ov., *Pont.* 2, 9, 46] *DNR* 2, 21 (p. 141W) *Nonne artes liberales antiquitus solis liberis servierunt? Ingenuis ingenuarum facultatum usus concessus est*; Geoffrey of Monmouth, *Vita Merlini* 1298-9 «*Volucres... / natura propria ditavit conditor orbis*».

44. **usus adest**: Ov., *Ars* 2, 676; **prompcior usus**: *LSD* 2, 615-6 (p. 387W) *Naturae virtus arti sedebat, at usus / Subsidiis opifer promptior esse solet.*

45. **ingenium...ars...vsus**: On the role of the triad (*ingenium / ars / usus*) in the development of Roman oratory and literary criticism, see Leeman and Pinkster, *M. Tullius Cicero*, 1: 209-11. The thought shifts from the formative role of *ars* in the avian world to the part it plays in shaping a literary creation. The stimulus for the latter arises from a writer's innate ability and poetic talent; technique helps to shape knowledge on any particular subject into a systematic treatise; constant exercizing of *ars* brings perfection. The first half of 45 could also mean: «the universe stimulates one's natural capacities»; for the sentiment cf. *SD* 1, 1257-8; *in Eccles.* f. 94vb *Amor igitur scientie naturaliter animo humano insitus est unde ad eius comprehensionem suspirat. Inquirit ergo rerum causas et per multorum similium inductionem naturam in artem transferre studet. In primordiis igitur sue inquisitionis uoti compos efficitur dum in-*

telligentie ipsius res inuestigare se subicere uidentur. Minio–Paluello 1954, 124, discusses Adam of Balsham's account of the development of the *ars disserendi*: through intellect (*ingenium*) man discovers reasons; *usus* expands the extent of knowledge, revealing the variety of discourse; understanding becomes easier, once rules are found to govern the discourse; cf. *LSD* 2, 617 (p. 387W) *Efficit ars, natura sed perficit usus; SD* 2, 1143-4 *Fallitur in multis assercio friuola uulgi; / Doctrine probat id ars, labor, usus, amor,* Matthew of Vendôme, *Tob.* 895-8 (ed. Munari, 2: 199) *Sunt assistrices doctrine quatuor: harum / Coniugio studium fructificare solet: / Prima parit natura quod ingenium fovet;auget / Vis exercicii, perficit usus opus* (= Walther, *Prov.* 30700a); **ingenium natura**: cf. Bernardus Silvestris, *Cosmographia* 1, 2, 2 (ed. Dronke, 99) *Et te, Natura, quia callida es ingenio...;* **ars iuuat**: cf. Boethius, *In topica Ciceronis comm.* 6 (*MPL* 64: 1155b) *Ratione quidem reperiri quiddam potest, sed melius atque facilius artifex faciet, si in opere construendo artis facultatem atque elegantiam comparet.*

45-46. **vsus / Perficit**: *LSD* 2, 617 (p. 387W) *Efficit ars, natura sed perficit usus.* Baudri, *Carm.,* 191, 45.

46. **repetatur) opus**: *Geta* 125 (ed. Cohen, 1: 39) *Propositum repetatur opus;* Baudri, *Carm.* 153, 26 *nec repetatur opus.*

47-76. The sounds birds make

48. **uarios...sonos**: *LSD* 2, 400 (p. 382W), 904 (p. 393W); cf. Isid., *Orig.* 12, 7, 9 *Varietas enim vocis eorum* (sc. avium) *docuit homines quid nominarentur, LSD* 2, 904 (p. 393W); for a survey of literary exercises based on words describing the characteristic sounds of birds and animals (*uoces animantium*) in medieval Latin prose and poetry, see Diaz y Diaz 148-55, Ziolkowski 1993, 36-8; for *uoces animantium* as an element in a 13th-c. travel poem, which post-dates the *LSD*, cf. *Novale* 215-62 (ed. Haye, 424-7), where an *accessus* points to the linguistic and didactic aspects of the component: *Nota quod causa materialis huius libri in parte est <laus> domini Henrici...; in quadam est gramatica et in quadam est moralis...; et in parte tangit proprietates avium et brutorum ad Latine eloquentie opulentiam et ad puerorum instructionem* (Haye, 408); Marcovich 411-2 argues that the catalogue in Hugutio derives, not from Suetonius, but from Osbern of Gloucester's *Derivationes* (b. 137-55 [1: 95]), a work known to Neckam, who borrowed liberally from it in writing the *SA.* Cambridge, UL, Ll. 1. 14, f. 46r, lists the *voces* as follows: *Aquila clangit / Accipiter pipilat / ... / Anas...tetrissat / Cignus dessitat uel dressitat / Ciconia gractulat uel grotolat / ... / Coruus crocitat uel craxat / Cornix buzat / Columba gemit / ... / Graculus... fringulat / Grus gruit / Hirundo minurrit... / Miluus miluit / ... / Merula frindit uel zurziat uel fringit / Noctua cucubit / Olor drensitat / ... / Pauo paululat / Perdix cacabat / Passer ticiat / Sturnus passitat* [parsitat **C**] */ Turtur gemit / Turdus* [Trudus **C**]*..socitat uel facillat / Wltur pulpat uel piopat uentilat tremit sibilat / ....*For the grammarian, these verbs, listed under the heading *De uoce* in Phocas, were categorized as *uoces* that signified naturally. Similar lists are found in Suet., fr. 161 (ed. Reifferscheid, 249-54), fr. 161b [311-2], 1-16 (*De philomela*); Aldhelm, *De metris* (*MGH, AA* 15: 179, 18-180, 19) presents them in alphabetical order in the section *De Ionico minori;* Eugenius, *Carm.* 41, 3-6 (*MGH, AA* 14: 257); *Carmen de philomela;* Eberhard, *Grecismus* 19, 32-40; Haye, 424, note on *Novale,* 215-63; **turba sonora**: cf. Matthew of Vendôme, *Ars* 1, 111, 117-62 (ed. Munari, 3: 123-5).

49. **Regia clangit auis**: cf. *SD* 1, 592; the eagle, the king of birds, heads the catalogue, just as it is given primacy in the bestiary at *SD* 1, 593.

49. **hirundo**: cf. *LSD* 2, 789 (p. 391W), 3, 61 (p. 396W) *minturnit hirundo.*

50. **turtur atque columba gemunt**: *Anth.* 762, 20 (ed. Buecheler, 1: 2, 248).

51. **rostro crepitans**: i. e. the clattering sound made by storks' bills cf. Ov., *Met.* 6, 97 *crepitante ciconia rostro* [Geoffrey of Monmouth, *Vita Merlini* 1327]; Juv., 1, 116; Isid., *Orig.* 12, 7, 32; Aldhelm, *Enig.* 31, 3 (*MGH, AA* 15: 110); *SD* 1, 131 *rostro crepitante*.

51. **crotalizat**: *ThLL*, 4: 1217, 15 s. v. *crotalisso* cites Cassiodorus, *De orthographia* (GLK, 7: 154, 8; cf. Petr., *Sat.* 55, 6 *gracilipes crotalistria*; *LSD* 2, 585 (p. 386W) *A crotalo crepitans nomen crotalistria sumpsit.*

52.. **Nugatur cuculus**: *LSD* 2, 865 (p. 393W); note the shortened second syllable of *cuculus*; *ThLL*, 4: 1281, 48, cites *Anth.* 762, 35 (ed. Buecheler, 1: 2, 248) *Et cuculi cuculant*; Neckam plays off a secondary meaning of *cuculus*, which refers to foolish men (cf. Hor., *S.* 1, 7, 31), to substitute a verb of similar meaning instead of *cuculat*; **laudat alauda diem**: for the etymology cf. *DNR* 1, 68 (p. 115W); *LSD* 2, 765 (p. 390W), 3, 58 (p. 396W); Bernardus Silvestris, *Cosmographia* 1, 3, 468 (ed. Dronke, 116); Hildebert, *De ornatu mundi MPL* 171: 1237c.

53. **Drensat olor**: cf. *Novale* 227 (ed. Haye, 425) *Non hic drensat olor*; **pulpat uultur**: cf. Eberhard, *Grecismus* 19, 33 *vultur pulpat*; *Novale* 255 (ed. Haye, 427); **coruum crocitare**: cf. *LSD* 2, 520 (p. 385W) *crocitans...avis*; *SD* 2, 1579 *Inter Ledeos crocitaui coruus olores.*

54. **lupire**: cf. *LSD* 2, 649-50 (p. 388W) *Milvius aerius lupus est, hunc rite lupire / Dicitur.*

55. **Iunonis...ales**: the peacock; cf. Juv., 7, 32; Claudian, *Carm.* 20, 330; *DNV* ed. T. Hunt, 1: 184 *pavones sive junonius ales.*

56. **Zinziat...merulus**: cf. Suet., fr. 161a, 13 (ed. Reifferschied, 308), *et merulus modulans tam pulchris zinzinat odis*; *Anth.* 733, 8 (ed. Buecheler, 1: 2, 218) *Haec inter merulae dulci modulamine cantus / Zinzilat.*

57. **Grus gruit**: cf. Suet. fr., 161a, 23 (ed. Reifferschied, 309), *Grus gruit*; **sclingens**: = *clingens* cf. *Novale* 225 (ed. Haye, 425) *Anser non clingit.*

58. **Perdices cacabant**: cf. Suet., fr. 161a, 19 (ed. Reifferschied, 309) *cacabat hinc perdix*; fr. 161b, 12 (ed. Reifferschied, 312) 12; Aldhelm, *De metris* (*MGH, AA* 15: 180, 13) *perdices cacabant.*

60. **Ticiat**: *LSD* 3, 61 (p. 396W) *Astutus passer titiat*; **nomen...trahens**: cf. *Glosule super Lucanum* 6, 129 (ed. Marti, 316) *passer a patiendo*; *LSD* 2, 786 (p. 391W) *Passer es, et nomen a patiendo trahis*; on *nomen* as an etymological marker cf. Cairns 30.

61. **Fringuliunt graculi**: cf. Suet., fr. 161a, 28 (ed. Reifferschied, 309) *fringulit et graculus*; Osbern, *Derivationes b* 149 (1: 95) *graculorum fringulire*; **cucubit**: cf. Aldhelm, *De metris* (*MGH, AA* 15: 180, 11) *noctuae cucubiunt*; **que**: i. e. the owl.

63. **dulcifluo**: *ThLL*, 5: 2187, 27 lists five occurrences of the adjective e. g. Venantius, *Carm.* 8, 19, 2 (*MGH, AA* 4: 199) *carmine dulcifluo*; **demulces aera**: cf. *SD* 1, 165.

64. **gesticulans**: cf. *SD* 1, 138, 1297.

65. **se conformat**: cf. Ov., *Am.* 2, 6, 1 *Psittacvs,...imitatrix ales*, 2, 6, 23 *non fuit in terris uocum simulantior ales.*

66. **Ludens**: for the playful behaviour of birds, animals and fishes cf. *SD* 1, 139, 148, 733, 1009; **proprios...habere**: cf. *SD* 1, 858.

67. **Hinnitu;** cf. Cambridge, UL, Ll. 1. 14, f. 46v *Equus hinnit*; cf. *LSD* 2, 237 (p. 378W) *Risum mentiris, hinnitum fingis.*

68. **putes**: cf. *SD* 1, 154, 206, 538, 920, 1020, 1152; 2, 985-6 *imam* (sc. partem) / *Cum Cereris genero uelle coire putes*, 1624 *Dedecus esse tibi fingere falsa putes*, 1677 *niueoque nitore / Blandiri placide candida fila putes*; for *putes* in this *sedes* cf. Ov., *Ep.* 9, 130.

69. **Turba...uolucrum**: Ov., *Met.* 10, 144 *turba volucrumque sedebat*; Aldhelm, *CDV* 437 (*MGH, AA* 15: 371); *SD* 1, 608; **Turba minor**: *LSD* 2, 411 (p. 382W); cf. *SD* 1, 608; 2, 1550-1 *fouet / Gaudia turba minor*, **dulci...modulatu**: cf. Martianus Capella, 2, 117 (ed. Willis, 33, 21-3) *ac tunc ille omnis chorus canoris vocibus dulcique modulatu praevertit omnes organicas suavitates*; *SD* 2, 1415-6 *En citharista Dauid dulci modulamine patres / Demulcet.*

70-2. cf. Suet., fr. 161a, 8, 14 (ed. Reifferschied, 309); **gratia lucis**: cf. *LH-L* 2: 462.

71. **in laudes exurgit**: a playful allusion to the divine office celebrated before dawn, Lauds; cf. *DMLBS* 5: 1571 s. v. *laus* 4; Prudentius, *Cath.* 3, 86-90.

73. **gaudia mentis**: cf. Mastandrea 331.

75. **Feminei mores**... / **Uirgo...marem**: Neckam plays with technical grammatical terms by attaching the epithet *feminei* to a masculine substantive and *mas* to a predominantly feminine noun cf. *Doctrinale* 139 *mas aut commune dabit oris femineumque*; **flectunt**: the verb also means «to sing in a modulated voice» cf. *OLD* s. v. *flecto* 11.

76. **Uirgo pudicicia**: Prudentius, *Psych.* 41 *uirgo Pudicitia speciosis fulget in armis*; **Uirgo...marem**: *uirgo*, as a noun of common gender, can be applied to a man without sexual experience cf. *OLD* s. v. *uirgo* 2a; *Doctrinale* 557 *est communis homo, pariter cum virgine latro*; 1119.

77-100. *What birds eat*

77. **Iunonius ales**: cf. Mastandrea 423.

77-8. **Non**... / **...sitim**: cf. Claudian, *Carm. min.* 27, 13-4 *non epulis saturare famem, non fontibus ullis / adsuetus prohibere sitim* [cited *DNR* 1, 35 (p. 86W)].

79-80. **Solis**... / **...uapor**: cf. Claudian, *Carm. min.* 27, 15-6 *solis feruor alit uentosaque pabula libat / Tethyos, innocui carpens alimenta uaporis* [cited *DNR* 1, 35 (p. 86W)]; in Hall's *apparatus criticus* PR attest *libat* for *potat*.

80. **equoreus...uapor**: e. g. the *aurifrisius* (95-6).

81. Ov., *Met.* 15, 394, describing the phoenix, who lived *non fruge neque herbis, / sed turis lacrimis et suco vivit amomi* [cited *DNR* 1, 35 (p. 85W)]; cf. Broek 335, note 2; *LSD* 2, 205 (p. 378W).

82. **dictis...fides**: cf. *LSD* 2, 538 (p. 385W); 4, 317 (p.427); 5, 324 (p. 447W), 796 (p. 459W), 920 (p. 462W); 8, 120 (p. 484W); *SD* 2, 708 *Maiorum dictis est adhibenda fides*, 1249-50 *dictis Ptholomei / ...est adhibenda fides*; *NA* 6, 4 *uix tumidis uerbis est adhibenda fides*; in Eccles. f. 144rb; *Ysopet* 57, 15; 63, 9; **uatum dictis**: cf. Ov., *Pont.* 3, 4, 65-6.

83-100. *The feeding habits of other birds.*

83. **Ficedulam**: *DNR* 1, 53 (p. 104W) moralizes the fig-pecker; *LSD* 2, 747-52 (p. 390W); **P** f. 195va has a marginal gloss *Quamuis ficedule det nomen gloria ficus*: Iuuenalis in satira que sic incipit: *Mergere ficedulus didicit nebulone parente*; **dulcibus uuis**: cf. Mart., 13, 49, 1 *cum pascar dulcibus uvis* [cited Isid., *Orig.* 12, 7, 73; *DNR* 1, 53 (p. 104W)]; cf. *SD* 2, 503 *vua...dulcisque creatur.*

84. **Frugifere**: cf. Claudian, *De raptu* 2, 138 *frugiferae...deae*; cf. *SD* 1, 1424; *DNR* 1, 56 (p. 106W) *purissimum granum eligit*; *SD* 1, 637.

85. **Exilem... / Predam**: cf. *in Eccles.* f. 90vb *Cernes alibi pisces in superficie aque natantes predam uolatilem et exilem uenari*; **hyrundo**: cf. McCulloch 174-5; *DNR* 1, 52 (pp. 103-4W); *LSD* 2, 789-800 (p. 391W); Neckam describes the behaviours of this and other birds, with moralizations, in *SD* 1, 799-808; to Alexander have been attributed three poems that relate the fable of the eagle and the tortoise *subcincte* (4 lines), *compendiose* (10 lines), and *copiose* (32 lines) cf. Hervieux, 3: 463-4; Mann 1986, 197; Ziolkowski 1993, 22; **solo...uolatu**: cf. *SD* 1, 799; Isid., *Orig.* 12, 7, 70 *Erundo dicta, quod cibos non sumat residens, sed in aere capiat escas et edat*; Sigebert of Gembloux, *Carm. in Eccles.* 133 (ed. Boutemy, 216) *Stans numquam comedit* (sc. hirundo), *uolitando per aera prandit*.

87. **Musca...cinifumque**: cf. *DNR* 1, 52 (p. 103W) *culicum et muscarum et apecularum infestatrix*; *LSD* 2, 795 (p. 391W) *Depopulatur apes, muscas, culices, cinifesque*.

88. **cibus...deliciosus**: cf. *SD* 1, 1301; M. Valerius, *Buc.* 3, 114 *Improba iam nidis vos* (sc. apes) *predam querit hirundo*, *SD* 2, 436 *delicious odor*.

89-93. The eagle's prey.

89. **lepores Iouis ales**: cf. Verg., *A.* 9, 563-4 *leporem... / Sustulit...Iouis armiger*, *DNR* 1, 23 (pp. 71-2W); *SD* 1, 593-604; *NE* 14, 1 *Dum moriendo lepus gemeret, Iovis alite captus...*; Ademar, *Phaedrus* 1, 9, 3-10 (ed. Bertini 1988, 174); Ov., *Met.* 6, 517 *deposuit nido leporem Iovis ales in alto*.

90. **Aufert**: cf. *NE* 7, 2; 23, 1-2 *In nidum vulpis catulos Iovis armiger olim / Sustulit, ut pullos pasceret inde suos*; **pignora grata sui**: cf. Verg., *E.* 8, 92 *pignora cara sui*.

91. **parens**: the ewe; **custode**: a shepherd cf. Hor., *C.* 4, 12, 9-10 *pinguium / custodes ovium*.

93. **Balatu**: the ewe calls for her abducted young cf. Cambridge, UL, Ll. 1. 14, f. 46v *Ouis balat*; Verg., *G.* 3, 554; **tantos...dolores**: Verg., *A.* 12, 880.

94. **genius**: *LSD* 2, 802 (p. 391W); *SD* 1, 668; John of Salisbury, *Enthet. maior* 223 (ed. van Laarhoven, 1: 121) *Hac sine sunt steriles verbi Genius ratioque*; **resim...suam**: *SD* 2, 123 *Attendas resim uerbisque licentia detur*, 1781-2 *Floribus est ornata suis resis uarioque, / Vt uulgo constat, picta colore nitent*.

95. **Aurifrisius**: cf. *LSD* 2, 689-90 (p. 389W); **unde**: = *undae*; **in esum**: cf. *SD* 1, 1425.

96. **ut ferrum strucio**: cf. *SD* 1, 685 *Deglutit ferrum*; *NP* 854 (ed. Orbán, 50) *ferrea frusta uorans* (sc. struthio).

97. **niso Cilla**: see note on *SD* 1, 40; cf. Verg., *G.* 1, 404-9; *CNP* 1299-1300 *insequitur...Nisus...Scillam*; *LSD* 2, 307 (p. 380W).

98. **Aere...ferunt**: cf. *LSD* 3, 17 (p. 395W) *Aere contentum descripsi chamaleonta*; Ov., *Met.* 15, 411; Plin., *Nat.* 8, 33, 122 (ed. Ian, 2: 120); *CPV* f. 142v *Est fera gameleon que uiuit in aere tantum*; *DNR* 1, 21 (p. 69W) *nec alimento alio quam haustu aeris vivat* (here the chameleon is moralized as an *adulator*. cf. Bambeck, 73); *LSD* 2, 113-8 (p. 376W) Urso, *De commixtionibus elem.* 6, 4 (ed. Stürner, 180) *Aliquando aer operatur in composito ad similitudinem loci et nutrimenti. Si ergo secundum superiora sui ad hoc conveniat, avis superiora aeris facile petit et aere nutritur ut gamaleon*; Solinus 40, 22 (ed. Mommsen, 170, 11-3): *hiatus eius aeternus ac sine ullius usus ministerio: quippe cum neque cibum capiat neque potu alatur nec alimento alio quam haustu aëris vivat*. Note the scansion of *cameleonta*.

99. **coruus...cadauere uili**: cf. Prudentius, *Tituli historiarum* 11-2 *Coruus enim ingluuie per foeda cadauera captus / Haeserat*; Baudri, *Carm.* 134, 136 *Putribus incumbis, corue, cadaueri-*

bus; *DNR* 1, 61 (p. 111W) *Cadavere...allicitur et eo vescitur* (sc. coruus); *LSD* 1, 430 (p. 367W), 2, 509-10 (p. 384W); *SD* 1, 637 *uile cadauer*.

100. **Alcinoi fructus**: i. e. apples; cf. Verg., *G*. 2, 87; *LSD* 2, 55 (p. 374W), 4, 664 (p. 435W); **plurima turba**: cf. *SD* 2, 116, 700.

102. **clangore suo**: cf. *DNR* 1, 23 (p. 73W); *SD* 1, 593.

101-24. *The powers of birds*

102. **clangore**: cf. *SD* 1, 593.

103. **In dumis latitantem**: cf. Marbod, *Carm. varia MPL* 171: 1717b *Et latet in dumis nova progenies sine plumis*; *LSD* 2, 181 (p. 377W) *Et praedam dumis latitantem cernit ab alto*; *DNR* 1, 23 (p. 71W); **cernit ab alto**: cf. *Glosule super Lucanum* 6, 129 (ed. Marti, 316) *aquila dicitur ab acumine oculorum*.

104. **strenuitate**: cf. *SD* 1, 158 *plus aquile strenuitatis inest*.

105. **Rupta prius**: cf. Ademar, *Phaedrus* 1, 20, 5-6 (ed. Bertini 1988, 48) *sed rupti prius / Periere quam quod petierant contingerent*; *SD* 1, 624 *mortificata prius*, 694 *neglecta prius*, 878 *Obscurata prius*; **Rupta...renodat**: cf. Alan of Lille, *De planctu* 13, 4-5 (ed. Häring, 857) *bellumque renodat / Ruptum*; *SD* 1, 810; **series fatorum:** cf. Luc., 1, 70 *fatorum series*; Claudian, *De raptu* 1, 52 *seriem fatorum pollice ducunt*; *DNR* 1, 34-5 (pp. 84-7W); *LSD* 2, 185-216 (pp. 377-8W); Berry, 198, note 185; **fila:** Claudian, *Carm. min.* 27, 109-10 (of the phoenix) *non stamina Parcae / In te dura legunt nec ius habuere nocendi*.

107-8. Cited in Lawn, *Salern. Questions*, 46, note 3.

107. **radii uirtute**: the ostrich has the power to hatch her brood by means of her vision alone; cf. *DNR* 1, 50 (p. 101W) *Nota quod mira est virtus radiorum visualium struthionis, qui visu solo ita fovet ova sua in arena recondita, ut ex illis egrediantur pulli in lucem*; *LSD* 2, 187-92 (p. 377W); *SD* 1, 679-700.

107-8. **strucio... / ...iubet**: cf. *SD* 1, 695-6.

108. **rumpere claustra**: Hor., *Ep.* 1, 14, 9 *amat spatiis obstantia rumpere claustra*; Verg., *A.* 9, 758; John of Salisbury, *Enthet. minor* 236 (ed. van Laarhoven, 1: 245).

109. **Accipitris**: cf. McCulloch 123-4; *DNR* 1, 25 (pp. 76-7W); *LSD* 2, 283-92 (pp. 379-80W).

109-10. **Accipitris clamor... / ...degenerare facit**: *LSD* 2, 722 (p. 389W) *Accipitris clamor degenerare facit*; *SD* 1, 652; 2, 1618 *Subtiles animos degenerare facis*; Matthew of Vendôme, *Tob.* 883-4 (ed. Munari, 2: 199) *adversa maritans / Rerum naturas degenerare facit*; **quibus incubat...oua**: cf. *Glosule super Lucanum* (ed. Marti, 345) *...aquila que nimii est caloris adeo quod oua quibus incubat coqueret nisi lapidem illum ad calorem suum reprimendum frigore lapidis nido apponeret* cf. *SD* 1, 601-2.

111. **perdicum**: The partridge hatches eggs stolen from other birds, but when the fledgelings hear their mother's call, they return to their own parents cf. McCulloch 152; Henkel 197-8; Jr 17, 11; *LSD* 2, 405-36 (pp. 382-3W); Berry 92-3, 199, note 405; see Diekstra 144 for other stories from *Physiologus* that derive from Jewish traditions; **tanta potestas**: cf. Mastandrea 839.

112-14. **Ad proprium...patrem**: cf. Isid., *Orig.* 12, 7, 63 *dum pulli propriae vocem genetricis audierint, naturali quodam instinctu hanc quae fovit relinquunt, et ad eandem quae genuit revertuntur*; *LSD* 2, 411 (p. 382W); *NP* 969-70 (ed. Orbán, 54).

113. **Instinctu genii**: *LSD* 2, 801-2 (p. 391 W) *gallus... / Instinctu genii;* **pulsantis ad hostia**: cf. Luc 13, 25; Hor., *S.* 1, 1, 10 *ostia pulsat.*

114. **Nutricem...suam**: cf. *DNR* 1, 43 (p. 96 W) *clamorem patris pulli eius agnoscunt,* 1, 44 (p. 96 W); **paruula turba**: cf. *LSD* 2, 411 (p. 382 W) *turba minor.*

115. **[Ciconia]**: The stork takes good care of its young, who return the affection to their parents when they are old cf. McCulloch 174; **Membra paterna fouet**: cf. *NP* 826 (ed. Orbán, 49) *Atque fouet menbris menbra patrina suis; DNR* 1, 65 (pp. 113-4 W); *SD* 1, 828-30.

116. **sub aquis**: cf. *Prose Salern. Questions* N 64 (ed. Lawn, 319, 18-21) *...quare ciconia in hieme precipitet se in aquam, et rostro pudendo infixo quasi mortua sub aqua...per totam hiemem iaceat; adveniente autem tempore reviviscat?* cf. N 64 (ed. Lawn, 321, 13-37).

117. **pietas**: Petr., *Sat.* 55, 6 attaches the epithet *pietaticultrix* to the stork cf. Connors 59 on the stork's association with *pietas* in antiquity; Isid., *Orig.* 12, 7, 17 *Eximia illis* (sc.ciconiis) *circa filios pietas;* .

118. **incipit esse parens**: cf. *LSD* 2, 552 (p. 385 W) *incipis esse parens; SD* 1, 687 *Desinit esse parens,* 829.

120. **Mater...patrem**: cf. *Doctrinale* 2552 *quam mater genuit, generavit filia matrem.*

121-2. The verses allude to the death of the Roman Crassus, who was killed by being forced to ingest liquified gold; **Cesareum munus**: i. e. gold cf. *DNR* 2, 53 (p. 162 W); the adjective is confined to poetry in the classical and late antique periods cf. *ThLL,* 2: 39, 61; Baudri, *Carm.* 98, 111.

121. **digestiua... / Vis**: cf. *LSD* 2, 491 (p. 384 W) *Exuperat ferrum vis digestiva potenter,* 3, 151 (p. 398 W); 7, 233 (p. 478 W); **caloris**: in medieval physiology fire was thought to aid digestion through a process of cooking in the stomach cf. Gerald of Wales, *Topographia Hibernica* 1, 14 (ed. Dimock, 46) *Avis* (sc. grus) *eadem tam calidum, tam igneum jecur habet, ut ferrum forte ingestum transire nequeat indigestum;* Urso, *De commixtionibus elem.* 1, 4 (ed. Stürner, 73) *...et virtus digestiva per calorem naturalem digerit et corrumpit.*

122. **exitiale**: cf. Stat., *Theb.* 4, 192 *hoc aurum vati fata exitiale monebant.*

123. **Corue**: cf. *LSD* 2, 509-58 (pp. 384-6 W); *SD* 1, 887-90; **tociens repetitum**: cf. *LSD* 2, 865 (p. 393 W) *Nugatur cuculus frustra tociens repetendo.*

123. **Corue...«chere»...repetitum**: cf. *LSD* 2, 557 (p. 386 W) *Corve salutator...Ave tibi, Caesar;* Mart., 95, 1-2 *Numquam dicis have sed reddis, Naevole, semper, / quod prior et corvus dicere saepe solet;* 14, 74, 1 *Corve salutator;* Persius, *choliambi,* 8 *quis expedivit psittaco suum chaere?;* Geoffrey of Monmouth, *Vita Merlini* 1364 *Intermiscet* (sc. psittacus) *'ave'verbis et 'chere' jocosis; SA* f. 25b *unde omelia, sermo, ad populum; coruu<m> salutantem Cesarem dixere: «chere, Cesar, anicos basilios,» idest «salue, Cesar, inuicte rex»; Appendix glossarum,* 123.

124. **larga...auara**: cf. *Aulularia* 210 (ed. Cohen, 1: 82) *Largus amicicias urget, auarus opes; SD* 1, 1196.

125-30. *Some birds lack guile*

125. **simplicitas...fauore**: cf. *LSD* 2, 475-80 (p. 384 W); 5, 842 (p. 460 W); for a contrast between *astutia* and *simplicitas* cf. *DNR* 1, 60 (p. 109 W); see Adrados 204 for the story of the *ignarae et simplices aves* and the one *ales astutior,* who had experienced every trick in the birdcatcher's repertory; **simplicitas...digna fauore**: Ov., *Ep.* 2, 64; *SD* 1, 902 *digna fauore,* 1063; 2, 230 *In facie multo digna fauore sedet* (sc. regia maiestas); cf. Mastandrea 220.

126. **cultrix eremi**: cf. *LSD* 2, 659 (p. 388W); Isid., *Orig.* 12, 7, 1 *aliae in desertis secretam vitam diligunt, ut turtur, LSD* 2, 659 (p. 388W) (of the pelican) *hec avis est eremi cultrix*; for other formations in *-ix* cf. *SD* 1, 139 *adulatrix*, 221 *seruatrix*, 1358 *circumuentrix*; 2. 1490 *precentrix*, 1585 *amatrix*, 1625 *uenatrix*, 1642 *inuentrix*.

127. **Phasis...nutrit**: i. e. pheasants; cf. Mart., 3, 77, 4 *nec Libye mittit nec tibi Phasis aves*; Bernardus Silvestris, *Cosmographia* 1, 3, 463-4 (ed. Dronke, 116) *Gallus uterque... / ...patria Phaside nomen habens*; *LSD* 2, 464 (p. 383W); *SD* 1, 161; **auis**: the dove cf. Mt 10, 16 *simplices sicut columbae*; *SD* 1, 643.

128. **ramus, oliua, tuus**: cf. *LSD* 2, 699-706 (p. 389W); *SD* 1, 647 Hor., *Epod.* 2, 56 *oliva ramis arborum*.

129. **astucia**: e. g. the partridge (cf. Isid., *Orig.* 12, 7, 1 *aliae astutae, ut perdix*) or the swallow cf. Adrados 202; Zander 63; cf. *SD* 1, 175 *callida passer*.

130. **Aucupis...retia**: cf. *SD* 1, 703.

131. **Cornix**: cf. McCulloch 108; *DNR* 1, 62 (p. 111W).

132. **officium...ducis**: cf. *DNR* 1, 65 (p. 114W) *cornices eas* (sc. ciconias) *duces praecedunt* [Isid., *Orig.* 12, 7, 16].

133. **Preuidet...casus**: cf. Isid., *Orig.* 12, 7, 44 *quam* (sc. cornicem) *aiunt...insidiarum vias monstrare, futura praedicere*.

134. **instare...fugam**: cf. the military terms in 133.

135. **casu lapidis**: cf. Isid., *Orig.* 12, 7, 15; *DNR* 1, 46-7 (pp. 96-7W); *SD* 1, 871-86; *NP* 911-2.

136. **saburra**: Cranes carry sand and small stones for ballast in strong winds cf. McCulloch 106; cf. *DNR* 1, 47 (p. 99W) *arenas devorant, sublatisque lapillulis ad moderatam gravitatem saburrantur, LSD* 2, 321-2 (p. 380W).

137. **mansuescat**: *SD* 1, 707-8; **prescriptio longi / Temporis**: in Roman law, *praescriptio* functioned to cure defects in property ownership; thus, if a person had good faith possession but not ownership of a piece of property, possession became ownership after a long period of time, which could amount to ten or twenty years; the term was originally parallel to *usucapio* for provincial land, but by Justinian's time *praescriptio* was a general term that had absorbed *usucapio*; for the legal phraseology cf. Cod. Iust. 7, 33, 1, 1 (sc. possessor) *non potest uti longi temporis praescriptione; ThLL*, 10: 833, 8 cites Iavol. dig. 41, 3, 21 *sequitur..., ut ne possessionem quidem locator retinuerit, ideoque longi temporis praescriptio duravit, praescriptio* rarely occurs in classical poetry (*ThLL*, 10: 831, 18 lists only Dracontius, *Romul.* 5, 250); cf. Latham, 369 s. v. *prescript / io*; **longi temporis**: Ov., *Fast.* 1, 104; Peter of Blois, *Carm.* 5, 3a, 6b, 1-3 *Rideo, / dum uideo / uirum longi temporis*.

139. **adulatrix**; rare word, also found in *DNR* 1, 19 (p. 65W) *blanda quadam et adulatrice verborum utens forma; ThLL*, 1: 877, 4 cites Tertullian, *De anima* 51, 23 *animae adulatrix* and two other prose examples; **nucibus**: = *nutibus*.

140. **apta**: etymological play on *grus* cf. Sedulius Scottus, *In Donati artem maiorem pars 2* ed. Löfstedt, *CCCM* 40B: 154, 97 *grus nomen est auis inde congruus id est aptus*; cf. *SD* 1, 1402 *grus comes apta grui*; Neckam favours this *sedes* for *apta* in the pentameters cf. *SD* 1, 166, 290, 508, 768, 1298, 1402, 1410; in hexameters cf. *SD* 1, 185, 231, 1363.

141. **tensis...alis**: cf. Claudian, *Carm.* 28, 174 *extentas...alas.*

143. **Remigio alarum**: Verg., *A.* 1, 301; *LH-L* 4: 506; Hunt ed. Gibson, 46, note 17.

145. **It, redit**: cf. Hor., *Ep.* 1, 7, 55 [*Ecbasis captivi* 975]; Ps.- Verg., *Elegiae in Maecen.* 1, 6 (ed. Clausen, 87) *it redit*; **equor metitur**: cf. Ov., *Ep.* 10, 28 *aequora...metior.*

149-72. *The forms of birds*

149-52. **Archanum... / ...apex**: cf. Claudian, *Carm. min.* 27, 17-20, (describing the phoenix) *arcanum radiant oculi iubar. igneus ora / cingit honos. rutilo cognatum uertice sidus / attolit cristatus apex tenebrasque serena / luce secat*; *LSD* 2, 201-2 (pp. 377-8W).

151-52. **serena / Luce**: cf. Aldhelm, *Enig.* 35, 3 *Raro me quisquam cernet sub luce serena*, *CDV* 500 (*MGH, AA* 15: 112, 374).

152. **igneus ambit**: Claudian, *Carm.* 22, 60; cf. *SD* 1, 149-50 *igneus... / Cingit honos.*

154. **Tincta...murice**: cf. Ov., *Ars* 1, 251 *de tincta murice lana.*

157. **Commendant**: cf. *SD* 1, 264; **gloria forme**: Ps.-Verg., *Culex* 408 (ed. Clausen, 36); cf. *SD* 1, 667; Orchard, 134, note 36, on Aldhelm, *Enig.* 6, 3; 96, 9.

158. **aquile strenuitatis**: cf. *NE* 40, 13 (ed. Hervieux, 2: 414) *Hec vires aquile magnas dedit.*

159. **Depingit... / Pauonem**:cf. *Ysopet* 34, 1 *inuenti picti pauonis amictu*; **ludens uario Natura colore**: cf. *NE* 40, 9-12 *Respondit Iuno: «Nature provida virtus / nulli vult vite commoda cuncta dare. / Illa tibi* (sc. pauoni) *formam tribuit variumque colorem»*; *SD* 1, 909 *lusit* (sc. natura); *SD* 1, 733 *Pauo nature decor.*

160. **superis...placet**: cf. *SD* 1, 162, 828, 1330; **forma...placet**: Ov., *Ars* 3, 480 *sermonis publica forma placet* [Baudri, *Carm.* 3, 7].

161. **Delectat uisum**: *LSD* 6, 23 (p. 464W), 153 (p. 467W); *CNP* 31 *flos specie uisum recreat*, 655; **Phasidos ales**: Stat., *Silv.* 2, 4, 27; 4, 4, 8; *LSD* 2, 464 (p. 383W).

162. **Accipitrix**: genitive = *accipitris*; **fateor...placet**: cf. *SD* 2, 1540 *fateor illa placere michi.*

164. **plurima restat auis**: cf. *LSD* 3, 669 (p. 410W) *Tot restant pisces*; 4, 782 (p. 438W); Matthew of Vendôme, *Ars* 1, 111, 111 (ed. Munari, 3: 122) *Plurima restat adhuc arbor*, note the *anaphora* of *restat / restant* in 165-8; **uisum recreat**: cf *SD* 2, 1741 *Aspectum recreat picture gratia.*

165. **fidus amans**: the turtledove; Matthew of Vendôme, *Piramus* 152 (ed. Munari, 2: 54); **rauco / Murmure**: *LSD* 3, 344 (p. 403W); 5, 76 (p. 442W); Verg., *G.* 1, 109; Ov., *Met.* 13, 567 *rauco cum murmure.*

167. **potentis / Nature**: cf. Boethius, *DCP* 3, M. 2, 2 (ed. Bieler, *CCSL* 94: 40) *natura potens*; Marbod, *De lapidibus* 111 (ed. Riddle, 42); *SD* 1, 117 *Nature ueneranda potestas*, 551-2 *studium...potentis / Nature*, 1101-2 *mira potestas / Nature*, 1125 *Nature dotes...potentis*; 2, 1657-8 *Proponit natura potens*; *NE* 27, 5 (ed. Hervieux, 2: 406) *«Si natura potens in avem me vertere vellet,...».*

168. **Palamedis aues**: cf. *SD* 1, 178.

169-70. **Et solus... / ...obit**: cf. Bernardus Silvestris, *Cosmographia* 1, 3, 449-50 (ed. Dronke, 116: cited *DNR* 1, 49 [p. 100W]); cf. *SD* 1, 187-8, 587-8, 1224-5, 1227-30, 1231-4 for other grafts of Bernard's poetry; cf. citation of *Cosmographia* 1, 3, 291-2 (ed. Dronke, 111) in Matthew of Vendôme, *Ars* 1, 111, 84a-84b (ed. Munari, 3: 121). McCulloch, 39 notes that the Third and Fourth Families of the *Physiologus*, much expanded bestiaries from the 13th-c., contain extracts from the *Megacosmus* of Bernard Silvestris; Muratova 1338 notes the presence of poetic fragments from Bernard's *Cosmographia* in New York, Pierpoint Morgan Library, MS 81.

171. **niueo candore nitet**: cf. *LSD* 2, 545 (p. 385W); Ov., *Met.* 3, 423 *in niveo mixtum candore ruborem*; Stat., *Ach.*, 315 *niveo candore iuvencam*; *SD* 1, 751.

173-78. *Birds display love towards their young*

173. **Ueneri**: cf. Isid., *Orig.* 12, 7, 61 *quas* (sc. columbas) *antiqui Venerias nuncupant.*

175. **Indulges soboli renouande**: cf. *SD* 1, 1149 *Indulget proli generande.*

178. **mensas ditat**: cf. *SD* 1, 797; **auis**: P's *aues* would require emending *ditat* to *ditant*; Neckam probably wrote *auis* (cf. *SD* 1, 596 *regia spernit auis*), which the scribe miscopied under the influence of the phrase *Palamedis aues* at *SD* 1, 168.

179-262. *Trees*

179. The bestiary attributed to Hugh of St Victor, *De bestiis* 3, 56 (*MPL* 177: 111b), includes a section on trees; McCulloch, 39 notes that Cambridge, UL, Gg. 6. 5, a 15th-c. bestiary manuscript, concludes with a chapter on trees; **Arboreos...fetus**: cf. Verg., *G.* 1, 55 *arborei fetus* [cited *DNR* 2, 57 (p. 164W)] cf. Theodulf, *Carm.* 74, 7 (*MGH, P. L.* 1: 573)]; Baudri, *Carm.* 126, 33; Ov., *Met.* 10, 665 (= Lawrence of Durham, *Dialogi* 2, 145); **herbas salubres**: John of Salisbury, *Enthet. maior* 1111-12 (ed. van Laarhoven, 1: 177) *Docta manus cavet urticas, herbasque salubres / tollit*; cf. Boethius, *DCP* 2, M. 5, 10 (ed. Bieler, *CCSL* 94: 29) *Somnos dabat herba salubres*; *SD* 1, 265-588; cf. *in Eccles.* f. 90va *Transeat quis per ortum deliciosum areolis distinctum decenter et herbis salubribus uestitum...inde herbarum salubrium uiror gratissimus et gratiosus lumina demulcet.*

181. **Humentique**: the *-que* suggests that a couplet has been lost; **loca saxea buxus**: cf. Bernardus Silvestris, *Cosmographia* 1, 3, 268 (ed. Dronke, 111) *Rupe rigens buxus.*

182. **nux...Phillidis**: Phyllis, the daughter of king Sithon of Thrace, was changed into an almond-tree cf. *LSD* 1, 807 (p. 484W) *Philli, tuae virtute nucis*; *DNV* ed. Wright, 102-3, glosses *nux Philidis* with *noyz de l'almaunde rapuant.*

183. **platanus...populus**: cf. Ov., *Rem.* 141, *Met.* 5, 590, *Ep.* 5, 25; *CNP* 513-5 *quam platanus riuo uel populus unda / ...tam Venus ocia amat*; *LSD* 8, 53 (p. 482W) *Et platanus vino laetatur.*

184. **uitis colles...amat**: cf. Bernardus Silvestris, *Cosmographia* 1, 3, 269 (ed. Dronke, 111) *vitis colle supino*; Verg., *G.* 2, 113 *Bacchus amat collis.*

185. **Sambuccus**: cf. *LSD* 8, 69-70 (p. 483W); Constantinus Africanus *De gradibus*, pp. 361-2, lists its medicinal qualities: *Haec arbor non omnino inutilis est....stomachum mollit, uomitum prouocat*; **est**: Matthew of Vendôme, *Ars* 4, 38 (ed. Munari, 3: 211) proscribed monosyllabic verse endings; in *SD* 1-2 monosyllables are absent from the end of pentameters, and in the hexameters Neckam allows only *est* (*SD* 1, 195; 2, 361, 607, 683, 1243) or *quo* (2, 877) / *qua* (2, 1693).

185-6. **apta... / ...bellis**: *LSD* 8, 53-4 (p. 482W) *fraxinus apta / Bellis.*

186. **Parthorum**: cf. Isid., *Orig.* 17, 7, 40 *Ex hac* (sc. taxus) *arcus Parthi...faciunt.*

186. **inuida taxus api**: *LSD* 8, 56 (p. 482W) *invida taxus api*; cf. Bernardus Silvestris, *Cosmographia* 1, 3, 276 (ed. Dronke, 111) *Et mala Cicropias perdere taxus apes.*

187-8. Bernardus Silvestris, *Cosmographia* 1, 3, 279-80 (ed. Dronke, 111).

189. **aspera...toga**: cf. Bernardus Silvestris, *Cosmographia* 1, 3, 212 (ed. Dronke, 109) *asperiore toga* [cited *SD* 1, 1230]; Matthew of Vendôme, *Ars* 1, 111, 104 (ed. Munari, 3: 122) *asperitasque toge*; *LSD* 8, 101-2 (p. 484W) *Persica velamen teneri lanuginis, hirtam / Castanae fructus gaudet habere togam.*

190. **lanugo**: in the sense both of 'down on fruit' and 'woollen garment' cf. *DMLBS* 5: 1551 s. v. *lanugo* 2b, 5d; **testa nucem**: cf. Geoffrey of Monmouth, *Vita Merlini* 741 *et quasi testa nucem circumdans omnia claudit.*

192. **nucleum**: cf. *Ysopet, prologus* 12 *...nucleum celat arida testa bonum.*

193. **baccis ditatur laurus**: cf. *LSD* 8, 41 (p. 482W) *laurus baccis decoratur*; *SD* 2, 23 *Et ditata stetit arbor fructu generoso.*

193. **Phebi / primus amor**: the nymph Daphne was metamorphosed into a laurel tree to escape being raped by Apollo cf. Ov., *Met.* 1, 452 *Primus amor Phoebi*; **laurus uiridissima**: cf. *LSD* 8, 147 (p. 485W).

195. **Anno...decies deno**: cf. *DNR* 2, 74 (p. 172W), *LSD* 8, 37-8 (p. 482W) *palma / Non nisi centennis fructificare solet*; *SD* 2, 493 *En cum maturo fructu stans palma creatur*, 495-6 *Temporibus nostris primos dat nobilis arbor / Fructus centennis*, 499 *Incipe centennis uel primos fructus.*

196. **gloria**: cf. *DNR* 2, 74 (p. 172W) *Palma fructu generoso gloriatur*; **Dactilici**: cf. Isid., *Orig.* 17, 7, 1 *fructus autem eius* (sc. palmae) *dactyli a digitorum similitudine nuncupati sunt*; *SD* 2, 494 *Dactile, dactilici nescius esto metri*; *DNR* 2, 74 (p. 172W); **fructus gloria**: cf. *LSD* 8, 73 (p. 483W) *gloria fructus.*

197. **inferior pars**: cf. *DNR* 2, 74 (p. 172W) *Non enim stipitis amplissima grossities est terrae vicina*; *LSD* 8, 39-40 (p. 482W) *Pars riget inferior, sed pars suprema decenti / Planitiae gaudens asperitate caret*; *SD* 1, 741.

198. **elate...comam**: cf. *Ct* 5, 11 *comae eius sicut elatae palmarum*; *DNR* 2, 74 (p. 172W) *Palma...dactylis videlicet et elatis decoratur*; *CPV* f. 153r *Dicitur elata ramus quia crescit in altum*; **poteris**: the copyist misread the abbreviation for the letters *er* in *pot'is* as a suspension bar over the first syllable to produce *pontis*; for the verb in this *sedes* cf. *LDS* 8, 90 (p. 474W) *In multis poteris hos reperire gradus*; for the metre cf. *SD* 1, 20, 26, 216.

199. **Effugat...uermes**: cf. *CPV* f. 153r *Illesum corpus aloes et mirra reseruant*; *DNR* 2, 69 (p. 170W); *LSD* 8, 81 (p. 483W); **redigique cadaver / In cinerem**: cf. Hildebert, *Carm. min.* 22, 67-8 *est hominis... / ...in cinerem redigi*; *SD* 1, 824 *in cinerem corpora versa*, 1215 *cutis in cinerem redigende.*

200. **Cinare**: Cinyras, king of Cyprus, father of Myrrha: cf. Ov., *Met.* 10, 298-502; *LSD* 8, 82 (p. 483W) *Quam Cinarae regis filia Myrrha creat*; Viarre 126.

201. **Uitis odora...odore**: cf. Ov., *Med.* 91 *bene olentibus...murris*; Peter of Blois, *Libellus*, 73, 1122 *mirtus odora.*

203. **cum stellis...contendere**: cf. *LSD* 4, 376 (p. 429W) *stellata volunt coelo contendere prata*; *SD* 2, 441 *Hic cum stellifero tellus contendit Olimpo*; Plin., *Nat.* 16, 40, 213 (ed. Ian, 3: 55) *Maxime aeternam putant ...cedrum*; Claudian, *Carm. min.* 27, 11-2 *par uolucer superis, stellas qui uiuidus aequat / durando.*

205. **Dissimilem... / ...nostri temporis esse putes**: *LSD* 2, 122 (p. 376W); **corrumpi nescia cedrum**: cf. *LSD* 8, 46 (p. 482W) *Nescia corrumpi* (sc. cupressus); Hildebert,

Biblical Epigrams 48, 6-7 (ed. Scott, 300) *Eterne uite corrumpi nescia cedrus / spem mihi designat;* SD 1, 978 *nescia stare.*

206. **nostri temporis**: for similar comments cf. *LSD* 5, 26 (p. 441W) *Languerent tenebris tempora nostra suis*; *SD* 2, 521-4 *O quot et quantos uoluent in corde dolores, / Cum sic corrumpi secula nostra scient. / Tantus erit mentis stupor ut uix credere possint / Nos tantis et tot fraudibus esse datos*; in *Eccles.* ff. 108ra-rb *Magnates uero nostri / temporis noctem verterunt in diem*; f. 124rb *Felicia erant tempora Nasonis qui dicere ausus est: Pascitur in uiuis Liuor; post fata quiescit* [Ov., *Am.* 1, 15, 39]. *Longe dissimilia sunt tempora nostra temporibus predecessorum. Persequitur enim hiis diebus liuor in cineratos*; **esse putes**: Ov., *Fast.* 5, 262.

209. **uirtus hebeni non cedit uiribus ignis**: cf. Plin., *Nat.* 12, 4, 20 (ed. Ian, 2: 383) *accendi* (sc. hebenum) *Fabianus negat*; *DNR* 2, 83 (p. 177W) *De ebeno: Ignis virtute dissolvi dedignatur*; *LSD* 8, 65-6 (p. 483W) *Flammae contemptrix ebenus*; *Prose Salern. Questions* B 121 (ed. Lawn, 58, 18-9) *Queritur quare ebenus sui soliditate resistit combustioni?* cf. N 64 (ed. Lawn, 320. 24-7); Urso, *De commixtionibus elem.* 6, 3 (ed. Stürner, 177); there are two 12th-c. references in vernacular literature to ebony's resistance to fire, the earlier in *Floire et Blanceflor* (written before 1170); Chrétien de Troyes *Roman de Perceval* (ed. W. Roach, [Geneva, 1959]), 3268-74, mentions trestles «made of ebony, a wood which one should not expect to rot or to burn»; cf. Hamilton 121-7; Cary 336; **uiribus ignis**: cf. Mastandrea 927.

210. **stupet**: cf. *LSD* 2, 188 (p. 377W) *Quod non intereat* (sc. phoenix) *Atropos ipsa stupet*; *SD* 1, 218, 221, 1263; Bynum 7 notes the connection between amazement and paradox made by medieval theologians and natural philosophers; **Lemnius**: Hephaistos (Vulcan), the son of Zeus and Hera, was thrown from heaven by his father for siding with Hera in a family quarrel; he landed on the island of Lemnos, which became sacred to the fire-god cf. Ov., *Met.* 13, 313; Claudian, *Carm.* 28, 572 *Lemnius auctor*; **queritur**: fire was essential to his craft as a forger of weapons for the gods cf. Serv., *A.* 8, 416 (ed. Thilo-Hagen, 2: 262, 16-8) *physiologia est, cur Vulcanus in his locis officinam habere fingatur inter Aetnam et Liparen: scilicet propter ignem et ventos, quae apta sunt fabris*; **Ethna**: the Sicilian volcano inside which, according to legend, Vulcan operated the forge where the Cyclopes (cf. *SD* 1, 212) produced Jupiter's thunderbolts cf. Ov., *Met.* 1, 259 *tela reponuntur manibus fabricata Cyclopum*; Walahfrid Strabo, *De cultura hortorum* 298-9 (*MGH, P. L.* 2: 346) *Lemnius aut altum quot in aera Mulcifer ire / Scintillas vastis videat fornacibus Aetnae.*

211. **ligno superari**: not the normal nature of things cf. Baudri, *Carm.* 92, 25-6 *Indefessus item ceptis ferrarius instat / Et ferrum ferro uincit et igne simul.*

212. **Cyclops**: cf. Verg., *G.* 4, 170-5; **durius**: P's reading, *purius*, refers to the refining of metal by smelting (cf. John of Salisbury, *Enthet. maior* 255 [ed. van Laarhoven, 1: 181]), but *Duriciam ferri* suggests Neckam wrote *durius* cf. Ov., *Met.* 14, 712 *durior et ferro, quod Noricus excoquit ignis*; *LSD* 6, 348 (p. 411W) *durius igne nocet*; *NE* 16, 5-6 (ed. Hervieux, 2: 401) *Ipsum perdurum mos est mihi rodere ferrum, / Et si quid ferro durius esse potest;* **ignis edax**: Verg., *A.* 2, 758; *CNP* 206; *LH-L* 3: 18.

213. **Philosophus nescit**: Bynum 24 emphasizes that among philosophers the element of amazement had a powerful cognitive aspect that stimulated further investigation; the allusion to Alexander the Great in *SD* 1, 216 suggests that *philosophus* refers to Aristotle, but the reference may be general rather than specific; cf. Urso, *De commixtionibus elem.* 4, 3 (ed. Stürner, 108-9) *Eodemque modo contingit, ut quoddam subiectum sic qualitatis agentis suscipiat principalem effectum, quod non secundarium, sic similem, quod non dissimilem, ut ebenus, que cale-*

fieri potest et non solvi vel igniri; **subsit causa**: cf. *LSD* 9, 372 (p. 494W), 406 (p. 495W); 10, 144 (p. 499W); Ov., *Fast.* 4, 140 *causaque...certa subest*; *DNR* 2, 21 (pp. 141-2) mentions Alexander the Great's curiosity about natural phenomena; **causa dolore**: cf. Mastandrea 113.

214. **Driades**: wood-nymphs cf. Verg., *G.* 1, 11; 3, 40 *Dryadum siluas...sequamur*, *SD* 2, 28 *Driadum gloria silua stetit.*

216. **Quam...cinxit**: cf. Mart., 9, 75, 2-3; Walter of Châtillon, *Alex.* 7, 93-4 *Terrarum domitor Ebactana cingere facta / Obsidione parat*; **Macedo**: i. e. Alexander the Great cf. *Glosule super Lucanum* 8, 694 (ed. Marti, 423) *Alexander qui dictus est Alexander Macedo*; for a list of other trees that astounded Alexander in India, including one that spoke Greek cf. *Brief Alexanders* 19 (ed. Pfister, 35, 15); Plin., *Nat.* 12, 4, 21-4 (ed. Ian, 2: 303-4); cf. *in Eccles.* ff. 85ra-rb *Macedo igitur quem animal glorie philosophus appellat qui omnes labores suos soli glorie mundane dicauit, cum uiam uniuerse carnis ingrederetur, quid de uniuerso labore suo amplius habuit quam lixarum aut kalonum extremus?* Cambridge, Trinity College, R. 16. 4, f. 122vb glosses *Macedo* with *idest Alexander.*

217. **Teda...cum fomentis ignita**: cf. Walter of Châtillon *Alex.* 3, 308-9 *et eo magis esurit ignis, / Quo plures tabulata cibos alimentaque prebent.*

219. **lignea materies**: cf. *SD* 1, 233 *materies abiegna.*

220. **septis**: = *saeptis* cf. *SD* 1, 696.

221. **Seruatrix**: cf. Stat., *Theb.* 12, 606; *LSD* 5, 315 (p. 447W), 8, 127 (p. 484W); **stupescit**: *OLD* cites one example (Cic., *de orat.* 3, 102); Plin., *Nat.* 12, 4, 21 (ed. Ian, 2: 383) *Nunc eas* (sc. arbores) *exponemus, quas mirata est Alexandri Magni victoria orbe eo patefacto*; Alexander's letter to Aristotle about the marvels of India circulated in the Middle Ages with a number of other Alexander texts cf. Smits 102 and note 44; *Brief Alexanders* 22 (ed. Pfister 37, 18-23).

222. **dehinc**: monosyllabic; cf. Verg., *A.* 9, 479-80.

223. **nigredo**: cf. Verg., *G.* 2, 116-7 *sola India nigrum / fert hebenum*; Isid., *Orig.* 17, 7, 36 *Cuius lignum nigrum est*; *Anth.* 353, 7 (ed. Buecheler, 1: 1, 278) *ebenum pretiosum atrum natura creauit*; *CMC* Oxford, Digby 221, f. 73rb *Alter Pluto scilicet ebenum id est nigrum ad similitudinem ipsius arboris propter terre obscuritatem*; *ThLL*, 5: 4, 46 on *ebenus* as a byword for blackness.

225. **Nigram...set formonsam**: cf. *Ct* 1, 4 *Nigra sum sed formonsa.*

226. **esse**: supply *se* from 225.

227. **exurit ignis**: cf. Verg., *A.* 6, 742 *exuritur igni*; **libidinis ardens**: Prudentius, *Ham.* 611-2 *sic felle libidinis ardens / inpletur uitiis perituro mixta marito*; **ignisue...libidinis**: cf. *SD* 1, 345.

228. **ire...inpacientis**: cf. Prudentius, *Psych.* 116 *Ira... / inpatiens*; **eam**: i. e. *dilectam.*

229. **Fraxinus**: cf. *SD* 2, 512 *Fraxinus bello commoda*; **artificis manibus**: cf. Verg., *A.* 12, 210; *De tribus puellis* 229 (ed. Cohen, 2: 240) *Hunc manus artificis mira sculptaverat arte*; Baudri, *Carm.* 134, 209; **parere parata**: cf. Verg., *A.* 4, 238 *parere parabat*; Matthew of Vendôme, *Tob.* 987 (ed. Munari, 2: 203) *parere paratus.*

229-30. cf. *LSD* 8, 53-4 (p. 482W); cited in Hunt ed. Gibson 79.

230. **tincta cruore**: cf. *SD* 1, 518; 2, 1774 *Hic rosa purpureo tincta cruore rubet.*

231. **funereis pompis**: cf. Prudentius, *Perist.* 12, 47 *pompa...funeris*; **cupressus**: cf. Hor., *Epod.* 5, 18 *iubet cupressos funebris...aduri*; Claudian, *De raptu* 2, 108 *tumulos tectura cu-*

pressus; Peter of Blois, *Libellus*, 73, 1120.

232. **Fetores...odore**: cf. Isid., *Orig.* 17, 7, 34 *Antiqui cypressi ramos prope rogum constituere solebant, ut odorem cadauerum, dum urerentur, opprimerent iucunditate odoris sui.*

233. **idonea...galeis**: cf. Isid., *Orig.* 17, 7, 32 *ex ea naves fiunt*; Peter of Blois, *Libellus*, 73, 1119 *apta fretis abies.*

235. **quernum robur**: for similar etymological play cf. Verg., *A.* 4, 441 *ualidam cum robore quercum*; Paschalis 7.

236. **tabulata gemant**: *LSD* 3, 349 (p. 403W) *saepe tamen tabulata gemunt.*

237. **foliis ornata**: cf. Verg., *G.* 3, 21 *foliis ornatus*; *SD* 1, 547.

237. **Mora...celsus**: *LSD* 8, 92 (p. 483W) *Mora tibi celsus, dat tibi mora rubris*; *Poems* 1, 87 (ed. Walther 1965, 114) *Celsus mora tibi*; *SD* 2, 507 *Non subruffa nitent que celsus mora dat* [gloss in **P**: *Celsus -si arbor mora ferens*].

238. **Pirrame**: cf. Matthew of Vendôme, *Ars* 1, 111, 105-6 (ed. Munari, 3: 122) *Ardua morus adest, cui momentanea proles / Sanguine Pirameo primitus alba rubet*, **sanguine tincta tuo**: cf. Ov., *Met.* 4, 126-7 *madefactaque...sanguine radix / purpureo tingit pendentia mora colore*; *NE* 16, 8 (ed. Hervieux, 2: 401) *Aspice, iam rubeo sanguine tincta tuo*; *Poems* 1, 89-90 (ed. Walther 1965, 114) *mora / Sanguine tincta tuo, Pyrame, linquo tibi* [cf. *Ibis* 54].

239. **exurgens**: = *exsurgens*; **pirus...ignea**: cf. Isid., *Orig.* 17, 7, 15 *Pirus vocata videtur quod in ignis speciem deformata est*; *DNR* 2, 78 (pp. 174-5W); *LSD* 8, 93-106 (pp. 483-4W).

240. **Fructus...nobilitate**: cf. *in Eccles.* f. 158rb *Sicut autem quedam arbores fructu carent, quedam fructu nobilitantur.*

241. **Ni Bachus desit**: cf. *DNR* 2, 78 (p. 174W) *Solet quaeri quare nociva sint pira, nisi vino conficiantur*; *Prose Salern. Questions* P 111 (ed. Lawn, 248, 14-20) *Si pira sumantur nisi vino conficiantur, est Ypocras testis, quoniam sequitur mala pestis....Debet (sc. pirum)...cum vino accipi ut calore vini tempereretur eorum frigiditas*; *Poems* 13, 8 *Post pira presbiterum quere vel adde merum*; 3, 105-6 (ed. Walther, 1965, 128, 120) *Et conferre solent pira, sed presente Lieo: / Sumpto non audent ista nocere mero*; the metonymy of wine-god (Bacchus) for wine is common in Roman poetry.

242. **Leticie potus**: i. e. wine.

243. **amigdale**: cf. *Doctrinale* 368 *sic et amygdala dic* [*-lum fructus, -lus dedit arbor*].

244. **reliquas...preis**: cf. Isid., *Orig.* 17, 7, 24 *ad inferenda poma arbusta sequentia praevenit* (sc. amygdala).

245. **uariis morbis...amigdala prosunt**: cf. Isaac Israeli, *De diaetis* pp. 434-5 *Vnde pectus mundificant, et pulmonem ab humore phlegmatico, et oppilationem splenis et hepatis aperiunt, et grossam ventositatem in colo intestino dissoluunt, et urinam prouocant, et renum ac matricis sordes mundificant, et etiam constipationem aperiunt, et...menstrua potenter educunt.*

246. **Lac:** subject of **confert**, referring to the beneficial effects of the almond's milky juice cf. *DMLBS* 5: 1533 s. v. *lac* 5.

247. **Coctana...uapore**: cf. Mart., 5, 78, 15 *lento castaneae uapore tostae*; *Poems* 3, 103 (ed. Walther 1965, 120) *Coctana si fuerint vino condita, iuvabunt*; Urso, *Aphorismi Glosula* 59, 2 (ed. Creutz, 98) *Caliditas etiam diminuit, dum humiditatem dissolvit et consumit; haec eadem intendit, dum grossiores partes dissolvendo substantiam remollit, ut videtur in ficubus et in uvis, quae primordiate sunt stipticae, postmodo actione caloris remolliuntur et dulcorantur.*

247-48. **lento... / ...placent**: cf. *LSD* 8, 139-40 (p. 484W) *volema volemi / Si fuerint lento cocta calore placent.*

248. **Castaneeque nuces**: cf. Verg., *E.* 2, 52.

250. **tunsio**: cf. *LSD* 8, 151-2 (p. 485W) *Fructu foecundam generoso reddit olivam / Tunsio, desidiam verbera saepe fugat.*

251. **Neptunus equum produxit...Athenis**: cf. *CMC*, Oxford, Digby 221, ff. 45rb-va *Est fabula quod Neptunus et Minerva de impositione nominis Athenarum contenderunt et quod diis placuit ut eius nomine civitas appellaretur qui melius munus mortalibus optulisset. Tandem [tamen MS] Neptunus percusso litore equum bellis produxit. Minerva iacta hasta olivam procreavit, que res melior probata est, quia pacis insigne est, et iccirco dea suum nomen urbi dedit...Conditis ergo Athenis auctorem earum Cy<c>ropem has duas urbis commoditates considerantem quod videlicet maris vicinam et olivarum haberet habundantiam diu credo dubium extitisse ab utraque civitati nomen imponeret. Unde Minervam fingimus concertasse. Tandem vero / 45va / olivarum fructum marinis preferens usibus ab earundem urbe videtur nominasse.Quare etiam olive Palladi deputentur, in sequentibus audies. Ideo vero equum dicitur invenisse Neptunus quod mare mobile et velox sit*; *Vat. Myth.* 1, 2 (ed. Zorzetti, 3) (= Serv., *G.* 1, 12 [ed. Thilo-Hagen, 3: 133, 15-134, 13]).

252. **tribuit Pallas**: Mart., 9, 24, 5 *Non solam tribuit Pallas tibi, Care, coronam.*

253. **furta, rapinas**: Stat., *Theb.* 4, 695.

254. **bella ciet**: cf. Verg., *A.* 1, 541; **gloria maior erit**: *LH-L* 2:441; John of Salisbury, *Enthet. maior* 292 (ed. van Laarhoven, 1: 125) *hosteque prostrato gloria maior erit.*

255. **Deliciis breuibus**: cf. *LSD* 5, 214 (p. 445W) *deliciaeque breves*; **cerasus**: cf. **P**'s gloss on **cerasis** in *SD* 2, 510: *Hoc* [hec **P**] *cerasum pro fructu, hec cerasus arbor. .*

257. **Mespila**: cf. *LSD* 8, 91-2 (p. 483W); *SD* 2, 509 *Mespila mollia sunt cum grato grata sapore*; Isaac Israeli, *De diaetis* p. 415 *De mespilis: Mespila...proprietatem habent stomachum confortandi, cholericam egestionem ac uomitum auferendi et urinam prouocandi: magis autem pertinent ad medicinam quam ad cibum, quia parum nutriunt*; **brumali...pruina**: cf. Pallad., *ins.* 91 *mespilus...niveo plena liquore.*

258. **constipent**: cf. Plin., *Nat.* 23, 7, 141 (ed. Ian, 4: 45) *Mespila...reliqua adstringunt stomachum sistuntque alvum*; Latham, 110, s. v. *constip / atio* lists *constipatus*: «'constipated' (med.) c. 1172»; **stipticitate**: note word play on *constipent*; Urso, *Aphorismi Glosula* 45 (ed. Creutz, 86) *Laxantia alia sunt laxativa virtute dissolvente ut scamonea..., alia stipticitate coartante ut sorba et mespila.*

259. **Cerea...pruna**: cf. Ps.- Verg., *Copa* 18 (ed. Clausen, 82) *sunt autumnali cerea pruna die*; Verg., *E.* 2, 53.

261. **Pampineas uites... / Vlmus**: cf. Ov., *Met.* 10, 100; *LSD* 8, 142 (p. 485W) *Ulmus, adest uiti conjuga, grata comes*; M. Valerius, *Buc.* 3, 105 *Gaudet...sociatis vitibus ulmus.*

263-588. *Plants*

263. **Noys**: in Bernardus Silvestris, *Cosmographia* 9, 7 (ed. Dronke, 140) herbs are the business of Physis; cf. *DNR* 2, 56 (pp. 163-4W).

264. **color, forma**: cf. Baudri, *Carm.* 134, 676 *Singula signabat forma colorque suus*; *SD* 1, 626 *forma colorque.*

265. **artemisia**: cf. *DNR* 2, 63 (p. 168W); *LSD* 7, 11-20 (p. 472W); 7, 11 *Matricis vitium levat artemisia*; Cameron 177.

265. **mater**: cf. Macer 2 (ed. Choulant, 28) *Herbarum matrem* (sc. artemisia); *DNR* 2, 63 (p. 168W); Bernardus Silvestris, *Cosmographia* 1, 3, 379-80 (ed. Dronke, 114); T. Hunt 1989, 171 s. v. *Mater Herbarum*: Artemisia vulgaris.

266. **uires**: Riddle in Schleissner, 152-3, cites ancient and medieval sources that classify wormwood as an abortifacient and as an emmenagogue; **deliciosus**: infrequent in classical literature cf. *ThLL*, 5: 449, 51; *SD* 1, 88.

267. **Abrotanum**: cf. *LSD* 7, 31-2 (p. 473W).

268. **contra sumpta uenena**: cf. *Theobaldi Physiologus* 14 (ed. Eden, 48) *sumpta venena fugat* [Hildebert, *Physiologus MPL* 171: 1220d]; *SD* 1, 300; Macer 40-1 (ed. Choulant, 29) *Serpentes nidore fugat* (sc. abrotanum), *bibitumque venena / Illorum extinguit*; **iuuat**: in a medical sense cf. Hor., *Ep.* 1, 2, 51 *iuuat illum sic domus...ut...fomenta podagram*; *SD* 1, 258, 286, 302, 369, 371, 380, 400, 412, 432, 457, 514.

269. **stomachum recreant**: cf. Macer 53 (ed. Choulant, 30) *stomachum corroborat herba*; Bernardus Silvestris, *Cosmographia* 1, 3, 407 (ed. Dronke, 114); **cocta liquore**: cf. Macer 55 (ed. Choulant, 30) *si sit decocta liquore*.

270. **nardus...epar**: cf. Macer 74 (ed. Choulant, 31) *Curat hepar, sibi si iungatur gallica nardus*; on the shortening of the first syllable of *epar* cf. *Doctrinale* 130; *SD* 1, 409, 415.

271. **spleni**: cf. Macer 75 (ed. Choulant, 31) *Splenque sibi iuncto potata iuvabit aceto*; *LSD* 7, 29 (p. 473W) *Prosunt...spleni*.

272. **Vulneribus**: cf. Macer 84 (ed. Choulant, 31) *Vulneribus prodest contrita recentibus illa*; **iuuamen**: a prose word from late antiquity cf. *ThLL*, 7: 727, 31; *SD* 1, 366, 370, 401, 438.

273. **Tussi**: cf. Macer 121 (ed. Choulant, 33) *Et tussim veterem curat, si saepe bibatur*. Constantinus Africanus, the author of *De omnium morborum qui homini accidere possunt cognitione et curatione*, has chapters *de tussi* 3, 6 (pp. 48-51), *de ictericia* 5, 11 (pp. 109-11), *de podagra* 6, 19 (pp. 137-9), *de morsu scorpionum* 7, 15 (p. 155), to note just a few of the ailments treated by *urtica*; **resumpta frequenter**: cf. *LSD* 3, 157 (p. 398W) *sumpta frequenter*.

274. **Ictericis confert**: *LSD* 6, 245 (p. 469W); **confert**: occurs often meaning *adiuuat* in medical writers cf. *ThLL*, 4: 186, 12; *SD* 1, 283, 287, 292, 298, 303, 313, 347; **mero**: cf. Macer 119 (ed. Choulant, 33) *Haec solet ictericos cum vino sumpta iuvare*; *LSD* 7, 12 (p. 472W), 118 (p. 475W); the administration of medicines in wine has a long history; Jackson 81-2 cites prescriptions recorded on wine amphoras from Roman Britain.

275. **semen...medetur**: Macer 120 (ed. Choulant, 33) *Illius semen colicis cum melle medetur*; cf. *LSD* 7, 47-8 (p. 473W).

276. **Stat cruor**: Claudian, *Carm. min. app.* 21, 16 *stat cruor in uenis*; Macer 138-9 (ed. Choulant, 33) *Quod si manentem cupias retinere cruorem, / Urticae succo frontem line*.

277. **podagra**: pain in the joints of the foot cf. Jackson 177-9, who synopsizes ancient accounts of the condition; Macer 132-3 (ed. Choulant, 33) *podagrae sic subvenit illa* (sc. urtica); Bernardus Silvestris, *Cosmographia* 1, 3, 401 (ed. Dronke, 114) *faciens urtica podagre*; *LSD* 7, 51 (p. 473W); *Doctrinale* 1702 *cum chiragra podagram quidam breviant, alii non*.

277-78. Martial 1, 98.

279. **Pulmoni**: cf. Macer 146-7 (ed. Choulant, 34) *pulmones adiuvat eius / Semen*; *LSD* 7, 50 (p. 473W).

280. **uenenatis morsibus**: Macer 650 (ed. Choulant, 54) *uenenatis...morsibus.*

281. **Sanant...ictus**: cf. Macer 164 (ed. Choulant, 34) *Curat, quos serpens vel scorpius intulit, ictus*; Dracontius, *De laudibus Dei* 1, 295 (*MGH, AA* 14: 38); *LSD* 7, 53-60 (p. 473W); **serpens uel scorpius**: a biblical congeries cf. Sir 39, 36; Lc 10, 19; Jerome, *Ep.* 22, 3 (ed. Hilberg, *CSEL* 54: 146, 13-4); according to Stannard 1974, 28, although scorpions are not found in Britain, a late 14th-c. English herbal lists many plants said to be effective in alleviating their painful stings; this he sees as part of the residual influence of the Greco-Roman herbal tradition.

282. **Lumbricos**: cf. Macer 168 (ed. Choulant, 35) *vermes ventris tineasque repellit.*

283. **Asmaticis confert**: cf. Macer 216 (ed. Choulant, 37) *iuvat asthmaticos*; for *conferre* with dative cf. *LSD* 7, 223-4 (p. 477W) *Spleneticis... / confert*; **sedat...tumores**: cf. Macer 213 (ed. Choulant, 37) *sedatque tumorem*; *LSD* 7, 61-8 (p. 473W).

284. **subuenit ydropicis**: cf. Macer 215 (ed. Choulant, 37) *Hydropicis...prodest*; **morsibus...canis**: cf. Macer 213 (ed. Choulant, 37) *Sola canis morsum curat*; *SD* 1, 290; Cameron 123-4 sets out the curative and antibiotic properties of plantain in treating wounds.

284. **morsibus apta canis**: cf. *LSD* 7, 58 (p. 473W); *SD* 1, 290.

285. **[Ruta]**: cf. *LSD* 7, 73 (p. 474W); on its medicinal effects see Cameron 125-6.

285-6. **Arteticos, sciazim... / ...iuuat**: Macer 276 *Arteticos sciasimque iuvat*; **matricem**: cf. Macer 279 *matricis prodest...tumori*; **menstrua, tussim**: cf. Macer 271 *Tussim...compescit, menstrua purgat* (ed. Choulant, 39).

285. **sciazim**: cf. Isid., *Orig.* 4, 7, 29 *ischiasis vocata a parte corporis, quam vexat*; Constantinus Africanus, *De ischiatica passione* 6, 18 (pp. 135-7).

286. **Pulmonem, pectus,...iuuat**: *LSD* 7, 71-2 (pp. 473-4W); Macer 274 *Pulmones iuvat et pectus*; **lumina**: cf. Macer 285 *oculos caligine curat* (ed. Choulant, 39).

286. **ruta**: cf. *LSD* 7, 69-78 (pp. 473-4W).

287. **apium**: cf. Isaac Israeli, *De diaetis* p. 454, *De apio: Valet secundum medicinam*; Macer 360-1 (ed. Choulant, 43) *Hydropicos et splen tumidum iuvat illa, iecurque / Si cum feniculi succo contrita bibatur*; *LSD* 7, 83 (p. 474W) *Confert hydropicis, spleni, jecorique.*

289. **emoptoicos**: **P** f. 209rb glosses *emoptoicis: sanguinem spuentibus*; cf. *DNR* 2, 59 (p. 166W); *LSD* 7, 91-6 (p. 474W).

289. **malua**: cf. *DNR* 2, 59 (p. 166W); *LSD* 7, 236 (p. 478W); *DMLBS* 4: 1128 s. v. *haemoptyicus*; Macer 385 (ed. Choulant, 44) *Et prodest haemoptoicis lapidesque repellit*; **lapidem**: cf. *LSD* 7, 96 (p. 474W); *SD* 1, 444 *Duricies lapidis*; Constantinus Africanus, *De lapide* 5, 17 (pp. 117-8).

290. **morsibus apta salus**: *LSD* 7, 96 (p. 474W); Macer 394; **Duricias sedat**: cf. Macer 392 *duricias mollit* (ed. Choulant, 44).

291. **Luminibus**: cf. Macer 421; **uirge curat... / Vlcera**: cf. Macer 417-8 (ed. Choulant, 45) *Ulcera praecipue membri curare virilis / Dicitur iste cinis*; *LSD* 7, 101 (p. 474W) *Seminis ejusdem curat cinis ulcera virgae*. The scribe may not have understood that *uirga* meant *penis*, and as a result copied *uulnera*

292. **lacte**: cf. Macer 397-8 (ed. Choulant, 44) *Lac dat abundanter eius decoctio sumpta / Nutrici*; *LSD* 7, 97 (p. 474W) *Ubera nutricis...foecundat anetum*; Isaac Israeli, *De diaetis* p. 479, *semen eius bibitum...lac augmentat.*

293. **Bethonica uirtus**: cf. *LSD* 7, 21 (p. 472W) *Betonicae vires*; *DNR* 2, 61 (p. 167W); **capitisque dolori**: cf. Hor., *S*. 2, 3, 29 *traiecto latens miseri capitisue dolore*; *SD* 1, 365.

293. **auris…dolori**: cf. Macer 435 (ed. Choulant, 46) *Auribus infusus varios fugat inde dolores*; Constantinus Africanus, *De dolore aurium* 2, 9 (p. 32); *DNR* 2, 61 (p. 167W); *LSD* 7, 21-6 (p. 472W).

294. **Fracture capitis**: cf. Macer 444 (ed. Choulant, 46) *Tritaque fracturae capitis haec sola medetur*; **ydropicis**: cf. Constantinus Africanus, *De hydropisi* 5, 5 (pp. 100-2); cf. Macer 468 (ed. Choulant, 47) *Prodest hydropicis*; 432 (ed. Choulant, 46).

295. **Vulneribus…antraci**: cf. Macer 494-6 (ed. Choulant, 48); *LSD* 7, 107-8 (p. 474W).

296. **morbis**: cf. Macer 501 (ed. Choulant, 49) *Omnibus et morbis prodest de frigore factis*; Urso, *Aphorismi Glosula* 60, 2 (ed. Creutz, 102) *Frigiditas variarum aegritudinum <causa> existit. Frigiditas enim de natura sui frigidorum morborum est inductiva, quorum unus est algor, qui frigidus morbus iudicatur et a frigiditate inducitur. Frigiditas opii etiam naturalem calorem suffocat et frigidum morbum inducit, qui etiam mortificat. Frigiditas constringit exteriora et fumositatem includendo effimeram febrem generat. Exulcerando membra nimiae siccitatis causa existit et frigidum morbum inducit, scilicet squaliditatem. Frigiditas constringit cerebrum et humiditas contenta per membra diffunditur et morbus humidus generatur. Frigiditas digestivam virtutem impedit in hepate et fit causa principalior in generando hydrope…Frigiditas causa est indigestionis….*

297. **conuicia det Fenenna**: cf. *LSD* 1, 211 (p. 362W), 7, 145-8 (p. 475W); *Poems* 2, 15 (ed. Esposito, 453) *tunc do conuicia mundo*; Elkanah had two wives, Hannah and Peninnah (cf. Hildebert, *Carm. min.* 39, 111, 13 *uxores sub lege duas simul Helcana duxit*); according to 1 Sm 1, the latter scorned and insulted the former because of her childlessness; Yahweh answered Hannah's prayer and she bore a son, Samuel; 1 Sm 1-2 *fueruntque Fenennae filii, Annae autem non erant liberi*; cf. Fulg., *De aetatibus* 7 (ed. Helm, 150, 19-152, 10); Berry, 184, notes 211-2; Macer 13 (ed. Choulant, 49) *Reddit* (sc. porrum) *fecundas mansum…persaepe puellas*; **Si porrum sumas**: cf. *LSD* 7, 146 (p. 475W) *porri sumptio*; Isaac Israeli, *De diaetis*, p. 459 *Caput eius* (sc. porri) *coctum…venerem suscitat.*

299. **Ebrietatis honus**: cf. Constantinus Africanus, *De ebrietate*, 1, 19 (pp. 17-8); *ebrietas* rarely occurs in classical verse cf. Hor., *Ep.* 1, 5, 16; *ThLL*, 5: 8, 5; **si crudum sumpseris**: cf. Macer 547 (ed. Choulant, 50) *Si crudum fuerit sumptum levat ebrietatem*; *LSD* 7, 126 (p. 475W) *relevans ebrietatis onus* (sc. foeniculus).

300. **Alleuiat**: a rare word found in the Itala and the Vulgate cf. *ThLL*, 1: 1673, 62; Act. 27, 38 *alleuiabant navem iactantes triticum in mare*; **uenena**: cf. Macer 530-1 (ed. Choulant, 50); Hor., *S*. 2, 4, 29 **sumpta uenena**: Macer 610 (ed. Choulant, 53); Isaac Israeli, *De diaetis*, p. 459 *Crudus cataplasmatus super morsum serpentis bene prodest*; **facit**: in a medical sense cf. Scribonius Largus 176 *antidotus…facit adversus toxicum.*

301. **Herba breuis**: cf. Macer 551 (ed. Choulant, 51) *haec multum redolens est et brevis herba*; Hor. *S*. 2, 4, 29; **lapillum**: cf. Macer 566 (ed. Choulant, 51) *Vesicae frangit lapides.*

301. **camamilla**: for the various spellings of the herb cf. T. Hunt 1989, 64 s. v. *Camomilla.*

302. **Dissipat**: for the verb in medical discourse cf. *ThLL*, 5: 1489, 39; **egilopas yctericosque**: cf. Macer 572 *Ictericis prodest*; 584 *Aegilopas curat* (ed. Choulant, 51-2); *LSD* 7, 109 (p. 474W) *Ictericis…camomilla medetur.*

303. **Nepta**: on the orthography of this herb cf. T. Hunt 1989, 185 s. v. *Nepeta*; *LSD* 7, 113-8 (p. 475W), 7, 113-4 *Vexatis tiasi confert... / ...nepta*; cf. *NG* M-N, 1209; **lepre**: cf. Macer 604 (ed. Choulant, 53) *Est leprae species elephantiasisque uocatur*; *LSD* 4, 856-7 (p. 440W).

304. **notum nomen**: note the etymological wordplay cf. Isid., *Orig.* 1, 7, 1 *Nomen dictum quasi notamen, quod nobis vocabulo suo res notas efficiat*; **nomen...trahit**: i. e. elephantiasis cf. *LSD* 7, 116 (p. 475W) *Leprae quae nomen ex elephante trahit*; *SD* 1, 382, 502; 2, 82 *Vis anime nomen a ratione trahens*; Constantinus Africanus, *De elephantiasi* 7, 17 (pp. 160-1); Jackson 182-4 discusses the form of leprosy identified with elephantiasis in ancient and medieval literature; cf. Dols 318.

305. Note the alliteration; **secundas**: **P** f. 209va glosses *secundas: Pelliculas que, si post partum remanent, ledunt matrem*; cf. Macer 630 (ed. Choulant, 54) *tardas haec extrahit herba secundas*; *LSD* 7, 119-24 (p. 475W); pennyroyal causes the uterus to move reflexively cf. Cameron 126; Riddle in Schleissner, 153.

306. **podagra**: cf. Macer 658 (ed. Choulant, 55); **uenena**: cf. Macer 650 (ed. Choulant, 54); Bernardus Silvestris, *Cosmographia* 1, 3, 393 (ed. Dronke, 114); **dira uenena**: Hor., *S.* 1, 9, 31; Ov., *Am.* 2, 14, 28; cf. Marbod, *De lapidibus* 46 (ed. Riddle, 36) *Atra venena fugat*; *SD* 1, 314, 383, 447, 500, 523.

307. **renibus**: cf. Macer 690 (ed. Choulant, 56); **ydropisis** = *ydropicis* cf. Macer 691; **luminibusque**: cf. Macer 682-3 (ed. Choulant, 56); *LSD* 3, 610 (p. 409W) *Vix oculis maratrum gratius esse potest*; Walahfrid Strabo, *De cultura hortorum* 211 (*MGH, P. L* 2: 342); Bernardus Silvestris, *Cosmographia* 1, 3, 389 (ed. Dronke, 114).

308. **stomacho**: cf. Macer 700 (ed. Choulant, 57).

309. **uirtus**: cf. Macer 716 *Virtus est illi*; **fastidia tollit**: cf. Macer 715 (ed. Choulant, 57) *ferunt, sibi quod fastidia tollat*; *LSD* 7, 131-6 (p. 475W); Constantinus Africanus, *De fastidio* 4, 9 (pp. 73-4); **herpes**: cf. Macer 718 (ed. Choulant, 57).

310. **fluxus uentris**: Macer, 727-8 (ed. Choulant, 58) *Omne genus fluxus ventris restringere mire / ...solet*; *LSD* 7, 132 (p. 475W).

311. **febrem que causon dicitur**: cf. Macer 752-3 (ed. Choulant, 59) *Febrem, quam causon Graecia dicit, / Inde iuvat*; *LSD* 7, 137 (p. 475W); **arcet**: in a medical sense cf. Plin., *Nat.* 27, 52 (ed. Ian, 4: 245) *nausiam maris arcet* (sc. absinthium) *in navigationibus potum*.

312. **soles**: cf. Plin., *Nat.* 12, 11 *soles aestate arcere*; Macer 760-1 (ed. Choulant, 59) *Fervorem solis aestate comesta nocere / Non sinit*; *LSD* 7, 137-8 (p. 475W).

313. **lactuca**: cf. Mart., 3, 89 for scatological wit on the laxative properties of *lactuca*; *LSD* 7, 141-4 (p. 475W).

313. **calorem**: cf. Macer 765-6 (ed. Choulant, 60) *Frigida Lactucae vis constat... / Unde potest nimios haec mansa levare calores.*

314 **nutrix sompni**: cf. Macer 768 *somnum dat*; Bernardus Silvestris, *Cosmographia* 1, 3, 369 (ed. Dronke, 113) *lactuca sopora*; **somnia uana**: cf. Macer 771 (ed. Choulant, 60) *Lactucae semen compescit somnia vana*; Marbod, *De lapidibus* 45 (ed. Riddle, 36) *somnia vana repellit*; *LSD* 7, 142 (p. 475W); *Poems* 1, 86 (ed. Walther 1965, 114); Ov., *Met.* 11, 614; Isaac Israeli, *De diaetis* p. 450 *De lactucis:...somnum laudabilem uigilias habentibus praestat.*

315. [**Rosa**]: cf. *DNR* 2, 66 (p. 168W); *LSD* 7, 295-314 (pp. 479-80W). Longer sections of sixteen verses describe the rose (315-30), the lily (331-46) and the violet (351-66), which

are grouped as a centrepiece. In the first two, extended mythological and / or allegorical material frame the medicinal benefits of the rose (325-6) and the lily (341-2); in the third, an allegorization of fourteen lines introduces the distich (365-6) on the violet's curative powers; **uernans**: cf. Baudri, *Carm.* 34,1 *uernans rosa* .

316. **roseus**: cf. *SD* 2, 450 *Inter quem roseus flosculus ille sedet*; **purpureusue**: cf. Hor., *C.* 3, 15, 15 *flos purpureus rosae*; *SD* 2, 445-6; *in Eccles.* f. 91va *Hinc inuitat purpureus rubor rosarum uernantium oculos ad sui conspectum*.

317. **Illa...gaudet**: accounts of the rose's origin include descent from the crimson of the rising sun or from Aurora's tresses cf. Dracontius, *De origine rosarum* (ed. Wolff, 82, note 1).

318. **superis...placet**: *LSD* 8, 28 (p. 482W) *munus, quod superis terrigenisque placet*; Mart., 11, 53, 7 *Sic placeat superis..*; *CNP* 1279-80 *succedens noctis tenebris aurora refulgens / terrigenis letum spondet adesse diem*; *Poems* 7, 6 (ed. Walther 1965, 124).

319. **specie**: cf. Macer 777 (ed. Choulant, 60) *Quod specie cunctos praecedat* (sc. rosa); Bond 80 translates Macer's section on the rose.

320. **aurore...hostis**: for use of *rosa / roseus* to describe Aurora cf. Verg., *A.* 6, 535 *roseis Aurora quadrigis*; 7, 26 *Aurora in roseis fulgebat lutea bigis*; Ps.-Verg., *Culex* 44; *Dirae (Lydia)* 73 (ed. Clausen 20, 14); Ov., *Met.* 2, 113.

321. **Tersites,...Birria,...Dauus**: cf. *CNP* 381-2 (ed. Walther, 1962, 37) *Desidiam testudineo gressu comitantur: / Davus, Tersites, Birria, Gnato loquax*; 391-4, 427-8; *LSD* 2, 120 (p. 376W), 7, 185 (p. 476W); for Thersites as a low character cf. John of Salisbury, *Enthet. maior* 1747 (ed. van Laarhoven, 1: 219) *Tersitae similes producit curia multos*; *Poems* 4, 41-2 (ed. Esposito, 455) *clarum / Tersitem reddit* (sc. uinum); Birria, a servant in the 12th-c. comedy *Geta*, became proverbial for sluggishness cf. *Geta* 61-9 (ed. Cohen, 1: 37) for a sharp exchange between Alcmena and Birria on the topic of the latter's laziness. Davus, the name of a Roman slave (cf. Hor., *S.* 1, 10, 40) and Birria appear together in *Baucis et Traso* 208-58 (ed. Cohen, 2: 78-80); cf. Walther, *Prov.* 25258 *Quidquid agunt alii, semper tu, Birria, dormis*; cf. Walther 1962, 38, note 9; Berry, 197, note 120.

323. **mira...uirtus**: Maximianus 5, 147 *mira tibi uirtus*.

324. **laudes utilitatis habet**: cf. *LSD* 7, 309-10 (p. 479W).

325. **Igni...sacro**: St. Anthony's fire, erysipelas cf. *DMLBS* 5: 1205 s. v. *ignis* 14b; Macer 78 *Compescit sacrum...ignem*; *LSD* 7, 311 (p. 480W) *sacroque medebitur igni*; **capiti stomachoque**: cf. Macer 782, 791, 793 (ed. Choulant, 60-1).

327. **quam...fugitiua / ...rosa**: the rose is linked to the theme of transience in Hor., *C.* 2, 3, 13-4; cf. *LSD* 7, 300 (p. 479W); *CNP* 733-4 *quod fugitiua decor res sit, quod uana, diserti / uatis quem genuit Mantua musa docet*. Neckam then quotes Ps.- Verg., *De rosis nascentibus* 35-50; cf. Baudri, *Carm.* 40, 5-6, 8 *Flos olim roseus nunc cinis est luteus*; 53, 9 *In Maio uernante rosa rosa marcuit ista*; Cropp 276. **P** f. 234rb adds a marginal gloss *Uirgilius de rosis* to three verses from *CNP*: *Mirabar celerem fugitiua etate rapinam / Et dum nascuntur consenuisse rosas. / Ecce et defluxit rutili coma punica floris.* Green 669 argues the case for assigning *De rosis nascentibus* to Ausonius. On the use of the rose as an emblem of time's passage in classical poetry cf. Gold 16, 18.

328. **Vernantis...rose**: cf. *LSD* 7, 295-6 (p. 479W); *SD* 1, 362; 2, 1608 *Vernantesque fugam iussit inire rosas*; Geoffrey of Monmouth, *Vita Merlini* 175 *vernantesque rosas*; **forma uenusta**: cf. *SD* 1, 1046 *forma uenustet*.

329. **Vespera cernit anum**: cf. Ps.- Verg., *De rosis nascentibus* 45-6 (ed. Clausen, 178) *quam modo nascentem rutilus conspexit Eoos, / hanc rediens sero uespere uidit anum*, for the thought cf. *Anth. De rosis* 72, 9 (ed. Shackleton Bailey, 1: 2, 76) *ne pereant, lege mane rosas. <cito> virgo senescit*; **puellam**: for later examples of the rose-young woman parallel to connote the flower's short life cf. Fleissner xix.

330.. **anum**: *mensis* and *dies* suggest word-play on *anum / annum*; **una dies**: cf Ps.-Verg., *De rosis nascentibus* 43 (ed. Clausen, 178) *quam longa una dies, aetas tam longa rosarum.*

331. **Lilia**: cf. *DNR* 2, 67 (p. 169W), 166 (pp. 274-5W); *LSD* 7, 315-334 (p. 480W); **designatiua**: see Matthew of Vendôme, *Ars* 2, 24 (ed. Munari, 3: 146) for comments on adjectives in *-ivus*.

332. **Vt rosa, martirium**: cf. *SD* 1, 358; 2, 164 *martyriique rose*; on the rose and lily as symbolic of aspects of Christian faith cf. Walahfrid Strabo, *De cultura hortorum* 415-8 (*MGH, P. L.* 2: 349) *Haec duo* (sc. rosae / lilia) *namque probabilium genera inclyta florum / Ecclesiae summas signant per saecula palmas, / Sanguine martyrii carpit quae dona rosarum / Liliaque in fidei gestat candore nitentis*; *LSD* 5, 105 (p. 442W) *rosa martyrii*, 5, 127-8 (p. 443W); *Poems* 3, 161-2 (ed. Walther 1965, 121) *Hic cruor est roseus, quem sic fudit rosa campi. / Que rosa? Martirii gloria, culmen, honos.*

333. **confessor lilia**: cf. *SD* 2, 59 *Non confessorum fulsissent lilia celo*; **lilia gestat**: cf. Ov., *Met.* 12, 411 *lilia gestet*; *SD* 1, 360-1.

334. **lilia uallis**: cf. *Ct* 2, 1 *ego flos campi et lilium convallium.*

335. **celestia lilia**: *LSD* 5, 455 (p. 451W).

336. **lilia**: to be taken with *uallis* and *montis*.

337. **Ciuibus angelicis**: cf. Venantius, *Vita Martini* 2, 122, *Carm.* 8, 3, 5 (*MGH, AA* 4: 318, 181) *coetibus angelicis hominum sociata propago*; *LSD* 5, 113-8 (p. 443W); **celibe uita**: Hor., *Ep.* 1, 1, 88; *LSD* 5, 114 (p. 443W); Matthew of Vendôme, *Ep.* 1, 7, 19 (ed. Munari, 2: 100); cf. Mastandrea 92.

338. **associandus erit**: cf. *LSD* 1, 4 (p. 357W).

341. **Exustis...membris**: cf. Macer 814, 818 (ed. Choulant, 62) *combustaque membra iuvantur*; *LSD* 7, 331 (p. 480W)...*usturis*; for the lily's power to assuage pain from burns cf. Cameron 128; **sedantque tumorem**: cf. *LSD* 7, 331-2 (p. 480W) *tumori / Sedando*; Walahfrid Strabo, *De cultura hortorum* 258-60 (*MGH, P. L.* 2: 344); *Poems* 3, 101 (ed. Walther 1965, 119) [Cambridge, UL, Gg. 6. 42, f. 231r] *Lilia succurrunt vino permixta tumori*; Cameron 122.

342. **simplicitas uera**: cf. Mart. 1, 39, 4.

347. **letargo**: an illness involving loss of memory or drowsiness; cf. Macer 852-7 (ed. Choulant, 63); *LSD* 7, 149-54 (p. 475W); **P** f. 232rb adds a marginal gloss on a verse from *CNP*: *Est in prelato uiolentus turbo frenesis*, as follows: Macer *Est quidam morbus letargus nomine dictus / Oppositum medici quem dicunt esse frenes<i>.*

348. **senes ad opus iuuenile**: cf. Bernardus Silvestris, *Cosmographia* 1, 3, 376 (ed. Dronke, 114) *Satiricon revocans ad iuvenile senes*; *SD* 1, 388 *Cipridis...opus*; Isid., *Orig.* 17, 9, 42 *pronos facit in Venerem* (sc. satureia); Macer 862 (ed. Choulant, 64) *Hocque modo mire venerem solet illa movere.*

347-8. **aceto / Iuncto**: cf. *LSD* 7, 151-2 (p. 475W) *aceto / Mixta* (sc. satureia).

349. **succurret iecori laterisque dolori**: cf. Macer 871 (ed. Choulant, 64) *iecoris prod-*

est...querelis, 877 *Compescit ...laterisque dolorem; LSD* 7, 155-60 (p. 476W); **laterisque dolori**: cf. Hor., *S.* 1, 9, 32 *laterum dolor; SD* 1, 417.

350. **condimentum**: cf. *LSD* 7, 155 (p. 476W) *Salvia grata cocis.*

351. [**Viola**]: cf. *LSD* 7, 335-40 (p. 480W); **Ecclesie..ornatur**: cf. Petrus Chrysologus, *Serm.* 22 (*MPL* 52: 262b) *et ornatur* (sc. thalamus) *...verecundiae rosis, liliis castitatis, pudoris violis;* **floribus ortus**: cf. Mastandrea 296.

352. **sunt...uiole**: cf. Ps.-Verg., *Copa* 13 (ed. Clausen, 81) *sunt etiam croceo uiolae de flore corollae; LSD* 5, 129-52 (p. 443W); Jerome, *Ep.* 54, 14 (ed. Hilberg, *CSEL* 54: 481, 7-9) *suscipe uiduas, quas inter uirginum lilia et martyrum rosas quasi quasdam uiolas misceas,* **lilia mixta rosis**: Dracontius, *Epithal. in fratribus dictum* 8 (ed. Wolff, 1); Matthew of Vendôme, *Ep.* 1, 7, 24, *Tob.* 166 (ed. Munari, 2: 100, 168); *SD* 2, 1698 *lilia mixta rosis* cf. 1694 *Lilia...associata rosis;* Marius Victorinus, *art. gram.* (GLK 6: 105, 15) *lactea sanguineis lilia mixta rosis; LH-L* 3: 197; see Fechter 48-61 on the comparison of roses and lilies.

353. **gradibus certis**: Hildebert, *Carm. min. supplementum* 3, 16 (ed. Scott, 57) *nec gradibus certis destitit esse bonus;* cf. *LSD* 10, 4-8 (p. 496W), 10, 4 *Hinc natura suos jussit adesse gradus; SD* 2, 285-6 *Corrupit corpus mox mens infecta ueneno; / Sic numerus graduum cepit habere locum.*

354. **ferrugineus flos, niueus, roseus**: cf. Macer 1345 *species tres esse leguntur earum,* 1347 *Nam sunt purpurei flores albique nigrique* (ed. Choulant, 83); Peter of Blois, *Libellus,* 73, 1100-1; *LSD* 5, 103 (p. 442W) *Dat violas dulci pictas ferrugine,* 7, 327-8 (p. 480W) *Dulcis ferrugo violas.. / Depingit;* in *Eccles.* f. 91va *Hinc uiole dulci ferrugine picte oculorum sibi uendicant officium;* Prudentius, *Psych.* 355 *et ferrugineo uernantes flore coronas?*

357. **Felices**: cf. *LSD* 5, 129 (p. 443W).

359. **uiole...uirtutis**: cf. Isid., *Orig.* 17, 9, 19 *Viola propter vim odoris nomen accepit; SD* 1, 363-4 *uiole...uirtus,* 557 *uiole uires;* **uirtutis honore**: cf. Mastandrea 929.

362. **lilia blanda**: cf. *LSD* 5, 128 (p. 443W) *Fiunt vernantes lilia saepe rosae;* in *Eccles.* f. 90va *inde blanditur niueus fulgor liliorum candentium.*

364. **concomitetur**: a rare word; *ThLL,* 4: 81, 51 cites three examples only, of which one occurs in verse cf. Venantius, *Carm.* 8, 3, 158 *Caesario concomitante suo.*

365. **podagram sedant**: cf. Macer 1368 (ed. Choulant, 84) *calidam dicunt sedare podagram; LSD* 7, 335 (p. 480W); **oculis capitisque dolori**: cf. Macer 1350-1, 1378 *Et capiti prodest, quocunque dolore laboret* (ed. Choulant, 83-4).

367. **Balnea**: In the *Isagoge,* Johannitius includes baths among the six factors listed as *occasiones* of health or sickness cf. Olson 42; *LSD* 3, 272 (p. 401W) *Confecto prosunt balnea nostra seni;* **ligustica**: cf. *LSD* 7, 161-4 (p. 476W).

368. **Radix**: cf. Macer 885 (ed. Choulant, 65) *Maior radicis vis est;* cf. *Prose Salern. Questions* B 277 (ed. Lawn, 133, 27) *Queritur quare quedam plantarum radices magis sint diuretice quam frondes vel rami, et e econverso? R. Hoc contingit ex maiori quantitate nutrimenti tracti ad radices quam ad folia vel ramos.*

369. **colicos**: cf. Macer 894; **stomachi**: cf. Macer 887-8 (ed. Choulant, 65); **stomachi sedare**: cf. *LSD* 7, 163 (p. 476W) *stomachi sedant...tumorem.*

370. **iuuamen**: cf. *SD* 1, 336.

371. **Ostrucium**: cf. T. Hunt 1989, 194 s. v. *Ostrutium:* ? Betony; ? Master-Wort.

371. **iuuat yctericos**: cf. Macer 910 (ed. Choulant, 65) *Ictericos...iuuat, LSD* 7, 165-70

(p. 476W); **depellit abortum**: cf. Macer 915 (ed. Choulant, 66) *Subdita matrici depellere fertur abortum.*

372. **splen**: cf. *LSD* 7, 166 (p. 476W); **tussis hanela**: Verg., *G.* 3, 497; Maximianus 1, 245 *hinc tussis anhela fatigat;* Macer 913 (ed. Choulant, 66) *tussique medetur.*

373. **cerefolii**: cf. T. Hunt 1989, 78 s. v. *Cerfolium.*

373. **cancris**: cf Macer 929 (ed. Choulant, 66) *Appositum cancris tritum cum melle medetur,* *LSD* 7, 171-2 (p. 476W); **sociati** to be construed with **cerefolii**: cf. *SD* 1, 400, 458; *LSD* 7, 172 (p. 476W) *o virtus, cancer obedit ei.*

374. **laterum...doloris**: cf. Macer 930-1 (ed. Choulant, 66) *Cum uino...lateris sedare dolorem / Saepe solet;* Isaac Israeli, *De diaetis* p. 456 *dolorem laterum...placat.*

375. **Lumbrici, tinee**: cf. Macer 935 (ed. Choulant, 67) *Lumbricos...tineasque repellis;* Constantinus Africanus, *De tinea* 1, 8 (pp. 6-7); **uenter, uomitus**: cf. Macer 941 (ed. Choulant, 67) *Saepe solet vomitum ventremque tenere solutum;* Walahfrid Strabo, *De cultura hortorum* 245-6 (*MGH, P. L.* 2: 344); Constantinus Africanus, *De uomitu* 4, 11 (pp. 75-6).

376. **uertigo**: cf. Macer 944 (ed. Choulant, 67) *Illius elixatura vertigo fugatur.*

377. **aluuum lenit**: cf. Macer 948 (ed. Choulant, 67) *Eius mollit cibus aluum;* *LSD* 7, 173-6 (p. 476W).

378. **podagram**: cf. Macer 954 (ed. Choulant, 67) *Dicunt appositam calidam sedare podagram.*

379. **Vnguibus...scabris**: cf. Macer 951 (ed. Choulant, 67) *Hocque superpositum scabros cito detrahit ungues.*

380. **Yctericos uino**: cf. Macer 955-6 (ed. Choulant, 67); Isaac Israeli, *De diaetis* p. 463, *utilis est habentibus icteritiam.*

381. **Ventrem..semina**: cf. Macer 965-6 (ed. Choulant, 68) *Illius semen ventrem stipare solutum / Fertur,* *LSD* 7, 177-80 (p. 476W).

381-2. **febrem / ...tercia**: cf. Macer 979-81 (ed. Choulant, 68) *febris ante tremorem / Si tria grana voret Coriandri seminis aeger, / Evadet febrem cui dat lux tertia nomen.*

382. **nomen...tercia**: cf. *LSD* 7, 263 (p. 478W) *At verbena febri, cui lux dat tertia nomen.*

383. **Antraci ueneri...sciasi**: cf. Macer 992 (ed. Choulant, 69) *Anthracas curat,* 989 *hac re venerem ceu ruta coercent,* 1004 *Haec contrita simul sciasis superadde dolori;* *LSD* 7, 181-4 (p. 476W), 7, 183 (p. 476W) *Anthraci, sciasi, tussi.*

384. **Horum**: sc. *nasturciorum;* **glabrio**: rare word; *ThLL,* 6: 1999, 58 notes Gloss. 5: 502, 35 = *is qui pilos evellit;* cf. Macer 995 (ed. Choulant, 69) *Illius succus crines retinere fluentes;* *SD* 1, 398; Cameron 22-3 describes the more bizarre medieval remedies for baldness.

384. **splene**: cf. Macer 1002 (ed. Choulant, 69) *Splen reprimit;* **poscit opem**: Hor., *Ep.* 2, 1, 134; *Ars* 411; Ov., *Fast.* 3, 594; *SD* 1, 397.

385. **Eruce**: cf. *LSD* 7, 185-90 (p. 476W); **urinam prouocat**: cf. Isaac Israeli, *De diaetis* p. 457, *De eruca: Dioscorides dicit quod urinam prouocat, quod Hippocrates negauit;* Macer 1018 (ed. Choulant, 70) *valet urinas...mouere;* the phrase recurs often in medical writings cf. Macer 348 (ed. Choulant, 42 *De apio*), 845 (ed. Choulant, 63 *De satureia*); *Regimen Sanitatis* 134, 137, 142.

385-6. **escas / Digerit**: cf. Macer 1017 (ed. Choulant, 70) *Cibus eius digerit escas;* *LSD* 7, 188 (p. 476W) *digeret ipsa cibos* (sc. eruca).

386. **maculas**: cf. Macer 1026 (ed. Choulant, 70) *Haec nigras maculas purgat*.

387. **lentigo**: cf. Macer 1021 (ed. Choulant, 70) *Tradunt et mundos lentigine reddere uultus*; Constantinus Africanus, *De lentiginibus* 2, 25 (pp. 42-3).

388. **Os fractum**: cf. *LSD* 7, 187 (p. 476W) *confractis ossibus*; **Cipridis...opus**: cf. Ps.- Verg., *Moretum* 84 (ed. Clausen, 162) *Venerem reuocans eruca morantem*; Isid., *Orig.* 17, 10, 21 *Eruca, quasi uruca, quod...in cibo saepe sumpta Veneris incendium moveat*; Macer 1033 (ed. Choulant, 71) *Non modice...venerem stimulare*; Bernardus Silvestris, *Cosmographia* 1, 3, 375 (ed. Dronke, 114) *Plena voluptatis eruca*; Matthew of Vendôme, *Ars* 1, 111, 39-40 (ed. Munari, 3: 118); *DNR* 2, 166 (p. 275W); *LSD* 7, 189-90 (p. 476W); *in Eccles.* ff. 109vb-110ra *Inimicus autem homo qui in agro terre liberi arbi / trii superseminauit zizania plantat per suggestionem...erucam incontinentie*; Isaac Israeli, *De diaetis* p. 458 *cum calore suo coitum augmentat*.

389. **niueo...candore**: Ov., *Met.* 3, 423; Dracontius, *De laudibus Dei* 1, 246 (*MGH, AA* 14: 34).

389-92. **papauer**: cf. Macer 1038-40 (ed. Choulant, 71) *Tres illi tribuunt species; flos unius albus / Alterius roseus, rubeus pallensque rubensque minoris / Flos est*; *LSD* 7, 191-6 (pp. 476-7W), 8, 169-70 (p. 485W).

391. **quod**: sc. *papauer*.

393. **rubet...pallet**: cf. Stat., *Ach.* 1, 309 *palletque rubetque*; *Pamphilus* 513, *Lidia* 63, 209 (ed. Cohen, 2: 213, 228, 234); **pallor...rubor**: cf. Dracontius, *Epithalamium* 8 (ed. Wolff, 1); Maximianus 4, 29.

395. **fluxum uentris**: cf. Macer 1057-8 (ed. Choulant, 72); *LSD* 7, 194-5 (p. 477W) *compescit fluxum ventris*.

396. **Indicitque fugam**: cf. *SD* 1, 530; **podagra**: cf. Macer 1084 (ed. Choulant, 73); *LSD* 7, 194 (p. 476W); **lenta podagra**: cf. Hor., *S.* 1, 9, 32; Mart., 7, 39, 7.

397. **dens, dissenteria, ficus**: cf. Macer 1115-6 (dens), 1119 (dysenteria),. 1123 (ed. Choulant, 74) *Hasque iubent haemorrhoidis superaddere tritas*; *LSD* 7, 197-204 (p. 477W).

398. **Nudatusque capud**: cf. Macer 1120-1 (ed. Choulant, 74) *Contritis Cepis loca denudata capillis / Saepe fricans capitis poteris reparare decorem*.

399. **mollit**: for the verb in medical discourse cf. Celsus 2, 12, 1c *qui ventrem molliant* (sc. cibi); 4, 27, 1c *si durities* (sc. alvi) *manet, mollire...videtur*; **soporem**: cf. Macer 1097 (ed. Choulant, 73) *Affirmant omnes mansas* (sc. cepas) *inferre soporem*.

400. **melli sit sociata**: cf. *SD* 1, 458.

401. **Cardiacis...sciasique**: cf. Macer 1130, 1134 (ed. Choulant, 75); *LSD* 7, 205-8 (p. 477W).

402. **Lingua bouis**: cf. Macer 34 (ed. Choulant, 74) *Lingua bouis graeco sermone Buglossa vocatur*; *DMLBS* 5: 1619 s. v. *lingua* 5e.

403. **conuiuas exhilarabit**: cf. Plin., *Nat.* 25, 8, 81 (ed. Ian 4: 142); Isid., *Orig.* 17, 9, 49 *Convivii quoque hilaritatem praebere fertur*; Macer 1136-8 (ed. Choulant, 75) *Vinum potatum, quo sit macerata Buglossa / Laetos convivas decoctio dicitur eius / Reddere, si fuerit inter convivia sparsa*; *SD* 1, 475.

404. **coleram purgat**: cf. Macer 1128-9 (ed. Choulant, 74) *coleram... / Purgat*; *LSD* 7, 205 (p. 477W) *Lingua bovis purgat choleram rubeamque nigramque*.

405. **spleni, tussi**: cf. Macer 1159, 1162 (ed. Choulant, 76); *LSD* 7, 209-10 (p. 477W).

406. **Scrofis**: cf. Macer 1190 (ed. Choulant, 77) *scrophas disperget*; **serpentis morsibus**: cf. Macer 1152 (ed. Choulant, 75) *Morsus serpentum*; *LSD* 7, 211-4 (p. 477W).

407. **Vulneribus**: cf. Macer 1208-9; **neruis**: cf. Macer 1220-1 (ed. Choulant, 78).

408. **brassica**: cf. Macer 1201-2 (ed. Choulant, 77); **ardentique febri**: cf. Macer 1236 (ed. Choulant, 79) *ardores nimios iuvat haec confectio febris*; *LSD* 7, 211 (p. 477W) *ardores febris*.

409. **testiculis**: cf. Macer 1271-2 (ed. Choulant, 80) *tumores...compescit testiculorum*; *LSD* 7, 215-6 (p. 477W); **leuamen**: in classical poetry the word is restricted to the last foot of the hexameter cf. *ThLL*, 7: 1192, 2.

410. **Votis...fauet**: cf. Macer 1275 (ed. Choulant, 80) *Accendit venerem* (sc. pastinaca); **Taidis**: the generic name for a mistress cf. Ov., *Ars* 3, 604; *Geta* 368 (ed. Cohen, 1: 50); *Ysopet* 66 *De iuuene et Thayde*.

411. **nigre colere**: cf. Macer 1293; **tussique**: cf. Macer 1297 (ed. Choulant, 81); *LSD* 7, 217-8 (p. 477W); Dioscorides p. 90 *De origano:...tussi cum melle linctum medetur*.

412. **Aures**: cf. Macer 1306 (ed. Choulant, 82); **ydropicos**: cf. Macer 1292; **ycteri-cosque iuuat**: cf. Macer 1300 (ed. Choulant, 81) *iuvat ictericos*; *LSD* 7, 219-20 (p. 477W)

413. **indignata frenesis**: cf. *SD* 1, 468 *indignans mania*.

414. **splen**: cf. Macer 1337 (ed. Choulant, 83).

415. **Pestifer**: cf. Bernardus Silvestris, *Cosmographia* 1, 3, 390 (ed. Dronke, 114) *Contra vipereum gramina nota genus*.

416. **uentris torcio**: cf. Macer 1336 (ed. Choulant, 83) *compescit tormina ventris*.

417. **auris laterum dolori**: cf. Macer 1452 *Auriculaeque grauem dicunt curare dolorem*, 1447 *Dicitur hoc bibitum lateris sedare dolorem* (ed. Choulant, 87); *LSD* 7, 225-6 (p. 477W).

418. **tisicis**: cf. Macer 1440 (ed. Choulant, 87) *phthisicos mire iuvat hausta*; Jackson 81 identifies phthisis as pulmonary tuberculosis.

420. **Yctericos**: cf. Macer 1451 (ed. Choulant, 87).

421. **sperica**: cf. Isid., *Orig.* 17, 9, 52 *una aristolochia rotunda dicitur*; Macer 1395 *Aristolo-chiae species tres dicimus esse*, 1397 (ed. Choulant, 85) *Dicta rotunda sequens, quod sit radice ro-tunda*; *LSD* 7, 221-4 (p. 477W); *LSD* 7, 221 *Aristologiae speciem medicina rotundam / Dicit*.

422. **uentris honus**: Mart. 1, 37, 1; 10, 48, 7-8 *exoneraturas ventrem mihi vilica malvas / adtulit*; Isid., *Orig.* 17, 9, 52; *SD* 1, 437; Macer 1412-3 (*dens, splen*), 1423 (*fistula*), 1425 (*sin-gultus*) (ed. Choulant, 86).

423. **Enula**; cf. gloss on *DNR* 2, 166 (p. 274W) *Haec hinula est scalonia*; **renibus**: cf. Macer 1497-8 (ed. Choulant, 89); *LSD* 7, 227-8 (p. 477W).

424. **abortus**: cf. Macer 1494 (ed. Choulant, 89) *depellit abortum*; on elecampane as an abortifacient cf. Riddle 1992, 115; *SD* 1, 521.

425. **uocem**: cf. Macer 1507 (ed. Choulant, 90) *Subvenit et voci raucae;* cf. *SD* 1, 431; *LSD* 7, 231-2 (p. 477W); **furetur uocem**: cf. *SD* 1, 1235.

426. **ysopus**: cf. Cambridge, UL, Gg. 6. 42, f. 231r (*DCV*) *Ysopus utilis est uix tamen ab-sque mero* with marginal gloss: Macer *Ysopus est herba tumidis pulmonibus apta*.

427. **Exhilarat faciem**: cf. *SD* 2, 131 *Spiritus exhilarat faciem*; *Poems* 3, 5 (ed. Walther 1965, 117) *Exhilarat faciem letus color* [cf. *SD* 1, 430 *letus...color*]; **pectus**: cf. Bernardus Sil-

vestris, *Cosmographia* 1, 3, 363 (ed. Dronke, 113) *Pectoris herba...ysopus*; **dilatat**: rare in poetry, but found often in the Vulgate.

428. **funereusque color**: Maximianus 1, 134.

429. **sumatur in esum**: cf. *LSD* 7, 185 (p. 476W) *si Birria sumat in esum.*

430. **color**: cf. Macer 1519 (ed. Choulant, 90) *Vultibus eximium fertur praestare colorem.*

431. **uocem...canoram**: cf. note to *SD* 1, 625.

432. **Lumbricos**: cf. Macer 1509 (ed. Choulant, 90).

434. **reserat...hostia**: cf. Macer 1515 (ed. Choulant, 90) *stipatum molliet alvum.*

435. **urinam...menstrua**: cf. Macer 2186 (ed. Choulant, 119) *urinas et menstrua pellit*;
Constantinus Africanus, *De gradibus* p. 348 *Spica nardi...menstrua et urinam provocat*; *DNR* 2,
166 (p. 274W) *Taceo et de cipra et nardo.*

437. **ellebori candentis**: cf. *SD* 1, 465.

438. **iecori**: cf. Macer 2184 (ed. Choulant, 119) *confortat potata iecur.*

439. **[Menta]**: cf. *LSD* 7, 233-6 (p. 478W); **Cererem**: the metonymy cues an allusion
to Proserpina's breaking of the fast imposed on her by the gods during her time in the underworld; **ieiunia soluas**: cf. Ov., *Met.* 5, 534-5 *ieiunia virgo* (sc. Proserpina) / *solverat, Fast.*
4, 607 (Mercury to Ceres) *'rapta tribus' dixit 'solvit ieiunia granis'*; *LSD* 7, 59 (p. 473W) *jejunia
solvat*; Flood 1977, 397-9.

440. **aer**: medieval medical writers classified air among non-natural things (*res non naturales*); it was subject to seasonal change and was viewed as a factor in conditioning bodily
health; it was also thought to act as an agent in spreading infectious diseases cf. *SD* 1, 1241-
2; Rather, 292.

441. **Lumbricis, mammis**: cf. Macer 1572 (ed. Choulant, 93) *Lumbricosque...depellere
fertur*; 1575 *Concretum solvit lac mammis*; **lingue**: 1577 *Asperitas linguae fugit illa saepe fricatae*;
Isaac Israeli, *De diaetis* p. 461 *linguam lenit asperam, si ex eo fricetur.*

442. **dolor...auris**: cf. Macer 1576 (ed. Choulant, 93) *Instillata fugat auris ...dolorem.*

443. **Vis ciperi**: cf. Macer 1585 *Vim Cypero*; *LSD* 7, 237-8 (p. 478W); **urinam laxare
meatus**: cf. Macer 1587 (ed. Choulant, 93) *Calculus, urinae purgat laxatque meatus.*

444. **Duricies**: a rare word in poetry cf. Juvencus 1, 672; Scribonius Largus 151 *per urinam extrahere lapides* (sc. uesicae).

445. **fantasmata uana**: cf. Macer 1615-6 (ed. Choulant, 94); *LSD* 7, 239-40 (p. 478W);
Aldhelm, *CDV* 1201 (*MGH, AA* 15: 403) *Qui liquor, ut dicunt, atrum fantasma fugabit.*

447. **Deliciis Bachi**: cf. *SD* 1, 1395.

447-8. **sociata stere... / Languorem**: cf. Macer 1639 (ed. Choulant, 95) *Post partum
potata steras vino sociata.*

448. **Lachesi...iubens**: for the dative after *iubeo* cf. *ThesLL*, 7: 577, 39; for *iubeo* followed by the accusative cf. *SD* 1, 810.

449. **Aristeo celestia dona**: cf. Ov., *Met.* 13, 289 *caelestia dona*; *LSD* 4, 770-1 (p.
438W), 7, 241-2 (p. 478W); *CNP* 687 *defert Aristeus celestia dona*; Macer 1643 (ed. Choulant,
96) *Prae cunctis apibus gratissima dicitur herbis.*

450. **asmaticisque placet**: cf. Macer 1657 (ed. Choulant, 96) *Asthmaticis...prodest.*

451. **Inferior regio**: euphemism for genitals cf. Cameron 63; **testes...foramen**: cf.

Macer 1671 (ed. Choulant, 97) *Haec simul apponas ani vel testiculorum*; **uesica**: cf. Macer 1679 (ed. Choulant, 97) *Morbis vesicae, plures ait ille probasse.*

452. **Yctericus**: cf. Macer 1676-8 (ed. Choulant, 97).

453. **uicio cordis iecorisque**: cf. Macer 1680 (ed. Choulant, 97) *Et cordis vitiis illam iecorisque dedisse.*

454. **Dentibus**: cf. Plin., *Nat.* 25, 13, 167 (ed. Ian, 4: 171); Macer 1686 (ed. Choulant, 97).

455. **Grata celidonie uis**: cf. *LSD* 7, 247 (p. 478W) *Mira chelidoniae virtus.*

455. **oculis**: cf. Isid., *Orig.* 17, 9, 36; Macer 1702 (ed. Choulant, 98) *Vtilius nullum dicunt oculis medicamen*; *LSD* 7, 247-8 (p. 478W); Cameron 121.

456. **uicium...dentis**: cf. Macer 1706 (ed. Choulant, 98) *Dentis...prohibet contrita dolorem*; **abire iubet**: cf. *LSD* 2, 12 (p. 373W), *SD* 1, 470.

457. **sciasi**: cf. Macer 1717-8; *LSD* 7, 249-50 (p. 478W); **neruisque**: cf. Macer 1720 (ed. Choulant, 99) *Fomento neruis eadem medicabitur aegris.*

458. **Lumina**: cf. Macer 1724 (ed. Choulant, 90) *Melle sibi iuncto caligine lumina purgat.*

459. **colubri...uenenum**: cf. Macer 1732-4 (ed. Choulant, 100) *Quod queat a simili colubrina uenena fugare / Quisquis se trita radice perunxerit eius, / Tutus ab incursu serpentum dicitur esse*; *LSD* 7, 251-4 (p. 478W).

460. **concreto sanguine**: cf. Ov., *Met.* 12, 270 *concretaque* (sc. *pars*) *sanguine pendet.*

461. **Vulnera...sanat**: cf. Macer 1769 (ed. Choulant, 101) *Vulnera...conglutinat*; **sedatque tumores**: cf. Macer 1770 (ed. Choulant, 101) *reprimit quoscunque tumores.*

462. **sacer ignis**: cf. Macer 1772 (ed. Choulant, 101) *sacro subvenit igni.*

463-4. **Ellebori geminas species**: cf. Isid., *Orig.* 17, 9, 24; Macer 1774-5 (ed. Choulant, 101) *Elleborum geminas species testantur habere / Album, quod sursum purgat, nigrumque deorsum.*

465. **album**: cf. *LSD* 7, 255-8 (p. 478W); **quartanas...tussique**: cf. Macer 1795 (ed. Choulant, 102) *Et tussi veteri, febribus super omnia prodest / Quartanis.*

466. **stare...iubet**: cf. Bernardus Silvestris, *Cosmographia* 1, 3, 430 (ed. Dronke, 115) *Quique sepulta diu surgere membra facit.*

467. **Lucina...lucem**: the goddess Lucina protected women in childbirth cf. Hor., *Epod.* 5, 5-6 *si uocata partubus / Lucina ueris affuit*; for the etymology cf. Ov., *Fast.* 3, 255 «*tu nobis lucem, Lucina, dedisti*»; Isid., *Orig.* 8, 11, 57; *Commentum super sex libros Eneidos Virgilii* 4 (ed. J. W. Jones [Lincoln, 1977]) *Juno...dicitur Lucina, quasi lucem natis prebens*; for the plant as an abortifacient cf. Macer 1779 (ed. Choulant, 101) *depellit abortum*; Riddle 1992, 115.

468. **Indignans**: cf. *SD* 1, 513, 546, 810, 1289, 1366, 1392; **mania**: rare word cf. *ThLL*, 8: 301, 3; Isid. *Orig.* 4, 7, 8.

469. **cedit uertigo**: cf. *LSD* 7, 257 (p. 478W) *vertigo recedit.*

470. **mures**: cf. Macer 1784 (ed. Choulant, 102) *mures pulvis necat eius.*

471. **paralisis**: **P** f. 210rb glosses *elleborum nigrum* by *miram sentit opem sumpta paraliticus illa*; cf. Macer 1839 (ed. Choulant, 104); *LSD* 7, 259-62 (p. 478W).

472. **Apostema**: cf. Constantinus Africanus, *De apostematibus* 7, 15 (pp. 158-9); Gaselee,

106, counts the noun among Neckam's «mistakes in prosody»; **articulare malum**: Bernardus Silvestris, *Cosmographia* 1, 3, 392 (ed. Dronke, 114); Matthew of Vendôme, *Ars* 2, 26 (ed. Munari, 3: 148) *Sevit in articulos articulare malum*; cf. Macer 1840 (ed. Choulant, 104) *Et varios bibitum morbos levat articulorum.*

473. **colere cum flegmate**: cf. Macer 1841 (ed. Choulant, 104) *Educit choleras varias et flegmata per alvum.*

474. **lepraque cum scabie**: cf. Macer 1853 (ed. Choulant, 104) *Emundat lepras, scabies quascunque repellit.*

475. **Conuiuas reddit hilares**: cf. Macer 1879-80 (ed. Choulant, 105) *Conuiuas hilares... / Reddere narratur, ut iam praescripta buglossa*; LSD 7, 263-6 (p. 478W).

476. **oris**: cf. Macer 1865 (ed. Choulant, 105) *oris bene vulnera purgat.*

477. **Oris fetorem**: cf. Contantinus Africanus, 2, 23 (p. 41 *De foetore oris)*; **uulnera curat**: cf. Stat., *Theb.* 11, 278; Mastandrea 961.

479. **[Millefolium]**: cf. LSD 7, 267-8 (p. 478W).

485. **Germandrea:** cf. Macer 1903-4 (ed. Choulant, 107) *Chamaedryos graece, quae Gamandrea latine / Dicitur,* LSD 7, 269-70 (p. 478W).

485. **caliginis umbram**: Macer 1914-5 (ed. Choulant, 107); cf. Mastandrea 97.

486. **calore**: cf. Macer 1917 (ed. Choulant, 107) *Pellet frigdorem, revocabit et ipsa calorem.*

487. **Morsibus occurrit**: cf. Macer 1910 *pestiferis occurrit morsibus illa*; **sordencia uulnera**: cf. Macer 1912 (ed. Choulant, 107) *Sordens purgatis vulnus.*

488. **menstrua, tussis**: cf. Macer 1906 *tussique medetur,* 1908 (ed. Choulant, 107) *purgat menstrua.*

489. **Mauro...auro**: Hor., *Epod.* 5, 27, plays on the two senses of *Punico*, alluding to an unspecified Carthaginian and to the Punic colour, purple; Neckam's punning allusion is similarly indeterminate; it evokes the name of Hrabanus Maurus (cf. Hrabanus, *Carm.* 5, 12 [MGH, P. L. 2: 169] *Maurus dicor ego*) and Maurus, the Salernitan medical writer and successor to Musandinus at the school of Salerno c. 1165-66 cf. Kristeller 1945, 157-8; Saffron 11-3; for the word meaning «black» cf. Isid., *Orig.* 12, 1, 55 *Mauron niger est*; the rhyme **Mauro / auro** occurs in the explicit of a manuscript containing Maurus's work: *hoc opus a Mauro restat, pretiosius auro* cf. Saffron 13; Reynolds, *Medieval Reading*, 86-7, notes how grammarians playfully generated verbal knowledge by means of etymologies based on association; **ab auro**: cf. LSD 3, 561 (p. 408W) *Gustum doreae, quae nomen sumpsit ab auro*; 7, 271-4 (p. 479W) *Contrahit a Mauro nomen maurella.*

490. **uires consule**: cf. SD 2, 53 *euentum consule,* 127 *consule causam,* 218 *sensum consule,* 329 *iusticiam diuinam consule*; Ov., *Ep.* 6, 105 *Non probat Alcimede mater tua − consule matrem!*; **nomen**: an etymological signal cf. SD 1, 304, 382, 502; on the study of words as part of the herbal tradition cf. Stannard 29.

491. **Apcius**: cf. SD 1, 766.

492. **caput**: i. e. the first letter of the word *maurella* cf. 493 *Parte tui dempta,* 494 *aurella*; **gloria maior:** because the plant would then be linked etymologically with *aurum* cf. 493 *aurea fias*; cf. Ov., *Fast.* 1, 714 *gloria maior eris, Ep.* 12, 78.

493. **Parte...dempta**: cf. Baudri, Carm. 189, 1-2; *Doctrinale* 276 *dempta carne per um facies a vel o*; **desses**: contracted form of second person singular imperfect subjunctive active of *desum* cf. ThLL, 5: 778, 50-4.

494. **aurella**: for etymological word play involving the removal of a single letter from the word for the festival, the Agonalia cf. Ov., *Fast.* 1, 325-6 *pars putat hoc festum priscis Agnalia dictum, / una sit ut proprio littera dempta loco*; Venantius, *Carm.* 1, 20, 5-6 (*MGH, AA* 4: 23) *si syllaba quarta recedat, / Praemiacum pollens, praemia nomen habes*; Doctrinale 1469 *dat Deus aureolam, quod nomen habetur ab auro.*

495. **capitis...dolorem**: cf. Macer 1923 (ed. Choulant, 108) *Istud idem dicunt capitis prodesse dolori.*

496. **prurigo**: cf. Macer 1926 (ed. Choulant, 108).

498. **strigni**: cf. Macer 1918-9 (ed. Choulant, 107) *Herbam, quam Greci Strignum dixere, Latini / maurellam dicunt.*

499-500. **igni / Sacro succurrit**: cf. *LSD* 7, 273 (p. 479W) *Igni succurrit sacro*; Macer 1929-30 (ed. Choulant, 108).

500. **egilopas**: cf. Macer 1922 (ed. Choulant, 107).

501. **infrigdat**: on the orthography of the verb cf. *ThLL*, 7: 1492, 14, *DMLBS* 5: 1364; *LSD* 3, 495 (p. 405W); Macer 1919 (ed. Choulant, 107) *vis eius frigida valde est*; Constantinus Africanus, *De gradibus* p. 365 *cataplasmatum super calidum stomachum mox eum refrigerat*; Urso, *Aphorismi* Glosula 52 (ed. Creutz, 14) *Calefacere, infrigidare, exsiccare, humectare, uniuscuiusque quatuor qualitatum est, formaliter seu causaliter*; **glaucos**: those suffering from the disease of glaucoma cf. Prudentius, *Apoth.* 20,

502. **aue**: i. e. the owl, alluding to glaucoma cf. Aldhelm, *CDV* 939 (*MGH, AA* 15: 393) *Glaucoma nec penitus lippos suffundat ocellos*; **nomen habet**: cf. Ov., *Met.* 13, 569-70 *locus exstat et ex re nomen habet.*

503. **solacia prebet**: *Pamphilus* 143 (ed. Cohen, 2: 199) *Incolumis leuiter egro solacia prebet.*

505-7. **species... / ...nigro**: cf. Macer 1935-6 (ed. Choulant, 108) *Tres habet haec species, semen profert prior album, / Altera subrufum, producit tertia nigrum*; *LSD* 7, 275-6 (p. 479W).

506. **pluris erit**: cf. *LSD* 7, 302 (p. 479W).

509-10. Constantinus Africanus, *De gradibus* p. 384 *albus convenit medicine et rufus albo non invento.*

510. **Accedet uotis...tuis**: cf. *SD* 1, 1373 *tuis uotis...accedet.*

511. **folium tere...polente**: cf. Macer 1940 (ed. Choulant, 108) *Iusquiami foliis contritis adde polentam.*

512. **tumidis...locis**: cf. Macer 1941 (ed. Choulant, 108).

513. **tumor omnis**: cf. Macer 1941 (ed. Choulant, 108) *Haec adhibendo potes quosvis curare tumores.*

516. **mammis**: cf. Macer 1958 (ed. Choulant, 109) *Mammas...dicunt curare tumentes.*

517-18. **Auribus infusi succi... / Vermes**: cf. Macer 1943 (ed. Choulant, 108) *Auribus infusus uermes succus necat eius.*

518. **sputa...tincta cruore**: cf. *SD* 1, 460 *sputaque...sanguine tincta.*

519. **uesice**: cf. Macer 1966 (ed. Choulant, 109); *LSD* 7, 91-6 (p. 474W).

520. **lixe**: the glossator of **P**, citing Luc., 9, 593, took the word to refer to a water-carrier (cf. *DMLBS* 5: 1628 s. v. 1 *lixa* «kitchen boy»); if so, the allusion escapes me; *lixa* can

also mean «lye, alkalized water» (*DMLBS* 5: 1628 s. v. 2 *lixa*) and may depend on *uis* in the previous verse. There is no evidence to equate a form *lixus* with *elixus*, a word often applied to parts of plants cooked in water for medicinal purposes cf. *ThLL*, 5: 394, 20.

521. **Denti**: cf. Macer 1973-4 (ed. Choulant, 110); **lenimen**: a rare word which occurs in classical poetry only in Hor., *C.* 1, 32, 15; Ov., *Met.* 6, 500; 11, 450 cf. *ThLL*, 7: 1140, 19; **depellit abortum**: cf. *SD* 1, 371.

522. **Egilopasque sacer…ignis**: cf. Macer 1980-1, 1988 (ed. Choulant, 110).

523. **Membra…quassata**: cf. Macer 1971-2 (ed. Choulant, 110) *malua potenter / Conquassata iuvat*; *LSD* 7, 91 (p. 474W) *Artubus elisis.* 524 **apum…tela**: cf. Macer 1982 (ed. Choulant, 110) *succoque medeberis eius / Puncturis apium*; **lesis** = *laesis*.

525. **combusturas**: cf. Macer 1989 (ed. Choulant, 110) *Et combusturis illo bene subvenis ignis*; *LSD* 7, 91 (p. 474W); for the construction cf. Scribonius Largus 1 *ad capitis dolorem…bene facit serpulli…quadrans*; **paratella**: cf. *LSD* 7, 279-80 (p. 479W); for the construction *facit ad* cf. Dioscorides, p. 94v *De ruta: facit ad pectoris laterumque dolores*; p. 311 *De rosa: aridis rosis et in uino decoctis expressus liquor facit ad dolores capitis.*

529. [**Nigella**]: cf. *LSD* 7, 281-2 (p. 479W); **Vulneris…sordes**: cf. Macer 2017-8 (ed. Choulant, 112).

530. **lepris**: cf. Macer 2019 (ed. Choulant, 112); **imperiosa**: cf. *SD* 1, 420.

531. **apostema**: cf. *LSD* 7, 282 (p. 479W) *apostemata rumpit* (sc. nigella); Macer 2022-3 (ed. Choulant, 112); **uota… / Lucine**: cf. Macer 2027-8 (ed. Choulant, 112); **uota secundat**: cf. Mastandrea 954.

532. **sciasis**: cf. Macer 2025-6 (ed. Choulant, 112).

533. **Ignes extinguit…cicuta**: cf. Pers., 5, 144-5 *calido sub pectore mascula bilis / intumuit, quam non extinxerit urna cicutae*; cf. Kissel 712; *SD* 1, 575; *LSD* 7, 283-4 (p. 479W). The medieval concept of allopathic medicine held that hot sicknesses were to be countered by cold medicines.

534. **frigiditate potens**: cf. *SD* 1, 602, 1109; hemlock causes the body to cool cf. Plin., *Nat.* 25, 151 (ed. Ian, 4: 165-6).

535. **Ignis…sacer**: cf. Macer 2044; **papillis**: cf. Macer 2045-7 (ed. Choulant, 113); *LSD* 7, 283 *Mammae turgenti tritam superadde cicutam* (*acutam* Wright).

536. **Terranee**:= *Therapnaeus*; Therapnae was the birthplace of Helen of Troy cf. Ov., *Ep.* 16, 198 *Rure Therapnaeo nata puella*; *Fast.* 5, 223; cf. *SD* 1, 1213 *forma Lacene.*

537. See Matthew of Vendôme, *Ep.* 2, 4, 69-70 (ed. Munari, 2: 128) on the topic of bustlines.

538. **uirginei pectoris**: cf. Ov., *Met.* 7, 17 *virgineo…pectore*; *SD* 2, 1705-8 *Pectore uirgineo geminus micat vnio surgens / Paulisper, gratus uirginitatis honos. / Exigue pectus ornant placideque mamille, / Quas magis acceptas forma rotunda facit*; *De tribus puellis* 48 (ed. Cohen, 2: 233) *Turgida* (sc. ubera) *namque nimis displicuere viris.*

539-40. **Si… / Lumina**: cf. Macer 2042 (ed. Choulant, 113) *Si frons contritis foliis sit operta virentis, / Vel si sint eius circumlita lumina succo.*

540. **lacrimis inmaduere**: cf. Ov., *Tr.* 1, 9a, 34 *lacrimis inmaduisse genas.*

542. **artericis**: cf. *SD* 1, 285.

543. **Laudibus:** in antiquity, hemlock was not normally included among herbs used for

healing purposes cf. Plin., *Nat.* 25, 13, 154 (ed. Ian, 4: 166) *remedia, in quibus bibenda* (sc. cicuta) *censetur, non equidem praeceperim;* **cicutam**: cf. Macer 2035-6 (ed. Choulant, 113).

544. **mundum sole**: for the metaphor cf. Cic., *de amic.* 47 (ed. W. A. Falconer, 158 [London, 1923]) *Solem enim e mundo tollere uidentur ei, qui amicitiam e vita tollunt;* for praise of Socrates cf. John of Salisbury, *Enthet. maior* 773-800 (ed. van Laarhoven, 1: 155-7).

545. **Socrati**: the most famous person to be executed by hemlock cf. Fleissner 25; Macer 2034 (ed. Choulant, 113) *Hac sumpta magnus Socrates fuit exanimatus;* Bernardus Silvestris, *Cosmographia* 1, 3, 413 (ed. Dronke, 115) *Socratice...cicute;* **pene** = *poenae*.

546. **Indignans...philosophia**: *LSD* 2, 484 (p. 384W); in Roman myth, Astraea, the virgin goddess of Justice, abandoned the earth cf. Ov., *Met.* 1, 150 *terras Astraea reliquit;* *SD* 1, 1287.

548. **Connexus blando federe**; cf. *CNP* 1342 *blando federe nexus adest.*

549. **depingit...ferrugo**: cf. Claudian, *De raptu* 2, 93 *dulci uiolas ferrugine pingit;* *LSD* 5, 103 (p. 442W); *SD* 2, 451 *Emula stat ueneti uiole ferrugo coloris.*

551-2. Cited by Hunt ed. Gibson 75 to suggest that personal observation played a still undetermined part in Alexander's scientific works.

552. **nobile...opus**: cf. *SD* 2, 36.

555. **preiudicat**: rare in poetry cf. Avienus, *ora* 35; Dracontius, *Romul.* 5, 249 (*MGH, AA* 14: 146).

557. **uiole uires**: cf. Isid., *Orig.* 17, 9, 19 *Viola propter vim odoris nomen accepit;* *SD* 1, 365-6.

559. **perstrinxi**: cf. Hugh of St. Victor, *De arca Noe morali* 3, prologus, (*MPL* 176: 647a) *Hic ipsius incrementi gradus, quos ibi breviter et summatim perstrinximus, latius in singula prosequendo explanabimus;* **presenti...carmine**: cf. *SD* 1, 565-6.

560. **scripte libelle**: the *Laus sapientie diuine.*

561-70. Cited in Hunt ed. Gibson 78; cf. Garbugino 1987, 38.

561. **alio... / Carmine**: Neckam lists the medicinal properties of violets in *LSD* 7, 335-40 (p. 480W); cf. *SD* 1, 563; so, e. g. Cic., *Off.* 2, 31 (ed. M. Winterbottom, 81 [Oxford, 1994]) gives a cross-reference to material covered in another work: *Sed de amicitia alio libro dictum est, qui inscribitur Laelius.*

563. **defectus... / Suplebit**: cf. *CPV* f. 141r *Non ab re nomen trahit a supplendo supellex / per quam defectus uarios supplere solemus;* **illius carminis**: the *Laudes sapientie diuine;* **istud**: the *Suppletio defectuum* cf. *SD* 1, 566 *istud opus.*

564. **Suplebit**: for the verb in the sense of completing an unfinished literary work cf. Matthew of Vendôme, *Ars* 4, 2 (ed. Munari, 3: 194 on *executio materie*) *Debent enim minus dicta suppleri;* **seruit...Noy**: cf. *SD* 2, 5-6 *Quod, diuina, tibi seruit, sapientia, carmen / Explicat ista.*

565. **Defectus...meos**: both moral and poetic deficits, which Neckam links in *SD* 1, 1038-66; cf. *in Eccles* f. 143rb *Vbi autem <ad>est peccatum, adest defectus. Ubi est defectus, necessarium est subsidium;* on the grammatical dimensions of the word, see S. Reynolds, *Medieval Reading,* 123, 196 and note 8; **prudens**: cf. *SD* 1, 1035, 1061, all in contexts which discuss the poem's composition.

567. **Prodeat in lucem**: thoughts about readers (*SD* 1, 562) lead Neckam to declare his

intent to publish the poem and, then, to thoughts about readers' responses to it; Carruthers, *The Book of Memory*, 212, notes that generosity and freedom from envy motivated medieval authors to offer their works to the public; composers who did not publish their writings were commonly thought to be acting against the interests of the community; cf. *SD* 2, 565-6 *Prodeat in lucem multis uigilatus ab annis / Detque fidem certam cum nouitate labor*, Bernardus Silvestris, *Cosmographia, dedicacio* (ed. Dronke, 6) *Viderit ergo discretio vestra si prodire palam, si venire debeat in comune*; Alexander of Châtillon, *Alex. prologus*, 17 *Tandem apud me deliberatum est / te in lucem esse proferendam*; in *Eccles.* f. 135va *Stultissimus autem est qui scientiam aliis inuidet impertiri...; felix suscipiat incrementum. Scientia igitur et sapientia secularis sunt diuitie conseruate in malum domini sui dum non prodeunt in lucem, nisi turpis questus gratia aut propter popularem fauorem*; *SD* 1, 1317; **lucis opus**: cf. *DNR* Prologue 1 (p. 2W) *In hoc enim opusculo lectorem ad opera lucis invitamus, ut abiectis operibus tenebrarum demum aeterna luce fruatur.*

568. **Liuor**: the envy motif (cf. Hor., *C.* 2, 16, 39-40) recurs in *SD* 2, 947-8 *Zoyle, quo uultum ridens auertis? Homerus / Nullus adest. Nouit serpere liuor humi*; in *Eccles.* f. 120ra-rb *Hec igitur debet esse causa inquisitionis causarum ut uberius nutriatur in nobis amor auctoris rerum et ut scientie thesaurum hilariter proximis distribuamus. / Relegetur procul inuidia tabescens...Scientie lumen putat liuor edax minui, si plurium mentes illustret. Set hilariter aliis conferendum est scientie munus*; Haye 1997, 89, interprets remarks of this type in the *LSD* not to be empty poses, but rather an index of Neckam's self-consciousness as a poet; **Ditis...fores**: cf. Mart. 7, 47, 7 *non tulit invidiam taciti regnator Averni.*

569. **superas euadat ad auras**: cf. Verg., *G.* 4, 486 *casus euaserat omnis,...redditaque Eurydice superas ueniebat ad auras.*

570. **cinice**: cf. *SD* 1, 1177-8; *LSD* 4, 519 (p. 432W) *Vis carmen cynico carpere dente meum*; **rodere**: cf. *C* f. 70bis v *Et fortassis erit aliquis mea carmina rodens, / Nam quandoque solet serpere liuor humi*; in *Eccles.* ff. 124rb-va *Etiam hoc opus nostrum uix inchoatum / iam cinici dentes corrodunt et alius ipsum arguit prolixitatis tediose, alius decise breuitatis.*

574. cf. Dioscorides, p. 10v *De croco: Omnium ad obsonia usus.*

575. **ignem sacrum**: cf. Dioscorides, p. 10v *Vergentes ad ignem sacrum inflammationes mulcet.*

577. **Solis sponsa**: cf. *SD* 1, 581, 588; Ov., *Met.* 4, 264-70 narrates the aetiological myth of heliotrope: the maiden Clytie was loved and then rejected by the sun, before she was changed into a sunflower as punishment for her jealousy. Her gaze followed the sun as it travelled across the sky; cf. Urso, *Aphorismi Glosula* 32 (ed. Creutz, 65) *Sic et flores solsequiae...clausi in die aperiuntur, dum sole repercutiente superficiem tenui humiditate exhausta eorum folia extra contracta flectuntur, in nocte vero humiditate infusa, laxata tensura, clauduntur*, cf. *DNR* 2, 58 (p. 165W), noted in Hunt ed. Gibson 71, note 29; **opes**: on the medicinal uses of heliotrope cf. Cameron 56-7.

579. **Solsequium**: cf. Plin., *Nat.* 2, 41, 109 (ed. Ian, 1: 165-6); Isid., *Orig.* 17, 9, 37; *DNR* 2, 58 (p. 165W); Lawn, *Salern. Questions*, 189, note 149; **ceruice reflexa**: Verg., *A.* 8, 633; *LH-L* 1: 327; Mastandrea 122.

582. **languet...amore**: cf. Ct 5, 8; *DMLBS* 5: 1549 s. v. *languere* 4a «to be weak or sick with love».

584. **delicias suas**: cf. *DNR* 2, 58 (p. 165W) *Sponsa...solis est curiosa ambitio, quae deliciarum suarum ostentatrix est*; in *Eccles.* f. 90va *Solsequium mirabitur oculus solis cursui obnoxium, dum delicias suas claudit ad solis occasum, easdem reserat ad ortum eiusdem*; Aldhelm, *Enig.* 51, 3 (*MGH, AA* 15: 120).

586. **Orbiculos**: restricted to prose in classical literature cf. *ThLL*, 9: 906, 2.

587-8. Bernardus Silvestris, *Cosmographia* 1, 3, 377-8 (ed. Dronke, 114).

589. **species paucas distinximus**: cf. *LSD* 7, 1 (p. 472W); *Doctrinale* 2362-3 *earum / quamlibet in proprias species distinguere debes*.

590. **stilo**: cf. *LSD* 3, 73 (p. 396W) *Sed stilus ad pisces nunc se transferat*; 5, 787 (p. 458W).

591. **Precedant**: cf. *LSD* 8, 3 (p. 481W) *Triticeum granum praecedat*; **descendit ab alto**: cf. Mastandrea 212.

592. **Pre foribus...clangit**: cf. *Poems* 448 (ed. Walther 1962, 38) *Pre foribus clamat mors: vigilate, viri!*; *SD* 1, 952; **regia...auis**: the eagle cf. *SD* 1, 596; Ov., *Met.* 4, 362 *regia...ales*.

593-890. *Birds*

593-604. *The eagle*

593. **aquile**: In old age the eagle, its eyes clouded with mist, flies up to the sun where heat dissipates it. After descending, it immerses itself in a fountain to renew itself. The eagle can look directly into the sun; it exposes its young to the sun's rays to determine which are worthy of the species. Eaglets who avert their eyes are considered degenerate cf. McCulloch 113-5; *LSD* 2, 157-84 (p. 377W); *SD* 1, 89-104, 940; Luc., 9, 902-5; Geoffrey of Monmouth, *Vita Merlini* 1310-9.

594. **doctoris**: cf. *SD* 1, 781.

595. **Solares radios**: cf. Matthew of Vendôme, *Ep.* 1, 1, 55 (ed. Munari, 2: 80); *LSD* 4, 70 (p. 424W).

595-8. Cited in Hunt ed. Gibson 79; cf. Plin., *Nat.* 10, 3, 10 (ed. Ian, 2: 221-2); Isid., *Orig.* 12, 7, 11 *unde et pullos suos...radiis solis obicit...*; *si quos vero inflectere obtutum, quasi degeneres abicit*; *DNR* 1, 23 (p. 71-2W) *Aquila etiam pullos suos radiis solaris fulgoris exponit...Eos vero quos natura potenti efficacia acuminis visus destituisse visa est, nido proturbat mater quasi degeneres et contemnit*; *CMC*, Oxford, Digby 221, f. 38vb *addunt etiam adeo acutum aquile esse obtutum, ut pro fulgentissimis solis radiis nunquam flectat obtutum; matres etiam, ut aiunt, pullos suos contra solis ortum obvertunt, ut si in ipsos solis radios lumina figere sustinuerint, in vitam reserventur; si non, a nido eiciantur*; *LSD* 2, 165-8; Urso, *Aphorismi Glosula* 38 (ed. Creutz, 69) *Aquila vero licet clara visus instrumenta habeat, tamen quadam conformitate naturae vel quia spiritus multus est visibilis...radiis solis oculos objicit et sine offensa ad videndum infigit*; *NP* 577-8; Lawn, *Salern. Questions*, 184, note 84; **degenerem:** Claudian, *Carm.* 6, 9-10 *degenerem refugo torsit qui lumine uisum, / unguibus hunc saevis ira paterna ferit*. Gerald of Wales, *Topographia Hibernica* 1, 13 (ed. Dimock, 39-45) moralizes the eagle.

597. **lumina mentis**: cf. Mastandrea 464.

599. **Instar auis dicte**: i. e. the eagle cf. *SD* 1, 701, 1143 *Belua dicta*; *LSD* 2, 157 (p. 377W) *Exuit igne nouo senium renovata juventus*; **reuocare iuuentam**: cf. Henkel 192-3; Dracontius, *De laudibus Dei* 1, 723-4 (*MGH, AA* 14: 64) *quem mox invitat ad escam / praepetis aut aquilae senio renovare iuventam*; Ambrose, *De mysteriis* 1, 8 (*MPL* 16: 420a); PsG 102, 5 *Revocabitur ut aquilae iuventus tua*; *SD* 1, 1279; *LSD* 9, 133 (p. 489W); *in Eccles*. f. 93va *Nonne item renouatur, ut aquila, is qui renouatur per gratiam?*; *NE* 7, 17-8; *Physiologus Lat.* VIII, 5-6 (ed. Carmody, 19) *descendens ad fontem trina uice se mergit, et statim renovatur tota* (sc. aquila);the scribe probably miscopied *renouare* as *reuocare* under the influence of *reuocare* in 594.

601. **calor ignitus**: cf. *SD* 1, 675 *Igneus...calor.*

601-2. cf. *Glosule super Lucanum* 6, 676 (ed. Marti, 345); *CMC*, Oxford, Digby 221, f. 38vb *aquila tanti caloris est ut etiam ova quibus supersedet decoquat nisi gagatem lapidem frigidissimum apponat*; *DNR* 1, 23 (p. 71W) *Aquila igitur ovis suis propter sui calorem lapides interponit frigidissimos, ut frigiditatis remedio calor ova non dissipet*; *LSD* 2, 173-4 (p. 377W).

602. **frigiditate potens**: *LSD* 4, 233 (p. 425W), 447 (p. 430W); **Temperat oua...frigiditate**: cf. *LSD* 2, 174 (p. 377W) *frigiditas temperat oua.*

605-24. *The pelican*

605. **[Pellicanus]**: When the pelican's young grow up, they strike their parents; when the parents hit back in turn, they kill them. The mother restores them to life by sprinkling them with her own blood cf. McCulloch 155-7; Henkel 194-6; *DNR* 1, 73-4 (pp. 118-9W); *LSD* 2, 657-74 (p. 388W); Geoffrey of Monmouth, *Vita Merlini* 1365-9; Gerhardt 1979, 13, 102, note 189.

605. **Soliuagi...macie**: cf. PsG 101, 7 *Similis factus sum pelicano solitudinis*; *Vita Aedwardi regis* ed. Barlow, 58, *ut uacuo solus domate pellicanus*; *DNR* 1, 74 (p. 119W) *Est enim avis ista macilenta...Avis etiam ista solitaria est*; **canora / ...pellis**: cf. *DNR* 1, 73 (p. 118W) *dicta sic eo quod pellis ejus tractata canere videatur propter sui asperitatem*; *LSD* 2, 657 (p. 388W).

607. **Natura ministrat**: cf. *Ysopet* 34, 11 *Qui plus posse putat sua quam natura ministrat*; *SD* 1, 1267-8; Mastandrea 545.

609. **equo** = *aequo.*

610.. **prolis inmemor...sui**: cf. *SD* 1, 688.

609-14. **seua**: cf. Isid., *Orig.* 12, 7, 26 *Fertur...eam occidere natos suos, eosque per triduum lugere, deinde se ipsam vulnerare et aspersione sui sanguinis vivificare filios*; *DNR* 1, 73 (p. 118W) *Pullos occidit* (sc. pellicanus); *LSD* 2, 659-60 (p. 388W).

611. **ad cor redit**: cf. *SD* 1, 692 *Ad cor ...redit* (sc. struthio).

612. **dilacerare**: cf. *LDS* 2, 666 (p. 388W) *corpus vulnerat ipsa suum.*

613-14. **sanguine**: cf. *Physiologus Lat.* VI, 4-5, (ed. Carmody, 17) *...effundit sanguinem suum super corpora filiorum mortuorum; et sic sanguine suo suscitat eos a mortuis*; *DNR* 1, 73 (pp. 118-9W) *Sanguine perfunduntur pulli, et sic reviviscunt*; *LSD* 2, 667-8 (p. 388W).

615-16. **proles / ...anime**: cf. *SD* 1, 615-6, 623.

619. **studii felicis**: cf. *SD* 1, 1153.

620. **perimit**: cf. *SD* 1, 432 *perimens*; note word play with *SD* 1, 619 *premit.*

621. **signata**: cf. *SD* 1, 648.

624. **mortificata**: cf. *SD* 1, 619.

625-30. *The parrot*

625. **Psitacus**: cf. McCulloch 151; **uoce sonora**: Prudentius, *Apoth.* 524; cf. Baudri, *Carm.* 99, 15; the gloss *uel canora* [cf. Ov., *Ars* 3, 311 *uoce canora*; *LSD* 3, 245 (p. 400W) *voces reddendo canoras*] is metrically equivalent to the lemma; for other examples of the phenomenon cf. Wieland 31.

625-26. cf. *DNR* 1, 36-8 (pp. 87-90W); *LDS* 2, 233-56 (pp. 378-9W).

627. **abhorret aquas**: cf. *SD* 1, 42; *DNR* 1, 36 (p. 88W) *siccitatis alumnus*; *LSD* 2, 247-8 (p. 379W).

627. **Orpheus alter**: cf. *LSD* 5, 756 (p. 458W) *Orpheus alter erit*; Baudri, *Carm. 3, 12*.

628. **Narcisus**: *Narcisus se ipsum non cognouit et ideo periit. Vmbram uidit, desiderauit et in hoc desiderio euanuit. Quilibet nostrum Narcisus est.* Neckam *Sermon 26*, cited in Hunt ed. Gibson 91, note 37; **Ulixis**: an allusion to the hero's dislike of sea travel.

630. **Vmbra...cinis**: cf. Hor., *C. 4, 7, 16 puluis et umbra sumus*; John of Salisbury, *Enthet. maior 926* (ed. van Laarhoven, 1: 167) *terra, cinis, vermis, faex, vapor, umbra, lutum!*; **alga**: for seaweed as an emblem for worthlessness cf. *OLD* s. v. *alga* 1 b; Hor., *S. 2, 5, 8*; Verg., *E. 7, 42 uilior alga*; Aldhelm, *Enig. 100, 26 (MGH, AA 15: 146) spretis vilior algis.*

631-46. *The dove*

631. **gemens**: the dove's song is traditionally mournful cf. Is 59, 11 *quasi columbae meditantes gememus*; Morson 162; **foramine petre**: cf. *DNR* 1, 56 (p. 106W) *columba in foraminibus petrae secure latitat*; *SD* 1, 39.

632. **nutrit amoris**; cf. *Ysopet 36, 35 Hispida lingua parit odium, pia nutrit amorem.*

634. **lateat...erit**: cf. *SD* 1, 747 for the future indicative in the apodosis and the subjunctive in the protasis.

634. **gemitus cantus**: cf. *DNR* 1, 56 (p. 106W) *Columba...gemitum habet pro cantu*; *LSD* 2, 729 (p. 389W) *Edit pro cantu gemitum.*

636. Mart., 1, 33, 4.

637. **Eligit**: the dove characteristically selects the better seeds and does not feed off dead bodies cf. *DNR* 1, 56 (p. 106W) *Non vescitur cadavere, sed purissimum granum eligit*; *LSD* 2, 705 (p. 389W) *renuitque cadaver*; **uile cadauer**: Mart., 8, 75, 9.

638. **diuinus sermo**: cf. *SD* 1, 1255.

639. **orto** = *horto*; cf. *SD* 1, 677.

641. **lactea...caro**: cf. Marbod, *Carm. uaria 4 (MPL 171: 1718B)*; Baudri, *Carm. 3, 18*; a witty epithet when applied to Thais, meaning both «milk white» and «spotless» (*DMLBS* 5: 1536 s. v. *lacteus 2b, 2c*); **Thaydis**: a generic name for a prostitute cf. Ov., *Rem. 383*; Hildebert, *Carm. min. supplementum 3, 48 Penelope donis altera Thais erit*; John of Salisbury, *Enthet. maior 1432* (ed. van Laarhoven, 1: 199) *munere capta Thais.*

642. **Carnem...uermibus...datam**: cf. the etymology of *cadauer* in *in Eccles.* f. 83ra *Vermes hereditatem suam adeunt et ecce cadauer merito dicitur quasi caro data uermibus*; *SD* 1, 1216.

643. **simplicitas...tanta**: cf. Ov., *Met. 5, 400 tantaque simplicitas*; Hrabanus Maurus, *Expositiones in Lev. 3, 5, 12 (MPL 108: 370d) Columba ergo simplicitatem, turtur indicat castitatem.*

643-4. **fouet...alienos**: cf. *LSD* 2, 721 (p. 389W) *Cum propriis natis alienos educat ova.*

645. **mores**: cf. *SD* 1, 689, 720, 760, 834, 928, 1038.

646. **auctori...suo**: i. e. God cf. *SD* 1, 1032; *LSD* 1, 78 (p. 359W) *Auctori studeat quisque placere suo.*

647-52. *The dove, again*

647. **auctor pacis oliue / ramo**: cf. Verg., *A*. 6, 230 *ramo...olivae*; 6, 808 *ramis insignis olivae*; *LDS* 2, 699-700 (p. 389W); *CNP* 17 *Felix ille locus quo pacis crescit oliua*; *Ysopet* 64, 1 *Optatam pacem ramus in ore tulit* (sc. columba).

649. **Gessemani**: for the scansion cf. *Doctrinale* 2029 *additur his hiemis, Alemannia, Getsemanique*; Gethsemani (cf. Mc 13, 42) was interpreted to connote richness cf. Jerome, *Lib. int. hebr. nom.* 61, 22 (ed. Antin, *CCSL* 72: 136).

650. **purus...cibus**: cf. *LSD* 2, 705 (p. 389W) *Vescitur ista cibis mundis*.

651. **uera quies**: cf. *SD* 1, 804; **uera...uerus**: cf. Verg., *A*. 3, 310 *verane te facies, verus mihi nuntius adfers*; **uerus Noe**: on *uerus* as an etymological marker cf. Cairns 30; Isid., *Orig.* 7, 6, 15 *Noe requies interpretatur*, **eandem**: sc. *pacem*.

652. **Accipitris**: the dove sits above the stream so that it can more easily detect the hawk's approach by its shadow cf. McCulloch 111; Ov., *Met.* 5, 605 *ut fugere accipitrem penna trepidante columbae*; *LSD* 2, 722, 731 (p. 389W) *Accipitris metuens umbram speculatur in undis*; **umbra uetus**: i. e. the Old Testament.

653-66. *The turtle-dove*

653. **Spernit**: cf. *DNR* 1, 59 (p. 108W) *Mortuo...compare suo, viroris aspernatur delicias*; *Prose Salern. Questions* B 292 (ed. Lawn, 139, 6) *Quare turtur marito perdito nunquam adheret alii?* *LSD* 2, 856 (p. 392W) *Delicias spernit*; for 12th-c. references to the dove's love of solitude and chastity after the death of its mate cf. Morson 162-3; **amena loci**: cf. *SD* 2, 440 *Depicti facies ridet amena loci*; **nemorosaque Tempe**: Luc., 8, 1, cited in *DNR* 2, 158 (p. 259W).

654. **Turtur**: cf. McCulloch 178; *LSD* 2, 855-64 (pp. 392-3W); **cui...fata tulere**: cf. *LSD* 2, 861 (p. 392W) *quem fata tulere*; Eugenius, *Carm.* 47, 1-2 (*MGH, AA* 14: 259) *Vtile coniugibus exemplum praebeo turtur: non repeto thalamum nec coniunx casta maritum.*

657. **regit...regitur**: witty use of a verb common in grammar and in medieval theories of syntax; *regimen* referred to the case imposed on the governed word by the governing word: see S. Reynolds, *Medieval Reading*, 100; *Doctrinale* 1247-8; 1270 *qui verbi regitur vi, passivis sociatur*, *tenetur* and *nomen* (656) are in the same key; cf. the use of grammatical terms *mobile fixo* in a marriage metaphor at *SD* 1, 1045.

658. **Inperio sponsi sponte**: as in the case of Heloise's voluntary decision to take the veil cf. Abelard, *Historia calamitatum* ed. Muckle, 81, 625-7 *Illa* (sc. Heloissa) *tamen, prius ad imperium nostrum sponte velata, et monasterium ingressa. Ambo itaque simul sacrum habitum suscepimus.*

660. **habitu**: for other indications of a monastic audience cf. *SD* 1, 718 *habitus humilis*, 880 *regula certa*, 1089 *te conclude*.

663. **Ludi**: present infinitive passive after *pensatur*.

665. **Adam**: cf. *SD* 2, 42 *O luctus tante posteritatis Adam!*

667. **phenicem**: The phoenix constructs for itself a pyre of aromatic spices, fanning the flames with its own wings. On the third day a reconstructed phoenix appears cf. McCulloch 158-60; Hassig 72-83; *DNR* 1, 34-5 (pp. 84-7W [Manitius, 3: 768, note 1]); *LDS* 2, 185-216 (pp. 377-8W).

667. **laus uatum**: poems devoted in whole or part to the phoenix include Ov., *Met.* 15, 392-407 [cited *DNR* 1, 35 (p. 85W)]; Lactantius, *De ave phoenice* (*Anth.* 485a [ed. Shackleton Bailey, 1: 2, 20-8]); Claudian, *Carm. min.* 27 [cited *DNR* 1, 35 (pp. 86-7W)]; Eugenius, *Carm.* 44 (*MGH, AA* 14: 258); Dracontius, *De laudibus Dei* 1, 653-82 (ed. Vollmer, *MGH, AA* 14: 60-1); Bernardus Silvestris, *Cosmographia* 1, 3, 451-2 (ed. Dronke, 116); *LSD* 2, 185-216 (pp. 377-8W); Geoffrey of Monmouth, *Vita Merlini* 1345-56; cf. Henkel 202-3; Viarre 150-1.

668. **uariis cultibus**: according to some, the phoenix's beauty was enhanced with precious jewels cf. Mermier 73.

669. **coitus ignara**: on the phoenix as an asexual creature, a Christian modification for theological purposes cf. Hassig 78-9; Broek 360, 421-2; *LSD* 2, 193-4 (p. 377W); **cibique**: cf. *SD* 1, 79-81; Lactantius, *De ave phoenice* (*Anth.* 485a, 109 [ed. Shackleton Bailey, 1: 2, 25]) *non illi* (sc.phoenici) *cibus est nostro concessus in orbe*; Broek 335-56; **cibique / ...potus**: cf. Eugenius, *Carm.* 14, 25 (*MGH, AA* 14: 243) *potus cibique nulla delectatio*.

670. **Purior...potus**: cf. Lactantius, *De ave phoenice* (*Anth.* 485a, 111 [ed. Shackleton Bailey, 1: 2, 25]) *Ambrosios libat caelesti nectare rores*; Claudian, *Carm. min.* 27, 14-5; **rarior usus**: cf. *SD* 1, 1260.

671. **sobrietas...annos**: cf. *LSD* 2, 206 (p. 378W) *Sobrietas annos multiplicare solet*; Plin., *Nat.* 29, 1, 29 (ed. Ian, 4: 378) sets the phoenix's lifespan at a thousand years; cf. Broek 69-70; Mermier 71 and notes 27-35.

673. **precordia cordis**: cf. Isid., *Orig.* 11, 1, 119 *Praecordia sunt loca cordis vicina quibus sensus percipitur; et dicta praecordia eo quod ibi sit principium cordis et cogitationis.*

674. **Ignis aromaticus**: cf. Lactantius, *De ave phoenice* 77-88;*in Eccles.* f. 93va *Fenix ex aromatibus renasci solet et ex aromatibus renascetur;* NP 649 (ed. Orbán, 44) *Fertur aromaticis glomerare struem speciebus.*

675. **Ignes...calor**: cf. *Miles gloriosus* 355 (ed. Cohen, 1: 209) *calor igneus.*

677. **Irrorans...fons**: dew and rain accompanied the phoenix's resurrection cf. Broek 212-4.

679-700. *The stork*

679. **Strucio**: The ostrich is unable to fly. It buries its eggs in the sand and forgets about them. They are hatched through the warmth of the sun's rays on the sand cf. McCulloch 146-7; Henkel 198-200; *LSD* 2, 485-96 (p. 384W); Geoffrey of Monmouth, *Vita Merlini* 1338-40 **certissimus index**: *LSD* 1, 189 (p. 361W), 442 (p. 367W); 3, 15 (p. 395W); 3, 623 (p. 409W).

680. **Aerias partes**: cf. Isid., *Orig.* 12, 7, 20 *de terra altius non elevatur* (sc. struthio); *DNR* 1, 50 (p. 101W) *Volatu brevi utitur* (sc. struthio).

681. **languenti...ictu**: cf. *SD* 1, 715 *languenti uolatu.*

682. **Aera... / ... Iunonis sub dicione**: cf. *SD* 1, 909; for *aer* as Juno's realm cf. *Glosule super Lucanum* 1, 546 (ed. Marti, 68) *unde dicitur* (sc. Vulcanus) *filius Iouis et Iunonis, id est etheris et aeris*; Baudri, *Carm.* 8, 25 *Turbata Iunone simul turbabitur aer.*

683. **uentrisque lacunar**: cf. *Alda* 185 (ed. Cohen, 1: 137) *Nil poterat uentris satiare capacis abyssum*; *LSD* 9, 93-4 (p. 488W) *Artubus humanis cupiens* (sc. hyena) *implere lacunar / Ventris....*

685. **Deglutit ferrum**: cf. *DNR* 1, 50 (p. 101W) *Quid quod ferri duritia a virtute struthionis digestiva superatur?*; *LSD* 2, 491 (p. 384W); *CPV* f. 142v *Pane nutritur homo, nutritur strucio ferro*; *SA* (T. Hunt 1991, 1: 268) *Strutionem miraberis ferrum in alimenta sumentem, raro remigio alarum utentem* [cf. *SD* 1, 681]; *Prose Salern. Questions* N 62 (ed. Lawn, 318, 31-2, of the *strutio*) *Et calidissimum est quod in effectibus ostenditur, quod etiam ferrum digerit*, **seua iuuant**: cf. *SD* 1, 1096 *feda iuuant*.

686. **Herodis...Neronis**: both men were bywords for cruelty; for *esse* with the genitive cf. *SD* 1, 1422; Sedulius, *Carm. pasch.* 2, 74 (ed. Huemer, *CSEL* 10: 49) *saeuumque tyrannum*; **Neronis**: cf. *SD* 2, 782 *Maiestas miseri nulla Neronis erit*; *LSD* 5, 918 (p. 462W) *Quamvis a saevo principe* (sc. Nero) *pressa foret* (sc. Roma); Juv., 8, 223 *Nero tam saeva crudaque tyrannide fecit?*; Ausonius, *Carm.* 21, 1, 10 (*MGH, AA* 5: 112) *Nero saevus*.

687. **Desinit esse parens**: cf. Hildebert, *Carm. min.* 27, 8 *propter Christum negligit esse parens*; *SD* 1, 844.

687-8. **Oua**: cf. Isid., *Orig.* 12, 7, 20 *Ova sua fovere neglegit* [cf. *NP* 855 (ed. Orbán, 50)]; *sed proiecta tantummodo fotu pulveris animantur*, *DNR* 1, 50 (p. 101W) *Struthio ova sua in sabulo aut arena linquens, diligentiam maternae sollicitudinis ignorare videtur*, *LSD* 2, 493-4 (p. 384W); **inmemor**: cf. Jb 39, 13-6; Jr 8, 7.

690. **neglectus**: a substantive.

691. **ne desperes**: Prv 19, 18 *erudi filium tuum ne desperes*; cf. Peter of Blois, *Carm.* 2, 5, 3b, 8 *Ne desperes, si criminis / in latens precipitium / pes labatur.*

692. **ad sese...redit**: cf. Hor., *Ep.* 2, 2, 138 *et redit ad sese*; Geoffrey of Monmouth, *Vita Merlini* 1167 'Nunc in me redii.'

693. **maternos affectus**: cf. *Alda* 107 (ed. Cohen, 1: 134) *In patre maternos affectus sentiat illa.*

694. **neglecta...oua**: cf. Isid., *Orig.* 12, 7, 20 *Ova sua fovere neglegit* (sc. struthio)

695. **ui nature**: cf. *DNR* 1, 50 (p. 101W); *LSD* 2, 493-4 (p. 384W) *radiorum mira potestas... / ...ova fovet*; Lawn, *Salern. Questions* 182, note 73, *Prose Salern. Questions* N 62 (ed. Lawn, 318, 32-4) *Unde ipsa strutio ova arene involvit, et calore arene magis calefiunt. Ipsa etiam visu eam trahit*; Lawn, xxii, surmises that Neckam incorporated this and other material into the *DNR*.

695-6. Cited in Lawn, *Salern. Questions* 45, note 3; *NP* 856 (ed. Orbán, 50) **scepta** = *saepta*.

698. **prompcior**: cf. *SD* 1, 756.

701-6. *The sparrow*

701. **Hostiles laqueos deuites**: *LSD* 2, 783 (p. 391W) *Subtiles laqueos devitas*; cf. *DNR* 1, 60 (pp. 109W) *Laqueos...aucupis deprehendit gnara, et deprehensos evitat* (sc. passer).

702. **Tot laqueos hostis**: cf. *SD* 1, 881, 958; 2, 1631-2 *tot habet fantasmata mundus, / Tot laqueos*; **parat arte**: cf. *Geta* 298 (ed. Cohen, 1: 47) *arte paras.*

703. **Fistula...auceps**: *Disticha Catonis* 1, 27, 2 (ed. Boas, 65); cf. *LSD* 2, 475 (p. 384W); *NE* 18, 14 *Retibus incaute decipiuntur aues*; Mart., 14, 217, 1-2 *Praedo fuit volucrum: famulus nunc aucupis idem / decipit*; *Disticha Catonis* 1, 27, 2 is assimilated and followed by a reference to the Sirens in *Ysopet* 9, 13-5: *Fistula dulce canit, alitem cum decipit auceps; / ... / Sirenici cantus, falerata melodia, stultos.*

704. **Dulce melos reddit**: cf. *SD* 2, 118 *Cum reddit dulcis musica dulce melos*; *LSD* 4, 667 (p. 435W), 10, 135 (p. 499W); **dulce Syrene malum**: Three types of Sirens are depicted in medieval illustrations, one singing, one playing the pipes, another the lyre cf. Hassig 104; cf. Jb. 20, 12; Claudian, *Carm. min. app.* 1, 1 *Dulce malum pelago Sirenae*; Marbod, *De decem cap.* 3, 60-5 (ed. Leotta, 107-8) *Haec est et Siren, quae stultos dulcia cantans / Allicit,...attractosque profundum / mergit in interitum, quem declinauit Ulixes / Praecludens comitum famosis cantibus aures, / Se quoque vi cohibens ne cursum flectere posset, / Nexibus artatus fugientis in arbore navis*; in Eccles. f. 88vb *Hic cantant Syrenes concupiscentiarum usque in exitium* [exicitium MS] *dulces* [cf. Boethius, *DCP* 1, 1, 11 (ed. Bieler, *CCSL* 94: 3)]; *De tribus puellis* 97-102 (ed. Cohen, 2: 235).

705. **Aures obturat**: Baudri, *Carm.* 77, 47; cf. PsG 57, 5 *sicut aspidis surdae et obturantis aures suas*; Prv 21, 13; Is 33, 15; Fulg., *Mitologiae* 2, 8 (ed. Helm, 48, 3) *Quas* (sc. Sirenas) *Ulixis socii obturatis auribus transeunt, ipse vero religatus transit*; Diekstra, 154; *LSD* 9, 289-90 (p. 492W); in Homer, *Od.* 12, 39-54, the sorceress Circe recommends that Odysseus block his companions' ears with wax to avoid hearing the Sirens' singing, which lured passing sailors to destruction on the rocky shores of the islands where they lived; for Ulysses and the Sirens cf. Hor., *Ep.* 1, 2, 17-26; Fulg., *Mitologiae* 2, 8 (ed. Helm, 48-9); the allegorical interpretation of the Circe myth, in which Circe stands variously for pleasure, lust or violent passion, has a long tradition cf. Kaiser *passim*; see Yarnall 80-6 for the symbolic role of Circe in Virgil's *Aeneid*; for Christian symbolism of the Sirens as representing lechery or worldly delights cf. Cherry 146; Hassig, figure 107, reproduces from London, British Museum, Harley 4751, an image of a Siren confronting Ulysses's ship; **munitus**: Ulysses was tied to the mast by his comrades so that he could hear the Sirens' song, but resist its fatal attraction.

706. **circumueniat**: cf. Claudian, *Carm.* 3, 153 *callida Circe*; **filia Solis**: i. e. Circe cf. Ov., *Met.* 14, 346; *Rem.* 276 *quod magni filia Solis eram*; Serv., *A.* 7, 19 (ed. Thilo-Hagen, 2: 127, 9-10) *Circe ...Solis fingitur filia*; Marbod, *De decem cap.* 3, 66-70 (ed. Leotta, 108) *Nec minus et Circes male dulcia pocula cavit, / Quae qui potarunt formas traxere ferinas / Effecti canibus similes suibusve lutosis; / Per quos degeneres enervatique notantur / Ducentes pecorum dominante libidine vitam*; Scherer 159-64; the Sirens and Circe appear together in Hor., *Ep.* 1, 2, 23; cf. *LSD* 4, 666-7 (p. 435W).

707-32. *Differentiation of birds in general*

707-16. **Sunt... / Sunt**: Isid., *Orig.* 12, 7, 1 sets out the different natures of birds in a series of contrasts, each introducued by *aliae...aliae*; *LSD* 4, 506 (p. 432W) *Sunt quibus ardor inest, sunt frigiditate nocivo*.

709. **Quedam**: e. g. the partridge cf. Isid., *Orig.* 12, 7, 1 *aliae astutae, ut perdix*; **lucellis**: the noun can mean both «small gain» and «pike, pickerel» cf. *DMLBS* 5: 1649.

710. **quas...simplicitatis amor**: e. g. the turtle dove cf. Isid., *Orig.* 12, 7, 1 *aliae simplices sunt, ut columbae*; *SD* 1, 126; Aldhelm, *CDV* 435-6, 492 (*MGH, AA* 15; 371, 373).

711. **noctuque dieque**: cf. Mastandrea 553-4.

714. cf. Suet., fr. 161a, 15 (ed. Reifferscheid, 309) *vere calente nouos componit acredula cantus*.

715. **languente uolatu**: the stork, for example cf. *SD* 1, 681; Urso, *De commixtionibus elem.* 4, 4, (ed. Stürner, 122) *Si autem animalia fiant de materia, cui dominantur superiora levium extrema, sed magis superiora aeris quam ignis, ad localem prosequendum motionem, leviora fiunt et non multum volantia ut fasiani, galline, perdices.*

718. **scema**: cf. *Novale* 34 (ed. Haye, 417) *Bene nuncquam cema notasti,* where the glossator explains *cema* [= *schema*] as *id est rhetoricum colorem.*

719. **delucidat**: rare word, found from Tertullian on, mainly in Christian writers cf. *ThLL,* 5: 1186, 25.

720. **Siluestres mores exue**: cf. Verg., *G.* 2, 49-51 *tamen haec quoque... / exuerint siluestrem animum.*

721-22. **brume / ...ueris**: cf. Adelard of Bath, *De eodem et diverso* (ed. H. Willner, *BGPM* 4: 1, 14, 27-8 [Münster, 1903]) *Ver, autumnus, hiems cur pingat, compleat, artet; / Prata, domos, latices, gramine, farre, gelu;* Marbod, *Carm. varia MPL* 171: 1717b.

723. **laudes**: cf. Marbod, *Carm. varia MPL* 171: 1717a *Certant* (sc. aues) *laude pari varios cantus modulari;* **hiis**: sc. *laudibus.*

724. **homo**: the shortening of the first syllable of **P**'s *huius* is unlikely; the second person singular verb, *tendis,* and *tibi,* suggest supplying a vocative; for homo at the diaeresis cf. *SD* 2, 176 *Ni medicus, nec homo, ni paterere, deus.*

725. **spaciatur in undis**: cf. *LSD* 3, 663 (p. 410W) *spaciando per undas;* M. Valerius, *Buc.* 2, 21 *Et pecus...spatiatur in herba.*

728. **fastus auis**: because the bird is *Ornatus pennis.*

729. **quo tendis**: cf. Verg., *A.* 5, 670 *quo tenditis.*

730. **Virtutum pennis**: Hildebert, *Biblical Epigrams* 52, 9 (ed. Scott, 303) *Virtutum pennis ut aues tolluntur ad astra;* cf. Boethius, *DCP* 4, 1, 9 (ed. Bieler, *CCSL* 94: 65, 31-2); **alta pete**: cf. *SD* 1, 924, 1413; Verg., *G.* 1, 142 *alta petens.*

731. **Reice**: cf. *SD* 1, 1070.

733-42. *The peacock*

733. **Pauo**: When the peacock cries out, it fills the listener with fear (*pauor*) cf. McCulloch 153; *DNR* 1, 39-40 (pp. 90-4W); *LSD* 2, 337-68 (p. 381W).

733. **nature...ostentacio**: cf. *DNR* 1, 39 (p. 90W) *Pavo...videtur esse naturae ostentatio;* **ludus**: cf. Bernardus Silvestris, *Cosmographia* 1, 3, 459 (ed. Dronke, 116) *Nature ludentis opus, Iunonius ales.*

734. **Iuno, gloria magna tibi**: cf. *LSD* 2, 339-40 (p. 381W); Mart., 14, 85, 2 *Iunonis avis; CMC,* Oxford, Digby 221, f. 40ra *pavonem in sua habet* (sc. Iuno) *tutela, quia divitum vita ornatum semper appetit et sicut pavo...posteriora...turpiter nudat, ita divitie et gloria secularis momentaliter quidem ornant, nudos relinquunt.*

735. **Magnatem**: cf. *LSD* 3, 175-86 (p. 399W) for criticism of the *curia magnatum.*

736. **Munitum**: cf. *SD* 1, 920.

737. **Voce minus grata**: *LSD* 2, 366 (p. 381W) *Horrida vox hosti displicet; SA* (T. Hunt 1991, 1: 268) *clamoris...horrore molestus est audientibus* (sc. pauo).

739. **furis gressibus**: cf. Theodulf, *Carm.* 45, 29 (*MGH, P. L.* 1: 543) *Gressibus it furum fallentum insania versis; LSD* 2, 367 (p. 381W) *Furtivo metitur iter gressu simulator; SA* (T. Hunt 1991, 1: 268) *Intueberis et pavonis incessum furtivum.*

740. **Magnatum fastus**: cf. *LSD* 3, 487-8 (p. 406W) *O si magnatum me numquam curia nosset! / Ha! multis mundi gloria uana nocet.*

741. **pars inferior**: cf. *SD* 1, 197; **florenti sydere**: cf. *SD* 1, 1211; **sydere fulgens**: Luc. 6, 393.

742. **gaudia uana**: cf. *LH-L* 2:405.

743-54. *The caladrius*

743. **Parce parcunt**: cf. Isid., *Orig.* 1, 37, 24 *'Parcas'...quod nulli parcant*; **caladrius**: The caladrius, an all-white bird, forecasts whether a sick person will die; if it averts its gaze from the patient, the patient is doomed, but if it directs its gaze at him, it takes the disease onto itself and flies to the sun where the illness is dissipated; cf. Druce 1912, 384-9; on the identity of the *caladrius* cf. Druce 1912, 398-407, McCulloch 99-100; Henkel 201-2; *ThLL*, 3: 995, 6 s. v. *charadrius*; *DMLBS* 2: 324 s. v. *charadrius*: «kind of bird»; Deut 14, 18; *Physiologus Lat.* V, 1 (ed. Carmody, 15) *Est uolatile quod dicitur caladrius*; *LSD* 2, 221-6 (p. 378W: translated by Druce 1912, 393); **caladrius aspicit egrum**: *LSD* 2, 221 (p. 378W); for illustrations of the caladrius from an early 12th-c. bestiary, see Kealey 10.

743-4. cf. *Physiologus Lat.* V, 4-7 (ed. Carmody, 15) *Si quis autem est in aegritudine constitutus, per hunc caladrium cognoscitur si uiuat an moriatur: si ergo est infirmitas hominis ad mortem, mox ut uiderit infirmum, auertit faciem suam caladrius ab eo, et recedit, et omnes cognoscunt quia moriturus est; si autem infirmitas eius non pertingit ad mortem, intendit faciem eius caladrius, et assumit omnes infirmitates eius intra se....*

749. **Uite uita**: cf. *SD* 2, 423 *Nam mors est anime, cum uite uita recedit*; cf. Verg. A. 4, 705 *uita recessit*. Hildebert, *Carm. min.* 39, IV, 24 *hoc verbo vite fieri vita ipsa fatetur.*

751. **candore nitescit**: Cic., *Arat.* 1, 174 *exiguo qui stellarum candore nitescit*; cf. *LSD* 2, 226 (p. 378W); *Physiologus Lat.* V, 2 (ed. Carmody, 15) *Physiologus dicit de hoc quia totus albus est, nullam partem habens nigram.*

752. **Dii bene**: Cropp, 107, note 21, lists occurrences of the phrase in *CNP* and *LSD*; cf. *SD* 2, 1580; Claudian, *Carm.* 15, 346 *di bene, quod....*

755-98. *The cock*

755. **gallus**: cf. McCulloch 104; *LSD* 2, 801-54 (pp. 391-2W); **uerberat alis / Corpus**: cf. Herrmann, «Gallus et Vulpes», 264, stanza 48 *Se ipsum prius exerit* (sc. gallus) / *dum latus alis perculit / ut ipse primum sentiat / quod subditis annuntiat*; *DNR* 1, 75 (pp. 120-1W); *LSD* 2, 801-54 (pp. 391-2W).

755. **excitat...alis**: cf. *LSD* 2, 803 (p. 391W) *Excitat* (sc. gallus) *a somno sese, se verberat alis*; *DNR* 1, 75 (p. 120W) *Seipsum gallus alis verberat ante cantum*; *SD* 1, 883; Lawn, *Salern. Questions*, 186, note 104.

761. **tellus inculta**: cf. Ez 36, 35 *terra...inculta.*

763. **Attritus uomer splendet**: cf. *LSD* 5, 93 (p. 442W); Verg., *G.* 1, 46 *et sulco attritus splendescere uomer.*

764. Ov., *Pont.* 1, 5, 6; cf. *in Eccles.* f. 157va *Aque statiue ut paludes facile corrumpuntur et uitium capiunt ne moueantur aque.*

765. **sistemata**: cf. *LSD* 10, 125 (p. 499W) *Musica vocales licet in systemata ducat.*

767. **Cantu distinguit**: cf. *DNR* 1, 75 (p. 121W) *Solet quaeri... quare gallus cantu suo horas distinguat*: Neckam explains the regularity of the cock's crowing as the result of the equally

regular movement of certain humours; *LSD* 2, 801 (p. 391W) *Gallus adest cantu distinguens...horas*; *NE* 40, 15 (ed. Hervieux, 2: 414); Lawn, *Salern. Questions*, 162, 105-7 ...*cur luciferi quasi iura / Vendicet usurpans sit gallus preco diei, / Necnon nocturnas distinguat cantibus horas?*; 186, note 104.

767. **preco diei**: *LSD* 2, 834-5 (p. 392W); Matthew of Vendôme, *Tob.* 1307-8 (ed. Munari, 2: 216) *preco diei / Gallus*; *DNR* 1, 75 (p. 120W) *Praeco diei*.

768. **usibus apta tuis**: cf. *LSD* 9, 248 (p. 491W) *usibus apta suis*; *SD* 1, 1363; **apta**: sc. *hora*.

769. **distribuenda**: cf. *SD* 1, 822.

770. **Rachel... Lya**: Jacob worked for seven years in order to win Rachel, the younger of Laban's two daughters, as his wife; tricked into marrying the elder daughter, Lia, Jacob agreed to labour for a further seven years to marry Rachel; cf. Gn 29, 15-30.

772. **certior esse tui**: cf. *SD* 1, 1088 *tucior esse sui*.

773. **Dat granum...purius**: cf. *Ysengrimus* 4, 937-8 (ed. Mann, 412); *DNR* 1, 75 (p. 120W) *Leni susurrio suas vocat ad esum grani puri*; *LSD* 2, 837-40 (p. 392W); *NP* 1033 (ed. Orbán, 56) *Gallus ad inuenta uocat uxores alimenta*; *Comparatio galli cum presbitero* stanza 8 (ed. Novati, 480).

777. **Prothdolor!**: for the spelling cf. *DMLBS* 3: 713 s. v. *dolor* 2b; **in senium...uergens**: cf. *LSD* 2, 845 (p. 392W); Luc., 1, 129-30 *alter uergentibus annis / in senium*; Hugh Primas 16, 97 *Etas enim mea uergit in senium*; Geoffrey of Monmouth, *Vita Merlini* 1264-5 *Mea non hoc exigit etas / in senium vergens*; a toad incubates the cock's eggs and produces the basilisk cf. *DNR* 1, 75 (p. 120W) *Cum item in senium vergit gallus, quandoque ovum ponit, quod bufo fovet, et ex ipso prodit basiliscus*; *LSD* 2, 845-50 (p. 392W); *Prose Salern. Questions* P 1, N 30, B 171, 105, 268 (ed. Lawn, 207, 1-12; 298, 9-22; 90, 5-7; 49, 10-17; 129, 18; 130, 6) *Queritur unde ex gallo generetur ovum unde fiat basiliscus? R.... Ex tanta siquidem siccitate sperma circa genitalia vel renes collectum, testa in superficie circumducitur, et ovum procreatur ex quo animal eiusdem generis effici non potest...Quare alterius generis animal efficitur, materia cuius venenosa est propter pessimas superfluitates in aliis etiam etatibus retentas... Quia ergo venenosa est materia, non est mirum si animal ex ea generatum sit venenosum*; Lawn, xxiv, dates the compilation of this question circa 1200.

779-80. **proles**: on the basilisk's generation from a cock's egg cf. McCulloch 93; Breiner 35 follows the basilisk's transformation ino the cockatrice and its subsequent influence on heraldry and alchemy; Urso, *Aphorismi Glosula* 14 (ed. Creutz, 38) *Imparum qualitatum actione violenta galli semen in eiusdem ovo conclusum sic aduritur, ut non in gallum sed corruptum transeat in serpentem*; *De commixtionibus elem.* 4, 1 (ed. Stürner, 90) *...et actu unam numero, sed potestate duplam transducit in duas diversas substantias, cum de semine fetus fiat et aliud animal vel de re eiusdem speciei duo diversa, ut de ovis galli et galline pullus et serpens*; 4, 3 (ed. Stürner, 113) *Accidentalis est illa, qua aliquid transit in id, cui naturaliter non innititur ut...ouum galli in animal alterius maneriei, quia in aspidem vertitur*; *LDS* 2, 845-54 (p. 392W); *NP* 1037-8 *Et post tercentos hic gallinacius annos / Ovvm producit, quo basiliscus erit*; 1101-2 (ed. Orbán, 56, 58); *Comparatio galli cum presbitero* stanza 10 (ed. Novati, 480 and note 1).

779. **proles infausta**: cf. *SD* 1, 1220; *LSD* 2, 849 (p. 392W).

780. **Heres**: cf. *DNR* 2, 120 (p. 198W).

781. **doctores deliri**: Arrius, for example, cited in *SD* 1, 783; just as the cock was thought to personify the doctors of the Church (cf. Novati, 470), the ill-omened offspring

of the cock is taken to symbolize those teachers who have deviated from Church doctrine; cf. Herrmann, «Gallus et Vulpes», 264, stanza 47, *Per gallum decentissime / doctores subintellige / qui uoce, gestis clamitant / auditores ne torpeant*; SD 1, 879, 975, 1276; Rowland in Goosens 1981, 351, notes the tradition that defined the cock «in doctrinal terms as signifying the teacher...of the Church».

782. **noxius error**: *Pamphilus* 638 (ed. Cohen, 2: 218) *Teque tuosque dies noxius error habet.*

783. **O quantum nocuit**: *LSD* 3, 490 (p. 406W); **infelix Arrius**: cf. Sedulius, *Carm. pasch.* 1, 300 (ed. Huemer, *CSEL* 10: 38) *Arrius infelix*; Arator 1, 444-5 (ed. McKinlay, *CSEL* 72: 39); SD 2, 1469; *LSD* 5, 531 (p. 452W).

784. cf. *LSD* 5, 451 (p. 450W); on the analogy between the cock and the soldier cf. Steadman 240-1.

785. **galeam**: i. e. the cock's comb cf. Theodulf, *Carm.* 72, 167 (*MGH, P. L.* 1: 567) *Pro galea crista est*; **calcaria**: cf. *LSD* 2, 807-34 (pp. 391-2W); *Comparatio galli cum presbitero* stanza 6, 2 (ed. Novati, 479) *in pede calcaribus, ut miles, armatur.*

788. **fera bella**: cf. Theodulf, *Carm.* 72, 160 (*MGH, P. L.* 1: 567) *in fera bella ruunt* (sc. volucres); **bella ciens**: cf. SD 1, 958; *LH-L* 1: 195-6; Mastandrea 81; the cock was famous as a warrior in antiquity cf. Rowlands in Goosens 1981, 341-2.

789. **Vxores regis**: on the cock's uxoriousness cf. Steadman 238-9; cf. Hor., *C.* 3, 24, 19-20 *nec...regit virum coniunx*; Alcuin, *Carm.* 49, 3-4 (*MGH P. L.* 1: 262) *huius* (sc. galli) */ Subditus imperio gallinarum regitur grex*; *Comparatio galli cum presbitero* stanza 4, 1 (ed. Novati, 478) *Gallus regit plurimam turbam gallinarum*; Baudri, *Carm.* 126, 57-8 *Vnus in ede mea gallus bis quinque maritet / Vxores noctis excubias celebrans*; Chauntecleer had numerous wives; **domas**: *Comparatio galli cum presbitero* stanza 9, 1-2 (ed. Novati, 480) *Gallus suas feminas solet verberare: / has quas cum extraneo novit ambulare.*

790. **Princeps...nanum**: cf. Matthew of Vendome, *Ars* 1, 111, 139 *Hic rex nanus adest,...*, a reference to the *regulus cristatus*, the golden-crested wren; **zelotipasse**: cf. Ysengrimus 5, 818, 17-8 (ed. Mann, 460) «*Gauisam scriptura refert his lusibus illam / Et mechum patruum zelotipasse suum*».

791. **subducunt...testes**: the cock is castrated to fatten him for eating cf. Isid., *Orig.* 12, 7, 50 *inter ceteras enim aves huic solo testiculi adimuntur*; Marbod, *De lapidibus* 74 (ed. Riddle, 39) *Ventriculo galli, qui testibus est viduatus...*; *DNR* 1, 75 (p. 120W) *Minus instructi putant gallum gallinaceum esse illum cui subtracti sunt testes sexus.*

792. **criste**: cf. Mart., 9, 68, 3 *cristati...galli.*

794. **Destituunt te**: *Ecloga Theodoli* 252 *Quod te destituunt vires, suspiria produnt*; **degenerare nequis**: in Ysengrimus 4, 939-42 (ed. Mann, 412) Reynard reproaches the cock, Sprotinus, for not measuring up to his father; Herrmann, «Gallus et Vulpes», 261, stanza 8, «*Cur ego, inquit* (sc. gallus), *degener / a patre meo aestimer / cum genitoris formulam / gestu, uoceque referam?*»

795. **Altilis**: *ThLL*, 1: 1763, 14 cites Nonius (ed. L. Müller, 72) *altile, non solum pingue, ab alendo, verum etiam opulentum*; Plin., *Nat.* 10, 50, 139 (ed. Ian, 2:261); **prenumeraui**: in SD 1, 793-4.

796. **Iacturam**: i. e. the cock's testes; **simplicitate**: in contrast to his former nobility.

797. **ditas mensam**: cf. *Geta* 190 (ed. Cohen, 1: 42) *Ditabis mensam praeda...meam.*

797-8. chors... / ...curia: cf. gloss on *cortem* in Cambridge, UL, Gg. 6. 42, f. 69v *hic chors* [chros MS] *chortis est curria uillanorum. Vnde Marcialis Cocus: Si Libie uolucres aut si michi Phasidos essent / accip<er>es at nunc accipe chortis aues*; Mart., 11, 52, 14 *chortis saturas et paludis aves.*

799-808. *The swallow*

799. [Hirundo]: The swallow hunts its food when flying cf. McCulloch 174-5; *DNR* 1, 52 (p. 104W); *LSD* 2, 789-800 (p. 391W); **tenuis esca**: the butterfly cf. *SD* 1, 86.

799. Progne: = Procne, the wife of Tereus cf. Ov., *Met.* 6, 424-674; *LSD* 2, 799-800 (p. 391W).

799. solo...uolatu: cf. *DNR* 1, 52 (p. 104W) *hirundo in ipso volatu cibo utitur.*

801. cf. *DNR* 1, 52 (p. 104W) *Adde etiam quod pullus hirundinis de nocte clamat; LSD* 2, 799-800 (p. 391W) *Adde quod et nati Prognes de nocte proterva / Voce petunt escas, cogit acerba fames.*

803. Presens...nisi: cf. *DNR* 2, 155 (p. 241W) *Sed quid est vita praesens, nisi...?*

805. cf. *DNR* 1, 52 (p. 103W) *Quid quod lapis multis utilitatibus deserviens in interioribus hirundinis latere perhibetur?*

807. Hec: sc. gemma; **lumine fulget**: cf. Mastandrea 467.

809-20. *The swan, likewise*

809. Cigno: The swan's song is sweetest just before it dies cf. McCulloch 176; *DNR* 1, 49 (pp. 100-1W); *LSD* 2, 369-82 (p. 381-2W); Geoffrey of Monmouth, *Vita Merlini* 1334-7; Gerald of Wales, *Topographia Hibernica* 1, 19 (ed. Dimock, 52); **mors astans**: cf. Peter of Blois, *Carm.* 1, 5, 10, 5 *Astat mors in ianuis.*

811. celo tegitur...urnam: cf. *in Eccles.* f. 137ra *Facilis iactura sepulchri materialis, celo tegitur qui non habet urnam*; Ov., *Met.* 1, 51 *quod tegit omnia caelum*; *Fast.* 5, 526 *urna tegit*; Dracontius, *Deliberativa Achillis* 29-30 (ed. Wolff, 42) *quas* (sc. animas) *urna polorum claudit*; Baudri, *Carm.* 26, 8 *Artus ingenuos hec habet urna tuos.*

812. diu uiuere: cf. Walther, *Prov.* 25010f *Quid est diu vivere quam diu torqueri?* cf. *SD* 1, 818.

813. Flora: cf. *LSD* 7, 358 (p. 481W).

815. Exequias celebrant... / ...exclamat: note the liturgical setting, with the *psitacus* as celebrant: cf. note on *SD* 1, 816; *SD* 2, 408 *Absque tropis sermo comicus esse nequid.* For parody of the Church's sacred texts cf. Bayless 177-212.

816. «Ilicet ire licet»: a ritual word used to conclude funeral ceremonies cf. Serv., *A.* 6. 216 (ed. Thilo-Hagen, 2: 40, 24-7) *corona quae tamdiu stabat...quamdiu consumpto cadavere et collectis cineribus diceretur novissimum verbum «ilicet», quod ire licet significat*; cf. *SA* f. 21b **Scilicet** *componitur a si et licet. similiter ilicet, quasi ire licet; expleto enim officio suo dicebat sacerdos clara uoce: «ilicet», quasi ire licet.*

818. uiuere pena grauis: cf. Eugenius, *Appendix* 50, 4 (*MGH, AA* 14: 281) *mors est iam requies, vivere poena mihi*; Maximianus 1, 4; *Ysopet* 54, 4 *Sed nece completa uiuere pena potest*; Peter of Blois, *Carm.* 1, 1, 9, 3a, 1-2 *Hanc uitam mori censeo, / nec nisi mori uoueo.*

821-34. *The hoopoe*

821. Vpupa: When the hoopoe sees its parents declining in old age, it extracts their old feathers and warms up their bodies with its own wings. Because of this behaviour, the bird became a byword for the need to honour one's parents cf. McCulloch 126-7; Henkel 200-1; Hassig 93-103; **succurre... / Orans**: cf. *Concordantia*, 2386 s. v. *succurro: nostrae precibus humanitatis...succurre.*

822. **distribuenda**: cf. Luc., 6, 20 *omni autem petenti te tribue*; **dato**: cf. *SD* 1, 945 *habeto.*

823. **dilectos... / Artus**: Ov., *Met.* 11, 737.

827. **colit coluber**: etymological wordplay cf. Isid., *Orig.* 12, 4, 2 *Colubrum ab eo dictum, quod colat umbras,...*; *SD* 1, 110 *Abruptas rupes...*

829. **obsequium...parentibus**: cf. *SD* 1, 118 *obsequiis...parens*; *Physiologus Lat.* X, 3-5 (ed. Carmody, 21).

830. **menbra fouet**: cf. Prudentius, *Psych.* 628 *suppeditare cibos atque indiga membra fouere.*

833. **nati sumus**: *SD* 1, 723.

834. **racione nocet?**: Neckam contrasts the kindly behaviour of irrational creatures with that of man, who is endowed with reason cf. Hassig 93; *Altercatio Ganimedis* 34 (ed. Lentzen, 177) «*Non aves aut pecora debet imitari / Homo, cui datum est ratiocinari*»; *Physiologus Lat.* X, 9 (ed. Carmody, 22) *Si hoc aues irrationabiles inuicem sibi faciunt, quomodo homines, cum sint rationabiles, parentum suorum nutrimenta uicem reddere nolunt?*

835-70. *Alexander addresses his mother*

839. cf. *LSD* 7, 360 (p. 481W) *Saepe placent animi seria mixta jocis.*

840. **gloria...amor**: cf. *SD* 2, 56 *Sanctorum creuit gloria, creuit amor.*

844. **Alexander...tuus**: Neckam names himself at the end of the *SMF*, cited in Hunt ed. Gibson, 17: *Fortasse tuo, liber, superstes eris Alexandro...tunc tuo Alexandro gratissimam recompensabis uicissitudinem*; **desinet esse**: Ov., *Fast.* 4, 229; *Ibis* 31.

846. **molliter ossa cubant**: Ovid, *Am.* 1, 8, 107-8 '*saepe rogabis / ut mea defunctae molliter ossa cubent*' [cf. Baudri, *Carm.* 45, 9; 97, 87]; *Doctrinale* 1459 *ut: mea defunctae da molliter ossa cubare.*

847. **cordis**: a long tradition associated the heart with remembrance cf. Varro, *De lingua Latina* 6, 46 *Recordari, rursus in cor revocare*; Jerome, *Comm. in Ezek.* 40, 4 (*MPL* 25: 373d-74a).

847. **mea menbra quiescent**: cf. *Anth.* 673, 10 (ed. Buecheler, 2: 1, 318) *quod patris homicii tene mea membra quiescunt*; *Ibis* 303; Mastandrea 493.

849-50. **cor cordis**: Neckam declines *cor* in the singular in the course of proclaiming love for his mother cf. *Doctrinale* 138 *cor cordis debet habere.*

851. **Dimidio cordis**: cf. Hor., *C.* 1, 3, 8 *animae dimidium meae.*

853. **Lux...lucens**: cf. Mt 5. 16 *sic luceat lux vestra*; *SD* 1, 868.

855. **iungitur illis**: cf. Theodulf, *Carm.* 46, 107 (*MGH, P. L.* 1: 547) *Ethica Grammaticae, Logica et mox iungitur illis.*

856. **uera dies**: cf. Walther, *Prov.* 14143a *Lux ubi vera dies, pax ibi vera quies.*

857. **mera**: **P**'s reading, *mora*, makes no sense here; the adjective *mera* is close to the paradosis and would complete the chiasmus *mera gratia:: gloria perpes*; **gloria perpes**: Prosper, *Epig.* 11 (*MPL* 51: 502c) *In Christo quorum gloria perpes erit.*

858. **habere diem**: Ov., *Fast.* 1, 324 *Nomen Agonalem credit habere diem*; *SD* 1, 862; cf. Isid., *Orig.* 5, 30, 10.

859. **«hodie genui te»**: Act 13, 33; Hbr 1, 5.

861. **luce diei**: cf. Mastandrea 459; cf. Isid., *Orig.* 5, 30, 9 *Apud Hebraeos autem dies prima una sabbati dicitur, qui apud nos dies dominicus est, quem gentiles Soli dicaverunt.*

864. **deus atque dies**: cf. *SD* 1, 859.

869. **flecte genu**: cf. Rm 14, 11 *quoniam mihi flectet omne genu*; **dulcissima mater**: cf. Mastandrea 236.

870. **gloria, gemma, decus**: *LSD* 1, 348 (p. 365W).

871-86. *The crane*

871. **gruum**: Cranes fly in a formation which resembles a letter. The leader directs the flight until his voice becomes hoarse; then another replaces him. At night the crane on watch carries small stones in his claws to prevent him from falling asleep cf. McCulloch 105-6; *LSD* 2, 315-36 (pp. 380-1W); **sibi succedens**: cf. *SD* 1, 1274 *sibi succedens ordine*; *CMC*, Oxford, Digby 221, f. 59v *congrua hoc uerbum tractum est a gruibus que congruunt id est conueniunt, sicut earum indicat natura*; **figuram**: a grammatical technical term cf. *OLD* s. v. *figura* 10; cf. Mart., 13, 75; Claudian, *Carm.* 15, 477-8 *ordinibus uariis per nubila texitur ales / littera pinnarumque notis inscribitur aer*; Isid., *Orig.* 12, 7, 14; *LSD* 2, 315-36 (p. 380-1W); Bernardus Silvestris, *Cosmographia* 1, 3, 457 (ed. Dronke, 116) *Queque figuratos apices inscribit eundo / ...grus*; *NP* 905 (ed. Orbán, 52) *Littera formata*; Gerald of Wales, *Topographia Hibernica* 1, 14 (ed. Dimock, 46-7).

872. **ortographia**: a technical term from grammar cf. *ThLL*, 9: 1060, 48; Mart., 9, 12, 7 *quod pinna scribente grues ad sidera tollant*; *LSD* 10, 42 (p. 497W); Geoffrey of Monmouth, *Vita Merlini* 1294-5.

874. **ne deliret linea**: cf. *SD* 1, 1034.

875. **uoce magistram**: Verg., *E.* 5, 48; cf. Isid., *Orig.* 12, 7, 15 *Castigat autem voce quae cogit agmen*; *LSD* 2, 325 (p. 380W); Geoffrey of Monmouth, *Vita Merlini* 1301-10 on *natura gruum*.

876. **cetera turba**: Ov., *Met.* 3, 23; Dracontius, *De raptu Helenae* 487 (ed. Wolff, 33).

877. **uenti rabies**: cf. *LSD* 4, 35 (p. 421W), 5, 43 (p. 441W); Ov., *Met.* 5, 7 *ventorum rabies*.

878. **Obscurata...littera...perit**: cf. Luc., 5, 716 (of cranes [cited Isid., *Orig.* 12, 7, 14]) *Et turbata perit dispersis littera pinnis*; cf. McCulloch 105, note 47; **littera tota**: Mart., 13, 75, 1 (grues) *Turbabis versus nec littera tota volabit*; Symphosius, *Aenig.* 26, 1 (*Anth.* ed. Buecheler, 1: 1, 228) (Grus) *Littera sum caeli pinna perscripta volanti.*

879. **preuia turba**: cf. SD 1, 875 (grus)*que precedit*; Ov., *Ars* 1, 542 *ecce leves satyri, praevia turba dei*; 2, 266 *columba est data...praevia duxque rati.*

880. **Illos**: object of *designat* in 879.

883. **Excitat a somno**: cf. Isid., *Orig.* 12, 7, 15 *nocte autem excubias dividunt, et ordinem vigiliarum per vices faciunt, tenentes lapillos suspensis digitis, quibus somnos arguant*; *LSD* 2, 327-30 (p. 380W); *NP* 910 (ed. Orbán, 52).

885. **prelia ducit**: cf. Mastandrea 698.

886. **Arma, quibus**: cf. *SD* 2, 275-6 *Arma, quibus potuit hostem uicisse, superna / Concessit subito gratia gratis ei.*

887-90. *The raven*

887. [**Coruus**]: The raven does not provide its young with food until it can see the black colour of thir feathers cf. *LSD* 2, 509-58 (pp. 384-6W); *DNR* 1, 61 (pp. 110-11W); **Apollinis ales**: cf. *DNR* 2, 126 (p. 206W) *Vulpes...coruum coepit demulcere, asserens Apollinem duabus auibus felicem censendum esse, coruo scilicet et cygno*; *LSD* 2, 529 (p. 385W); McCulloch 108, 161.

888. **nigra...ueste**: cf. Ct 5, 11 *comae...nigrae quasi coruus*; **corpora ueste tegi**: Ov., *Ep.* 13, 32, *Med.* 18, *Fast.* 3, 214; *Ibis* 102.

888. **nigra...tegi**: cf. Isid., *Orig.* 12, 7, 43; *DNR* 1, 61 (p. 110W) *Pullos enim suos non sustentat alimentis antequam in colore patrissent*; *LSD* 2, 527-8 (p. 385W); *NP* 933-4 (ed. Orbán, 53); Alan of Lille, *De planctu* ed. Häring, 815, 173 *Illic coruus...suos fetus non sua esse pignora fatebatur usque dum nigri argumento coloris hoc quasi secum disputando probabat.*

890. **relatiuo...honore**: cf. Matthew of Vendôme, *Ars* 2, 24-5 (ed. Munari, 1: 147) *Iusta relativo gaudet honore fides*; *Ep. prologus*, 46, *Tob.* 824, 2010 (ed. Munari, 2: 196, 245).

891-1172. *Animals*

891-930. *The bat*

891. **Sollicitant**: cf. *SD* 1, 1258; **leuium spectacula rerum**: Verg., *G.* 4, 3; cf. Maximianus 1, 175 *Quid quod nulla levant animum spectacula rerum*; *LSD* 2, 305 (p. 380W), 4, 434 (p. 430W) *Visum delectant levium spectacula rerum*; *CNP* 1259 *demulcent puerum leuium spectacula rerum*; cf. *Alda* 161 (ed. Cohen, 1: 136); Mastandrea, 814.

892. **seria mixta iocis**: Neckam adheres to the poetic tradition in which the Horatian distinction between delight (*delectare*) and utility (*prodesse* cf. *Ars* 333) as the aim of poetry is recast in terms of games and seriousness. Neckam states that he had sometimes discharged the two functions separately, focussing exclusively on serious matters (*SD* 1, 906 *seria*) or on trifles (*SD* 1, 892 *ioca*, 906 *ludicra*); here, however, he argues for a kind of discourse that combines *ioca* with edifying material in the service of serious thought. In the bestiary, delight is found in animal lore, while the moral profit is located in the allegorizations cf. *Accessus ad auctores* (ed., Huygens, 21) *Accessus Phisiologi: intentio eius est delectare in animalibus et prodesse in figuris* cf. Olson 27-8; *Ysopet, prologus* 1-2 *Vt iuuet et prosit, conatur pagina praesens; / Dulcius arrident seria mixta iocis*; cf. Peter of Celle, *Ep.* 69 (*MPL* 202: 515a) *Miscuisti siquidem jocos seriis, sed temperatos et sine detrimento dignationis et uerecundiae*; Matthew of Vendôme, *Ars* 2, 35 (ed. Munari, 3: 154) *varietas tollit fastidium, ad fastidii remediale blandimentum diversis partibus arma damus, et gravibus dulcia et seriis iocunda possunt interponi*; for a contrary view cf. Geoffrey of Vinsauf, *Poetria Nova* 1917-8 *Seria si tractes, sermo sit serius et mens / Seria*; *CNP* 341-2 *set non diffiteor michi ludicra sepe placere, / dummodo sint ludis seria mixta meis*; for the issue elsewhere in Neckam's poetry cf. Cropp 254; Mart., 8 *praefatio: quam* (sc. materiam) *quidem subinde aliqua iocorum mixtura variare temptavimus*; 7, 68, 2-3; Claudian, *Carm.* 22, 165 *seria quisque iocis...miscet.*

893. **Seria**: Neckam repeatedly raises the topic in the master text cf. *LSD* 3, 945 (p. 417W); 4, 252-69 (p. 426W), 366 (p. 428W), 389 (p. 429W), 515 (p. 432W), 10, 291-2 (p. 502W); *in Eccles.* f. 82ra *Cum seria proponuntur, grauitatem ipsorum ludicra repente orta relaxant. Non nunquam cum uerbum exhortacionis ad morum edificationem et fratrum consolationem proponitur, curiositas partes suas interponit*; f. 89ra *Urtice proxima sepe rosa est et uanitatibus sese associant seria. Ludicris sese intermiscent autentica, leuibus interseruntur grauia*; f. 91rb *Dum igitur seria pro-*

ponuntur aut ad fugam uitiorum impellentia auditores aut ad eleccionem honesti inuitantia, tedio afficiuntur auditores. Si uero uerba proferantur eleganti et uenusta compositione ordinata quibus nec uicia reprehendantur nec uirtutes commendentur, non replebitur auris auditu, **ioca**: cf. *NE* 25, 13 *Ista iocosa monent homines ne, dum mala vitant, / non provisa satis pessima sponte petant.*

894. **dico**: cf. *LSD* 4, 515 (p. 432 W) *Naturae ludos seria jure voco*; cf. Curtius, *European Literature*, 417-35, 478-9.

895. **Seria...repellunt**: cf. *LSD* 3, 945-6 (p. 417 W) *Non aures semper demulcent seria, saepe / Quae non delectant utilitate juvant.*

896. **Eacidem cithara**: i. e. Achilles cf. Ov., *Tr.* 4, 1, 15-6 *fertur...tristis Achilles / Haemonia curas attenuasse lyra*; *SD* 2, 1732 *Eacide Stacius arma dedit*; Stat., *Ach.* 1, 188-94; *in Eccles.* f. 154ra *Interdum pila lusit Achilles, interdum cytare fidibus canoris* [cf. *SD* 1, 897] *se recreauit.*

897-902. Cited in Hunt ed. Gibson, 49.

897. **crinitus Apollo**: Verg., *A.* 9, 638; cf. *LSD* 1, 530 (p. 369 W) *Tunc cithara mulcet superos crinitus Apollo*; Berry, 191, note 530.

898. **Uirgilii musa**: Alan of Lille, *Anticlaudianus* 1, 142 *Virgilii musa mendacia multa colorat*; **musa iocosa**: Ov., *Tr.* 2, 354; Mart., 2, 22, 2; cf. Schaller 85, note 43, for the Ovidian tag in Carolingian literature; *Cena Cypriani* 4, 12 (*MGH, P.L.* 4: 900); Baudri, *Carm.* 1, 29.

899-900. Ps.- Verg., *Copa* 37-8 (ed. Clausen, 82); cf. Matthew of Vendôme, *Tob.* 617 (ed. Munari, 2: 187) *«Pone merum, talos» caro noxia clamitat.*

901. **'Est et non'**: the initial words of the pseudo-Virgilian poem entitled *De est et non* (ed. Clausen, 173-4); 'Ver erat': the incipit of the poem *De rosis nascentibus* (ed. Clausen, 177-8); Mart., 14, 185 *Accipe facundi Culicem, studiose, Maronis, / ne nucibus positis ARMA VIRUMQUE legas.*

902. **'Iam nox hibernas'**: the incipit of the *Moretum* 1 (ed. Clausen, 158); cf. *LSD* 5, 613-4 (p. 454 W) *scripsit* (sc. Hildebertus) / *Sicut hyems laurum, Pergama flere nolo*; for allusions to the ps.- Vergilian *Ciris* and *Moretum* in *DNV*, see Ellis 1889, 160-1.

903. **Detinuit Sceuolam pila**: P. Mucius Scaevola, pontifex maximus and Roman consul in 133 BCE; cf. *RE* 16: 1, 425-8 s. v. *Mucius* no. 17; his expertise in ball-playing is noted by Cic., *De orat.* 1, 217, a work included by Neckam among curriculum authors listed in *SA* f. 48b: *Nam si ut quisque in aliqua arte et facultate excellens aliam quoque artem sibi adsumpserit, is perficiet ut, quod praeterea sciet, id eius, in quo excellet, pars quaedam esse videatur, licet ista ratione dicamus pila bene et duodecim scriptis ludere proprium esse iuris civilis, quoniam utrumque eorum P. Mucius optime fecerit*; cf. V. Max., 8, 8, 2 *Scaeuola autem ...optime pila lusisse traditur, quia uidelicet ad hoc diuerticulum animum suum forensibus ministeriis fatigatum transferre solebat;...ut enim in rebus seriis Scaeuolam, ita in lusibus hominem agebat, quem rerum natura continui laboris patientem esse non sinit*; Dyck 40-1 notes Valerius Maximus's practice of searching Cicero's philosophical works for examples to fill his rhetorical handbook; **circos cerne Catonem**: V. Max., 2, 10, 8, relates that at the Floralia in 55 BCE Cato left the theatre when he learned that his attendance inhibited the actors' license: *Quem abeuntem ingenti plausu populus prosecutus, priscum morem iocorum in scenam reuocauit*; cf. Mart., 1, 0, 15 *non intret Cato theatrum meum aut si intrauerit, spectet*, 20-1 *cur in theatrum, Cato severe, venisti? / An ideo tantum veneras, ut exires?* cf. Mart., 9, 28, 1-3; *LSD* 4, 566 (p. 433 W); cf. *in Eccles.* f. 154ra *Stultitiam simulare loco prudentia summa est. Cato Censorinus circum intrauit, set tempestiue* [tempestatiue MS] *recessit.*

904. **Minerua iocis**: cf. *in Eccles.* f. 154ra *...iocis quibusdam recreatur etiam sapientia.*

905. **regia maiestas**: cf. Claudian, *Carm.* 10, 198 *laxet terribiles maiestas regia fastus*; *LSD* 10, 315 (p. 503W); *CNP* 225; *SD* 1, 944 *maiestas regia*; *SD* 2, 229-30 *Regia maiestas humane nobilitatis / In facie multo digna fauore sedet*; *regia* can also qualify *sceptra* cf. Geoffrey of Monmouth, *Vita Merlini* 229-31 *nec vivere more ferino / velle sub arboribus dum regia sceptra tenere / posset*; Baudri, *Carm.* 134, 166.

906. **ludicra cano**: cf. Hor., *Ep.* 1, 1, 10; Verg., *E.* 7, 17; *LSD* 2, 697-8 (pp. 388-9W) *Ludit in effectu vario sapientia summa; / Fas erat ut ludat nostra Thalia semel*, 4, 252 (p. 426W) *En dum naturae considero ludicra, ludos / Ejus maturos seria jure voco*, *CNP* 341 *set non diffiteor michi ludicra sepe placere*, 1629-30 (ed. Walther 1962, 42) *deliqui ludicra uana / edens, delirus ridiculusque senex*; *SD* 1, 1015-20; but cf. Marbod, *De decem cap.* 1, 16-7 (ed. Leotta, 62) *Ergo propositum mihi sit neque ludicra quaedam / Scribere.*

908. **uolucrum...nescia iuris**: cf. Alan of Lille, *De planctu*, ed. Häring, 816, 192 *Illic uespertilio, auis hermafroditica,...locum inter auiculas obtinebat.*

909. **lusit** (sc. Natura): medieval authors developed the idea of *natura ludens* to explain anomalies or singularities in the physical world as a jest; the bat is both bird and a quadruped; it flies with the aid of a membraneous wing and, unlike other birds, it has teeth; cf. *DNR* 2, 129 (p. 210W) *Simia...naturae ludentis opus*; *SD* 1, 221 *ridet Natura*; *Poems* 1, 15 (ed. Esposito, 453) *Cum gaudet uenter ludit natura potenter*, Gerald of Wales, *Topographia Hibernica*, 1, 16 (ed. Dimock, 49) *naturae ludentis opera contulit admiranda* (on the two different feet of the osprey); Alan of Lille, *De planctu*, ed. Häring, 815, 168 *Illic noctua tante deformitatis sterquilinio sordescebat, ut in eius formatione Naturam fuisse crederes sompnolentam*, **uesperte**: = *uespertine* cf. *Novale* 237 (ed. Haye, 426) *Non vespertilio vesperte blacterat hora*, where, however, the glossator explains *vesperte* as *dee vespertine*; *uesperta* is unattested in CL; for *uespertilio* etymologically linked to *uesper* cf. Isid., *Orig.* 12, 7, 36 *Vespertilio...nomen accepit, eo quod lucem fugiens crepusculo vespertino circumvolet*; Hugh of St Victor, *De bestiis* 3, 34 (*MPL* 177: 96c) *Vespertilio animal ignobile a vespere nomen sumpsit*, *Ysopet* 45, 3 *Linquit aues que sumit auis de uespere nomen*; *NE* 2, 11-2 *...dum vespere pausant, / antique fraudis conscius ipse* (sc. uespertilio) *fugit.*

910. **uolucrem...genus**: cf. McCulloch 94; cf. Ov., *Fast.* 4, 99,

911. **girando circinat auras**: *LSD* 2, 769 (p. 390W); cf. Ov., *Met.* 2, 721; *CNP* 1421.

913. **Adde quod**: on the use of this phrase in catalogues of didactic material, see Haye 1997, 205; cf. *Poems* 3, 27 (ed. Walther 1965, 118) *Adde, quod actis est precellere gloria*, Walther notes seventeen instances of *Adde quod* in the *LSD*; cf. *SD* 1, 1241, 1433; 2. 585, 1063, 1309; Ov., *Ep.* 17, 201; Claudian, *Carm.* 18, 187.

915. **pennis aut plumis...carebit**: cf. Symphosius, *Aenig.* 28, 2 (*Anth.* ed. Buecheler, 1: 1, 229) (Vespertilio) *Pluma mihi non est, cum sit mihi pinna volantis.*

916. **bis geminos...pedes**: cf. Isid., *Orig.* 12, 7, 36 *specie quoque volatilis simul et quadrupes, quod in aliis avibus reperiri non solet*; cf. *SD* 1, 1128; *NE* 2, 1-3 *Quadrupedes et aves gererent dum bella furentes / et modo quadrupedes, nunc fugerent volucres, / versutus vespertilio se iunxit utrisque / ....*

917. **Soricis**: cf. Isid., *Orig.* 12, 7, 36 *animal murium simile.*

918. **Vt pisces**: the sawfish, for instance.

919. **Dentibus ornatus**: cf. Plin., *Nat.* 11, 37, 164 (ed. Ian, 2: 335) *volucrum nulli dentes praeter vespertilionem.*

920. **Aures**: cf. *NE* 2, 5 *Auribus...se quadrupedem simulabat, /* (sc. uespertilio).

921. **mentitur ypocrisis**: cf. *DNR* 2, 129 (p. 210W) *Nonne...hypocrisis mendax religionem veram in multis mentitur?*

924. **terrena sapit**: cf. Phil 3, 19 *et gloria in confusione ipsorum, qui terrena sapiunt; SD* 1, 978.

928. **cinico dente**: cf. *LSD* 4, 519 (p. 432W) *Vis carmen cynico carpere dente meum?*; *SD* 1, 1177; *CNP* 1589 *penetrat uix dente canino / quicquam.*

929. **Arrectas...aures**: Verg., *A.* 12, 618; Claudian, *Carm.* 1, 210 *Adrectis auribus.*

931-64. *The lion*

931. **ueniam**: cf. Plin., *Nat.* 8, 16, 48 (ed. Ian, 2: 94); Isid., *Orig.* 12, 2, 4, 6; *DNR* 2, 148-9 (pp. 227-31W); *LSD* 9, 11-46 (pp. 486-7W); *NE* 41, 19-20 *Supplicibus uerbis flexus lacrimisque rogantis, / Nobilis optatam mox leo dat ueniam;* Lawn, *Salern. Questions*, 188, note 138; 164, 138 *Cur leo prostratis parcens instantibus instet?*

931. cf. Isid., *Orig.* 12, 2, 6 *Prostratis...parcunt; DNR* 2, 148 (pp. 228-9W) *Notum est autem quod «Parcere subjectis scit nobilis ira leonis.»...Sic et regia nobilitas supplicibus veniam erogat; NP* 76 *sternitque rebelles; LSD* 9, 31 (p. 485W) *Parcere supplicibus...gaudet;* **arcens**: cf. *SD* 1, 1225.

932. **uincit nobilitate**: cf. *NE* 41, 16 *qui* (sc. leo) *cunctas superas nobilitate feras;* Isid., *Orig.* 12, 2, 3; **leo**: The lion's attributes include sparing the defeated, sleeping with its eyes open, and reviving its dead cubs by breathing new life into them. However, the noise of wheels and the sight of a white cock terrify him. It has the ability to capture its prey by describing with its tail a circle on the ground that traps them cf. McCulloch 137-40.

935. For the thought cf. Alcuin, *Carm.* 85, 5, 8 (*MGH, P. L* 1: 304) *Vincere nos ipsos non est victoria parva.*

936. **uinci...uincere**: cf. Mart., 14, 213, 1; Prosper, *De providentia divina* 233 (*MPL* 51: 622c) *Est etenim ambarum vinci, est et vincere posse;* **sic uinci**: cf. *SD* 1, 937.

938. **uictor ero**: cf. *Ysopet* 55, 14 *Argum si poteris uincere, uictor eris.*

939. **Describit...circum**: cf. *SD* 2, 439 *Circum describit florum iocunda uenustas;* **cauda...minaci**: *SD* 2, 1105-6 *caudaque minaci / Exurgens.*

939-40. cf. *DNR* 2, 148 (p. 229W); *Prose Salern. Questions* C 23 (ed. Lawn, 334, 22-3, 26-8) *Cur si leo circumvenerit tractu caude, alia animalia non audent transire circulum? Responsio: ...Odorantes igitur bestie leonis vestigia, timentes eum prius adesse, ferocitatis ipsius recordantes, non audent transire, et videntes non moventur.*

941. **Luminibus...uigilans**: cf. Ov., *Met.* 15, 101 *uigilans oculis;* **Luminibus...apertis**: cf. Henkel 165; *Physiologus Lat.* 1, 10 (ed. Carmody, 11) *Secunda natura leonis: cum dormierit, oculi eius uigilant, aperti enim sunt; Theobaldi Physiologus* (ed. Eden, 26, 9); Hildebert, *Physiologus MPL* 171: 1217c; *DNR* 2, 148 (p. 227W) *Leo dormiens apertos habet oculos; LSD* 10, 45 (p. 487W); cf. Orbán, 71, note 80).

942. **Erroremque suum...habere**: cf. Ov., *Fast.* 1, 32 *erroremque suum...habet.*

945. **Rugitu**: cf. Henkel 166; Isid., *Orig.* 12, 2, 5; *Physiologus Lat.* 1, 14-5 (ed. Carmody, 11-2); *Theobaldi Physiologus* 7 (ed. Eden, 26); Hildebert, *Physiologus MPL* 171: 1217b; *DNR* 2, 148 (p. 228W) *Leo...rugitu suo catulum suum excitat; LSD* 9, 35-6 (p. 486W); Orbán, 71, notes 88-90; Lawn, *Salern. Questions*, 183, note 76; Urso, *De commixtionibus elem.* 5, 1 (ed. Stürner, 129) *effectu vero coniunctionis trium tantum elementorum natura mota trium temporum*

spatio semel in composito suam actionem exercet. Inde est, quod fetus leonis non animatus exortus tertio die natiuitatis per naturam patris tamen cooperante rugitu vivificatur, **patris proles**: cf. Matthew of Vendôme, *Tob.* 1057-8 (ed. Munari, 2: 206) *proles / Patris amore gemit.*

946. **leo fis**: cf. Mart., 12, 92, 4 *dic mihi, si fias tu leo, qualis eris?*; Marbod, *Carm.* 3, 5-8 (ed. Bulst, 189); Giovanni Orlandi *per litt.* suggests reading **sis** in view of the preceding **habeto** cf. *SD* 1, 721 *Sis philomena*; **formaque iusticie:** cf. *SD* 1, 1169.

947. **tutum**: supply *sit.*

949. **elacio ceca**: *NA* 5, 3 (ed. Hervieux, 3: 466) *Euehit in preceps stultos elacio ceca*

949-50. **strepitus rede**: cf. Isid., *Orig.* 12, 2, 4 *Rotarum timent strepitus; DNR* 2, 149 (p. 231 W) *Cantus gallinaceorum et rotarum timent strepitus, et ignem magis; LSD* 9, 21-2 (p. 486 W); *NP* 69.

951. **Pallida mors**: Hor., *C.* 1, 4, 13; Walther, *Prov.* 20578; *LSD* 2, 443 (p. 383 W); 3, 23 (p. 395 W); *SD* 2, 1358 *Sic et pallida mors, nox quoque ceca datur, Poems* 1, 137 (ed. Walther, 1965, 115) *mors astat pallida*; **instans:** cf. *Poems* 6, 7 (ed. Walther 1965, 123) *Insta! mors instat.*

951-2. **mors... / Pre foribus clamat**: cf. *Poems* 448 (ed. Walther 1962, 38) *Pre foribus clamat mors: vigilate viri!*

952. **clamat..:time**: cf. *LSD* 3, 340 (p. 402 W); Hildebert, *Carm. min.* 55, 112 *postquam clamas 'exi foras.'*.

953. **albus...gallus**: cf. *NP* 68 (ed. Orbán, 27) *candentem...gallum*; cf. Rowland in Goosens 1981, 340-1, 352; *Comparatio galli cum presbitero* stanza 6, 4; 7a, 1-4 (ed. Novati, 479 and note 2); **gallus terroris ymago**: cf. Plin., *Nat.* 10, 21, 47 (ed. Ian, 2: 233) *itaque terrori sunt* (sc. galli) *etiam leonibus....*

954. **'defuncti, surgite'**: cf. 1 Cor 15, 52.

955. **Verbere...caude**: Luc., 1, 208 *se saeuae stimulauit* (sc. leo) *uerbere caudae*; Lawn, *Salern. Questions*, 164, 138-9 *Cur leo... / Exacuatque suas cum caude motibus iras?*

961. **Febricitat**: cf. *DNR* 2, 148 (p. 228 W) *in aestate qualibet febricitat, in hiemem sanus esse uidetur; LSD* 9, 17 (p. 486 W) *aestu febrili quauis aestate laborat.*

961-62. **Tempore successus**: cf. *DNR* 2, 148 (p. 228 W) *Sic et superbus in diebus prosperitatis impatientia vexatur.*

963. **nubila... / Tempora**: Ov., *Tr.* 1, 1, 40 *nubila sunt subitis pectora nostra malis*; 1, 9a, 6; *SD* 1, 1446 *Seu sors nubila sit.*

965-86. *The elephant*

965. **elephas**: The elephant, lacking joints, is unable to get up once it has fallen. Consequently, it sleeps leaning against a tree for support. The hunter weakens the tree by partially cutting through it, so that when the elephant rests against it, both fall to the ground. Unable to rise, the elephant is lifted with the help of a young elephant cf. McCulloch 115-9; Hassig 129-44; **Nescius...membra**: cf. Henkel 178-9; Cass., *Var.* 10, 30 (ed. Å. J. Fridh, *CCSL* 96: 412, 10-23); *LSD* 9, 47 (p. 487 W) *Artus non flectit elephas; Theobaldi Physiologus* 9 (ed. Eden, 64) *non habet* (sc. elephas), *ut surgat, quia nunquam crura recurvat* (Lawn, *Salern. Questions*, 41, dates this work to c. 1100); *DNR* 2, 143-4 (pp. 222-5 W); *LSD* 9, 47-90 (pp. 487-8 W); *NP* 138 (ed. Orbán, 29); Druce 1919, 28-9; **potestas**: with this moralization cf. *SD* 1, 1144-6.

967-72. cf. *Theobaldi Physiologus* 11-6 (ed. Eden, 64) *Cum vult pausare vel somno se recreare, / Incumbit ligno arboris exiguo, / Quam notat atque secat venator et obice celat / Clamque sedens spectat, dum requiem repetat. / Ille velut quondam securus ad arboris umbram / Cum venit, incumbit cumque ruente ruit; LSD* 9, 49 (p. 487W).

968. **stando**: cf. Aldhelm, *Enig.* 96, 16 (*MGH, AA* 15: 143) (Elefans) *Quin potius vitam compellor degere stando.*

969. **barrus**: cf. Isid., *Orig.* 12, 2, 14 *Apud Indos...a voce barro vocatur* (sc. elephas).

970. **Mollis**: the epithet is suitable for a tree (*arbor* in 969) in which rest is thought to reside cf. Verg., *G.* 2, 470 *mollesque sub arbore somni non absunt;* 3, 435 *mollis...somnos.*

971. **succidit...robur**: cf. *LSD* 9, 49 (p. 487W) *succiso robore; SD* 1, 977 *robur succidit.*

971. **robur...uenator**: cf. *NP* 140 (ed. Orbán, 29) *Quam serrat prudens eboris venator amore.*

973. **Surgere...nequid**: cf. *DNR* 2, 143 (p. 222W) *...tanto pondere supinatus nequit propriis viribus surgere...Humano solatio consurgit, cujus arte jacuit,* p. 224W *per se...resurgere non potest;* Hildebert, *Physiologus MPL* 171: 1222c; *LSD* 9, 47-8 (p. 487W) *casus ei, sum / Desit subsidium, perniciosus erit; NP* 144-5 (ed. Orbán, 29); **ui...arte**: cf. *NE* 41, 23 *quem cum non posset nec vi superare nec arte /* ....

974. **domino**: cf. *DNR* 2, 143 (p. 222W) *In magistrum quippe recipit quem sibi subvenisse cognoscit.*

975. **Lucrum uenatur**: *LSD* 3, 179 (p. 399W); cf. 3, 523 (p. 407W) *lucri venator.*

978. **nescia stare**: cf. Verg., *G.* 3, 84 *stare loco nescit.*

979. **casus**: in the literal sense «falling» and the figurative sense of «chance»; cf. the same pun on *casus* in Juv. 3, 273.

984. **Ipsius**: i. e. *gratie.*

985. **Augustum**: the Roman emperor, Augustus cf. *LSD* 5, 209 (p. 445W) *Salvator voluit sub tanto principe nasci; Scholia in Horatium* ed. Botschuyver, 4: 8, 11-4 *Hoc hic intellegitur dictum de Augusto, sed in veritate quamquam nescienter loquebantur et quasi prophetabant de Christo. qui in tempore Augusti natus fuit....;* **torue**: cf. Sedulius Scottus, *In Donati artem maiorem* ed. B. Löfstedt, *CCCM* 40C: 338, 14 *Nam nomen neutri generis posuit pro aduerbio quod est torue id est terribiliter;* **cernit**: sc. gratia; **directo sydere**: in classical Roman times, a star was thought to be most favourable when it shone from directly above.

986. **Neronis**: cf. Luc., 1, 55 *obliquo sidere Romam* [of Nero].

987-92. The camel

987. **Gibbosam**: see Matthew of Vendôme, *Ars* 2, 20 (ed. Munari, 3: 143) for comments on adjectives in *-osus; DNR* 2, 141-2 (pp. 221-2W); *LSD* 9, 109-12 (p. 488W); **camelo**: cf. McCulloch 101-2.

988. **Plus...aqua**: When camels do not have muddy water available, they produce it by stirring up clear water with their hooves cf. *DNR* 2, 142 (p. 222W) *...nisi coenosior liquor fuerit, ipsi assidua proculcatione limum excitant ut turbidetur, LSD* 9, 111-2 (p. 488W); **turbat aqua**: cf. Hor., *S.* 1, 1, 60 *turbatam...aquam; NE* 10, 3 «*Cur michi, dum biberem, turbasti, perfide, rivum?*»

992. **recti tramitis...iter**: cf. *LSD* 9, 74 (p. 487W) *recto tramite...iter*, *NA* 3, 8; Orchard 216-7; *SD* 1, 1111.

993-96. *The fox*

993. **uulpis**: cf. McCulloch 119-29; Hassig 62-71; **amfractus...recuruos**: because *uulpis* was thought to derive from *uolupes*, the fox never travels in a straight line cf. Isid., *Orig.* 12, 2, 29 *numquam rectis itineribus, sed tortuosis anfractibus currit, fraudulentum animal insidiisque decipiens*; *DNR* 2, 125 (p. 204W); *NP* 409 (ed. Orbán, 37); Claudian, *Carm.* 1, 105 *curuis anfractibus*; **uulpis astuta**: cf. Hor., *S.* 2, 3, 186; Avianus 6, 9 *Tunc uulpes pecudum ridens astuta quietem....*

994. **taxo**: cf. *DNR* 2, 127 (p. 207W) relates how the fox induces the badger to leave his underground house; *LSD* 9, 163-4 (p. 490W).

995. **heresim**: On the fox's association with heresy and the broad definition of that term, see Hassig 67.

996. **fraus aliena rapit**: cf. *DNR* 2, 127 (p. 207W) *Sic sic multi sunt qui turpiter res alienas invadunt.*

997-1008. *The hare*

997. **Forme ...leporis conplexio**: on the hare's constitution cf. *LSD* 4, 764-7 (p. 438W); Jacquart, 415 and note 30, identifies Constantine (*Pantegni: Theorica* 1, 6) as the first to use the word *commixtio* in discussing the question of temperament: *Illud autem complexionem esse dicimus quod ex elementorum commixtione conficitur*, cf. Jacquart 1984; Urso, *Aphorismi* Glosula 2 (ed. Creutz, 22) *Patet ratione juridica, quod omnis actio tripliciter variatur, scilicet secundum naturam, vel complexionem rei agentis et secundum formam eiusdem variam et secundum diversitatem rei patientis*, Glosula 6 (ed. Creutz, 28-9) *Parva vero...sunt habilia ut lepus, canis, simia et his similia, nisi membrorum gravitate...vel inflexibilitate praepediantur*, Prose Salern. *Questions* P 117 (ed. Lawn, 250, 7-10) *Quare lepus...pre ceteris animalibus tam cito currit? Responsio. Animalium quedam sunt habilia ad cursum et velocia per complexionem, ut leo et similia; quedam pro habilitate instrumentorum, quamvis complexio discordet, ut lepus*; *DNR* 2, 134 (pp. 215-6W); *LSD* 9, 151-2 (p. 489W) *Tardos efficeret lepores complexio, si non / Formula membrorum cursibus apta foret.*

999. **colere** = *cholere* cf. *SD* 1, 1103, 1107; **timor**: cf. *DNR* 2, 134 (p. 216W); Lawn, *Salern. Questions*, 172, 47 *timidi leporis que causa timorem / Aumentet...?*, 198, note 47; *NE* 34, 4 (ed. Hervieux, 2: 410); see Diekstra 153 for the theory of the four elements applied to stories about the lion, dog and the cock in the *DNR*; **pedibus... / Addidit**: Verg., *A.* 8, 224; Walther, *Prov.* 21132.

1000. **celerem...fugam**: cf. *LSD* 4, 766 (p. 438W) *Huic* (sc. lepori) *...dat celerem membrorum formula sic sic / Depositis membris cum levitate fugam*, Hor., *C.* 2, 7, 9; **celerem cogit inire fugam**: cf. *SD* 2, 1470 *celerem cepit inire fugam* (sc. Arrius), 1608 *Vernantesque fugam iussit inire rosas*; *NA* 5, 10 *Terror uelocem iussit inire fugam*, Isid., *Orig.* 12, 1, 23.

1001. **Vrgens articulus**: cf. *SD* 2, 841 *Vrgens articulus hunc errorem reuocabit*, on the symbolism of the hare in the scientific and popular tradition, see Lauzi 539-46; 549 for its metaphorical associations.

1003. **natura...te reddit**: cf. *Novale* 449 (ed. Haye, 435) *Ergo natura te reddit iure nocentem*; Dracontius, *De laudibus Dei* 1, 680 (*MGH, AA* 14: 60-2) *redditque... / depositum natura suum.*

1007. **Infirme carni**: cf. Mt 26, 41 *spiritus quidem promptus est, caro autem infirma.*

1008. **prebet…opem**: cf. *SD* 1, 1029, 1302.

1009-66. *The section on the sawfish leads to reflections on composition, literary borrowing and morals*

1009. **Perplicito**: not attested in CL; *OLD* lists *perplicatus* «tangled, intertwined»; **serre**: Neckam omits all mention of the usual story of the sawfish's race against a ship, after which it lowers its wings and allows itself to be carried back out to sea cf. McCulloch 163-5; Henkel 180-1; the sawfish was depicted either as a winged dog or as a flying fish or siren; cf. McCulloch Plate VII for an illustration of a sawfish in flight over a boat; Clark 49, Figure 2, 5, reproduces a similar drawing from the Harvard Bestiary; Isid., *Orig.* 12, 6, 16 *Serra nuncupata, quia serratam cristam habet*; cf. Geoffrey of Monmouth, *Vita Merlini* 844-6.

1010. **fruticum densa corona**: for an illustration of the foliage on the sawfish's tail, see figure 13, facing p. 23, in Druce 1918-19; Muratova in Goosens 1981, 237 and note 53; *SD* 1, 1013 *fruticum…corona*; Ov., *Met.* 1, 122 *densi frutices.*

1011. **superbe**: cf. *Physiologus Lat.* IV, 9 (ed. Carmody, 15); Druce 1918-19, 29-32, lists moralizations of the sawfish from Latin and vernacular sources.

1014. **sollicitudo uigil**: cf. *SD* 2, 202 *Inpendit studiis sollicitudo uigil.*

1015. **Ludus…lasciuia**: cf. Hor., *Ep.* 2, 2, 214-6; *SD* 1, 1009.

1017. **Ludum…iuuenis**: cf. Mart., 9, 26, 10 *lascivum iuvenis cum tibi lusit opus*; **lasciua senectus / Est monstrum**: cf. Marbod, 35-6 (ed. Bulst, 297-8) *Lasciuum pectus non debet habere senectus / Et contemptibilis solet esse libido senilis*; Matthew of Vendôme, *Tob.* 795 (ed. Munari, 2: 195) *Hec tria displiceant: lasciva senecta*; in *Eccles.* f. 160vb *Adolescentia enim uoluptuosa, uana est. Set o dolor! o dedecus! cum adolescentiam uanam monstruosa sequitur senectus. Aliquem habet colorem excusationis iuuentus illecebris exposita carnalibus. Senectus autem lasciua monstrum est*; *CNP* 1001 *par monstro senium reddit morosa iuuentus*; Claudian, *Carm.* 20, 327 *lascivique senes.*

1017. **iuuenis**: cf. Marbod, *De decem cap.* 1, 47-50 (ed. Leotta, 69) *Praeterea iuvenem cantare iocosa decebat, / Quod manifesta seni ratio docet esse negatum, / Cuius morali condiri verba sapore / Convenit et vitiis obsistere fronte severa.*

1018. **turpe seni**: Maximianus 1, 101; cf. Ov., *Am.* 1, 9, 4 *turpe senex miles, turpe senilis amor.*

1019. **Lusimus…ludum**: cf. Hor., *Ep.* 1, 14, 36 *nec lusisse pudet, sed non incidere lusum* [cited Matthew of Vendôme, *Ars* 1, 48 (ed. Munari, 3: 64]; Peter of Blois, *Carm.* 2, 2, 1, 1-4 *Non te lusisse pudeat, / set ludum non incidere / et, que lusisti temere, / ad uite frugem uertere*; 4, 11, 1, 3-4; cf. *LSD* 2, 97-8 (p. 375W), 697-8 (p. 389W); *Carmina Burana* 75, 1, 5-6 (ed. Hilka, 1: 2, 48) *res est apta senectuti / seriis intendere.*

1022. **querens quem uoret**: cf. 1 Pt 5, 8.

1024. **sceptum**: = *coeptum*; **sceptum…opus**: Ov., *Fast.* 4, 16 *et 'coeptum perfice' dixit* «opus».

1025-26. **Utilis est aliis**: *LSD* 3, 234 (p. 400W); in another context Neckam wrote: *Set scribens aliis scribo michi. Disco docendo; Sic michi sic aliis vtilis esse uolo* cf. **C** f. 70bis v; **Utilis… / Utilis**: cf. Ov., *Fast.* 6, 224 *utilis et nuptis, utilis esse viris.*

1026. **Utilis...sibi**: *LSD* 6, 222 (p. 468W).

1027. **Materialis**: see Matthew of Vendôme, *Ars* 2, 15-9 (ed. Munari, 1: 140-3) for comments on adjectives in -*alis*; **polit**: cf. Baudri, *Carm*. 92, 31-2 *limas parat ad poliendum; hic polit, hic acuit....*

1031. **comes uite**: cf. Aldhelm, *Enig.* 14, 3 (*MGH, AA* 15: 104) *Cum mihi vita comes fuerit nihil aurea forma.*

1032. **Auctori**: the word includes the sense of God, the author of the book of nature cf. Marbod, *Carm.varia MPL* 171: 1717b *Invidet auctori, cuius subservit honori / Bruma rigens, aestas, autumnus, veris honestas.*

1033. **cos...ferrum**: cf. Hor., *Ars* 304-5; *LSD* 3, 233 (p. 400W) *Ferrum cos acuit;* for *quos = cos* cf. John of Garland, *Dictionarius*, ed. Wright, 127 *Coquinarii quocunt* [= cocunt] *et vertunt in verubus colurnis anseres.*

1035. **Lima mordaci...utor**: cf. Ov., *Pont.* 1, 5, 19 *scilicet incipiam lima mordacius uti.*

1035-66. Cited in Hunt ed. Gibson 16-7.

1037. **lima iudiciali**: cf. Baudri, *Carm.* 131, 13 *Et sua complacuit sententia iudicialis.*

1038. **Cum uerbis mores**: cf. *SD* 2, 1533-6 *Si uicium lingue purgas, purgare memento / Cum lingua uicium pectoris atque manus. / Barbariem uita sermonis cum uiciorum / Barbarie, ne mens barbara fiat.*

1039. **corripio mores**: cf. *LSD* 2, 839 (p. 392W) *Corripit errantes* (sc. gallus); **emendo**: in a moral sense also.

1040. **pingo uerba:** cf. Camargo 1992, 183, 1 <*F*>*loribus rethoricis uerba non facile depinguntur;* Matthew of Vendôme, *Tob.* 2161-2 (ed. Munari, 2: 252) *Vera loquens non pingo metrum, ne picta supellex / Carminis incurrat ambitionis onus,* 2165 *Vera negant pingi, quia vera relatio nescit, / Nescit adulari floridiore sono.*

1041. **adapto**: cf. Camargo 1992, 202, 318-9 «*Iste nouit dictiones dictionibus cum quodam decenti matrimonio adaptare*».

1042. **cum faleris uerba**: cf. *LSD* 6, 363 (p. 472W) *Verborum phaleras...relinquo;* 10, 309 (p. 503W) *Spretis verborum phaleris devotio simplex, / Sermonem purae simplicitatis amat;* Camargo 1992, 202, 329-30 «*Est* <*huic*> *in promptu uerba quelibet inaurare,* <*falerare,*> *pingere, purpurare*»; Marbod, *De decem cap.* 1, 52-3 (ed. Leotta, 70) *Iam nunc experiar scripturus seria verbis / Non exquisitis sed nec trivialibus uti.* For a near-contemporary debate about words (Greek, unusual, common, abstract, modern, novel) between Adam of Petit-Pont and his critics, see Lendinara 164.; cf. 166, note 28, where she cites an *accessus* to Adam's *Oratio* in Berlin, Staatsbibliothek Preussischer Kulturbesitz, MS lat. 607: *Quamvis Moyses perceperat quo[modo] in carminibus verba falerata .i. ornata et exotica...eantur, magister Adam de parvo Ponte per verba aliquantulum inusitata proponit se scribere;* cf. William of Malmesbury, *De gestis* (ed. Hamilton, 344) on Aldhelm's style:...*nec nisi perraro et necessario verba ponit exotica.*

1043. **Barbariem...uerborum**: the grammarian traditionally warned against defects, such as barbarisms and solecisms cf. S. Reynolds, *Medieval Reading*, 22, 122; a barbarism was an error within a word resulting from removing, adding, replacing or transferring a syllable or letter (Donatus, *Barbarismus* [ed. L. Holtz, 653] *una pars orationis uitiosa in communi sermone*); cf. *SD* 1, 1051; 2, 1509-10 *Soloes deuito querelam / Et uicium fugio, barbara lingua, tuum,* 1535 *Barbariem uita sermonis;* cf. Neckam's apology for using the Irish names of rivers at *LSD* 3, 941 (p. 417W) *barbaries sibi barbara nomina fingit;* Mart., 1, 65, 1 *barbara uerba* [cf.

Lawrence of Durham, *Dialogi* 3, 331 *Barbariem biberas, et barbara verba resudas*]; *CP* ff. 150va-51ra discusses the fours kinds of *barbarismus*; cf. Matthew of Vendôme, *Tob.* 2159 (ed. Munari, 2: 252) *Verborum placeat macies, infantia metri / Floris egens, carens scemate, nuda tropis*, **turgida** cf. *DNR* 2, 174 (p. 311W) *Quid vanius quam verbis ampullosis, quae jam abierunt in desuetudinem, operosam diligentiam impendere?*

1044. **sedent animo**: Cambridge, UL, Ll. 1. 14, f. 49r lists as synonymous phrases: *Apparet mihi / Liquet mihi / Sedet animo / Persuasum est*; cf. *SD* 2, 1532 *Turpia femineo turpius ore sedent*; **publica uerba**: cf. Donatus, *Vita Virgilii* 180-3 *novae cacozeliae repertorem, non tumidae* [cf. *SD* 1, 1043 *turgida*] *nec exilis, sed ex communibus verbis, atque ideo latentis*; Lyne 1-4, 7-13, discusses the views of ancient theorists about the use of ordinary language or common words in poetry; Haye 1997, 86, notes that the prologues to didactic works draw attention to the importance of adopting a low style with lucid language to ensure quick comprehension of the contents; cf. Ov., *Ars* 1, 144 *et moueant primos publica uerba sonos*; Sen., *Ep.* 79, 6 (ed. L. Reynolds, 1: 257 [Oxford, 1965])) *Praeterea condicio optima est ultimi: parata verba invenit, quae aliter instructa novam faciem habent. Nec illis manus inicit tamquam alienis; sunt enim publica.*

1045. **Scinthasis**: = *synthesis*: cf. *SD* 2, 1511-2 *Scribendi michi lex, intellectus michi seruit; / Hunc finem merito sinthasis omnis habet*; *CP* f. 153rb; **nubat**: cf. Matthew of Vendôme, *Ars* 1, 1 (ed. Munari, 3: 43-4) *Versus est metrica oratio succincte et clausulatim progrediens venusto verborum matrimonio...*; **mobile fixo**: cf. Matthew of Vendôme, *Ep.* 1, 5, 32 (ed. Munari, 2: 94); *Doctrinale* 1531 *iungere non poterit coniunctio mobile fixo*; 250, 1434; *NG* L-M, 665 s. v. *mobile* D) gramm. 1) declinable 2) *nomen mobile* cites Conrad of Hirsau, *Didasc.* p. 31, 4 *ut his partibus* (sc. orationis)*...fixis, mobilibus, comparativis assuescerent.*

1046. **materies**: cf. Ov., *Am.* 1, 1, 2 *materia conveniente modis*; *Tr.* 5, 1, 6 *materiae scripto conveniente suae.*

1047. **sociata marito**: cf. *Anth.* 387, 2 (ed. Buecheler, 2: 1, 180); a fanciful elaboration of Horace's remarks about combining words to produce a poetic effect cf. Hor., *Ars* 46-8.

1049-50. **coniugium**: for marriage as a metaphor in the language of criticism cf. Peter of Blois, *Libellus*, ed. Camargo, 50, 177-8 *Propria translacio...est quando quodam matrimonio verborum dic*ciones sibi invicem *maritantur*; Carmargo 1992, 191, 136-8; 201, 317-9; Hor., *Ars* 45-8 *Hoc amet, hoc spernat promissi carminis auctor / in verbis etiam tenuis cautusque serendis. dixeris egregie...*; Lyne, 3-4, explains what happens in «combination».

1051. **barbariem uiciorum**: cf. Baudri, *Carm.* 99, 161 *Barbaries siquidem uiciorum mox inolescit*; 134, 1243 *Barbariem siquidem linguam dicit uiciatam*; Cambridge, UL, Ll. 1. 14, f. 45v, glosses *barbarismus* with *Coruptus sermo* and *barbaralexis* with *Barbara diccio*; on the distinction between the grammatical faults of *barbarismi* and *soloecismi* (cf. *SD* 1, 1052), see S. Reynolds, *Medieval Reading*, 22 and note 25.

1052. **uicium soloes**: a solecism occurs in any phrase that contravenes the rule of grammar: cf. Donatus, *Barbarismus* ed. L. Holtz, 655; *Doctrinale* 2375-6 *est soloëcismus incongrua copula vocum / ut, si dicatur, vir bellica, sponsa pudicus*; *SD* 2, 1509-10 (Grammatica speaks) *Soloes deuito querelam / Et uicium fugio, barbara lingua, tuum* [cf. *Doctrinale* 2369-70]; 1531 *num uicium Soloes purgare teneris?*; John of Salisbury, *Enthet. maior* 137 (ed. van Laarhoven, 1: 115) *admittit soloen, sumit quod barbarus affert*; *Novale*, 114-5 (ed. Haye, 420) *In reliquis horis est dictio plena pudoris / Vel soloe – moris vicii vel deterioris.*

1053-54. **mores / Uix sub iudicium conuoco, uerba uoco**: Ov., *Pont.* 1, 5, 20 *et sub iudicium singula verba vocem.*

1055. **studiis**: cf. *LSD* 5, 335-6 (p. 448W) *libros / Diligo; in Eccles.* f. 150rb *Dulcescit michi*, *fateor, librorum inspectio, set utinam michi dulcescat orandi studium!* **feliciter**: construe with *dandum*; cf. Baudri, *Carm.* 99, 153-4 *Sed malo libris incumbere carminibusque / Quam par iumentis ducere tempus iners.*

1056. **dilato...breuianda**: allusions to the rhetorical tropes *amplificatio* and *abbreuiatio.*

1057. **Dissimulo, sileo**: cf. Mart., 11, 108, 4 *taces dissimulasque?*

1057-58 **corripienda / Producens**: witty use of verbs that refer to the shortening and lengthening of syllables in metrics as well as to the process of revision cf. *SD* 1, 1039 *Corripio mores*; the verbs pick up ideas inherent in *dilato* and *brevianda* (1056); cf. *Doctrinale* 2416.

1059. **carpens aliena** (sc. carmina): Neckam criticized (*OLD* s. v. *carpo* 9b) other writers' efforts, even as he culled (*OLD* 4) excerpts from the texts he read for possible future use; Baudri, *Carm.* 99, 178; 126, 71-2 *Nec michi librorum nec desit copia carte / Excerpamque legens, carta quod excipiat*; see M. Carruthers, *The Book of Memory*, 214, who discusses the intimate connection between reading and composing for medieval writers.

1060. **nobile...opus**: Mart., 9, 93, 6 *sacrae nobile gentis opus*; cf. note on *SD* 1, 2.

1062. **apposite dicta**: cf. *SD* 2, 158 *Apposite dicit* (sc. rethorica); *Poems* 4, 53 (ed. Esposito, 455) *Apposite dicis, allegas, Bache, peroras.*

1064. **furtim...insero multa**: a reference to the literary grafting of material borrowed from numerous authors [cf. Isid., *Orig.* 10, 44 *Conpilator...aliena dicta suis praemiscet*]; Neckam sometimes names the source text e. g. *Uirgilii musa* (898), *Nasone docente* (1405); cf. Sen., *Suas.* 3, 7 (ed. Winterbottom, 2: 554) on Ovid's use of Virgilian language: *Hoc autem dicebat Gallio Nasoni suo valde placuisse; itaque fecisse illum quod in multis aliis versibus Vergilii fecerat, non subripiendi causa, sed palam mutuandi, hoc animo ut vellet agnosci*; cf. the same metaphor from arboriculture at *SD* 1, 893-4 *ioca rite / Interserta locis seria dico suis*; implicit in *furtim* is the notion of literary plagiarism (*furtum*) cf. John of Salisbury, *Metalogicon* 1. 24 (*MPL* 199: 855b) *quis autem ad splendorem sui operis, alienum pannum assuerat, deprehensum redarguebat* (sc. Bernardus) *furtum*; on medieval attitudes to plagiarism, see M. Carruthers, *The Book of Memory*, 218-20; she notes how a web of textual allusions and transformations constituted a dialogue between the *memoria* of the composer and the audience; **reseruo**: cf. Peter of Blois, *Libellus*, 68, 900-1 *Excerpant sibi quasi quosdam flosculos a libris Tullii, Senecae, Terentii, Oracii, Persii et Iuuenalis.*

1065. **censor**: cf. Baudri, *Carm.* 86, 37 *Erratus nostros ut clemens corrige censor*, 153, 11-2; Marbod, *Liber decem capitulorum* 1, 14-5 (ed. Bulst, 210); **me iudice**: Hor., *Ars* 244; Ov., *Ars* 3, 491 *iudice me*; *SD* 2, 1048 *Iudice me*; *Poems* 8, 1 (ed. Esposito, 460).

1066. **ingeniosus erit**: *Ibis* 187; Mart., 1, o, 8 *improba facit qui in alieno libro ingeniosus est.*

1067-72. *The beaver*

1067. **Castora cum Polluce**: i. e. the testicles; Hassig 86 notes how the enlargement of the beaver's testicles in several illustrations underlines the lesson about the dangers of sexual temptation; cf. Hor., *Ep.* 2, 1, 5; Matthew of Vendôme, *Ars* 1, 53, 77-8 (ed. Munari, 3: 77) *Venus excitat egra bilibres / Fratres* [= *testiculi*]; *LSD* 9, 99-102 (p. 488W); Lawn, *Salern. Questions*, 184, note 88; cf. the long excursus on the twins in the section *De superbia* in *CNP* 1423f; **castor**: The beaver, when hunted, severs its own testicles and throws them away; the hunter collects them and gives up the chase cf. McCulloch 95; Henkel 189-90; Hassig 84-92; *DNR* 2, 140 (pp. 220-1 W).

1068. **euadat**: cf. Juv. 12, 34 *Qui se / eunuchum ipse facit, cupiens evadere damno testiculi* [cited Isid., *Orig.* 12, 2, 21]; Hassig 85 and note 12; **sequentis**: i. e. the hunter, who sought a medicine (*castoreum*) produced from the beaver's inguinal glands cf. Cameron 25-6; Getz 319.

1069. **castus**: on the beaver as an emblem for chastity, see Hassig 86; *LSD* 7, 75-6 (p. 474W) *Fervor ea Veneris ut aneto vincitur, agno / Casto vim similem Castoreoque dabis, Physiologus Lat.* XVII, 10 (ed. Carmody, 32-3) *Sic et omnis qui...caste uult uiuere, abscidit a se omnia uitia et omnis impudicitiae actus*; **quod te uexat**: cf. Ov., *Fast.* 6, 524 'an numen, quod me, te quoque vexat?' ait.

1070. **hanc cum matre relinquas**: cf. Mc 10, 7 *propter hoc relinquet homo patrem suum et matrem.*

1071. **matre relinquas**: cf. Verg., *G.* 4, 328.

1073-90. *The hedgehog*

1073. **Hericius:** The hedgehog climbs a vine and shakes free the grapes. After coming down, he fixes the grapes to his quills by rolling on them. He then takes the fruit to feed its young. Under threat, the hedgehog curls itself into a ball cf. McCulloch 124-5; Henkel 192; **spinis**: cf. Isid., *Orig.* 12, 3, 7 *Ericium animal spinis coopertum*; Symphosius, *Aenig.* 29, 1 (*Anth.*, ed. Buecheler, 1: 1, 229) (Ericius) *Plena domus spinis.*

1074. **Cui desunt uires**: cf. Ov., *Pont.* 3, 4, 79; *Ecbasis captivi* 374 *Si desunt vires....*

1078. **Horrens**: with play on the literal meaning «to bristle» (*OLD* 1).

1080. **arma ministrat ei**: *SD* 1, 1166; Verg., *A.* 1, 150 *furor arma ministrat*; *LH-L* 1: 127.

1081. **uitis fructu generoso**: cf. Isid., *Orig.* 12, 4, 7 *nam dum absciderit uvam de vite, supinus* (sc. ericius) *se volutat super eam, et sic eam exhibet natis suis, SD* 2, 487 *uitis generosa.*

1082. **pomis**: cf. *Ecbasis captivi* 150 *Cursitat ericius, pomis revehatur onustus.*

1088. **Conclusus**: rare word; *ThLL*, 4: 80, 46 records a single occurrence of the noun in Caelius Aurelianus, *chron.* 1, 4, 77.

1089. **concludatur...conclude**: note word-play on the philosophical sense of the word; *DNR* 2, 36 (p. 149W) *Sic et vir claustralis intra septa murorum tutus erit, qui multas reperit insidias.*

1090. **Experto credas**: cf. Ov., *Ars* 3, 511 *experto credite*; Alexander did not enter the Augustinian abbey of Cirencester until after 1197 cf. Hunt ed. Gibson 11-2.

1091-96. *The sow*

1091. **Svs inmunda luti**: cf. Hor., *Ep.* 1, 2, 26; Claudian, *Carm.* 5, 487 *hunc suis inmundi pingues detrudit in artus*; Sedulius, *Carm. pasch.* 3, 81-4 (ed. Huemer, *CSEL* 10: 70); **luti**: cf. Isid., *Orig.* 12, 1, 25 *Ingurgitat enim se caeno, luto inmergit, limo inlinit.*

1092. **limosa...humo**: cf. Ov., *Rem.* 142 *limosa canna palustris humo*; **philosophatur**: cf. Pamphilus, *Gliscerium et Birria* 96 (ed. Cohen, 2: 96) *Et miser ante fores philosophatur equus*; note the lengthening of the first syllable cf. *De Vetula* 1, 696 (ed. P. Klopsch, 219 [Leiden, 1967]).

1095. **deliciatur**: rare word cf. *ThLL*, 5: 449, 17 cites Mutianus Chrysost., *hom.* 29, 4 *non itaque deliciemur deliciis corporis.*

1097. **Seuiciam...aper**: cf. Verg., *G.* 3, 248 *saevus aper*; **potentum**: e. g. Herod and Nero in *SD* 1, 686 cf. *SD* 1, 1145-6 *potestas / Seuiciam* .

1098. **Frendens...aper**: cf. McCulloch 97; *LSD* 9, 139-44 (p. 489W) *Frendit aper dum fulmineo desaevit in hostem, / Dente ferox*; Mart., 13, 93; Cambridge, UL, Ll. 1. 14, f. 46r *Aper frendit*; **dente timendus aper**: Ov., *Ep.* 4, 104 [*Ecbasis captivi* 648]; Bernardus Silvestris, *Cosmographia* 1, 3, 210 (ed. Dronke, 109).

1099. **Densa...silva**: cf. Ov., *Met.* 15, 488 *densis...silvis*; **iaculorum silva**: cf. *SD* 2, 110 *silua capillorum*, 1505 *Prisca supercilia* (sc. Grammatice) *tegit horrida silua pilorum*; 1, 1113; **silua minacem**: cf. Claudian, *Carm. min.* 9, 10-2 *stat corpore toto / silua minax, iaculisque rigens in proelia crescit / picturata seges*; **porcum**: cf. Claudian, *Carm. min.* 9, 6-7 *os longius illi / adsimulat porcum* (of the porcupine).

1100. **Abruptas rupes**: *LSD* 9, 147 *Dum petit abruptas onager rupes*; for the etymological link between *rumpo* and *rupes* cf. Paschalis 128, 339.

1101. **mira potestas / Nature**: cf. *LSD* 4, 410 (p. 429W). Bynum 7 observes that wonder (*mira*) is associated with the coincidence of opposites (*mixta*) in the works of theologians and natural philosophers.

1102. **mixtus...humor**: cf. *DNR* 1, 75 (pp. 120-1W) for the application of the theory of humours to explain certain characteristics of the cock.

1104. **picta colore**: cf. Ov., *Fast.* 4, 275 *picta coloribus... / ...puppis habet.*

1105. cf. Claudian, *Carm. min.* 9, 12-5 *corium cute fixa tenaci / alba subit radix alternantesque colorum / tincta vices, spatiis internigrantibus exit / in solidae speciem pinnae* (of the porcupine).

1108. **Humor...aquosus**: cf. *SD* 1, 1265 *aquaticus humor.*

1111. **directo tramite**: cf. Aldhelm, *CDV* 645, 846, *Enig.* 59, 3 (*MGH, AA* 15: 380, 389, 124); *SD* 1, 992.

1112. **Arcu lunato**: *LSD* 1, 456 (p. 367W); cf. *SD* 2, 621-3 *Affirmant lunam... / Arcu lunato pontificumque mitra / Ornatam*, 1000-1 *Fratres quos terret missa sagitta minax / Arcu lunato Centauri*; cf. Ov., *Am.* 1, 1, 23 *lunauitque...arcum*; Claudian, *Carm. min.* 9, 21-2 *interdum fugiens Parthorum more sequentem / uulnerat* (of the porcupine); 42 *sese utitur arcu*; 47-8...*Parthosque retro didicisse ferire / prima sagittiferae pecudis documenta secutos*; **Parthica tela**: *CNP* 1388 *Parthica tela uolant.*

1114. **docta...manu**: cf. Claudian, *Carm. min.* 9, 32-4 *certum sollertia destinat ictum / nil spatio fallente modum, seruatque tenorem / mota cutis doctique regit conamina nisus.*

1115-48. *The crocodile and the hydrus*

1115. **cocodrillus**: The crocodile is a quadruped, armed with claws and teeth. Its hide is so tough that weapons cannot penetrate it. It sheds tears after devouring a man. When the hydrus, the crocodile's enemy, comes upon the animal sleeping with its mouth open, it rolls itself in the mud in order to slip into the jaws more easily. Once swallowed, it consumes the crocodile's entrails, killing it. It then emerges cf. McCulloch 106-8; Henkel 171-2; **Ore...patulo**: cf. Ov., *Met.* 15, 513 *patulo partem maris evomit ore*; *Ep.* 16, 56; *DNR* 2, 100-1 (pp. 185-6W), *LSD* 9, 155-162 (pp. 489-90W).

1116. **ydrus**: cf. McCulloch 129-30; Breiner 30-3 charts the transformation of the croc-

odile's enemy from the ichneumon (Plin., *Nat.* 8, 25, 90 [ed. Ian, 2; 108-9]) into the hydrus, a water snake; over time the enemy was variously identified with the ichneumon, en-
hydros, hydrus, trochilos and the Hydra; see Druce 1909, 321-4, on the sources and symbolism of the conflict between the two animals.

1117. **humo...tenaci**: cf. *LSD* 3, 612 (p. 409W) *tenax limus*; Claudian, *Carm.* 20, 443
caeno subnixa tenaci / mergitur, the *ydrus* rolls in mud so that it can slide more easily into the
crocodile's jaws.

1117-8. **Corpus**: cf. *Physiologus Lat.* XIX, 3-6 (ed. Carmody, 35) *...cum uiderit* (sc. hydrus) *crocodilum in littore fluminis dormientem aperto ore, uadit et inuoluit se in limum luti, quod
possit facilius illabi in faucibus eius, et ueniens insilit in ore eius;...ille autem dilanians omnis uiscera
eius exit uiuus de uisceribus crocodili iam mortui ac disruptis omnibus interraneis eius.*

1118. **Hostis**: i. e the crocodile: cf. *Physiologus Lat.* XIX, 2 (ed. Carmody, 35) *hoc animal*
(sc. hydrum) *inimicum est crocodilo.*

1119. **absumptis extalibus exit**: cf. Solinus 32, 25 (ed. Mommsen, 143, 14-8) *strophilos
auis paruula est: ea reduuias escarum dum adfectat, os beluae huiusce paulatim scalpit et sensim...adi-
tum sibi in usque fauces facit. quod ichneumon conspicatus penetrat beluam populatisque uitalibus ero-
sa exit aluo*; Aldhelm, *CDV* 976-7 (*MGH, AA* 15: 394-5) *uentris dum uiscera foeda / Turpiter
egessit ruptis extalibus ani.*

1127. **Oua fouet**: Matthew of Vendôme, *Tob.* 268 (ed. Munari, 2: 172); cf. Isid., *Orig.*
12, 6, 20 *Oua in terra fouet; masculus et femina uices seruant*; *DNR* 2, 100 (p. 185W) *In partu
fouendo mas et foemina uices seruant.*

1128. **bis geminos...pedes**: a quadruped cf. Plin., *Nat.* 8, 25, 89 (ed. Ian, 2: 108); **fertur habere**: cf. *SD* 1, 1206.

1129. **distenti**: cf. *SD* 1, 1137 *extensi*; **linea recta**: cf. *SD* 2, 10.

1130. **Quinque quater cubitos**: cf. Isid., *Orig.* 12, 6, 19 *animal quadrupes* [cf.
1128],*...longitudine plerumque uiginti cubitorum*; *DNR* 2, 100 (p. 185W) *Plerumque ad uiginti ul-
nas magnitudinis eualescit.*

1131. **Vnguibus armatur...dente**: cf. Ov., *Met.* 10, 540 *armatosque unguibus ursos uitat*;
Isid., *Orig.* 12, 6, 19 *dentium et unguium inmanitate armatum*; *SD* 1, 919 *Dentibus armatur*, 1303
Vnguibus armatus ursus.

1132. **cutem**: cf. Isid., *Orig.* 12, 6, 19 *tantaque cutis duritia ut quamuis fortium ictus lapidum
tergo repercutiat*; cf. *DNR* 2, 100 (p. 185W) *Circumdatur maxima firmitate cutis...ut ictus...reper-
cutiat*; *LSD* 9, 157 (p. 489W).

1035-66. Cited in Hunt ed. Gibson 16-7.

1135. **cinico...dente**: cf. *SD* 1, 1177.

1137. **corporis extensi**: cf. *SD* 2, 1703-4 *nitor extensique decenter / colli.*

1139. **cutis aspera**: cf. *LSD* 9, 157 (p. 489W) *asperitate cutis illatos excipit ictus*; **tela**: supply *signant.*

1141. **Ulixes / Uerbis**: Ulysses serves here as a figure of a persuasive speaker cf. Matthew of Vendôme, *Ep.* 2, 1, 37-8 (ed. Munari, 2: 109) *falero uel sicut Ulixes / Verba*; Ov.,
Met. 13, 92 *ubi nunc facundus Ulixes?*

1142. **Cicero**: the Roman figure *par excellence* of eloquence cf. *LSD* 5, 195 (p. 444W)
Artis rhetoricae fuit arx; 8, 21-2 (p. 481W); *in Eccles.* f. 108vb *Si nomen Antonii cuius iussis pre-
cisum est caput auctoris Romani eloquii* [cf. Luc., 7, 62-3] *detestatur orbis...Ille* (sc. Cicero) *tuba*

fuit eloquentie; John of Salisbury, *Enthet. maior* (ed. van Laarhoven, 1: 185) 1215-46; **Quintiliane**: cf. *LSD* 10, 95-6 (p. 498W); *Poems* 4, 55 (ed. Esposito, 455) *Scis quod Tullius es, Ysocrates, Quintillianus*; on the diffusion of Quintilian's work in the 12th-c., see Mollard *passim*.

1143. **uorans hominem**: cf. *DNR* 2, 101 (p. 186W) *crocodrillus hominem vorat, et plorat*; **sua fletibus ora**: Arator, *De Actibus* 2, 996 (ed. McKinlay, *CSEL* 72: 134); cf. Mastandrea 294; *LSD* 9, 159-60 (p. 489W) *Vescitur humano nonnumquem corpore, sed tunc / Tanquam compatiens fletibus ora rigat* [Boethius, *DCP* 1, M. 1, 4 (ed. Bieler, *CCSL* 94: 1) *fletibus ora rigant*]; Claudian, *De raptu* 1, 268 *maduerunt fletibus ora*; *LH-L* 2: 300.

1144. **compacientis**: cf. *NE* 21, 2 *Astitit huic, veluti compatiendo, lupus*.

1147. **Herodes**: cf. *in Eccles.* f. 108vb *Ha! Herodes Herode tru[n]culentior, quid nobili precursoris capite mensam infelicem cruentas? Certe certe indigna fuit mensa tyranni tam nobili ferculo. Hec lasciua saltatrix capite Baptiste uirginis fuit remuneranda*; Peter of Blois, *Carm.* 1, 1, 7a, 17-19 *arripit Herodem post uinum mors aliena; / femina dat saltus, fert cibula, fit philomena; / set nece Baptiste fedatur regia cena*; **nate**: the un-named daughter of Herodias and Herod, who performed the dance which brought her the head of John the Baptist on a platter: cf. Mc 6, 14-29; Mt 14, 1-12; Prudentius, *Tituli historiarum* 133-6.

1149-72. *The elephant, again*

1149. **proli generande rara uoluptas**: Elephants copulate rarely; to deliver their young, the female takes to the water to prevent dragons from eating her offspring cf. McCulloch 115; Henkel 177-8; Hassig 129-30; Druce, *AJ*, 1919, 25, assembles the classical sources on the subject of the elephant's reluctance to mate; *DNR* 2, 145 (p. 226W) *elephas...raro soboli procreandae tempus impendit*; *Physiologus Lat.* XXXIII, 2 (ed. Carmody, 57) *concupiscentiam fetus minime in se habet* (sc. elephas).

1150. **barri**: P f. 198ra *Barros dicitur elephas propter grauedinem sui unde et barro dicitur, quia grauis est persona et auctentica*; **in amne parit**: *LSD* 9, 90 (p. 488W); cf. *DNR* 2, 145 (pp. 255-6W); *Physiologus Lat.* XXXIII, 7-11 (ed. Carmody, 57); Hildebert, *Physiologus MPL* 171: 1222b; *NP* 132 (ed. Orbán, 28); for an illustration, see Druce, *AJ*, 1919, Plate 11, No. 2, facing p. 10.

1151. **draconis**: *LSD* 9, 77-8 (p. 487W) mention the dragon and the rhinoceros as enemies of the elephant; on the legend of the *draco* see Druce, *AJ*, 1919, 33-41; *id.*, «The Medieval Bestiaries», 63-4.

1153. **Felicis studii**: cf. *LSD* 5, 129 (p. 443W) *Sunt violae qui iam studiis felicibus instant*.

1154. **spiritus almus aquam**: cf. *DNR* 2, 145 (p. 226W) *Sic sic antiquus draco hominem persequitur, sed ad aquas gratiae se transferat homo*.

1157. **hostis... / Infestans**: cf. *DNR* 2, 145 (p. 226W) *hostis infestat*.

1159. **Cum congressuras acies**: cf. *LSD* 3, 841 (p. 414W) *Jam congressuros fratres..*; Aldhelm, *Enig.* 96, 1-6 (*MGH, AA* 15: 142-3); **prelia**: though **P**'s reading *plurima* could be the subject of *poscunt* (cf. Hildebert, *Carm. min.* 50, 1 *Plurima cum soleant sacros evertere mores*), it probably covers some such word as *prelia*.

1160. **Ostenso...sanguine**: cf. *LSD* 9, 67-8 (p. 487W) *visoque cruore / Armatos tumido pectore turbat atrox*; Druce, *AJ*, 1919, 26, quotes a marginal note in a 13th-c. bestiary: «According to the testimony of the Book of Maccabees [1, 6, 34], they showed the elephants the 'blood' of grapes (and mulberries) to the end that they might provoke them to fight»;

see Hassig 136 and note 42, for a moralization based on´1 Macc 6, 34-7 that is attached to the elephant.

1161. **iram concipit**: cf. Ov., *Met.* 1, 166 *concipit iras.*

1166. **arma ministrat**: cf. Ov., *Met.* 15, 471 *arma ministret.*

1168. **uera fides**: cf. Claudian, *Carm.* 10, 240; **lancea longus**: a possible allusion to the name of Longinus, a soldier alleged by tradition to have been present at the Crucifixion and to have driven a spear into Christ's side cf. Smith, *A Dictionary of Christian Biography,* 3: 739.

1068. **sequentis**: cf. Bernardus Silvestris, *Cosmographia* 1, 3, 229-30 (ed. Dronke, 110) *Prodit item castor, proprio de corpore velox / Reddere, quas sequitur hostis avarus, opes.*

1169. **iuuamen**: a word found mostly in the prose of late antiquity cf. *ThLL,* 7: 727, 34; *SD* 1, 366.

1172. Note the word-play on *cedet* (= caedet) and *cedit*; **Amalechita**: the Amalechites attacked the Israelites at Raphidim near Mt. Sinai: cf. Ex 17, 9 *dixitque Moses ad Iosue: «Elige viros et egressus pugna contra Amalech;»* cf. 1, Sm 15, 7-8.

1173-84. *To the reader*

1173-84. **Lectori...tetrico**: cf. *LSD* 2, 696 (p. 389W) *Subsunt judicio carmina nostra tuo; CNP* 333-8 *set scribens aliis scribo michi, disco docendo; / sic michi, sic aliis utilis esse uolo. / proficiens prodesse uolo tibi, candide lector, / discipulusque mei set tibi doctor ero. / qui me commorit, melius non tangere clamo! / dum michi succenses, inuide, parce tibi.*

1173. **Lectori tetrico**: cf. Mart., 11, 2, 7 *Lectores tetrici salebrosum ediscite Santram; LDS* 3, 3-4 (p. 395W); *SD* 1, 1175 *candide lector,* 2, 127 *Ciuilis lector,* 968 *lector...censeat,* 1249 *Si michi succenses, lector, nolens / ...uolens*: cf. *CNP* 887 *set data suscepit Balaam nolensque uolensque.*

1175. **candide lector**: *LSD* 2, 695 (p. 389W); 4, 150 (p. 423W), 671 (p. 435W); 5, 403 (p. 449W); 9, 246 (p. 491W); cf. Mart. 7, 99, 5 *Dicere de nobis, ut lector candidus, aude;* **C** f. 70bis v *Proficiens prodesse uolo tibi, candide lector.*

1173-84. cf. *CNP* 331-40.

1175. **Grates persoluam**: cf. Verg., *A.* 1, 600 *grates persoluere dignas.*

1176. **uultu placido**: cf. Ov., *Met.* 15, 692 *officium placido uisus dimittere vultu.*

1177. **cinico...rodit dente**: cf. Hor., *Ep.* 1, 18, 81-2 *qui / dente...circumroditur;* the literary critic, like the Roman satirists, is portrayed as a biting dog cf. Ov., *Tr.* 4, 10, 123-4 *nec...Liuor iniquo / ullum de nostris dente momordit opus; LSD* 4, 519 (p. 432W) *Vis carmen cynico carpere dente meum;* 522-5 (p. 432W) *Carpere si gaudes aliena volumina, tanquam / Jurisconsultus, consulo jure tibi. / Ne scribas, aut si coepisti, desine, judex, / Lector es, at scriptor incipis esse reus;* cf. *LSD* 5, 1-34 (p. 440W) for Neckam on his critics.

1179. cf. *NP* 1341-2 (ed. Orbán, 66) *Nil consum<m>atum, nichil omni parte beatum / Extat in hiis rebus* (a poet defends his work); **solacia mundo / Prebet:** cf. *Poems* 4, 3 (ed. Esposito, 454) *Humano generi prebet solacia leta.*

1180. **habet neuos forma decora suos**: cf. Seneca the Elder's report of Ovid's remark concerning faults (*uitia*) in his own poetry: *Contr.* 2, 2, 12 (ed. Winterbottom, 1: 264) *Aiebat* (sc. Ouidius) *interim decentiorem faciem esse in qua aliquis naevos esset.*

1182. **nodos scirpus**: cf. Walther, *Prov.* 17081a *Nodum in scirpo queris.*

1183. **Cur me succensens**: cf. *LSD* 5, 11 (p. 440W) *Cur mihi succensus*; *SD* 2, 633-4 *istud / Qui michi succenses, Zoile, stare nequit,* 1249 *Si michi succenses, lector,* **C** f. 70bis v *Dum michi succenses, inuide, parce tibi.*

1184. **mea scripta legis?**: *Doctrinale* 1461 [cf. Ov., *Pont.* 3, 4, 91].

1185. **limaci**: cf. Isid., *Orig.* 12, 5, 7 *Limax uermis limi...unde et sordida semper et inmunda habetur*; *SD* 1, 1187 *feda,* 1187 *inmundiciam.*

1191–1222. *Observations on avarice*

1191. **Estus auaricie**: John of Salisbury, *Enthet. maior* 889 (ed. van Laarhoven, 1: 163) *aestus avaritiae gignit plerumque rapinas*; 1491; for denunciation of money-grubbers cf. *Enthet. minor* 263-82 (ed. van Laarhoven, 1: 247).

1192. **aspis**: cf. *DNR* 2, 114 (p. 194W); *LSD* 9, 289-90 (p. 492W).

1193. **letale uenenum**: Eugenius, *Carm.* 6, 4 (*MGH, AA* 14: 236); *LH-L* 3: 189.

1194. **Buffonis**: cf. *SD* 1, 778; cf. Peter of Blois, *Carm.* 1, 1, 7a, 9 *Bufo, rana, culex tres dant tria quisque uenena.*

1196. **auara manus**: *Ysopet* 52, 8 *...nil dat auara manus*; *LH-L* 1:167.

1197. **uirus... / Effundit**: cf. *SD* 2, 384 *Effundit serpens uirus ab ore uirens*; Camargo 1992, 200, 296-9 *Si aliquis aliquem contumelijs affecerit uel ei in aliquo incomodauerit, hec inducantur: ...»Hic uirus sue nequitie <in me> fudit,»* Marbod, *De lapidibus* 63 (ed. Riddle, 38) *Iste* (sc. achates) *nempe uirus fugat, et quod uipera fundit*; Geoffrey of Monmouth, *Vita Merlini* 659-60 *donec Erinus / ...uirus diffundet in ipsos.*

1200. **Crasse**: *SD* 2, 471-4 *Frugifer Eufrates, Iudee terminus, illam / non potuit Crassi diminuisse sitim. / Si non transisses amnem, miserande sititor / Auri, cessisset Parthia tota tibi*; in *Eccles.* f. 85rb *Parthi Crasso aurum propinauerunt; nec sic sitis morientis sedata est*; John of Salisbury, *Enthet. maior* 1171 (ed. van Laarhoven, 1: 181) *captat opes Crassus, ut eas convertat in aurum*; Hunt ed. Gibson 90, note 32.

1201. The verse is repeated at *SD* 2, 41; cf. *SD* 1, 1291; **causa pudoris**: cf. Mastandrea 114.

1202. **misere...condicionis, homo**: cf. *LSD* 2, 462 (p. 383W), 644 (p. 387W); *Poems* 1602 (ed. Walther 1962, 41) *misere conditionis homo*; *SD* 2, 455-6 *at in se / Exarsit misera condicione miser.*

1204. **merx miseranda**: i. e. poison.

1205-6. **uirus... / ...uires**: similar verbal play in *SD* 2, 384 *Effundit serpens uirus ab ore uirens.*

1207. **Ethiopi**: **P** f. 212ra records a marginal gloss in the section entitled *De dracone*: Dauid *Dedisti eum escam populis ethiopum* [PsG 73, 14] ad litteram, quamuis subsit misterium, on the verse: *Ethiopum populus recreatur carne draconis*; **merx...preciosa**: *LSD* 6, 274 (p. 469W).

1208. **capitis thalamo**: cf. *SD* 2, 105-6 *Principium motus motor c<e>rebro dominatur / A cuius thalamo censibus apta uia est,* 137 *In cordis thalamo fulget sapientia.*

1209-10. **censes / ...censor**: cf. Isid., *Orig.* 9, 4, 13 *Est enim nomen censoris dignitas iudi-*

cialis. Censere enim iudicare est.

1213. **Lacene**: i. e. Helen of Troy cf. Hor., *C.* 2, 11, 23; *CNP* 1015 *nouit id obscene describens probra Lacene.*

1216. **paries...parens**: for similar word play cf. *SD* 2, 306 *Et fieret pariens absque dolore parens*, 1465-6 *Pelagius pelagus heresum Faustusque recedit / Infaustus.*

1218. **ocula blanda**: cf. Ov., *Am.* 2, 6, 56 *oscula dat cupido blanda columba mari*; *LH-L* 4: 85.

1219. **caro...cara**: cf. Hilarius poeta, *Carm.* 9, 20 *cuius nitet caro cara candens uti lilium*; Matthew of Vendôme, *Tob.* 1971-2 (ed. Munari, 2: 243) *quamvis / Cara sit, heu carie non caritura caro?*; *SD* 1, 852.

1223-1458. *Animals*

1223-26. *The dog*

1223. **canis**: Dogs guard their master's property and are devoted to their owners cf. McCulloch 110-1; cf. *DNR* 2, 157 (pp. 252-8W); *LSD* 9, 169-70 (p. 490W).

1223-24. Bernardus Silvestris, *Cosmographia* 1, 3, 223-4 (ed. Dronke, 109-10), cited *DNR* 2, 157 (p. 252W).

1225. **Blandus adulator**: *LSD* 1, 450 (p. 367W); *CNP* 951 *Blandus adulator nomen contraxit ab aula*; Jerome, *Ep.* 22, 2 (ed. Hilberg, *CSEL* 54: 146, 7-8) *adulator quippe blandus inimicus est*; **custos**: cf. Isid., *Orig.* 12, 2, 26 *dominorum tecta defendunt*; *DNR* 2, 157 (p. 253W); *DNV* (ed. Wright, 111) *assit...magale, in quo canis fidelis custos secum pernoctet*; **custos tutissimus**: cf. *Ysopet* 51, 5-6 *tutam / Seruo domum* (sc. canis).

1226. **amator heri**: cf. Isid., *Orig.* 12, 2, 26 *dominos suos diligunt*; **heri**: = *eri*.

1227-28. *The ape*

1227-28. Bernardus Silvestris, *Cosmosgraphia* 1, 3, 227-8 (ed. Dronke, 110), cited *DNR* 2, 129 (p. 211W); *LSD* 9, 107-8 (p. 488W); **deformis... / Simia**: cf. *Ecbasis captivi* 656 *Simia deformis.*

1228. **Simia...homo**: the ape exemplifies a natural deformity cf. *SD* 1, 1295 *monstra.*

1229-30. *The sheep and the goat*

1229. **ouis**: cf. McCulloch 166.

1229-30. Bernardus Silvestris, *Cosmographia* 1, 3, 211-2 (ed. Dronke, 109); cf. *DNR* 2, 161 (pp. 266-7W).

1231-32. *A squirrel (?) and the marten*

1231-32. Bernardus Silvestris, *Cosmographia* 1, 3, 231-2 (ed. Dronke, 110); **cisimus**: cf. *SD* 2, 1714 *preclarum cisimus ornat opus.*

1232. **Matrix**: = *martix icis* m. cf. *NG* L-M, 227 s. v. *martur*; **beuer**: see Hassig 90-1 on the use of beavers' hides as clothing for rich ecclesiastics.

1233-34. *Oxen and the hare*

1233-4. Bernardus Silvestris, *Cosmographia* 1, 3, 219-20 (ed. Dronke, 109).

1234. **res fugitiua**: John of Salisbury, *Enthet. maior* 880 (ed. van Laarhoven, 1: 163).

1235-56. *The wolf*

1235. **predatur**: cf. Verg., *G.* 1, 129-30 *ille... / praedarique lupos iussit*; **uetus incola silue**: i. e the wolf cf. *Ecbasis captivi* 110 «*Laudes dic superis, silve novus incola surgis*»; people lose their voice if a wolf sees them first cf. McCulloch 188-9; cf. Geoffrey of Monmouth, *Vita Merlini* 105 *Tu prior has silvas coluisti* (sc. lupe); Petrus Pictor, *De sacramentis* 289 (ed. L. van Acker, *CCCM* 25: 30) *Iam paradisiacam repetit uetus incola sedem*; *LSD* 2, 609 (p. 387W); **Vocem predatur**: cf. Plin., *Nat.* 8, 22, 80 (ed. Ian, 2: 105) *Sed in Italia quoque creditur luporum visus esse noxius vocemque homini, quem priores contemplentur adimere ad praesens*; Symphosius, *Aenig.* 33, 3 (*Anth.*, ed. Buecheler, 1: 1, 230) (*Lupus*) *Multa cum rabie vocem quoque tollere possum*; Isid., *Orig.* 12, 2, 24; *DNR* 2, 132 (p. 213W); *LSD* 9, 117-8 (p. 488W) *At lupus aspectu subito tibi praeripit usum / Vocis*; Lawn, *Prose Salern. Questions* B 284 (ed. Lawn, 137, 15) *Quare viso lupo, homo perdit vocem?*

1236. **radius**: cf. Verg., *E.* 9, 53-4; *LSD* 9, 119 (p. 488W) *Nam vitio radii medius corrumpitur aer*; Lawrence of Durham, *Dialogi* 2, 33 *An fortasse lupi nos aspexere priores?*; cf. Lawn, *Salern. Questions*, 160, 63-4 *Cur raucescat homo subito quem luce lupina / Perstringit facies?*

1238. **causa timoris**: Ov., *Fast.* 5, 248 *ira Iovis magni causa timoris erat*; Pamphilus, *Gliscerium et Birria* 176 (ed. Cohen, 2: 100) *gladii causa timoris erant.*

1239. **infrigidat artus**: cf. *Poems* 1, 15 (ed. Walther 1965, 112) *Artus infrigidas placide placidoque calore / Letificas*. **artus...occupat**: cf. Verg., *E.* 4, 190; Mastandrea 584; *LSD* 2, 449 (p. 383W), 723 (p. 389W); 9, 120 (p. 488W) *At qui membra recens occupat, unde stupor*; Aldhelm, *CDV* 630 (*MGH, AA* 15: 379); Pamphilus 55 (ed. Cohen, 2: 196).

1241. **inficitur aer**: cf. *LSD* 9, 119 (p. 488W) *Nam vitio radii medius corrumpitur aer*; Urso, *Aphorismi Glosula* 39 (ed. Creutz, 72) *Inde fit quod aliquis venenosos habens spiritus vulnerans aliquem etiam ex levi vulnere ipsum inficiendo occidit...Sicut lupus et quaecunque venenosa animalia mordendo, pungendo, videndo infectione suae malitiae infectos turbant, corrumpunt et aliquando corrumpendo occidunt*; *Prose Salern. Questions* B 284 (ed. Lawn, 137, 18-24 *Dicimus ergo quia eius aspectus est causa perditionis vocis, sed non quolibet modo...Ut ergo hoc fiat oportet ut aciem luminis directe figat in faciem hominis. Tunc igitur aer medius inficitur corrupta lupi humiditate, et frigiditate complexionis eius aliquam contrahit malitiam. Ex eo igitur quod lupus linea recta dirigit aspectum suum in hominem, fortius infundit aeris mediantis malitiam*; cf. P 75 (ed. Lawn, 234, 19-21).

1243. **fur nocturnus**: cf. *Liber sacramentorum Engolismensis* LVIII, 2102, 5-7 (ed. P. Saint-Roch, *CCSL* 159C: 323) *...ne ouile Domini praedo uiolentus inrumpat et dispersas absque pastore oues fur nocturnus inuadat*; Ademar, *Phaedrus* 1, 23, 3 (ed. Bertini 1988, 100) *Nocturnus cum fur panem misisset cani....*

1243-44. **Fur... / Suggillat**: cf. *DNR* 2, 132 (p. 214W) *Nonnumquam canis et lupus...confoederantur, adeo ut et ipsi fures in noctis furvo incedentes caulas subintrent, ovesque strangulent*; cf. Sada 793-4.

1245-6. **sedare sitim**: cf. Ov., *Met.* 3, 415 *dumque sitim sedare cupit, sitis altera crevit*; **ille sititor... / Sanguinis**: cf. *NA* 1, 15-6 *Deliciis sedare famem sitit* (sc. lupus) *ille sititor / Sanguinis*; Bernardus Silvestris, *Cosmographia* 1, 3, 215-6 (ed. Dronke, 109) *lupusque sititor / Sanguinis.*

1246. **lassus non saciatus abit**: cf. Juv., 6, 130 *et lassata viris necdum satiata recessit* (of the Roman empress, Messalina)

1247. **Predo rapax**: the wolf cf. Mt 7, 15 *lupi rapaces*; Hor., *Ep.* 16, 20; see Sada 783, note 17 on the etymology of *lupus*.

1251. **En lupus!**: cf. M. Valerius, *Buc.* 3, 119 Meris: *Heu male consuetus nostro lupus instat ovili.*

1252. **baculi**: cf. *Carmina Cantabrigiensia* 35, 8, where a priest uses a stick to beat a wolf; **desit copia**: Mart., 7, 74, 3 *sic tibi lascivi non desit copia furti*; **Meri, fuge**: in Verg., *E.* 9 the singing shepherd, Moeris, is said to have lost his voice after wolves cast eyes on him: cf. Verg., *E.* 9, 53-4 *uox quoque Moerim / iam fugit ipsa: lupi Moerim uidere priores.*

1255. **Fistula dulce canens**: cf. SD 1, 703 *Fistula dulce canit.*

1256. **pastoris**: Sada 786-7 relates the appearances of the wolf in the New Testament to images of Christ as the good shepherd.

1257-66. *Transition*

1257. **arbitrio uisus obnoxia:** cf. Urso, *Aphorismi Glosula* 41 (ed. Creutz, 78) *Hinc aperte monstratur, quod ille qui haec eorum oculis sensibiliter demonstrabat ipsorum mentes ad eorum cognoscendam significationem flectebat*; SD 1, 925 *uisus tantum considerat exteriora*; **uisus**: the faculty of sight connects the role of vision in the section on the wolf (SD 1, 1236, 1242) and the following contrast between appearances and reality.

1257-66. Although the miracle at Cana was cited by Augustine and John of Salisbury, among others, in discussions of miracles and natural processes (cf. Bynum 13), the points they wanted to make by rhetorically juxtaposing the two differ from Neckam's focus here. The emphasis on the element of wonder and its presence or absence, linked to unusual or quotidian events and defined in terms of miracles and natural processes, respectively, suggests Urso Salernitanus as a possible intertext cf. Urso, *Aphorismi Glosula* 1 (ed. Creutz, 10) *Consuetum et ordinatum rerum naturalium processum non miramur, sed insuetum et momentaneum. Qui enim solius uerbi imperio et de nichilo cuncta produxit ad miraculum hominibus imprudentibus, monstrare potuit insueta et quod per temporum interualla perficitur, subito efficere ualet*; (ed. Creutz, 1, 19) *Consuetum et ordinatum rerum processum non miramur, scilicet quae cotidie per naturam in rebus ipsis fieri noscuntur, et quae ex ipsis saepius producuntur, sed inconsuetum et momentaneum, scilicet cum res in rem nulla naturae actione sed sola creatoris uoluntate mutetur, ut habetur ab Elisabeth, quae in senectute concepit et de Aaronis arida uirga quae floruit.*

1259. **Nature...miracula**: cf. SD 2, 707 *Nature solitum uincunt miracula cursum*; LSD 3, 315 (p. 402W); 6, 131 (p. 466W); 10, 1 (p. 496W).

1258. **Haut umquam**: P's *Haut numquam* appears to be a variation of *non numquam* (cf. SD 1, 177), though it is not needed for metrical reasons. In view of the following point (1259-64), a negative statement seems called for here. The implied contrast is with 1263 where the occurrence of a miracle in the world does cause a ferment among people. Neckam sets up the *uulgus* as a foil for the natural philosopher, who is awed by the hidden processes of nature which he discovers while investigating the causes of things (cf. SD 1, 1265-6).

1259-60. **uulgus / ....miratur**: cf. Ov., *Am.* 1, 15, 35 *uilia miretur uulgus*; LSD 1, 551 (p. 370W) *uulgus fingere multa solet*; 5, 323 (p. 447), 7, 33-6 (p. 473W) *Exilis meriti reputat communia uulgus, / Sed quae commendat rarior usus habet. / Sed num judicium plebis natura tenetur /*

Velle sequi? virtus maxima saepe latet; 7, 286 (p. 479W), 9, 175 (p. 490W); *SD* 1, 1381, 1390; 2, 1143 *Fallitur in multis assercio friuola uulgi*; for criticism of the common people (*uulgus*) as a foil cf. Ov., *Fast.* 6, 25 *ne tamen ignores volgique errore traharis...*; Adelard of Bath, *Quaestiones naturales* 49, 12 (ed. Mueller, 15, 29).

1260. **rarior usus habet**: Juv. 11, 208 *voluptates commendat rarior usus*; *LSD* 10, 120 (p. 498W); cf. *SD* 2, 1558. *rarior usus adest*; *rarior usus* refers to the miracle cited in 1261-2.

1261. **In uinum mutauit aquam**: the vine's natural process of transforming water into wine is connected with the miracle at Cana in Augustine, *De Genesi ad litteram* 6, 13 (ed. Zycha, *CSEL* 28: 188) and John of Salisbury *Policraticus* 2, 12 (ed. Keats-Rohan, *CCCM* 118: 91-2); cf. Bynum 13; Sedulius, *Carm. pasch.* 3, 4 (ed. Huemer, *CSEL* 10: 65) *In uinum conuertit aquas*; Urso, *Aphorismi* Glosula 1 (ed. Creutz, 20) *Et aqua ad vitis nutrimentum attracta per sui corruptionem vini pocula subministrat, quae omnia et similia hominibus magnum praebent spectaculum, nisi longa consuetudo subtrahet admirationem. Sed quoniam rectus status hominis primiparentis peccato erat deperditus, delicti onere aggravatus coepit miser et miserabili illico incurvari statu...Nostrae igitur miseriae compatiens...Dei filius assumpto nostrae carnis indumento ad nos occultus pugnaturus cum hoste advenit... Verumtamen ante suae passionis tempora inter homines aliquamdiu conversatus, hominis rationem malitie summa inebriatam primo ad sui cognitionem per miracula voluit excitare, ut non solum verba sed inusitata opera deitatis suae redderent testimonium, dum aquam in vinum sine temporis interstitio commutaret. Pauxillos panes multiplicavit...Patet ex his exemplis paucis sic sui creantis imperiis paruerunt, ut prorsus naturae conditione cursu nescio illico mutarentur in ea quae rata per se ratione valeant, ut ex hac subita et insueta mutatione rationis metas excedente humanum genus illum crederet creatorem, qui creaturas prout voluit et non secundum ut eas instituit et ad agenda statuta miraculo se ministrat*; Peter of Blois, *Carm.* 1, 1, 7, 9-10 *In uinum conuertit aquas prece matris aquarum / conditor*, **uitis generosa**: referring both to the vine and to Christ cf. Augustine *In Iohannis euangelium tractatus* 80. 2 (ed. Willems, *CCSL* 36: 528, 5) *ego sum uitis uera* (Jo. 15, 1)... *secundum hoc ergo uitis Christus*; *Poems* 3, 39 (ed. Walther 1965, 118); *SD* 2, 487.

1262. **mundator**: a word often used by ecclesiastical writers cf. *ThLL*, 8: 1624, 6-18; cf. Augustine, *In Iohannis euangelium tractatus* 80, 2 (ed. Willems, *CCSL* 36: 528, 18) *ecce et ipse mundator est palmitum, quod est agricolae, non uitis officium*; the allusion is to Christ's miracle at the wedding in Cana cf. Jo 4, 46 cf. Claudian, *Carm. min. app.* 21, 5-6 *permutat lymphas in uina liquentia Christus, / quo primum facto se probat esse deum.*

1263. **insigne...opus**: cf. *SD* 2, 67 *Non effulsissent miracula tanta per orbem.*

1264. **Ignorans**: construe with *orbis* in 1263.

1267-82. *The stag*

1267. **[Ceruus]**: The stag sheds its horns and nature replaces them every year. When stags ford a river, one rests its head upon the haunches of another in front; when the one in front tires, it retreats to the rear cf. McCulloch 172-4; Henkel 186-7; Hassig 40-51; *DNR* 2, 135-6 (pp. 216-7W); *LDS* 9, 131-6 (p. 489W); *Prose Salern. Questions* B 168 (ed. Lawn, 86, 23) *Queritur quare cervus singulis annis unum cornu accrescit?* Dracontius, *De laudibus Dei* 1, 639 (*MGH, AA* 14: 58) *Frontibus arboreis amittunt cornua cervi, / anguibus assumptis sed mox palmata resurgunt*; **Cornibus...ceruum**: for the derivation of *ceruus* from *cornu* cf. Isid., *Orig.* 12, 1, 18.

1267-68. **Natura... / ...ministrat**: cf. *SD* 2, 193, *nomen natura ministrat*, 485 *delicias natura ministrat*.

1268. **noua**: sc. *cornua* cf. Ov., *Met.* 1, 640-1.

1269. **Innouat**: picking up *noua* in preceding verse cf. *SD* 1, 1282.

1270. **Fabri...manus**: cf. *LSD* 7, 319-20 (p. 480W) *Filius ille fabri qui solem condidit, atque / Auroram fabri filius atque faber.*

1271-75. Hassig 44 notes that artists of illustrations for bestiaries frequently depicted the way in which stags crossed rivers; cf. *Theobaldi Physiologus* 19-26 (ed. Eden, 50); *DNR* 2, 135 (p. 216W) *Cum item cervorum agmen vadum fluvii ingentis transire disponit, prenatat fortior, ita quod caput sequentis praecedentis clunibus innititur,* Hildebert, *Physiologus MPL* 171: 1220d-1221a; *NP* 232-7 (ed. Orbán, 31).

1275-6. Different moralizations are recorded for this activity by Hassig 45.

1278. **indignans**: cf. *SD* 1, 1284, 1289.

1279. **renouare iuuentam**: cf. *LSD* 9, 133 (p. 489W) *Serpentis virtute soles reparare juventam*; Lawn, *Salern. Questions*, 200, note 69.

1281. **uermes**: cf. Plin., *Nat.* 8, 32, 118 (ed. Ian, 2: 119); *DNR* 2, 136 (p. 217) *Serpentes hauriunt, et spiritu narium extrahunt de latebris cavernarum;* Mart., 12, 28, 5 *cervinus gelidum sorbet sic halitus anguem.* Tradition held that stags drew snakes from their holes by means of breathing through the nose; Neckam appears to use *uermis* and *coluber* interchangably at *SD* 1, 826-7; **cornibus herent**: cf. Ov., *Met.* 12, 269; Mastandrea 164; Gn 22, 13 *viditque...arietem inter vepres herentem cornibus;* *Ecloga Theodoli* 107 *rapitur, qui cornibus haeret / In dumis, aries.*

1282. **Cura...curis**: cf. *LSD* 3, 185 (p. 399W) *Curia se curis agitat;* **sollicitare novis**: cf. Ov., *Am.* 2, 4, 45 *me noua sollicitat* (sc. *aetas*).

1283-86. *The tiger*

1283. **delusus ymagine**: cf. *SD* 2, 453 *Narcisus delusus ymagine; LSD* 2, 477 (p. 384W), 9, 127-30 (p. 489W); **uitrea delusus imagine**: cf. *LSD* 7, 365 (p. 481W) *delusus imagine formae;* Claudian, *De raptu* 3, 268 *uitreae tardatur imagine formae.*

1284. **Orbate... / Tigridis**: cf. Juv. 6, 270; McCulloch 176-7; **delusus**: Pursuing her abducted young, the tiger is deceived when the hunter throws down a mirror; when the tiger catches sight of her own reflection, she ends the pursuit, believing she has recovered her cub. See Druce, «The Medieval Bestiaries», 52 and Plate V, an illustration depicting the hunter on horseback holding the cub, while he looks back at the tiger, who is clutching the mirror.

1287. **[Simia]**: Neckam omits the usual story of the ape who gives birth to twins. One it loves, the other it loathes. When hunted, the female carries her favourite in front of her, while the other clings to her back. When she tires, she drops the favoured child and the other survives cf. McCulloch 86-8; *Ysopet* 16 (p. 246); *DNR* 2, 128-29 (pp. 207-11W); *LSD* 9, 107-8 (p. 488W); Claudian, *Carm. min.* 53; **tellure relicta**: cf. Ov., *Ep.* 10, 129 *sola tellure relictam; LH-L* 5: 370; Mastandrea 846.

1288. **Ops**: cf. *LSD* 4, 567 (p. 433W) *Omnibus una parens Ops;* **spoliata**: cf. *SD* 1, 829-30.

1289. **fouet alto corde dolorem**: cf. Verg., *A.* 1, 209 *premit altum corde dolorem*; *LH-L* 1: 447; Mastandrea 163.

1290. **tristis adire domum**: cf. *Ecloga Theoduli* 317 *dum tristes adit Proserpina sedes*; *SD* 1, 1338.

1290. **Nature**: cf. *DNR* 2, 129 (p. 210W) *Simia..., naturae ludentis opus*.

1292. **uotis..adesse**: Ov., *Ep.* 6, 152 *adest votis Iuppiter*; Claudian, *Carm.* 23, 24.

1293. **tellus pariat**: cf. Verg., *G.* 1, 278-80; **Gigantes**: the gigantic sons of Earth and Tartarus were defeated by Jupiter when they assaulted the heavens cf. Ov., *Met.* 1, 151-62, *Fast.* 5, 35-6 *Terra feros partus, immania monstra, Gigantas / edidit ausuros in Iovis ire domum*; epic narratives on the theme, called Gigantomachies, were popular in antiquity; Claudian, for example, composed both Greek and Latin poems on the subject; cf. *De tribus puellis* 79-80 (ed. Cohen, 2: 234) *Illa canit fera bella Iovis, fera bella gigantum / Atque refert illos igne perisse Iovis*; **tellus**: cf. Ov., *Fast.* 5, 35 *terra feros partus, immania monstra, Gigantas / edidit*; Hor., *C.* 2, 12, 7 *Telluris iuuenes* (= Giants); *in Eccles.* f. 122ra *ut ad figmenta poetarum descendam, uideor mihi uidere Gigantes infestare superos*.

1294. **Qui...parent**: cf. Theodulf, *Carm.* 72, 151-2 (*MGH, P. L.* 1: 567) *Inter utramque aciem legatos ire putares, / Qui pugnae aut pacis iura referre parent*.

1295. **Obsequitur iussis**: cf. *SD* 2, 1419; Prudentius, *Symm.* 2, *praefatio*, 32 *Iussis obsequitur Petrus*; **monstra**: cf. Verg., *G.* 1, 184-5 *quae plurima terrae / monstra ferunt*; together with the Giants, monstrous and demonic creatures, earth produced the ape.

1296. **Contractis...naribus**: cf. Isid., *Orig.* 12, 2, 30 *Simiae Graecum nomen est, id est pressis naribus; unde et simias dicimus, quod suppressis naribus sint*.

1297-98. cf. *NP* 312-40 (ed. Orbán, 34-5).

1298. **Contraxit**: note play on *contractis* in 1296; **lusibus apta**: cf. Ov., *Am.* 2, 3, 13 *sunt apti lusibus anni*.

1299. **Risum mentiri**: cf. *LSD* 2, 237 (p. 378W) *Risum mentiris*; *DNR* 2, 129 (p. 208W) *Simia non solum gestibus sed et lineamentis hominem mentiens...*; *LSD* 9, 107 (p. 488W) *Simia ridiculis imitatur gestibus actus*; Claudian, *Carm.* 18, 303 *humani qualis simulator simius oris*.

1301. **Deliciosus...cibus...murena**: cf. *LSD* 3, 550 (p. 407W) *Isto se reficit simia laeta cibo*; Bernardus Silvestris, *Cosmographia* 1, 3, 421 (ed. Dronke, 115) *Suspectus murena cibus*; *DNV* ed. Wright, 97, glosses *murena* with *lampré*; *SD* 1, 1428.

1303-6. *The bear*

1303. **ursus**: After giving birth to an amorphous piece of flesh, the bear licks it into shape cf. McCulloch 94-5; *DNR* 2, 130-1 (pp. 211-3W); *LSD* 9, 103-6 (p. 488W); **Vnguibus armatus**: cf. *LSD* 2, 295 (p. 380W of the *falco*); Ov., *Met.* 10, 540 *armatosque unguibus ursos / vitat*; Dracontius, *De laudibus Dei* 1, 457 (*MGH, AA* 14: 48); **deseuit in hostem**: cf. *LSD* 2, 299 (p. 380W); Cambridge, UL, Ll. 1. 14, f. 46v *Vrsus...seuit uel fremit*.

1304. **languens...capud**: cf. Isid., *Orig.* 12, 2, 22 *Vrsorum caput invalidum*; *NP* 268 (ed. Orbán, 32) *Debilis est capite.*.

1305. **carni partus informis**: cf. Verg., *G.* 3, 247 *informes ursi*; Plin., *Nat.* 8, 36, 126 (ed. Ian, 2: 122); Claudian, *Carm.* 24, 310; Isid., *Orig.* 12, 2, 22 *Nam aiunt eos informes generare partus et carnem quandam nasci quam mater lambendo in membra conponit*; *DNR* 2, 131 (p.

213W)...*et ita nascuntur informes*; LSD 9, 103 (p. 488W); NP 259-65 (ed. Orbán, 32); Lawn, *Salern. Questions*, 183, note 77.

1307-10. The wild-cat

1307. **que uis**: cf. Plin., *Nat.* 8, 38, 137 (ed. Ian, 2: 126); Isid., *Orig.* 12, 2, 11; *Prose Salern. Questions* N 2 (ed. Lawn, 276, 8) *Questio. Si uncia momorderit aliquem, omnes sorices de confinio concurrant et mingant super eum, et sic moriatur.*

1308. **uncia**: cf. LSD 9, 273-8 (p. 492W).

1311. **[Linx]**: The lynx's urine hardens into a precious stone, which it hides from view cf. McCulloch 141; **Vertitur in lapidem**: cf. Ov., *Met.* 15, 414-5 *quidquid vesica remisit, / vertitur in lapides*; Solinus 2, 38 (ed. Mommsen, 40, 16-7) (*lyncum*) *urinas coire in duritiem...calculi*; **lincis liquor**: LSD 6, 246 (p. 469W); **inuida nostris / Usibus**: cf. Ov., *Met.* 9, 486 *coeptis invida nostris.*

1311-12. cf. Plin., *Nat.* 8, 38, 137 (ed. Ian, 2:: 126)...*invidentes urinam terra operiunt*; Isid., *Orig.* 12, 2, 20 *Huius urinam convertere in duritiam pretiosi lapidis dicunt, qui lyncurius appellatur ...Nam egestum liquorem harenis...contegunt, invidia quadam naturae ne talis egestio transeat in usum humanum*; DNR 2, 138 (p. 219W); LSD 6, 246 (p. 469W) *lyncis...liquor.*

1316. **utilitatis habet**: cf. Ov., *Pont.* 1, 5, 54 *quae nil utilitatis habent*, *Tr.* 4, 1, 38 *sed quiddam furor hic utilitatis habet*; **Gemma latens**: cf. Boethius, DCP 2, M. 5, 29 (ed. Bieler, CCSL 94: 29) *gemmasque latere volentes.*

1317. **Prodeat in lucem**: cf. SD 2, 565 *Prodeat in lucem*, 1177, 1599 *Prodiit in lucem.*

1319. **Obducant solem**: cf. *In Eccles.* f. 94ra *Quid igitur miratur quis solis fulgorem quem nobis subducit quandoque etiam exilis nubecula?*; SD 2, 701 *Set solem tantas dabis obduxisse tenebras.*

1321. **sub modio**: cf. Mt 5, 15 *neque accendunt lucernam et ponunt eam sub modio*; Arator 2, 1-2 (ed. McKinlay, CSEL 72: 77); Sedulius, *Carm. pasch.* 3, 276-82 (ed. Huemer, CSEL 10: 85); Baudri, *Carm.* 77, 177; Matthew of Vendôme, *Ep.* 1, 2, 95 (ed. Munari, 2: 86); Peter of Blois, *Carm.* 1, 10, 2a, 12-3 *nec tegitur / sub modio lucerna.*

1323-1420. The mouse: a tale of arrogance

1323. **tumor...fastus:** cf. SD 1, 344; 2, 50 *Vicit Adam fastus pestis*, 619-20 *Sed sunt quos reddit prediues uena superbos; / Ingenium fastus degenerare facit.*

1325. **fabula**: Neckam had tried his hand at the genre early in his career; the *Nouus Esopus* is a versification of selected fables from *Romulus*, itself an influential prose version of fables written by Phaedrus cf. Ziolkowski 1993, 19-20; the tale of the mouse has all the characteristics of a fable: a fiction with an animal protagonist, preceded and concluded (1323-4 *promythium*; 1419-20 *epimythium*) with an explicit moral; Neckam treats the fable of the frogs and their request for a king in DNR 2, 191 (p. 348W) [cf. Dicke 174-80] and LSD 2, 621-44 (p. 387W); NE 5, 15 *Fabula nostra docet cunctis non cuncta licere*, 16, 9 (ed. Hervieux, 2: 401) *Mordacem prohibet morderi fabula nostra*; **Informare...mores**: Isid., *Orig.* 1, 40, 3-6 defines the functions of *fabula*, including fictions written *ad mores hominum* by Horace and Aesop: *Ad mores, ut apud Horatium mus loquitur muri..., ut per narrationem fictam ad id quod agitur verax significatio referatur*; *in Eccles.* f. 97ra *Proposui enim in animo meo querere et inuestigare non curiose, non arroganter set sapienter, humiliter et discrete de omnibus generibus rerum que fiunt* *sub sole ad informationem morum*; on the usage of *informatio* and *informare* in John Gower's *Confessio amantis* and Alain of Lille's *Anticlaudianus* cf. Simpson 1-10.

1326. **Prebet...fabella fidem**: cf. Ademar, Phaedrus 1, 5, 2 (ed. Bertini 1988, 62) *Testatur haec fabella propositum meum.*

1327. **mus**: linked etymologically with *humus* cf. McCulloch 143.

1331. **uirtute**: meaning both «lineage» and the «force» of an element.

1333. **rex**: note the ironic use of *rex*, a term usually reserved for the lion e. g. «*Aegrum fama fuit*», 27, 4, 39, 41, 45 (*MGH, P. L* 1: 62-3); cf. *SD* 1, 1338, 1365, 1375, 1386, 1399; **ab ore / ...pendet**: cf. Ov., *Ep.* 1, 30 *narrantis coniunx pendet ab ore viri.*

1334. **curia tota**: cf. *SD* 2, 1464 *mirans curia tota stupet.*

1336. **uariis**: sc. *sententiis*; **turba fauet**: Ov., *Fast.* 2, 654 *linguis candida turba favet.*

1338. **solis adire**: Ov., *Ep.* 12, 70 *vix illuc radiis solis adire licet.*

1339. **emensus iter**: Ov., *Fast.* 1, 544 *emensus...orbis iter*; Stat., *Theb.* 2, 375; Claudian, *Carm.* 7, 166 *hinc Phoebi longum permensus iter*; *DNR* 2, 148 (p. 229W).

1340. **Gemmarum**: the interpretation of Apc 21, 18-21 formed one base for medieval interest in precious stones.

1340-52. An ekphrasis of the Sun's Palace.

1341-2. Ov., *Met.* 2, 1-2 (cited *SA* f. 19b); cf. *SD* 2, 231-3 with Ov., *Met.* 1, 84-6; *SD* 2, 383 with Ov., *Met.* 3, 407; *SD* 2, 897 *Tempestiua suis ueniet narratibus hora* with Ov., *Met.* 5, 499; *SD* 2, 1481-2 with Ov., *Pont.* 2, 5, 61-2.

1342. **stelliferis**: rare word cf. *SD* 2, 441 *Hic cum stellifero tellus contendit Olimpo* [cf. Sen., *Phaedra* 785 (ed. O. Zweierlein [Oxford, 1986]) *stellifero...polo*].

1343-52. Neckam devotes *LSD* 3 to precious stones; instead of treating them individually, as in the bestiary (*De bestiis* 3, 58 [*MPL* 177: 115d-119a]), he describes them as part of the ekphrasis; **Irradians...carbunculus ardet**: Dracontius, *De laudibus Dei* 1, 322 (*MGH, AA* 14: 40) *carbunculus ardet honore*; Marbod, *De lapidibus* 341 (p. 62 Riddle) *Ardentes gemmas superat* (sc. carbunculus); *LSD* 6, 241 (p. 469W) *Illustrat tenebras radians carbunculus*; *SD* 2, 1716 *carbunculus ardens.*

1343-44. **achatem / Non pallere**: cf. Isid., *Orig.* 16, 11, 1 *Est autem nigra* (sc. achates), *habens in medio circulos nigros et albos iunctos et variatos....*

1344. **flammiger**: rare word cf. *ThLL*, 6: 873, 13.

1345. **Examitum**: cf. *SD* 2, 1713-4 *Examitum fulgens mordaci pectine nectit / Fibula...*; **laurum**: cf. *LSD* 7, 18 (p. 472W) *lauri iunge virentis opes.* **smaragdi / ...uiror**: cf. *CMC* Oxford, Digby 221, f. 72va *smaragdus gemma est viridissima ultra omnes herbas et frondes*; Marbod, *De lapidibus* 134 (ed. Riddle, 45) *Omne virens superat forma viridante smaragdus.*

1346. **uiror**: cf. *LSD* 6, 153 (p. 467W)...*recreatque virore smaragdus.*

1347. **Crisolito...cedit**: cf. *SD* 2, 452 *Iacincto cedit*; Isid., *Orig.* 16, 15, 2 *Chrysolitus auro similis*; Marbod, *De lapidibus* 185 (p. 49 Riddle) *Auro crisolitus micat*; *LSD* 6, 179 (p. 467W) *Nomen chrysolito color aureus indidit*; Prudentius, *Psych.* 854; **fului...metalli**: gold cf. *LSD* 5, 907 (p. 461W); 6, 17 (p. 463W); *SD* 2, 1772 *gemmis fulua metalla nitent*; Claudian, *Carm.* 10, 57 *fulvo defendit prata metallo.*

1348. **unio**: cf. *LSD* 6, 317-20 (p. 471W).

1349-50. **confer / Celo saphirum:** cf. *LSD* 6, 135 (p. 466W) *Contendit coelo saphirus*, 139 (p. 466W) *Coelestis color est*; Marbod, *De lapidibus* 104 (ed. Riddle, 42)...*puroque simillima coelo*.

1349. **celi facies ridet**; cf. *SD* 2, 440 *facies ridet...loci*.

1352. **Contendunt...tuos:** cf. *LSD* 6, 340 (p. 471W) *Dum certant* (sc. gemmae) *radios vincere, Phoebe, tuos*.

1355. **Sole salutato:** cf. Stat., *Ach.* 1, 57 *rege salutato*; **causaque uie reserata:** cf. Alan of Lille, *De planctu* 7, 41 (ed. Häring 832) *Tu uie causam resera petenti*; Ov., *Met.* 10, 23 *causa viae est coniunx*, *Ep.* 16, 28; 17. 158; Stat., *Ach.* 1, 734; Claudian, *Carm.* 1, 129 *quae causa uiae?*; *SD* 1, 1377.

1357. **non gloria uexet inanis:** cf. *Disticha Catonis* 2, 16, 2 (ed. Boas, 117) *quos gloria uexat inanis*; *Ysopet* 15, 11 *Hoc faciunt stulti quos gloria uexat inanis*; *Gal* 5, 26 *non efficiamur inanis gloriae cupidi*; *NA* 5, 1-2 *De facili menti stulte surrepit inanis / Gloria, que miseros precipitare solet*.

1358. **fallere:** cf. *NA* 1, 21 *Spes fallax multos fallit*.

1363. **Vsibus apta:** Ov., *Fast.* 3, 666 *humanis usibus apta Ceres*; *LSD* 9, 248 (p. 491W).

1365. **uoluens sub pectore curas:** cf. Claudian, *Carm.* 28, 147-8 *pectore curas / uoluebat*; *LH-L* 4: 172-4; Mastandrea 638. **P**'s gloss, *yronia*, a species of *allegoria*, draws attention to the narrator's mocking tone; see S. Reynolds, *Medieval Reading*, 136-7.

1367. **uelatam...amictu:** cf. Ov., *Met.* 10, 1 *croceo velatus amictu*.

1368. **pandit ordine cuncta:** cf. Verg., *A.* 6, 723 *ordine singula pandit*; Claudian, *Carm.* 20, 235; *NE* 20, 22 (ed. Hervieux, 2: 403) *Querenti pastor ordine cuncta refert*; *LH-L* 4: 114.

1369. **Illa...refert:** cf. *SD* 2, 1508; **uiribus inpar:** *LSD* 2, 413 (p. 382W); Avianus 18, 10; Ov., *Ep.* 19, 5; *LH-L* 5: 642-3; Mastandrea 927.

1370. **nutu concutit:** cf. Ov., *Met.* 2, 848-9 *ille pater... / ...qui nutu concutit orbem*.

1371. **menia, templa, domos:** *LSD* 3, 852 (p. 415W); 5, 80 (p. 442W); 3, 982 (p. 418W); *SD* 1, 1436; for a similar *congeries* before or after diaeresis cf. Matthew of Vendôme, *Tob.* 1840 (ed. Munari, 2: 238) *Restituet Dominus menia, rura, domos*; Lawrence of Durham, *Dialogi* 2, 108 *Maenia, saxa, domos, quae male ludis, habet*; Mart. 9, 25, 4 *aspicimus solem, sidera, templa, deos*; **Arthos / ...Nothus:** on the form *Arthos* for *Arctos* in the manuscripts of Claudian cf. the *apparatus criticus* of Claudian, *Carm.* 1, 22; 8, 51; *De raptu* 2, 189 (ed. Birt, 4, 152, 371); cf. *ThLL*, 2: 470, 59; cf. Luc., 4, 70 *vacat imbribus Arctos / Et Notos*.

1375. **spe delusus:** cf. *NA* 1, 12 *spe lusus, gaudia vana fouet*; **consumit gaudia uotis:** cf. Stat., *Theb.* 1, 323 *extrahit et longo consumit gaudia uoto*.

1376. **Eolii carceris:** cf. Ov., *Fast.* 2, 456.

1378. **perpetuo federe uinctus**; cf. *SD* 2, 1719-20 *Paulus... / ...perpetuo federe iunctus*.

1379. **Quid miri:** cf. *SD* 2, 747.

1381. **desunt uires:** cf. Ov., *Am.* 2, 4, 7 *nam desunt uires ad me mihi iusque regendum*; *NA* 2, 9-10 *Inuidisse michi Naturam sencio, uires / desunt*; *LH-L* 2: 46-7.

1384. **conpos uoti:** Ov., *Ars* 1, 486 *uoti...compos eris*; *NA* 2, 25; *SD* 2, 1756 *Et uoti compos redditur ipsa sui*.

1387. **Publica priuate:** cf. *SD* 2, 151-2 *iuris / Priuati faciat publica*; Hor., *Ars* 131 *publica materies privati iuris erit*; Ov., *Tr.* 4, 2, 74 *causaque privata publica maior erit*; Claudian, *Carm.* 21, 299.

1388. **vera referre**: *NE* 31, 21 *Ista docent veros non semper vera referre.*

1389-90. **Cibele...potens,...deorum / Mater**: cf. Fulg., *Mitologiae* 3, 5 (ed. Helm, 65, 14) *Ergo ideo et turrita pingitur* (sc. Cybele), *quod omnis potentiae elatio sit in capite; ideo et leonum curru praesidens, quia omnis potentia etiam uirtuti dominatur; ideo et multiplici ueste, quod omnis potentia ornata sit; sceptrum etiam fert, quod regno uicina sit omnis potentia. Ob hanc rem etiam mater deum dicta est, ...ergo potentia diuitum mater est*; Mythographi Vaticani 1, 225.

1390. **cunctis nobilitate preest**: cf. *SD* 2, 485-6 *Has dat opes quas delicias natura ministrat / Menti qui reliquos nobilitate preit.*

1391. **inexhaustas uires**: cf. Sil. 16, 498 (ed. L. Bauer, 2: 154 [Leipzig, 1892]) *inexhaustas effundit turbine uires*; **cataclisme**: cf. *LSD* 5, 45 (p. 441 W) *aquas cataclismi*; a rare word in Classical Latin: *ThLL*, 3: 587, 35 lists only *Carmen adv. Marc.* 4, 44 and Ps.-Eugenius, *Carm. app.* 20, 30 (*MGH, AA* 14: 276).

1393. **absorbet**: cf. *SD* 2, 481-2 *Has edit paradysus aquas quas concaua tellus / Absorbet*; **rebus habundat**: cf. Mastandrea 728.

1394. **plumis, Sardanapalle, tuis**: cf. Juv. 10, 362 *pluma sardanapalli*; *Poems* 1, 74 (ed. Walther 1965, 113) *Tunc renuo plumas, Sardanapalle, tuas*; *SD* 2, 773 *plume tibi, Sardanapalle, nocebunt.*

1395. **Delicias Bachi**: *LSD* 4, 356 (p. 428W); *Poems* 1, 92 (ed. Walther 1965, 114)*Delicias Bachi semper adesse precor.*

1396. **mel...Alcinoo**: cited in *CP*, O f. 99ra; cf. *LSD* 4, 664-5 (p. 435W) *Ludens Alcinous pueris sic poma ministrat / Sic mel Aristaei*; Ov., *Pont.* 4, 2, 9-10 *Quis mel Aristaeo... / ...poma det Alcinoo?*; Mart. 7, 42, 6 *Alcinoo nullum poma dedisse putas?*

1398. **nota referre pudet**: cf. *CNP* 1046 *nota referre licet.*

1399. **causa laboris**: *LH-L* 1: 302; Mastandrea 113.

1400. **talibus orsa**: cf. Ov., *Met.* 4, 54 *talibus orsa modis lana sua fila sequente*; *LH-L* 5: 349.

1401. **Iungit amor**: cf. Ov., *Ep.* 20, 228.

1405. **Nasone docente**: Neckam names the source cf. Ov., *Fast.* 4, 98 *et docuit iungi cum pare quemque sua*; *Fast.* 3, 193, 526; *SD* 2, 1729-30 *Naso / Cui dulces elegos scribere ludus erat.* For this language in a marriage context cf. Ausonius, *Septem sap.* 30 (*MGH, AA* 5: 248) *par pari iugator coniunx; quicquid inpar, dissidet.*

1406. Ov., *Ep.* 9, 32 [Walther, *Prov.* 28890]; **nube pari**: cf. Walther, *Prov.* 29404 *Si vis nubere, nube pari*; for the motif in *epithalamia* cf. Claudian, *Carm. min. app.* 5, 12, 51-3, 79.

1407. **Prodeat in medium**: cf. *LSD* 5, 524 (p. 452W) *Prodiit in medium*; **terre soboles**: etymology linked *mus* with *terra* and *humus*: cf. Isid., *Orig.* 13, 3, 1 *Alii dicunt mures quod ex humore terrae nascantur, nam mus terra, unde et humus*; McCulloch 143.

1408. **Ridet Iupiter**: cf. Ov., *Ars* 1, 633; Mart., 9, 34, 1 *Iuppiter...risit*; Claudian, *Carm. min.* 51, 1-2; Jupiter appears in the fables of Avianus e. g. 8, 11 *Iupiter arridens postquam sperata negauit*; 14, 1; 22, 1; **acta placent**: *Aulularia* 10; *Alda* 8, 565 (ed. Cohen, 1: 74, 130, 151).

1409. **donacio propter / Connubium**: on the medieval reality of *donatio propter nuptias DMLBS* 3: 722 cites *Acta Henrici* 11. 11, 275 (dated 1186) *compositio...tam super...[terris] quas petebam nomine maritagii...quam super aliis que nomine donationis propter nuptias petebam in Normannia vel in Anglia.*

1410. **Dos datur**: cf. Isid., *Orig.* 5, 24, 25 *Dictam...dicunt...dotem quasi do item.*

1411. **cedris...mirica**: cf. *SD* 2, 554-5 *Cum cedris... / ...certat*; Peter of Blois, *Libellus*, 73, 1122 *pigmea mirica.*.

1412. **ulule cignis**: cf. Verg., *E.* 8, 55 *certent et cycnis ululae*; *SD* 2, 553 *subdis cum cignis, ulule*; **saliunca rosis**: cf. Verg., *E.* 5, 17 *puniceis humilis quantum saliunca rosetis*; *SD* 2, 282 *uernans fit saliunca rosa*; Baudri, *Carm.* 41, 6; 80, 4; *Miles Gloriosus* 275 (ed. Cohen, 1: 206); *LH-L* 5: 21.

1413. **fumus...euanescit in auras**: cf. *LSD* 1, 87 (p. 359W); *NA* 2, 29 *tenues miser euanescit in auras*; Ov., *Met.* 14, 432, *Ep.* 1, 79.

1414. **Sceptra...regia**: cf. *LSD* 5, 632 (p. 455W) *illis regia sceptra dedit*.

1415. **Pelle leonina...asellus**: John of Salisbury, *Enthet. minor* 196 (ed. van Laarhoven, 1: 243) *pelle leonina dic quid asellus agat* [cf. Avianus 5]; *NA* 5, 15 *Est asinus, quamuis indutus pelle leonis*; **leonina**: rare word cf. *ThLL*, 7: 1169, 70.

1416. **segnicies**: cf. Peter of Blois, *Libellus*, 51, 225-6 «*Tarditatem asini stimulus accelerat*».

1417-18. **repulsam / passus es**: cf. Ov., *Met.* 2, 97 *nullam patiere repulsam.*

1418. **latebrasque colis**: cf. Verg., *G.* 1, 181-2 *exiguus mus / sub terris posuitque domos.*

1420. **fastus**: cf. *SD* 2, 50 *Vicit Adam fastus pestis*; the tale of the mouse and its association with darkness plays against the archetypal story of pride, the fall of Lucifer.

1421-36. *The mole*

1421. **[Talpa]**: cf. *DNR* 2, 122 (p. 200W); **natura creauit**: cf. Mastandrea 545.

1423. **talpam**: The mole lives underground, in darkness and blind cf. McCulloch 143; **in talpam uersa puella**: witty allusion to Proserpina, who lived six months of the year in the Underworld cf. Ov., *Fast.* 4, 417-620; *CMC* Oxford, Digby 221, f. 73va *Pluto secum ducit puellam id est Proserpinam.*

1424. **Triticee Cereris**: cf. *LSD* 8, 3 (p. 481W) *Triticeum granum*; 8, 6 (p. 481W) *hic est Cereris deliciosus honos.*

1426. **gravem culpam pena**: cf. Ov., *Am.* 2, 14, 44 *poenam culpa secunda ferat*; *Ars* 2, 604 *At contra grauis est culpa tacenda loqui.*

1431. **Luminibus capti...talpe**: cf. Verg., *G.* 1, 183 *aut oculis capti fodere cubilia talpae*; *DNR* 2, 122 (p. 200W) *Subterraneos fodiunt cuniculos talpae oculis capti*; Urso, *De commixtionibus elem.* 6, 4 (ed. Stürner, 179) *Si autem secundum inferiora sui / ad iam dictos effectus terra conveniat, hoc animal profunda terre inhabitat et terra fovetur ut talpa.*

1431. **talpe**: cf. Isid., *Orig.* 12, 3, 5 *Talpa dicta, quod sit damnata caecitate perpetua tenebris*; **fodere**: = *foderunt.*

1433. **comitatur egestas**: Claudian, *Carm.* 3, 36 *infelix humili gressu comitatur Egestas* [Peter of Blois, *Libellus*, 48, 127]; cf. *Poems* 2b, 8-9 (ed. Walther, 1962, 116) *tam liberas artes, tam honestas / infelix humili gressu comitatur egestas*; in *Eccles.* f. 87vb *luxum infelix humili gressu comitatur egestas.*

1435. Nebuzardan was Nebuchadnezzar'commander of the guard (Jr 39, 9 *magister militum*), who after the seige of Jerusalem deported the surviving population to Babylon; cf. Serlo of Bayeux, *Non uis armorum sed princeps ipse cocorum / Ierusalem muros destruxit uix ruituros* (ed. Boutemy, 257, 52-3).

1437–46. *The larus*

1437. **larus**: cf. Lv 11, 16.

1438. **aqua...tellus**: cf. Walahfrid Strabo, *Epitome in Lev. MPL* 114: 814d *Larus et in aquis et extra aquam conversatur*, *Glossa ordinaria in Lev. MPL* 113: 329b; *CPV* f. 142v *Nunc terra, nunc degit aquis larus aera findens.*

1446–58. *The fox, once more*

1447. **[Vulpis]**: cf. *DNR* 2, 125 (pp. 204-6W); *LSD* 10, 163-4 (p. 490W); **prenuntiat**: cf. Peter of Blois, *Ep.* 20 (of bishop Rainald of Chartres) *munificentiam enim a tenera prenuntiavit infantia.*

1449. **Hinnulus... / Ceruum**: cf. gloss on *DNR* 2, 166 (p. 274W) *Hic hinnulus est foetus cervae*; **indiciis certis**: *Ecbasis captivi* 739; cf. *DNR* 2, 36 (p. 150W), 125 (p. 204W); *CNP* 1403.

1450. **rampno**: cf. *SD* 2, 291-2 *Mens ramnos morum paliuros atque nociuas / Herbas et frutices monstraque uana parit.*

1451. **soboles**: cf. *DNR* 2, 125 (p. 205W) *Catuli in utero materno unguibus pelliculam ventris materni penetrant, et dum jam matrem infestant asperitatem subsecuturam praenuntiant* [cf. *SD* 1, 1447 *prenuntiat*].

1457-8. The fox plays dead by lying on its back; when birds land on him, the fox captures and eats them cf. McCulloch 119; Henkel 188-9. Diekstra 147 notes that this observation on fox behaviour is grounded in fact; cf. Isid., *Orig.* 12, 2, 29 *Nam dum non habuerit escam, fingit mortem, sicque descendentes quasi ad cadaver aves rapit et devorat* (sc. vulpis); *DNR* 2, 125 (p. 205W); *Physiologus Lat.* XV, 1-8 (ed. Carmody, 29); *Theobaldi Physiologus* 1-10 (ed. Eden, 44); Hildebert, *Physiologus MPL* 171: 1220a-b; *NP* 415 (ed. Orbán, 37) *Insidias tales auibus struit exiciales*; Herrmann, «Gallus et Vulpes», 261, stanza 13; Druce 381 and plate 1 for an illustration of a stone over a 12th-c. doorway of the nave of Alne Church, Yorkshire, with the *titulus* VULPIS; it depicts a supine fox feigning death in order to catch birds.

1458. **aucupis arte**: Mart., 0, 11, 6 *si captare feras aucupis arte placet*; *SD* 1, 703.

APPENDIX

While **P** contains a much more complete copy of both books of the *Suppletio defectuum* and offers a better quality of text overall, **M** preserves a number of true readings among its excerpts, most notably at 51 *Que*, 84 *cereris*, 169 *solus*, 181 *buxus*, 198 *poteris*, 787 *geris*, 875 *Se*, 900 *aurem*, 904 *ipsa*, 1033 *cos*, 1191 *quid*, 1233 *animalque*. **M** ff. 151v-165v presents extracts from *Suppletio defectuum* I in the following order (square brackets indicate the omissions): 1-56, [57], 58-106, [107-8], 109-120, [121-2], 123-209, [210], 211-68, [269-82], 283-86, [287-92], 293-4, [295-306], 307-8, [309-46], 347-8, [349-66], 367-70, [371-76], 377-80, [381-406], 407-8, [409-58], 459-60, [461-528], 529-32, [533-88], 589-646, [647-52], 653-661, [662-4], 665-72, [673-700], 701-2, [703-32], 733-46, [747-50], 751-70, [771-2], 773-4, [775-6], 777-806, [807-8], 809-12, [813-4], 815-20, 871-90, 821-70 (with two verses added between vv. 842-3, which are absent from **P**'s text), 891-930, [931-92], 993-1096, [1097-8], 1099-1114, [1115-48], 1149-51, [1152-8], 1159-72, [1173-90], 1191-1212, [1213-4], 1215-20, [1221-2], 1223-34, [1235-1302], 1303-10, [1311-1420], 1421-58.

Orthographical variants are excluded from the following report of **M**'s readings:

1-100

1 *M corrects* Ornuta *to* Ornata? 7 rerum] ferer 14 iusta] certa 18 Vsum] Visum 19 mutat] munit 22 docet] decet 23 Scootillant 25 est istis; *second* est *omitted* 28 aera 32 Artom 33 distinguetur 35 lecus 37 Mergus amor aquas *with expunction marks under* amor; siluaque; polumbes 40 mistra; fictaque] ruraque 41 amat coruus; cornix] cornu 42 nidum uolucres regit psitacus *with expunction marks under* uolucres regit; horret 43 M *corrects* ass *to* ars 49 clausit; minturnit 51 Que 53 uultur] turtur 58 cacabant *with the first two letters inserted by the copyist above the line*; trecrissat 59 sturnus] turdus 61 graculi] *omitted in* M 62 noctes] noctos 63 Psitace] Perfiotate 65 Nunc] Quem 67 risibus] usibus 68 turis 69 minor in laudes uolucrum *with expunction marks under* in laudes 71 quanto 72 Desuper] Desy 73 aures 76 M *adds the superscripts letters* ci *before the final letter*; probat 77 epul; sotulare; M *omits* famem; cicanius 78 Que nullo 79 eum] enim 80 equs reus 81 iuuat 82 Si] Set 83 ficus recreat 84 cereris 86 medico 87 bibo; cinifemque; pepellus 88 est 89 Veneratur 90 grata] cara 92 Depones; fetu d stat 94 resiui 95 Aurigfrigius *with an expunction mark under the first* g 97 perdrix; M *corrects* fuit *to* fit; M *omits* esus 98 calnaleonca 99 Allicitur

101-200

101 Ioui 102 M *omits* Que 103 Induuimis *with expunction marks under the letters* -ui 109 Accipitrix; columba 111 perditum 112 augmina *with an expunction mark under the second letter*

116 M *corrects* clausit *to* claudit   125 fauor   126 heremis *with an expunction mark under final letter*   127 quos grecia; nutrit; auisque *with the first letter added superscript* 128 ramis...tuis

130 M *corrects* recitat *to* recia; doles   131 crepitatos   133 Preuibet 135 casu] cau *with a suspension bar over the second letter*   136 salubria   137 longa   139 nutibus   140 mortibus   141 Nunc] Hinc; excelsis; alis] abs   143 Remisio   144 gires   146 notos 147 supirat   150 rutila uirtute; M *corrects* flaget *to* fulget   151 Auirea *with an expunction mark under the third letter*; cerenas *with an expunction mark under the final letter*   152 cecat   153 Cerileo; depingi] respersi   157 Commendant   158 strenuitatis habet inest   162 Accipitis; *after* placet *M writes on the next line* Delectat uisum, *before placing expunction marks under both words*   163 maculus; pulmas   169 solus   172 Piscatus; cum   174 patrem   177 Nonnumquam *with* num *added superscript*; supertbit *with an expunction mark under the second* r   178 sensu *with expunction marks under the last two letters*   179 Arbores   181 Humnitique; buxus   185 flori; laudalis *with an expunction mark under the second* l   186 bellus   187 Fuscus; in horensis; ramus   188 extimuere] ytinere   189 ornat] instar *with expunction marks and* ornat *written above.*

190 nucem] mitem   193 Bracis   195 tibi dices decies, *with expunction marks under* dices   198 poteris   199 ab ustis   200 synare

201-300

203 contendere   205 Dissimile   209 cedat   211 a   213 sumsit   214 Afferectus? 219 Lingnea *with an expunction mark under the first* n; conseruauit *with the letters* -ua *added superscript.*

220 ceptis   224 poterit *is corrected to* potest   225 delecta   229 M *corrects* perire *to* parere.

230 Quam   231 funereis *with the second* e *added above*; M *corrects* ponitis *to* pompis 233 abiegna] ab ignea   235 Ad   238 suo   241 gatissima   242 M *corrects* subditr, *with a bar over the final letter, to* subsidium   247 Wcani   248 M *corrects* Constaneeque *to* Castaneeque   250 causio   255 casus   258 constupent; stipiditate   265 artanesia   266 uires]uicis; delicosus   267 non uos] meros; lumbos   268 Soluatur; iuuant   283 Asmaticis *with the letters* ci *added above*; cedat   284 opta 285 Artethicos *with the letter* h *added superscript*; M *corrects* maternitatem? *to* matricem   286 rura

301-400

307 ydropicis   308 uis]his; maratri *corrected from* marafri   347 lertargo *with the first* r *added superscript*; saturena   348 Iucta   367 rectant; ligustria   370 iuamen   379 superaddita *with the second* d *added superscript*   380 Intericos; sit

401-500

407 camgis (*no hairlines over the minims*)   460 M *omits* que

501-600

529 sorde   530 M *corrects* Imdicit *to* Indicit   532 eius] ouis   589 paucis   590 M *omits* stilo 591 M *omits* ea; descendit] precedit   592 clausit   597 verm   599 dicte] deest

601–700

601 ignitus actus deformet honestos *with expunction marks under* actus deformet honestos *and* ea cogat degenerare *written above the deleted words*   603 ignitus   604
celebris   610 suis   614 Fometisque   616 M *corrects* que *to* qua   620 pereunt   622
contricti; uiuificabitur   624 reuiuscit   625 canora   628 M *corrects* nasciscus *to*
narciscus; ulixes   635 teste] testes   636 M *corrects* testes *to* teste *with an expunction
mark under the final* s   637 hoc   642 M *corrects* datum *to* datam   643 hoc   644 Qua;
simplicitate   653 tempore   654 suam ?   655 annum   657 Hic] Hec   660 tranfert;
esse] ipsa   668 uarios cultilibus

701–800

735 ampluarum   736 sensu   738 M *corrects* mimis *to* nimis   739 Melior; M *corrects*
in sensus *to* in sessus; furibus   741 scidere   743 caldarius; aspersit   745 respisceret
752 Dii] Dum 754 uernat] cremat   755 Exitat   757 cultus] cautis   762 M *corrects*
mente *to* mense   764 M *omits* aque   765 exercicior wererbles sistemata   767
Cauta   768 Hornas   770 Illa sibi] Ista sibi   773 purius] pluribus   777 uergens
iam   779 infausta *with the first* a *added above the line*   780 prodisziosa   786 confuso
787 formam geris impiger   788 sciens   789 domos   790 uarium] uanum (*or
nanum?*)   791 te sub seducunt   792 triste; premant   794 Destituit   798 M *corrects*
Delicians *to* Delicias   799 tenus

801–900

801 possit   804 uera *with* e *written superscript*   805 hrundo   809 Cogno; mor   815
cuntisque; paratus   818 Cui mors] Cum mores   819 tamen] cum   826 quandam
827 Mauseola   831 ciba   832 in uaco   835 dignatur   836 felix mater   840 M
corrects uiuet *to* uiuit   842 nescius *with the letter* s *added above the line*; exat   842 *After*
842 *in* M *there follows a couplet:* Tu michi uiuis ad huc uiuo tibi set tibi uiuam/Inque
meo regnans pectore uiuet amor; *the text of* M *then continues with v.* 843   844 tuuus
845 Mens] Mors; erat   847 quiescunt   849 miri] uiri   852 docet   855 iugiter
857 mora   864 atque   865 Hic] Hunc   866 Equale; consimileque; M *corrects* tibi
to sibi   873 Deuita; spacioiis   pporcio   874 quoque 875 Et] Se   879 preuia]
prima   881 hostiis; fatiscit   883 Exitat   884 ille   885 acles   889 colori 891
Sollicitant *with the first* i *written above the line*; lenitum   893 rete   894 Interserta]
Inter seria   895 icos   896 Eaciden; *after v.* 896 *there follows this verse*: Priamidem
helenum graias regnasse per urbes   899 Pone] Pene

901–1000

900 aurem; Venite   901 calicis; M *omits* et   902 canunt] carent *with expunction
marks, after which* cancer *is added on the same line*   903 cernere   904 ipsa; mineruia
909 ridens
911 auras *with the letter* r *inserted above the line*   912 numquam; arca   915 M *omits*
ala   916 socitur *with an expunction mark under the letter* o   924 M *omits* non   930
fustus

993 uulpes   996 lucris inians inhyans *with expunction marks under* inians   997 M
corrects Fore *to* Forme   999 M *corrects* catus *to* casus; colore; umor

1001–1100

1000 celem   1001 articulis   1002 uolidos   1003 natura] non; redit   1004 suma
1005 M *omits* corpora   1007 dominatur   1009 nexu] ueru   1010 comis] connus
1011 supere   1013 fructum; perpexa   1016 ludit] ridet   1017 M *corrects* sustinuo
to sustineo   1021 decretio] decetero   1023 sera   1024 ceptum   1027 Materiaalis
with an expunction mark under the third a   1029 Aptat *with final* t *added above the line*
1034 Lumine   1037 M *omits* michi   1041 apto   1042 nolla   1044 publica
1045 Sinthasis   1046 Sustinet; uenustaque   1048 M *corrects* resputat *to* respuat; ipse
1050 nouo] suo   1054 Vir   1055 felicibus; arcto   1057 corripiendam   1058
tremor   1063 sint] fuit   1064 frutum   1078 curis *with the abrreviation for* ur *written*
above the letter u   1079 cuncta *with the second* c *written above the line*   1082 subueit
1084 recres   1086 Intra hac se *with expunction marks under* hac; potest] putat
1091 Suus; fece se feda   1092 philosophantur   1095 Fece uoluptatum] Ex uolun-
tatum   1096 agit] amat   1099 mincem   1100 Arbutas acies rubes

1101–1200

1105 est   1151 Notas declinat fraudes necesse promtus adest   1159 plurima   1160
barrus] rarius   1162 peccora   1165 in heremis   1166 uigilat; armat; M *omits* ei
1171 pugnabat   1172 sic cedet] sic sedet   1191 quid   1192 Questus] Estus; aspicis
1198 pelui   1200 perferri

1201–1300

1203 contendit; latidando   1205 Pluribus; gemma quam *with transposition marks to*
change to quam gemma   1208 flulgida *with an expunction mark under the first* l   1210
cunta   1211 gemam M   1215 tutis *with the second* t *inserted above the line*; cinerem]
nichilum   1216 parens] pens   1217 teneri   1224 Parturit   1227 Perfodit; fisus
1231 Scisimus; obrescit   1232 Martrix   1233 animalque qtimoris   1234 Crescit]
Tres

1301–1400

1304 debitate caput   1305-6 M *copies out in the order* 1306-5 *with transposition marks,*
b *against* 1306, a *against* 1305, *indicating the corrected order*   1308 infaustibus   1309
rumpes

1401–1458

1423 eperta   1425 tantum] fm   1429 disparlicet   1431 capiti   1433 commutatur
1434 Prodigia; annus   1440 dura] datur   1442 asper   1447 actus] nrcis *with a*
suspension bar over n?; premiciat   1450 ramo   1452 M *corrects* erat *to* erit   1454
ungvibus   1455 malingna   1458 prit

INDEX NOMINUM

Numbers refer to the verses of the present edition.

GENERAL INDEX

Numbers refer to pages of the present edition and 'n.' to a note on the specified page.

CONTENTS

Stampa: Tipografia Artigiana Tuderte - Todi

SISMEL

EDIZIONI DEL GALLUZZO

Siena, Stresa. A cura di Carla Casagrande, Maria Antonietta Casagrande Mazzoli, Mariella Curandai, Simona Gavinelli, Silvana Vecchio

Paulus Venetus, *Super primum Sententiarum Johannis de Ripa lecturae. Abbreviatio*. Ed. par Francis Ruello

Paulus Venetus, *Logica parva*. Ed. by Alan R. Perreiah

EZIO FRANCESCHINI E LA RESISTENZA

3. *L'archivio di Ezio Franceschini sulla Resistenza. Il carteggio del Gruppo Frama (1943-1945)*. A cura di Francesca Minuto Peri, 1998, pp. XXII-852

MANOSCRITTI DATATI D'ITALIA

1. *I manoscritti datati della Provincia di Trento*. A cura di Maria Antonietta Casagrande Mazzoli, Lorena Dal Poz, Donatella Frioli, Silvano Groff, Mauro Hausbergher, Marco Palma, Cesare Scalon, Stefano Zamponi, 1996, pp. XVI-110 con 87 tavv. f. t.

2. *I manoscritti datati della Biblioteca Riccardiana di Firenze, I: Mss. 1-1000*. A cura di Teresa De Robertis e Rosanna Miriello, 1997, pp. XXVI-146 con 180 tavv. f. t.

3. *I manoscritti datati della Biblioteca Riccardiana di Firenze, II: Mss. 1001-1400*. A cura di Teresa De Robertis e Rosanna Miriello, 1999, pp. XXII-108 con 126 tavv. f. t.

◆ in preparazione:

I manoscritti datati della Provincia di Vicenza e della Biblioteca Antoniana di Padova. A cura di Nicoletta Giovè e Cristiana Cassandro

I manoscritti datati della Biblioteca Nazionale Centrale di Firenze, Fondo Conventi Soppressi. A cura dei bibliotecari della Sala Manoscritti della BNCF, coordinati da Marco Palma e Stefano Zamponi

MICROLOGUS' LIBRARY

1. Jacques Berlioz, *Les catastrophes naturelles au Moyen Age*, 1998, pp. 244

2. *The Regulation of the Evil. Social and Cultural Attitudes to Epidemics in the Late Middle Ages*. Edited by Agostino Paravicini Bagliani and Francesco Santi, 1998, pp. 212

3. Pinella Travaglia, *Magic, causality and intentionality. The doctrine of the rays in al-Kindi*, 1999, pp. 176

◆ in preparazione:

Alessandra Sorci, *«La forza de le linee». Prospettiva stereometrica in Piero della Francesca*

Piero Morpurgo, *L'armonia della natura e l'ordine dei governi (secoli XII-XIV)*

MILLENNIO MEDIEVALE

1. *Glossae diuinae historiae. The Biblical Glosses of John Scottus Eriugena*. Edited with an Introduction by John J. Contreni and Pádraig P. Ó Néill, 1997, pp. XXX-254

2. Alcuino, *De orthographia*. Edizione critica a cura di Sandra Bruni, 1997, pp. LXXXII-46

3. *Entre Dieu et Satan: les visions d'Ermine de Reims*. Recueillies et transcrites par Jean Le Graveur. Présentées, éditées et traduites par Claude Arnaud-Gillet. Préface d'André Vauchez, 1997, pp. 286

4. *Gli Umanesimi Medievali*. Atti del II Congresso dell'«Internationales Mittellateinerkomitee» (Firenze, Certosa del Galluzzo, 11-15 settembre 1993). A cura di Claudio Leonardi, 1998, pp. VIII-884

5. *Testi, manoscritti, ipertesti. Compatibilità informatica e letteratura medievale*. Atti del Convegno di studi (Firenze, Certosa del Galluzzo, 31 maggio - 1 giugno 1996). A cura di Lino Leonardi, 1998, pp. VIII-210

6. Iacopo da Varazze, *Legenda aurea*. Edizione critica a cura di Giovanni Paolo Maggioni, 1998, voll. 2, pp. LXVI-1368. SECONDA EDIZIONE RIVISTA DALL'AUTORE, 1999, voll. 2.

7. Massimo Bernabò, *Il Fisiologo di Smirne. Le miniature del perduto codice B. 8 della Biblioteca della Scuola Evangelica di Smirne*. Con la collaborazione di Glenn Peers e Rita Tarasconi, 1998, pp. XXVIII-128 con 115 tavv. f. t.

8. Stefania Bertini Guidetti, *I Sermones di Iacopo da Varazze. Il potere delle immagini nel Duecento*, 1998, pp. X-174

9. Paolo Luotto, *Il vero Savonarola e il Savonarola di L. Pastor*. Ristampa anastatica della II edizione rivista dall'autore, 1998, pp. VI*-XVI-624

10. *La Bibbia in italiano tra Medioevo e Rinascimento. La Bible italienne au Moyen Age et à la Reinassance*. Atti del Convegno di studi promosso dalla Fondazione Ezio Franceschini e dall'École Française de Rome (Firenze, Certosa del Galluzzo, 8-9 novembre 1996). A cura di Lino Leonardi, 1998, pp. X-442

11. *Gesta Karoli Magni ad Carcassonam et Narbonam*. Untersuchungen und Neuedition von Christian Heitzmann, 1999, pp. CXXIV-120

12. *Un leggendario fiorentino del XIV secolo*. Edizione critica a cura di Antonella Degl'Innocenti, 1999, pp. XLII-122

13. Angela Frascadore, *La scomunica e la scrittura. Un'indagine sulla cultura grafica di notai, giudici testimoni nella Puglia nel primo Trecento*, 1999, pp. VIII-196 con 12 tavv. f. t.

14. *Il Testamentum* alchemico attribuito a Raimondo Lullo. Edizione del testo latino e catalano del MS Oxford, Corpus Christi College, 244. A cura di Michela Pereira e Barbara Spaggiari, 1999, pp. CLXVIII-632

♦ in preparazione:

Raimondo da Capua, *Legenda beate Agnetis de Monte Policiano*. Edizione critica a cura di Silvia Nocentini

Tradizioni patristiche nell'Umanesimo. Atti del Convegno di studi promosso dalla Società Internazionale per lo Studio del Medioevo Latino (Firenze, 6-9 febbraio 1997). A cura di Mariarosa Cortesi

Anima e corpo nella cultura medievale. Atti del V Convegno di studi della Società Italiana per lo Studio del Pensiero Medievale (Venezia, 25-28 settembre 1995). A cura di Carla Casagrande e Silvana Vecchio

Gian Carlo Garfagnini, *«Questa è la terra tua». Savonarola a Firenze*

Bartolomeo da Trento, *Liber epilogorum in gesta sanctorum*. Edizione critica a cura di Emore Paoli

Storia di Barlaam et Iosafat. Volgarizzamento italiano dalla lingua d'oc (secondo la versione del ms. Riccardiano 1422). Edizione critica a cura di Giovanna Frosini

Raffaele Argenziano, *Agli inizi dell'iconografia sacra a Siena*

Mariella Curandai, *Fonti agiografiche latine medievali di Siena. I passionari*

Gli studi di agiografia medievale (1978-1997). Repertorio bibliografico da «Medioevo latino» e altre fonti. A cura di Antonella Degl'Innocenti e Silvia Nocentini

Les études sur le prophétisme médiéval (Xe-XVe siècles). Répertoire bibliographique à partir du «Medioevo latino» et d'autres sources. Par André Vauchez

Gli studi sul papato da Alessandro III a Bonifacio VIII. Repertorio bibliografico. A cura di Agostino Paravicini Bagliani

Ser Matteo di Biliotto, *Imbreviature. I registro (anni 1294-1295)*. A cura di Manila Soffici e Franek Sznura

11. *Carmelo Cappuccio maestro di letteratura*. A cura di Claudio Leonardi (con saggi di W. Binni, C. Cappuccio, G. Sbrilli), 1998, pp. 40

12. *La buona lingua della polvere. Cataloghi, repertori e lessici tra erudizione, narrativa e politica*. Atti della III tavola rotonda della Fondazione Ezio Franceschini, in collaborazione con la Sovrintendenza Archivistica per la Toscana (Certosa del Galluzzo, 4 dicembre 1995). A cura di Francesco Santi, 1998, pp. VII-80 con 7 tavv. f. t.

◆ in preparazione:

Leone Borsotti, *Storia della natura e storia dell'uomo*. Tre saggi sulla tradizione cristiana nella crisi del pensiero moderno

Giornata commemorativa per i primi dieci anni di attività della Fondazione Ezio Franceschini alla Certosa del Galluzzo (Firenze 1987-1997)

Il cimelio. Ordine e disordine del 'pezzo unico' nelle sistemazioni documentarie e nella ricerca storica. Atti della quarta tavola rotonda della Fondazione Ezio Franceschini, in collaborazione con la Sovrintendenza Archivistica per la Toscana (Firenze-Certosa del Galluzzo, 10 dicembre 1996). A cura di Francesco Santi.

4. Vittore da Tunnuna, *Chronica. Chiesa e Impero nell'età di Giustiniano*. A cura di Antonio Placanica, 1997, pp. LXVI-146

5. Teodulo, *Ecloga. Il canto della verità e della menzogna*. A cura di Francesco Mosetti Casaretto, 1997, pp. CXXVIII-70

6. Girolamo Savonarola, *Verità della profezia. De veritate prophetica dyalogus*. A cura di Claudio Leonardi. Traduzione di Oddo Bucci, 1997, pp. LXIV-232 con 1 tav. f. t.

SAVONAROLA E LA TOSCANA

8. *Verso Savonarola. Misticismo, profezia, empiti riformistici fra Medioevo ed età moderna.* Atti della giornata di studio (Poggibonsi, 30 aprile 1997). A cura di Gian Carlo Garfagnini, 1999, pp. XX-152

9. Rita Librandi, Adriana Valerio, *I* Sermoni *di Domenica da Paradiso.* Studio e testo critico, 1999, pp. CLXXX-170

♦ in preparazione:

I processi del Savonarola (1498). A cura di Ida Giovanna Rao, Paolo Viti, Raffaella M. Zaccaria

Ludovica Sebregondi, *La fortuna iconografica del Savonarola*

Roberto Ridolfi, *Prolegomena alla «Vita di Girolamo Savonarola»*

Savonarola e la mistica. Atti del quarto seminario (Firenze, 22 maggio 1998). A cura di Gian Carlo Garfagnini

Una città e il suo profeta. Firenze di fronte al Savonarola. Atti del Convegno Internazionale di studi (Firenze, 10-13 dicembre 1998). A cura di Gian Carlo Garfagnini

LA TRADIZIONE MUSICALE
STUDI E TESTI

1. Clemente Terni, *Armonia dell'amore. Ragione della vita nell'esperienza francescana*, 1998, pp. XX-80

2. *Un inedito trattato musicale del Medioevo (Vercelli, Biblioteca Agnesiana, cod. 11).* A cura di Anna Cornagliotti e Maria Caraci Vela, 1998, pp. 116 con 7 tavv. f. t.

3. Guiot de Dijon, *Canzoni.* Edizione critica a cura di Maria Sofia Lannutti, 1999, pp. LXXX-234

4. *Col dolce suon che da te piove. Studi su Francesco Landini e la musica del suo tempo in memoria di Nino Pirrotta.* A cura di Antonio Delfino e Maria Teresa Rosa Barezzani, 1999, pp. XII-664 con 17 tavv. f. t.

♦ in preparazione:

Psallitur per voces istas. Scritti in onore di Clemente Terni in occasione del suo ottantesimo compleanno. A cura di Donatella Righini

Francesco Giomi, Marco Ligabue, *L'istante zero.* Conversazioni e riflessioni con Pietro Grossi

PERIODICI

Documenti e studi sulla tradizione filosofica medievale, 1, 1990 -
voll. 1-6:
c/o Centro Italiano di Studi sull'Alto Medioevo, p.zza della Libertà 12, I-06049 Spoleto (PG)
TEL. 0743-23271 FAX 0743-232701

voll. 7-9:
c/o Brepols Publishers
Steenweg op Tielen 68, B-2300 Turnhout
TEL. 0032-14-40.25.00 FAX 0032-14-42.89.19

Sommario dell'ultimo volume pubblicato (10, 1999, pp. 494): J. Whittaker, *Does God Have a Soul?* – R. Chiaradonna, *ΟΥΣΙΑ ΕΞ ΟΥΚ ΟΥΣΙΩΝ. Forma e sostanza sensibile in Plotino (*Enn. VI 3[44], 4-8) – G. Galluzzo, *Il tema della verità in Plotino. Fonti platoniche e presupposti filosofici* – J. Pépin, *La hiérarchie par le degré de mutabilité (Nouveaux schèmes porphyriens chez saint Augustin, I)* – G. Madec, *Le christianisme comme accomplissement du platonisme selon saint Augustin* – G. Leroux, *Vestiges et empreintes. La causalité dans l'interprétation de* Timée, 53*b par Calcidius* – D. Gutas, *The 'Alexandria to Baghdad' Complex of Narratives. A Contribution to the Study of Philosophical and Medical Historiography among the Arabs* – S. Fazzo, *Frammenti da Alessandro di Afrodisia* In De generatione et corruptione *nel* Kitab al-Tasrif*: problemi di riconoscimento e di ricostruzione* – A. Bertolacci, Metafisica A 5, 986 *a* 22-26 *nell'*Ilahiyyat *del* Kitab al-Sifa *di Ibn Sina* – S. Donati, *Il commento alla* Fisica *di Adamo di Bocfeld e un commento anonimo della sua scuola. Parte II* – J.-P. Torrell, *Philosophie et théologie d'après le Prologue de Thomas d'Aquin au* Super Boetium de Trinitate. *Essai d'une lecture théologique* – W. Goris, *Die Anfänge der Auseinandersetzung um das Ersterkannte im 13. Jahrhundert: Guibert von Tournai, Bonaventura und Thomas von Aquin* – T. Dorandi, *La* versio latina antiqua *di Diogene Laerzio e la sua recezione nel Medioevo occidentale: il* Compendium moralium notabilium *di Geremia da Montagnone e il* Liber de vita et moribus philosophorum *dello ps. Burleo* – M. Bertagna, *La definizione delle modalità nella seconda parte della* Logica *di Richard Ferrybridge. Parte II* – S. Perfetti, Docebo vos dubitare. *Il commento inedito di Pietro Pomponazzi al* De partibus animalium *(Bologna,* 1521-24) – D. De Smet, *Le Souffle du Miséricordieux (*Nafas ar-Rahman*): un élément pseudo-empédocléen dans la métaphysique de Mulla Sadra as-Sirazi* – Indice dei manoscritti – Indice dei nomi

Hagiographica, 1, 1994 -
voll. 1-4:
c/o Brepols Publishers
Steenweg op Tielen 68, B-2300 Turnhout
TEL. 0032-14-40.25.00 FAX 0032-14-42.89.19

Sommario dell'ultimo volume pubblicato (5, 1998, pp. 300): S. Schein, *The «Female-Men of God» and «Men who were Women». Female Saints and Holy Land Pilgrimage during the Byzantine Period* – J. Elfassi, *Germain d'Auxerre, figure d'Augustin de Cantorbéry. La réécriture par Bède de la «Vie de saint Germain d'Auxerre»* – F. Mosetti Casaretto, *Santità virtuale e «petitio» agiografica nell'«Epistola ad Grimaldum» di Ermenrico di Ellwangen* – W. Berschin - A. Häse, *Rückblick auf die neue Ausgabe der ältesten Ulrichsvita* – L. Moulinier, *Hildegarde exorciste: la «Vie de Hildegarde» en français et sa principale source inédite* – C. Krötzl, *Prokuratoren, Notare und Dolmetscher. Zu Gestaltung und Ablauf der Zeugen-einvernahmen bei spätmittelalterlichen Kanonisationsprozessen* – A. Ferreiro, *Simon Magus and Simon Peter in a Baroque Altar Relief in the Cathedral of Oviedo, Spain* – J. Marí Arcelus Ulibarrena, *Carteggio di José María de Elizondo relativo al «Floreto de Sant Francisco»* – P. Chiesa, *Recuperi agiografici veneziani dai codici Milano, Braidense, Gerli ms. 26 e Firenze, Nazionale, Conv. Soppr. G. 5. 1212* – Indice dei santi – Indice dei nomi di persona – Indice degli autori antichi, medievali e moderni – Indice degli studiosi – Indice dei nomi di luogo

Micrologus. Natura, scienze e società medievali / Nature, Sciences and Medieval Societies, 1, 1993 -
voll. 1-4:
c/o Brepols Publishers
Steenweg op Tielen 68, B-2300 Turnhout
TEL. 0032-14-40.25.00 FAX 0032-14-42.89.19

Sommario dell'ultimo volume pubblicato (6. *La visione e lo sguardo nel Medio Evo / View and Vision in the Middle Ages*, II, 1998, pp. 281): Jean-Claude Schmitt, *Les dimensions multiples du voir. Les rêves et l'image dans l'autobiographie de conversion d'Hermann le Juif au XIIe siècle* – Michele Camillo Ferrari, Imago visibilis Christi. *Le volto santo de Lucques et les images authentiques au Moyen Age* – Christian Heck, *Du songe de Jacob aux visions de saint dans l'art médiéval. Théophanie et géographie sacrée* – Vera Segre Rutz, *Astrazione e modalità narrative nell'illustrazione delle Apocalissi spagnole di Beato de Liebana* – Jérôme Baschet, *Vision béatifique et représentations du Paradis (XIe-XVe siècle)* – François Boespflug, *La vision de la Trinité de Christine de Markyate et le* Psautier de Saint-Alban – Jean Wirth, *Peinture et perception visuelle au XIIIe siècle* – Michael Camille, *The Eye in the Text: Vision in the Illuminated Manuscripts of the Latin Aristotle* – Michel Pastoureau, *Voir les couleurs au XIIIe siècle* – Francesca Cecchini, «Le misure secondo l'apparenza». *Ottica e illusionismo nella scultura del Duecento: tracce figurative e testimonianze letterarie* – Jean-Yves Tilliette, «Amor est passio quaedam innata ex visione procedens». *Amour et vision dans le* Tractatus amoris d'André le Chapelain – Christopher Lucken, *L'imagination de la dame. Fantasmes amoureux et poésie courtoise* – Denis Renevey, «See by ensaumple»: *Images and Imagination in the Writings of the Author of* The Cloud of Unknowing – Carra Ferguson O'Meara, *Francesco Petrarca and the Renaissance Idea of Artistic Vision* – Indice dei nomi e delle cose notevoli – Indice lessicale – Indice dei manoscritti.

◆ in preparazione:

vol. 7, 1999, «Il cadavere. Antropologia e immaginario sociale / The corpse. Anthropology and Social Imaginary»
vol. 8, 2000, «Il mondo animale e la società degli uomini / The World of Animals and Human Society»

Medioevo musicale. Bollettino bibliografico della musica medievale, 2, 1999, pp. XXXII-708
Pubblicazione promossa dalla Fondazione Ezio Franceschini. A cura della sezione musica Matilde Fiorini Aragone diretta da Clemente Terni.

Medioevo latino. Bollettino bibliografico della cultura europea da Boezio a Erasmo (secoli VI-XV), 1, 1980 -

voll. 1-18:
c/o Centro Italiano di Studi sull'Alto Medioevo, p.zza della Libertà 12, I-06049 Spoleto (PG)
TEL. 0743-23271 FAX 0743-232701

vol. 20, 1999, pp. XXXVIII-1179

◆ in preparazione:

Compendium Auctorum Latinorum Medii Aevi (CALMA).
Curantibus: Cantabrigiae Michael Lapidge; Florentiae Gian Carlo Garfagnini et Claudio Leonardi; adiuvantibus Lidia Lanza, Rosalind Love et Simona Polidori

SISMEL
EDIZIONI DEL GALLUZZO
via di Colleramole 11 - 50029 loc. Bottai
Tavarnuzze - Impruneta - Firenze
TEL. 055-23.74.537 FAX 055-23.73.454
E-MAIL: galluzzo@sismel.it
INTERNET: www.sismel.it

PUBBLICAZIONI

promosse dalla

FONDAZIONE EZIO FRANCESCHINI

AUTOGRAPHA MEDII AEVI

c/o Brepols Publishers
Steenweg op Tielen 68, B-2300 Turnhout
TEL. 0032-14-40.25.00 FAX 0032-14-42.89.19

1. *Liutprando da Cremona e il codice di Frisinga Clm* 6388. A cura di Paolo Chiesa, 1994, pp. 86 con 42 tavv. f. t.

2. *Guibert de Nogent et ses secrétaires*. Cura et studio Monique Cécile Garand, 1995, pp. 88 con 14 tavv. f. t.

3. *The Authographs of Eriugena*. Edited by Edouard Jeauneau and Paul Dutton, 1996, pp. 224 con 99 tavv.

4. *The Autograph Manuscript of the «Liber Floridus». A Key to the Understanding of the Work*, by Albert Derolez, 1998

BIBLIOTECA DEL MEDIOEVO LATINO

c/o Giunti Gruppo Editoriale
via Bolognese 165, I-50139 Firenze
TEL. 055-66.79.201 / 66.79.202
FAX 055-66.79.397

1. Dante Alighieri, *Epistola a Cangrande*. A cura di Enzo Cecchini, 1995, pp. LII-52

2. Marbodo di Rennes, *Vita beati Roberti*. A cura di Antonella Degl'Innocenti, 1995, pp. LXXVI-97

3. Letaldo di Micy, *Within Piscator*. A cura di Ferruccio Bertini, 1995, pp. XXIV-80 con 6 tavv. f. t.

Per la prosecuzione della collana, si veda SISMEL - EDIZIONI DEL GALLUZZO (PER VERBA. Testi mediolatini con traduzione)

OPUSCOLI

c/o Fondazione Ezio Franceschini
Certosa del Galluzzo I-50124 Firenze
TEL. 055-20.49.749
FAX 055-23.20.423

1. *La Fondazione Ezio Franceschini*. Atti e cronaca della costituzione della Fondazione e dell'inaugurazione della sede (13 dicembre 1987), 1988, pp. 42

2. *A cinquant'anni dalla prima cattedra di Storia della letteratura latina medievale (Padova 25 novembre 1988)*, 1990, pp. 88 con 11 tavv. f. t.

3. *Nel segno di Francesco. A proposito di una raccolta di scritti di Ezio Franceschini*, 1990, pp. 44 con 4 tavv. f. t.

4. *La Fondazione Ezio Franceschini. Notizie 1987-1990*. Resoconto delle attività del triennio. A cura di Lina Nicoletti e Francesco Santi, 1990, pp. 40

5. *La Fondazione Ezio Franceschini. Notizie 1991-1992*. Resoconto delle attività del biennio. A cura di Silvia Cantelli, 1992, pp. 36

6. Isabella Gualandri - Claudio Leonardi, *Ezio Franceschini e la storia di Else Valgimigli*, 1992, pp. 30

7. Clemente Terni, *Frate Francesco. Retablo musicale in dodici quadri per soli, coro, strumenti e percussioni. Omaggio a Pietro Parigi nel centenario della nascita*, 1993, pp. 36

8. *Specchi di carta. Gli archivi storici di persone fisiche: problemi di tutela e ipotesi di ricerca*. A cura di Claudio Leonardi, 1993, pp. 120

9. *Il verso europeo*. Atti del seminario di metrica comparata (4 maggio 1994). A cura di Francesco Stella. Prefazione di Claudio Leonardi, 1995, pp. 166

10. *Segreti in vetrina. Utilità e danno per la storia delle mostre di libri, documenti e cimeli*. A cura di Claudio Leonardi, 1996, pp. 114

Per la prosecuzione della collana, si veda SISMEL - EDIZIONI DEL GALLUZZO

QUADERNI DI CULTURA MEDIOLATINA

c/o Centro Italiano di Studi sull'Alto Medioevo
p.zza della Libertà 12, I-06049 Spoleto (PG)
TEL. 0743-23271 FAX 0743-232701

1. Birger Munk Olsen, *I classici nel canone della scuola altomedievale*. Prefazione di Claudio Leonardi, 1991, pp. X-138

2. *Gli studi francescani dal dopoguerra ad oggi*. Atti del Convegno di studio (Firenze, 5-7 novembre 1990). A cura di Francesco Santi, 1993, pp. X-418

3. *La scuola di Erse. Lettere e documenti di Manara Valgimigli, Ezio Franceschini e Lorenzo Minio Paluello*. A cura di Giovanni Benedetto e Francesco Santi. Premessa di Claudio Leonardi, 1991, pp. XVI-66

5. *Gli autografi medievali. Problemi paleografici e filologici*. Atti del Convegno di studio della Fondazione Ezio Franceschini (Erice, 25 settembre - 2 ottobre 1990). A cura di Paolo Chiesa e Lucia Pinelli. Premessa di Claudio Leonardi, 1994, pp. X-320

6. Lorenzo Minio Paluello, *Luoghi cruciali in Dante. Ultimi saggi. Con un inedito su Boezio e la bibliografia delle opere*. A cura di Francesco Santi. Premessa di Claudio Leonardi, 1994, pp. VIII-174

7. *Il mestiere di storico del Medioevo*. Atti del Convegno di studio dell'Associazione «Biblioteca dei frati» (Lugano, 17-19 maggio 1990). A cura di Fernando Lepori e Francesco Santi, 1994, pp. X-126

8. Bruno Nardi, *Trattato dell'unità dell'intelletto di S. Tommaso. Testo, traduzione e commento*. Nuova edizione a cura di Paolo Mazzantini, 1998, pp. XXX-284

9. Ezio Franceschini, *Limiti e compiti di una nuova disciplina. Profilo letterario del Medioevo latino*. Ristampa anastatica della prolusione del 1939, con note autografe e il carteggio di

studiosi ed amici. A cura di Claudio Leonardi e Francesco Santi, 1993, pp. X-58 con 2 tavv. f. t.

10. *Macchine per leggere. Tradizioni e nuove tecnologie per comprendere i testi.* Atti del Convegno di studio della Fondazione Ezio Franceschini e della Fondazione IBM Italia (Certosa del Galluzzo, 19 novembre 1993). A cura di Claudio Leonardi, Marcello Morelli e Francesco Santi, 1994, pp. VIII-252

11. Clelia Maria Piastra, *La poesia mariologica dell'Umanesimo latino. Repertorio e incipitario.* Presentazione di Claudio Leonardi, 1994, pp. XL-262

12. *I re nudi. Congiure, assassini, tracolli ed altri imprevisti nella storia del potere.* Atti del Convegno di studio della Fondazione Ezio Franceschini (Certosa del Galluzzo, 19 novembre 1994). A cura di Glauco Maria Cantarella e Francesco Santi. Premessa di Ovidio Capitani, 1996, pp. XVIII-184 con 16 tavv. f. t.

13. *Fabula in tabula. Una storia degli indici dal manoscritto al testo elettronico.* Atti del Convegno di studio della Fondazione Ezio Franceschini e della Fondazione IBM Italia (Certosa del Galluzzo, 21-22 ottobre 1994). A cura di Claudio Leonardi, Marcello Morelli e Francesco Santi, 1995, pp. X-482 con 83 tavv. f. t.

14. *Album. I luoghi dove si accumulano i segni (dal manoscritto alle reti telematiche).* Atti del Convegno di studio della Fondazione Ezio Franceschini e della Fondazione IBM Italia (Certosa del Galluzzo, 20-21 ottobre 1995). A cura di Claudio Leonardi, Marcello Morelli e Francesco Santi, 1996, pp. XII-252

15. *Modi di scrivere. Tecnologie e pratiche della scrittura dal manoscritto alla scrittura elettronica.* Atti del Convegno di studio della Fondazione Ezio Franceschini e della Fondazione IBM Italia (Firenze, Certosa del Galluzzo, 11-12 ottobre 1996). A cura di Claudio Leonardi, Marcello Morelli e Francesco Santi, 1997, pp. VIII-266

◆ in preparazione:

José Ruysschaert, *Études sur l'histoire de la Bibliothèque Vaticane et des bibliothèques médiévales.* A cura di Paolo Vian

EZIO FRANCESCHINI E LA RESISTENZA

c/o Edizioni Piemme
via del Carmine 5, I-15033 Casale Monferrato (AL)
TEL. 0142-55648 FAX 0142-74223

1. Ezio Franceschini, *Uomini liberi. Scritti sulla Resistenza.* A cura di Francesca Minuto Peri. Premessa di Francesco Margiotta Broglio, 1993, pp. LVI-448 con 7 tavv. f. t.

2. *L'archivio di Ezio Franceschini sulla Resistenza. Regesto dei documenti.* A cura di Francesca Minuto Peri, 1993, pp. XIV-338 con 9 tavv. f. t.

Per la prosecuzione della collana, si veda SISMEL - EDIZIONI DEL GALLUZZO

PERIODICI

Filologia mediolatina, 1, 1994 -
c/o Centro Italiano di Studi sull'Alto Medioevo, p.zza della Libertà 12, I-06049 Spoleto (PG)
TEL. 0743-23271 FAX 0743-232701

Sommario dell'ultimo volume pubblicato (5, 1998, pp. 340): G. Orlandi, *Le statistiche sulle*

FONDAZIONE EZIO FRANCESCHINI

Certosa del Galluzzo I-50124 Firenze

TEL. 055-20.49.749 FAX 055-23.20.423 E-MAIL: fef@cesit1.unifi.it

INTERNET: http://sismel.meri.unifi.it

PUBBLICAZIONI

promosse dalla

SOCIETÀ INTERNAZIONALE PER LO STUDIO DEL MEDIOEVO LATINO

BIBLIOTECA DI «MEDIOEVO LATINO»

c/o Centro Italiano di Studi sull'Alto Medioevo
p.zza della Libertà 12, I-06049 Spoleto (PG)
TEL. 0743-23271 FAX 0743-232701

1. Silvia Cantelli, *Angelomo e la scuola esegetica di Luxeuil*, 1990, 2 voll., pp. VIII-53; XXIV-526

2. Paolo Chiesa, *Le versioni latine della «Passio sanctae Febroniae». Storia, metodo, modelli di due traduzioni agiografiche altomedievali*, 1990, pp. XVIII-402

3. Antonella Degl'Innocenti, *L'opera agiografica di Marbodo di Rennes*, 1990, pp. VIII-218

4. Agostino Paravicini Bagliani, *Medicina e scienze della natura alla corte dei papi nel Duecento*, 1991, pp. XVIII-490

5. *La critica del testo mediolatino.* Atti del Convegno (Firenze, 6-8 dicembre 1990). A cura di Claudio Leonardi, 1994, pp. VIII-456 con 2 tavv. f. t.

6. Jacques Dalarun, *«Lapsus Linguae». La légende de Claire de Rimini*, 1994, pp. 534 con 12 tavv. f. t.

7. Michela Pereira, *L'oro dei filosofi. Saggio sulle idee di un alchimista del Trecento*, 1992, pp. VI-266

8. Giovanni Paolo Maggioni, *Ricerche sulla composizione e sulla trasmissione della «Legenda aurea»*, 1995, pp. XIV-610

9. Francesco Stella, *La poesia carolingia latina a tema biblico*, Spoleto 1993, pp. XXXII-592

10. *Liber miraculorum sancte Fidis.* Edizione critica e commento a cura di Luca Robertini, 1994, pp. XII-478

11. *Modern Questions about Medieval Sermons. Essays on Marriage, Death, History and Sanctity*, by Nicole Bériou - David L. D'Avray, with P. Cole, J. Riley-Smith, M. Tausche, 1994, pp. XII-410

12. Emma Condello, *Una scrittura e un territorio. L'onciale dei secoli V-VIII nell'Italia meridionale*, Spoleto 1994, pp. XIV-166 con 26 tavv. f. t.

13. José Manuel Díaz de Bustamante - María Elisa Lage Cotos - José Eduardo López Pereira, *Bibliografía de Latín Medieval en España (1950-1992)*, Spoleto 1994, pp. XII-516

14. Adele Simonetti, *I Sermoni di Umiltà da Faenza.* Studio ed edizione, 1995, pp. XCIV-196

15. *The Classical Tradition in the Middle Ages and the Renaissance.* Atti del Convegno (Firenze, 26-27 giugno 1992). A cura di Claudio Leonardi e Birger Munk Olsen, 1995, pp. X-284

16. Osberno, *Derivazioni.* A cura di Paola Busdraghi, Maria Chiabó, Andrea Dessì Fulgheri, Paolo Gatti, Rosanna Mazzacane, Luciana Roberti, 1996, 2 voll., pp. XXX-464; 514

17. Chiara Crisciani - Michela Pereira, *L'arte del sole e della luna. Alchimia e filosofia nel Medioevo*, 1996, pp. VIII-356

18. Helena De Carlos Villamarín, *Las antigüedades de Hispania*, 1996, pp. 342

19. Luigi Canetti, *L'invenzione della memoria. Il culto e l'immagine di Domenico nella storia dei primi frati predicatori*, 1996, pp. XVI-558

20. Luigi Giovanni Giuseppe Ricci, *Problemi sintattici nelle opere di Liutprando di Cremona*, 1996, pp. XXII-218

21. Giulia Goi, *La tavola di sant'Agata da Cremona,* 1998, pp. VI-136

PERIODICI

Documenti e studi sulla tradizione filosofica medievale, 1, 1990 -
voll. 1-6:
c/o Centro Italiano di Studi sull'Alto Medioevo, p.zza della Libertà 12, I-06049 Spoleto (PG)
TEL. 0743-23271 FAX 0743-232701

voll. 7-9:
c/o Brepols Publishers
Steenweg op Tielen 68, B-2300 Turnhout
TEL. 0032-14-40.25.00 FAX 0032-14-42.89.19

vol. 10: si veda SISMEL - EDIZIONI DEL GALLUZZO (Periodici).

Hagiographica, 1, 1994 -
voll. 1-4:
c/o Brepols Publishers
Steenweg op Tielen 68, B-2300 Turnhout
TEL. 0032-14-40.25.00 FAX 0032-14-42.89.19

vol. 5: si veda SISMEL - EDIZIONI DEL GALLUZZO (Periodici).

Medioevo latino. Bollettino bibliografico della cultura europea da Boezio a Erasmo (secoli VI-XV), 1, 1980 -
voll. 1-18:
c/o Centro Italiano di Studi sull'Alto Medioevo, p.zza della Libertà 12, I-06049 Spoleto (PG)
TEL. 0743-23271 FAX 0743-232701

voll. 19-20: si veda SISMEL - EDIZIONI DEL GALLUZZO (Periodici).

Micrologus. Natura, scienze e società medievali / Nature, Sciences and Medieval Societies, 1, 1993 -
voll. 1-4: c/o Brepols Publishers
Steenweg op Tielen 68, B-2300 Turnhout
TEL. 0032-14-40.25.00 FAX 0032-14-42.89.19

voll. 5-6: si veda SISMEL - EDIZIONI DEL GALLUZZO (Periodici).

SOCIETÀ INTERNAZIONALE PER LO STUDIO DEL MEDIOEVO LATINO
Certosa del Galluzzo I-50124 - Firenze
TEL. 055-20.48.501 FAX 055-23.20.423 E-MAIL: sismel@cesit1.unifi.it
INTERNET: http://sismel.meri.unifi.it